The City Rehearsed

The City Rehearsed examines architecture and print culture after the Reformation. Centered on the strange Netherlandish painter Hans Vredeman de Vries (1526–1609), it discusses changes in the definition of perspective and ornament under Protestant critiques of the image, and looks at some of the fascinating ways architecture was redefined by the ability of art to circulate globally.

The first sustained study of Vredeman in English, Heuer's book tracks the movement of his works to Spain, Mexico, and beyond, arguing for a new way of writing about European art around 1600. Aside from criteria like beauty and humanism, it turns to categories like collaboration, copying, and failure to map the intellectual horizons (and art-historical afterlife) of a moment after the "Renaissance" had matured. This engaging book will be of interest to any student of architectural history, art history, philosophy, or early modern culture.

Christopher P. Heuer is Assistant Professor in the Department of Art and Archaeology at Princeton University.

The Classical Tradition in Architecture

Series Editor: Caroline van Eck, Leiden University, Netherlands

Classical architecture not only provided a repertoire of forms and building types capable of endless transformation; it was also a cultural actor and provided cultural capital, and was used to create political and religious identities. This series provides a forum for its interdisciplinary study, from antiquity to the present day. It aims to publish first-class and groundbreaking scholarship that re-examines, reinterprets, or revalues the classical tradition in the widest sense. The series will deal with classicism as a cultural phenomenon, a formal language of design, but also with its role in establishing the agenda, method and grammar of inquiry in Western history of art and architecture and recent reconsiderations of these roles.

Power & Virtue:
Architecture and Intellectual Change in England 1660–1730
Li Shiqiao

Landscapes of Taste:
The Art of Humphrey Repton's Red Books
André Rogger

The Picturesque:
Architecture, Disgust and Other Irregularities
John Macarthur

The Florentine Villa:
Architecture History Society
Grazia Gobbi Sica

Architecture, Print Culture, and the Public Sphere in Eighteenth Century France
Richard Wittman

Festival Architecture
Edited by Sarah Bonnemaison and Christine Macy

The City Rehearsed:
Object, Architecture, and Print in the Worlds of Hans Vredeman de Vries
Christopher P. Heuer

Architecture, the City, and the Public in Eighteenth Century France:
A Reader
Edited by Richard Wittman

The City Rehearsed

Object, architecture, and print in the worlds of Hans Vredeman de Vries

Christopher P. Heuer

Routledge
Taylor & Francis Group
LONDON AND NEW YORK

First published 2009
by Routledge
2 Park Square, Milton Park, Abingdon, Oxon OX14 4RN

Simultaneously published in the USA and Canada
by Routledge
711 Third Avenue, New York, NY 10017

Routledge is an imprint of the Taylor & Francis Group, an informa business

First issued in paperback 2013

Typeset in Univers by
RefineCatch Limited, Bungay, Suffolk

Cover design by Mark Rakatansky Studio, Brooklyn

This book was made possible by a grant from the Graham Foundation for Advanced Studies in the Visual Arts

British Library Cataloguing in Publication Data
A catalogue record for this book is available from the British Library

Library of Congress Cataloging in Publication Data
Heuer, Christopher P.
The city rehearsed : object, architecture, and print in the worlds of Hans Vredeman de Vries / Christopher P. Heuer.
p. cm. – (The classical tradition in architecture)
Includes bibliographical references and index.
1. Vredeman de Vries, Hans, 1527-ca. 1604–Criticism and interpretation. 2. Architecture and society–Netherlands–History–16th century. 3. Architecture–Aesthetics. 4. Architecture– Philosophy. I. Title.
NE670.V74H48 2008
769.92–dc22
2008014932

ISBN13: 978–0–415–43306–8 (hbk)
ISBN13: 978–0–415–54232–6 (pbk)

for EAM, who waited

Contents

Acknowledgments

"What's the verb behind it all?" Dennes Boon's simple question drove the first incarnation of this book, which was submitted as a doctoral dissertation to the Department of History of Art at Berkeley in December 2003. Subsequent reading, thinking, and traveling for the project have been possible only through the generosity and the support of many people and institutions. For funds assisting with photography, permissions, and production costs, I am grateful to Columbia University, the Spears Fund of Princeton's Art & Archaeology Department, and the Graham Foundation for Advanced Studies in the Visual Arts. The last two entities transformed this study from an unwieldy thesis into a grown-up publication. Research and travel was underwritten by the Samuel H. Kress foundation and the Kunsthistorisch Instituut Leiden, and was facilitated by grants from the Deutscher Akademischer Austausch Dienst and the Bibliographic Society of Great Britain. Without the assistance of staff at the Stadsarchief Antwerp, the Rijksprentenkabinet Amsterdam, and the Rare Book Room at the Universiteit Amsterdam, this book would not have been finished.

Two fortunate years at the Getty Research Institute in Los Angeles in 2002–04 permitted time and space to write, and the intellectual hospitality provided by Thomas Crow, Charles Salas, and the scholars around the theme-year "Biography" shaped this book's arguments in unexpected and helpful ways. I am indebted to Cassie Albinson, Tatiana Senkevitch, Isabelle Tillerot, and, above all, Andrew Perchuk and Sebastian Zeidler as sources of criticism and advice. Elizabeth Honig, a teacher, advisor, and friend, continued to inspire the book through her sustained intellectual unselfishness and her own writing on Netherlandish art. Matthew Jesse Jackson, whom I met on my first day of graduate school, made work possible at Berkeley and the Getty by reminding me what mattered, and what, ultimately, did not.

This manuscript was completed in the Department of Art & Archaeology at Columbia University and at the Centre Canadien d'Architecture in Montréal. I am grateful to both institutions, and to Mario Carpo, Jonathan Crary, Vittoria di Palma, and Phyllis Lambert for making the respective stays happen. At Avery Library, particularly, I owe thanks to Gerald Beasley. Elsewhere at Columbia, Graham Bader, Francesco Benelli, Kate Bentz, Nikolas Bakirtzis, David Freedberg, Clemente Marconi, Keith Moxey, Amy Powell, John Rajchman, Tanya Sheehan, and Alicia Walker were important sources of encouragement, and at the CCA, Alexis Sornin an irrepressible host. Final edits were completed during an exhilarating first year at Princeton, where I have benefited enormously from the questions of students, from the patience of Susan Lehre and her staff, and specifically from the erudition and wit of Danny Curčic, Rachel DeLue, Brigid Doherty, Thomas da Costa Kaufmann, Thomas Leisten, Esther da Costa Meyer, John Pinto, Jerome Silbergeld, and Nino Zchomelidse. As chairs, Patricia Brown and Hal Foster supported this book at every opportunity.

I am particularly grateful to five scholars who withstood late drafts of individual chapters: Cammy Brothers, Hanneke Grootenboer, Paul Taylor, Christopher S. Wood, and Rebecca Zorach. Their friendly criticisms, corrections, and proddings made this an immeasurably better book—what errors surely remain, however, are mine and mine alone. Caroline Mallinder and Georgina Johnson at Routledge have remained steadfast throughout the entire publication process, as has series editor Caroline van Eyck, who kindly took an early interest in the project. Finally, for conversation and support, for everything from bibliography to bike repair, the project will always be indebted to the following individuals: Holm Bevers, Heiner Borggrefe, Karel Bostoen, Britta Bothe, David Brafman, Taco Dibbits, Nina Dubin, Peter Furhing, Thomas Fusenig, Hartford Gongaware, Glenn Harcourt, Johanna Heinrichs, Barbara, Jared, and Schuyler Heuer, Charles van de Heuvel, Doug Hildebrecht, Ann-Sophie Lehmann, Piet Lombaerde, Mark Meadow, Candace and John Monroe, Luke Morgan, Koen Ottenheym, Loren Partridge, Dan Pearson, Mark Rakatansky, Peter Relic, Stephanie Schrader, Eric Jan Sluijter, Claudia Swan, Stephen Tobriner, Nancy Troy, Barbara Uppenkamp, Angela Vanhaelen, Jan de Vries, Anne Wagner, Suzanne Walker, Bronwen Wilson, Wim de Wit, and Sophie Zimmermann. An earlier version of Chapter 2 appeared in *Hans Vredeman de Vries and the Artes Mechanicae Revisited* (Turnhout, 2005), and bits of Chapter 5 as "Perspective as Process in Vermeer," *Res: Anthropology and Aesthetics* 38 (Autumn 2000). I am grateful to Brepols Press and to the President and Fellows of Harvard College for permission to republish.

Helen, lastly, requested that this project be ended quickly. Elizabeth, however, lived with it the longest; this book is for her.

List of abbreviations

AA	*Antwerpsche Archivenblad*, vol. 1, 1864–
H	Friedrich Wilhelm Heinrich Hollstein, *Hollstein's Dutch and Flemish Etchings, Engravings and Woodcuts, ca 1450–1700*, vol. 1, 1949–
SAA	Stadsarchief, Antwerp
UBA	Universiteitsbibliotheek, Amsterdam
Van Mander	Karel Van Mander. *Het schilder-boek: het leven van der doorluchtige Nederlandsche en Hoogduitsche schilders*, 6 vols, Haarlem: Paschier van Wesbuch, 1604, Hessel Miedema (ed.), Michael Hoyle, J. Pennial-Boer, and C. Ford (trans.), Doornspijk: Davaco, 1994–99

All measurements are given in centimeters.
Unless otherwise noted, all translations are mine.

The question now is what artists are to do.

Boris Arvatov

Introduction

Iconoclasm's faces

On February 9, 1604, the regents of Leiden University considered a written application for a faculty position. In a short letter, a 77-year-old man from Friesland presented himself as potential professor of "*perspective, Ingenie, en de architecture*" (perspective, engineering, and architecture). The request was supported by a recommendation from the *stadhouder* of the Dutch Republic, Maurits of Nassau, and alluded to a vast experience with art and architectural practice. The applicant claimed he had authored "numerous books, which disclose the secrets of many diverse subjects, all using copper engravings." Prints or no, the regents of Leiden were unimpressed. They turned the old man's application down, dispatching a polite note and a consolatory gift of 25 guilders.[1] Within five years the applicant was dead.

The writer, an artist and architect recorded in the Leiden archives as one "*Hans Vredeman de Vriese,*" is the subject of this book. Arguably the most prolific Netherlandish print designer of the sixteenth century, Hans Vredeman (1526–1609)

0.1
Hans Vredeman de Vries, *Perspective,* II, no. 42, 1605. Engraving, H.560. Centre Canadien d'Architecture, Montréal.

wrote and illustrated one of the strangest, most influential, and most misunderstood tracts on art ever published (Figure 0.1), a book touted by turns as "a failure," "surreal," and "protofilmic."[2] It went through 26 separate editions after his death. As the Leiden affair demonstrates, however, Vredeman knew professional disappointment well. In 1561, his proposed design for a new Antwerp town hall had, in fact, been rejected. In 1589, he had been, without explanation, abruptly fired from a position as court architect at the town of Wolfenbüttel. In 1592, having been lured to the Hanseatic port of Danzig (now Gdańsk) by the promise of work as a fortifications engineer, Vredeman was sacked after petitioning the town council to found a painters' guild. The same year the city even installed a rival Netherlander in Vredeman's place—again without explanation—who seems to have pirated fortification projects Vredeman had spent a year drafting. By 1598, old and poor, Vredeman drifted to Hamburg, where, claimed the Netherlandish biographer Karel Van Mander (who knew the artist personally), he worked so diligently on a painting of the *Tower of Babel* that he ruined his eyes.[3]

It is, however, far from the figure of a wandering melancholic that Hendrick Hondius depicted in his series of artist's portraits published in 1610 (Figure 0.2). In plate 47, Vredeman looks into the distance, stern and interrupted, his left hand just

0.2
Hendrick Hondius, *Theatrum Honoris* (Amsterdam, 1610) no. 47. Engraving.
Herzog-August Bibliothek, Wolfenbüttel.

withdrawn from a cloak opened to six unfastened buttons. He has stopped to place his finger upon a paper sheet that curls at its two top edges. His right hand delicately grasps dividers (*passer*) in the midst of tracing an arc. Pencil-holding compasses were unusual in North Europe before the seventeenth century,[4] but in Hondius's print, Vredeman's tool makes a mark. A hexameter verse below praises Vredeman as "*pictor*" and perspectivist, as his compasses—medieval attributes of the mason[5]—bespeak his work as a builder. Petra-Sophie Zimmermann has noted that Vredeman's image is the only portrait in Hondius's series to include a geometer's tools.[6] Here, however, the compass has become an engraver's burin, the arc an etched line. Vredeman points to himself at work, and, resting the tip of his left index finger on the very paper being inscribed, signals the result of that work by touch. He gestures, as if teaching, and looks out to his left. The presentation of perspective, in this image, invokes Vredeman's hands as much as his vision.

Near the end of his life, Vredeman enjoyed the prestige of sponsorship at the most dazzling artistic colony of his day: Rudolf II's court in Prague. Painted *trompe l'oeil* programs Vredeman executed there, the artist Samuel van Hoogstraten reported in a treatise of 1678, not only "ingeniously deceived," (*daer veel konstig meede misleyt*) but "astonished" (*verwonderen*) viewers lucky enough to encounter them.[7] Nor was Vredeman unique in his roamings; the landscape painters Lucas van Valkenborch and Martin van Steenwyck, too, traveled from city to city in the Holy Roman Empire in the 1580s, fleeing, in Van Mander's metaphor, "art-destroying Mars"—Antwerp's 1566 iconoclasm and its aftermath.[8] But Vredeman's wanderings and intermittent failures, more than his triumphs, introduce the most compelling and illuminative aspects of his work in that they consistently occurred in the cracks between the practices of painting, printing, and building. "Perspective, engineering, and architecture"—the triumvirate cited in Vredeman's unsuccessful Leiden application, had become, by 1600, not just overlapping subjects in a potential university curriculum, but, as this book will argue, fundaments for crafting a new kind of artist.

*

Art is only possible, wrote Adorno, in an antagonistic world.[9] In sixteenth-century Europe, Protestant hostility to images begat many of the strangest polemics against painting and sculpture in Western history, polemics which often spilled over into violence and iconoclasm, and which forced artists and architects to rethink what they did and why. The physical violence of the Reformation, as art history is increasingly making clear, also changed the idea of what pictures could do.[10] In fact, for the late sixteenth century, the Calvinist correlation of visual images with devotional mendacity spurred breathtaking reconfigurations for perspective, ornament, and color, for the idea of how, for example, a painting might be "reformed" rather than annihilated outright.

What Hegel once decried as the "crisis of the image" wrought by Calvinist doctrine increasingly seems more like the precociously modern (and equally problematic) moment the Renaissance artwork slipped from its interest in the observed world alone.[11] Writing around 1604, Karel Van Mander claimed that his day was one where painting began to seek out its *own* terms for explaining itself, instead of borrowing them from science or rhetoric. Indeed, in the wake of the Reformation, the more modern story goes, painting often became proudly unbeautiful and obtuse, less interested in presenting grace than in its own feats of composition. As new methods of engraving, for example, drained images of mimetic pretense, art reveled in its detachment from religious ritual, replacing it with new, even more dazzling and mystifying performances centered on markets, courts, and art-making itself, rather than the church. In this shedding of aura, art became not crudely secular, however, but rather attuned to its equally enchanting relations with other kinds of image—a facility easily mappable on to modernity.

Yet today, an early modern art which twentieth-century historians called "mannerism"—an art emphatically *about* art—seems less the language of solipsism or political complacency it used to be. The appeal of the style at courts in the Netherlands, Bohemia, and France, as Rebecca Zorach has shown,[12] appears less complicit in consolidating royal power than long assumed. Forms like grotesqueries, for example, cloaked potential for courtiers' aesthetic subterfuge and criticism, insurrection which—while of an assuredly aesthetic character—challenged without adopting a clear oppositional relationship to, say, a monarch. The tension art historians associate with mannerism as a category has traditionally remained wrapped up with worry about *profuse* rather than over-elaborate artworks, images that in their sheer numbers became capricious or outrightly forgetful about their origins: in 1935, Julius von Schlosser, writing about replicas of Quattrocento paintings, decried "mannerist copyists and counterfeiters," who produced things which, as identicals, could not be art.[13] The sixteenth century, Schlosser argued, was the first real century of the copy. In such a scenario, vast numbers of replicas in print, paint, and particularly in the Spanish New World, in architecture, formed chains of versions that were similar but slightly different; they threatened to crowd out the "real" maker, story, or site which lay behind a single model's existence.

But as Schlosser of course knew, the relation between art's status as a thing and its role as a sign for something else was a quandary that predated the "late" Renaissance. It was merely politicized, rather than invented, in the wake of Luther and Calvin. Indeed, the late sixteenth-century realization—through the writings of Vasari and Van Mander—that art and architecture, too, had their own histories, was, in part, spurred by a question raging even in church circles of Europe after the Council of Trent: what paintings, prints, and sculpture might do besides *re-present*. This is an issue which, while daunting, ultimately besets the work of art only secondarily. On a functional level it must first be contemplated by the artist.

Early modern subjects

Hans Vredeman de Vries spent much of his career dealing with prints and paintings of buildings. There is an engraving from his *Perspective* treatise published at Leiden and The Hague in 1604–05 that shows an architectural landscape (Figure 0.3). The print is

0.3
Hans Vredeman de Vries, *Perspective*, I, no. 44, 1604. Engraving, H.562.
Centre Canadien d'Architecture, Montréal.

19.8 × 29.4 centimeters and oblong—large for an illustration from a pattern-book.[14] A simple barrel vault thrusts vertiginously into a recessed courtyard, with a colonnade of four Doric columns and a supporting cross-vault—what Vredeman, in an accompanying description, calls a "*cruys-welssel.*" The archway is garnished with a curling strapwork capstone beneath a terrace with sixteen balusters, two just disappearing at the top edge. At lower left a door with six panels creaks open, overlaid with three specked instruction lines indicating joining-points for the horizon, here marked in italics as "*orison*" just right of center. The etched shadows cast by the columns, indicating an unseen light source from the left, are diagonally cross-hatched, separating the black of the floor from the grays of the building itself, which themselves are done in vertical strokes. The left facade is rendered with choppy left-right dashes. Six dotted rays suck through this porch towards a second arch, where they meet beneath a dome-structure lined with three niches. In the right foreground a stairway opens to a downward basement. There are no human figures; Vredeman's "horizon," his point of view, inhabits the place alone.

Amidst all these surfaces lie three *repoussoir* plaques. The first, fastened to the upper left edge, reads simply "*Vrise Invent,*" the other two are framed at chest-height indicating "*Anno*" and then "*1604.*" The first plaque, while a printmaking convention,[15] seems to picture Vredeman's place, and activity, in two commingled sites of authorship; first, Vredeman figures as author of the flat print (*inventio*—to devise), and second, via the sham inscription, as architect behind its depicted structures. The lonely signature is pressed up against the surface of the page in a framed plaque itself, gating the outside viewer from Vredeman's invented world—the signature, floating in a cartouche, even has a different white background than the rest of the building. It seems simultaneously part of the perspectival fiction and the flatness of the printed surface.

What is, in fact, this image? Karsten Harries likened the work to surrealist painting.[16] De Chirico has been invoked more than once to describe Vredeman's prints, yet the notion of dreamlike figuration alone is suspect when speaking of the seventeenth century. When the prints are included as modern illustrations in books on science, optics, comparative literature, and even linguistics, they have been described with a sense of non-sense: as grotesques, "architectural fantasies," or *capriccios*.[17] Their exaggerated deployment of perspective seems particularly unsettling when it upends a supposedly "neutral" system of representation—linear *prospettiva* itself. Indeed, distinguishing between images *naer het leven* (of the life) and *uyt zijn selve* (of one's self), Van Mander discussed the story of Parrhasius and Zeuxis, a topos that, even by the early seventeenth century, was already a cliché.[18] Pliny's story, retold by Horace and Cicero, was known in the Netherlands through Antwerp rhetoricians' plays. It famously described one ancient artist's ability to deceive another. Using a painted *trompe l'oeil* curtain, Parrhasius had fooled Zeuxis into thinking that his painted surface was not a false cloth but a "real" curtain. In the pendant to this fable, Zeuxis was commissioned to paint a portrait of the mythical Helen, the most beautiful woman in Troy. For this he assembled the loveliest maidens of Croton and selected from them the most beautiful features of each, "for he did not," as Cicero described, "think that he could find all the component parts of perfect beauty in one person."[19] This recombinant approach to creativity—wherein the artist takes bits from the viewed world and reshuffles them to suit his own ends—simply supplied another version of painting in the Parrhasian mode, that is, of painting *naer het leven* by duplicating viewed experience, however reconfigured it may be. In the Netherlands, the phrase's very etymology suggested that to make art *near het leven* (or *ad vivium*, or *nach dem Leben*, or *al vif*) meant not just to make images *from* life, but, to make images *to* the life, that is, to make images prefacing new things as much as documenting extant ones.[20] One of the earliest appearances of the term *al vif*, in fact, is in Villard de Honnecourt's sketchbook, a suite of drawings intended specifically to model buildings and sculpture. Vredeman's *Perspective* illustration itself was meant to be copied out, excerpted, and used to shape something new.

As the "Flemish Parrhasius," (Van Mander) Vredeman de Vries's own origins remain elusive. Vredeman seems to have been born in Leeuwarden, the capital of Friesland, around 1526. There he was apprenticed to a mediocre glass painter from Amsterdam named Reyner Gerritsen.[21] His father, an artilleryman, died in 1540, and soon Vredeman moved south to Mechelen, in Brabant, then spent two intermediary years in the small town of Kampen as part of his *Wanderschaft*. Vredeman seems to have been registered as a *schrijnwerker*, or joiner, in the Antwerp guilds by 1548, and, in 1549, he helped design festival decoration for a colossal *blijde inkomst* of Philip II and Charles V in that city.[22] Yet by 1550, Vredeman was back in Friesland in Kollum, where he found himself earning money as an oil painter—yet not at the status of full master.[23] Around 1552, he moved to Mechelen, where, lodging with an art dealer, Claude Dorici, he married a local woman, Johanna von Muysen, and, in 1555, began to produce drawings for ornament prints for the Antwerp publishing firm of Gerard de Jode. In May of 1561, still in Mechelen, Vredeman was paid 92 guilders to design decorations for an Easter procession.[24] It was recently discovered that in Mechelen Vredeman was also a designer of woodwork,[25] and appears to have been employed in the local tapestry industry; he meanwhile collaborated with the canvas painter Michael Coxcie and may even have produced an altarpiece.[26]

Sometime around 1562, Vredeman moved to Antwerp, where he identified himself on a print as a member of a rhetorician's guild. As Van Mander tells it, Vredeman also collaborated with Pieter Bruegel the Elder on a now-lost painting for the city treasurer and art collector, Aert Molckemann.[27] Like Bruegel, Vredeman began to have his designs published by Hieronymus Cock's "Aux" *Quatre Vents* firm, etched by Jan and Lucas van Doetecum. Through Cock, Vredeman may have become affiliated with a spiritualist sect with roots in his native Friesland, known as the *Huys ter Liefde*, or Family of Love. Involvement with the much-persecuted Familists may have been the reason Vredeman fled Antwerp quite suddenly in 1570, heading first to Aachen and then to Liège. Little is known of this first "exile" period, although, around 1575, Vredeman did write to the Antwerp guild complaining of wretched (*verachtig*) working conditions abroad.[28] He returned to the city in 1577 when a Reformed government had been installed, but left Antwerp again in 1586, a year after Hapsburg forces reclaimed power. He then traveled to Hamburg, Wolfenbüttel, Frankfurt, and the Protestant city of Danzig. Dismissed from an engineering post there, Vredeman was invited to Rudolf II's court at Prague in 1596, but seems to have left in 1598 after petitioning the emperor unsuccessfully for a project payment. He settled in Amsterdam around 1601. Finally, around 1605, Vredeman moved back to Hamburg, where he died in 1609, five years after being thwarted, as we have seen, in his attempt to teach at the newly founded University of Leiden.

Recent writing on Vredeman by Heiner Borggrefe, Piet Lombaerde, and Peter Fuhring has contributed to a complete re-evaluation of his place in early modern art and architecture. The present study would not have been possible without their work. Yet at the same time, the same research which has supplied many long-needed answers to Vredeman's eccentric career has also assumed that the questions that need to be asked of his *works* remain traditional, that the scope of the problems has always been clear, and that his role as an artist or an architect, a Catholic or a Protestant, an engineer or a printmaker, can simply be taken for granted, bracketed off along disciplinary boundaries.[29] The present book attempts, however humbly, to rethink these assumptions, to revisit the very terms under which Vredeman and his milieu have been queried.

Architecture as allegory, repetition as form

What do images of "empty" architecture mean? On the rare occasions when Vredeman's contemporaries *did* in fact talk about *pictures* of buildings, it was chiefly as embellishments to larger compositions. For painters, architecture was crucial: ". . . bases, columns, capitals, façades, fleurons, canopies, and the whole range of the masons' craft," Cennino Cennini had written in 1380, "should be executed with great delight . . . but bear in mind they must follow the same system that you have in the figures . . ."[30] In the *Lives*, Giorgio Vasari linked perspective and architecture, and urged the inclusion of "perspective views, or buildings" in the background of compositions, although he deemed the subject "a wearisome theme and difficult to explain." Rather, he claimed, "it is enough to say that perspectives [*prospettivi*] are beautiful insofar as they appear correct when looked at, and diminish as they retire from the eye, and when they are composed of a varied and beautiful scheme of buildings."[31] Northern writers drew associations between architecture, linear perspective, and adornment: Van Mander described the Courtrai painter Pieter Vlerik as "excellent in architecture [*Metslyrye*], that is, painting temples and perspectives,"[32] and elsewhere noted the usefulness of "stairways of stone, and architectural columns" as supplementary vehicles for directing the viewer inward towards a narrative subject.[33] Even earlier, Vasari had praised the charm of buildings (*casamenti*) as something separate from "the beauty of the *storia*" in a painting.[34] Like landscape, architecture—and more explicitly architecture in perspective—was clearly understood as an important *additive* of a painting's background, at once a structuring principle and, paradoxically, an ornament. It was never a genre of subject matter.

Empty architectures could be sacrally charged. An anonymous group portrait of c.1520, now in Utrecht (Figure 0.4, Color Plate I), depicts a view of the grotto of the Nativity in Bethlehem, flanked by members of an Amsterdam pilgrim confraternity.[35] The tiled interior hosts a tiny mandorla encircling the letters "IHS," and a compacted, stylized

0.4 **North Netherlandish.** ***Four Members of the Brotherhood of Jerusalem before the Grotto of the Nativity*, c.1520. Oil on panel, 99 × 230.** Museum Catharijneconvent, Utrecht.

room stands in for the birthplace of Christ. The four pilgrims are well-to-do members of the Amsterdam Brotherhood, who themselves had journeyed to Bethlehem—Wouter van Hoogsteyn, Jan Bennink, Jacob Heyn, and Meinert Willems, as identified on the work's original frame.[36] They kneel outside the miraculous space of the grotto. Two pilasters frame a second inscription that reads simply: "This is the figure [*figuer*] of Bethlehem wherein God was born." This titulus, denotively pointing to the grotto as a historical place, at the same time poses the architecture as, quite literally, a substantive "figure" itself, a claustrophobic room that intercedes between the realms of man and earth. The open grotto is not a sign—it does not just point to the divine but marks the site of Christ's very real impression on earth. As Karl Birkmeyer once argued, many early Netherlandish paintings relied upon architectural views precisely to mark the presence of an invisible reality.[37] This was not a juxtaposition of real/ideal, but of body and trace; according to twelfth-century theologians, the "figure" was a space and significance *beyond* history, a "figment" or a "dream image" left behind by a spiritual presence.[38] Pushed up against the specifically located here-and-now of the four *Jeruzalembroeders*, the "figure" in the Utrecht painting extracts the empty architecture—even as a specifically viewed site—from a merely symbolic link to the real Bethlehem grotto. Instead, its connection to the Netherlandish present is a bodily one. Here architecture, as *figura*, uniquely collapses time.

Roman antiquity remained a steadfast source of pictorial forms and architectural *exempla*. Prints of ruins illustrated Rome and allegorized its loss. The distinction Vitruvius drew in the *Ten Books* between the tragic, comic, and satiric scenes of the theatre was familiar to patrons as well as to artists in the sixteenth century. In Vitruvius's Book V, the classification of the tragic's "columns, pediments, and statues" as "kingly" objects, and the comic's "private buildings, balconies, and rows of windows"[39] as "common" ones raised the possibility of a purely connotative architecture itself, buildings serving no function aside from, as it were, actors. At the same time, the physical ruins of Rome themselves continued to fascinate artists and antiquarians alike, particularly in viewers from Vredeman's Antwerp. In 1558, Hieronymus Cock published Sebastian van Noyen's studies of the Baths of Diocletian (Figure 0.5).[40] These prints contained precise illustrations of ground plans, measurements, and elevations of the ruined complex, accompanied by commentary. Van Noyen, court architect to the Hapsburgs in Brussels, isolated the buildings on papers that could be assembled into a frieze reconstructing the baths, treating them as vast specimens of purely archaeological import. Cock himself, meanwhile, had drawn and etched the ruins of the Colosseum and the Capitoline hill as early as 1551, and went on to issue subsequent series in 1561 and 1562.[41] Cock's images of the Palatine differed from van Noyen's in that they were only loosely documentary (Figure 0.6); instead he fragmented views of multiple monuments, blurred distances between buildings, and dotted the ruins with travelers, tiny animals and human figures, among them (as in the extreme lower right corner of the third view of his series) spindly figures who sit upon, touch, and draw the monuments. Mantled with weeds, Cock's archways foregrounded the effects of time and decay rather than antiquity's structural glory. Further, they raised the possibility of locatable architecture alone

0.5
Jan and Lucas van Doetecum after Sebastian van Noyen, *Elevations and Section of Baths of Diocletian*, 1558. Etching and engraving, H.64. Prentenkabinet, Leiden.

evoking temporality or loss, even when no discernable *storia*, or even history, nestled among the rubble.

Cock's prints, well known to Vredeman (they shared an etcher, as we shall see in Chapter 1), incorporated Roman buildings as an ingredient of landscape rather than archaeology; a dedicatory quatrain appended to the suite of Cock's ruins by the humanist Cornelius Grapheus pondered the city's destruction as the "Queen of the World" at the hands of barbarians.[42] This pathos was itself echoed in contemporaneous depictions of Biblical architecture. Two famous paintings of the *Tower of Babel* executed by Pieter Bruegel in the 1550s, for example, handled the mythical building as an independent subject, which by its very complexity captured the linguistic dissimulation heralded by its conceit.[43] Through Cock, Vredeman's publisher, and Pieter Bruegel, his one-time collaborator, architecture gained force and marketability as a pictorial subject, for both painting and print.

Yet the specificity of these Roman and Old Testament buildings imparted them a status and a "story" that the supplementary architectures mentioned by Cennini, Vasari, and Van Mander lacked. What, then, should we make of pictures of solo buildings more ordinary, or worse—as in Vredeman's case—exaggeratedly imaginary? When, in 1558, Cock published a series of fantastic landscapes after his brother Matthys, for example, he entitled it: "Various landscape compositions with fine histories [*historien*] placed into them."[44] The publisher here actually inserted scriptural narratives, like the

0.6
Hieronymus Cock, *Third View of the Ruins on the Palatine*, 1561. Etching and engraving, H.210.
Rijksprentenkabinet, Amsterdam.

Sacrifice of Isaac, into the imaginary hillsides of his employee, in order to make the prints comprehensible. Later, Cock peopled a landscape drawing by Pieter Bruegel with the *Temptation of Christ*.[45] Why did this not occur with Vredeman? Subsequent art history assumed that without a primary narrative such work was just preliminary or unfinished—particularly so in the case of a print. Indeed, one of the questions which consistently arises when Vredeman's works are invoked as "Dutch" is what his engravings really are.

Vredeman has never fitted smoothly into histories that posit a sharp divide between Netherlandish and Flemish architectural traditions, or between real and unreal architecture. E. H. ter Kuile, bewildered by Vredeman's 1565 etchings, dismissed them as "impossible daydreams."[46] In Lewis Mumford's interwar *Culture of Cities* they fared slightly better, as "crazy copybook simulacra," which portended possibilities for urban redesign.[47] Since the nineteenth century, Vredeman's prints have been placed in a broader tradition of architectural pictures in Northern oil painting. Jan van Eyck, Jan Gossaert, and Albrecht Altdorfer all deployed elaborate architectural backdrops for religious narratives, and it is as a fulfillment and stabilization of their experiments that Vredeman's output initially drew notice. In 1866, Gustav Friedrich Waagen described Vredeman as "*die Schöpfer der Architekturmalerei*" on the basis of the paintings in Vienna and Berlin.[48] Hans Jantzen, writing in a sprawling 1910 survey of architectural painting, bound this appellation of "creator" to a project of architectonic control: as he put it: "Vredeman's drawings presented architectural representation with a solid scaffold, whereby it took on structural certainty [*konstruktive Sicherheit*] for the first time . . ."[49] For Jantzen, a devotee of Alois Riegl, Vredeman's prints established a morphological paradigm of tactile, "Flemish picture space" (*Vlämischer Bildraum*), which indirectly cleared the way for the "optical" practices of the great Dutch church painters of the seventeenth century—Pieter Saenredam, Gerard Houckgeest, and Emmanuel de Witte.[50] In his dissertation Jantzen even cited Riegl's (then-) recently published *Das holländische Grüppenportrait* (1902) approvingly in this respect, and took Vredeman's work as the decisive split between an "objective" Flemish mode of picture making and the entry into a Dutch "subjective" one, in which perspective begins to fracture and dissolve into a set of pictorial effects. Riegl had, in fact, lectured on Vredeman in a course of 1896.[51] For Jantzen, this dissolution was not a modern move, but a look backward, retrenching painting in its medieval origins, in the surfaces of ornament design, filigree, and early Netherlandish devotional images. In this trajectory Vredeman hardened perspective into a woody lattice ("*Gerüst*"), deriving its worth from a construction that was tacitly "architectural" and transferable from form to form.

Lurking within Jantzen's obscure reading is the idea that early modern perspective processes—particularly when reified by fantastic architecture—lay bare the essentially self-referential character of *all* painting. They do this allegorically. Some of the best new work on Netherlandish art has traced the way certain paintings make a subject of perspective "alone."[52] Hanneke Grootenboer has argued that perspective in certain Dutch still-lifes can allegorize the near-religious "presence" of representation itself, falling between the grammar (signs) and content (signification) of a work. With a nod to Walter Benjamin and Paul de Man, Grootenboer suggests that perspective challenges humanist ideas of symbolism based upon either identity or homology between material and image. Perspective, she insists, uniquely *avoids* fixed reference, alluding to nothing but painting's incapacity to adequately re-present something not there. In this, perspective uniquely articulates painting's essential difference from any single meaning or substance—and hence its truth. Grootenboer's interpretation has the strength of attending to the import of the pictorial "emptiness" in pictures like Vredeman's. In addition, it nuances many older interpretations of perspective offered by Northern art history, which demonstrate a particular obsession with recoupable and stable "realities" behind its works—variously iconologic (symbol), or connoisseurial (authorship, dating, condition). Within the reading of perspective as an image of the "un-representable," perspective, then, comes to re-inscribe the aura supposedly lost in the image by pre-mechanical reproduction.[53] Perspective re-sacralizes painting precisely in a milieu where it had become exuberantly secular—the Dutch Republic. Functioning as a rhetoric, that is, perspective comes to enchant pictorial discourse once again.

The idea of rhetoric (which de Man defined as the study of tropes and figures) engages elements of art theory which Vredeman himself used on the sixteenth-century stage—structures like the figure, the allegory, and even the sign. Yet, until recently, surprisingly little attention has been paid to the debts Vredeman's images owed to disciplines outside the circumscribed areas of early modern building history and theory.

A goal of the present study is to suggest that architectural images are inextricable from a Renaissance context in which fields like painting, woodwork, and urban planning were interlinked. The last subject, specifically, emerged as a coherent discipline for the first time in the sixteenth century, and, attendant to Vitruvius, found itself embracing the practices of the theater as well as the architectural treatise. This borrowing was not simply an appropriation of form; physical cities like Antwerp lifted the more immaterial strategies of visual manipulation and rhetorical address for the design of streets and buildings, and consistently recalled the perspectival shape of the stage.

In early modern Europe, the fables of Parrhasius and Zeuxis mapped twin paths to architectural or artistic invention: one could mimic the seen world, or make something from various parts of it. Leonard Barkan has pointed out that the incessant retelling of the Parrhasius and Zeuxis anecdotes was, itself, a rehearsal of their didactic: the fables' allusion to two different modes of imitation (*of the life* vs. *of the spirit*) was actually less important than their relentless repetition and refashioning in the present. Even with a minor artist like Vredeman, professional success in art and architecture hinged upon the continual re-invention of conventional motifs like, say, the antique orders. As Barkan puts it: "the twice-told story . . . the image . . . and not some set of 'meanings' variously attributed to them, *are* the objects of cultural transmission."[54] Indeed, in moving away from "classical" rhetoric as a sole mode of aesthetic theory, sixteenth-century Netherlanders (as we shall see in Chapter 2) often prized the enunciatory task of visual form alone—styles or *elocutio* were not appendages to content in northern Europe, but in their sheer formal diversity emerged *as* tradition. In this, I want to argue in what follows, might lie the best way to think about the "subject" of a work like Vredeman's 1604 engraving (Figure 0.3). The tiny nothingness at its center speaks not only to Vredeman but to the other perspective demonstrations physically stacked "behind" it within the book, to those versions which came before and will come after it. "Copper engravings," "secrets," "many different hands"—the things cited by Vredeman in his Leiden letter—these are the real stuff of art around 1600: a *series* of iterations whose repetition, in part, *is* their actual content.

Iconoclasm and the early modern artist

It was precisely in the later sixteenth century that theologians—and increasingly, artists—began to write about how values like disfigurement and even anachronism could both plague and inspire visual imagery.[55] A key obsession of many writers was with *fantasia*—images that seemed to veer from ancient prototypes as well as from forms found in nature. Springing pre-made from an artist's imagination, *fantasia* were potentially dangerous if unchecked.[56] In the *Sophist*, Plato had drawn a distinction between *icastic* and *fantastic* imitation—between imitation of things that exist in nature and things that exist solely in the mind.[57] Augustine disapproved of certain kinds of *fantasia* precisely *because* they collaged nature rather than mirrored it:

> By taking away some things from objects which the senses have brought within its knowledge and by adding some things, it is possible for the mind to produce in the exercise of imagination something which as a whole was never observed by any of the senses.[58]

The unrestrained mind, combining bits of reality—like the mythical portrait of Helen by Zeuxis—effects a gap between sensory data and the image it produces. This is potentially dangerous in a Christian framework, for it portends a departure from the natural order of things. It also grants considerable freedom to humanity's own intellect.[59] Unlike mimesis, *fantasia* foments a turn away from the real world through its internal re-invention—it deals precisely, with what is *not* seen. Augustine's combinatory scheme, perhaps, imagined a kind of art that shunts viewers not to some transcendent beyond, but back inward, perilously, to an individual and internal *mind*.

In Vredeman's day, the central issue with many image critiques lay in charges of incomprehensibility, or excess. In 1553, the reformer Jan Gerrtiz Vestege, dismayed at "over-elaborate" images in church, castigated the equally strange spectacle of removing them by force. Calvin did not condemn all art, only that which did not aspire to anything besides instruction or pleasure, for "it is an unfitting and absurd fiction, [when] the incorporeal is made to resemble corporeal matter," he wrote, since "God's majesty is far above the perception of the eyes, and debased through unseemly representations."[60] Calvin assailed the claim of mere material to presence something divine as "delusion."[61] Reformers in the Netherlands proposed removing altarpieces altogether and replacing them with "good maxims [*spreeken*] in large letters written on the walls."[62] But when iconoclasm came to Vredeman's Antwerp in August of 1566 it took relatively subtle forms.[63] Unlike the massacres accompanying image-breaking in Huguenot France, where monks were beheaded and church treasuries ransacked, in the Netherlands individuals tended to be the ones who stole away with sculptures, quietly, and often in the night. One English witness to the 1566 Antwerp iconoclasm, Richard Clough, marveled at how "the thing was done so quiet and still," and that "so few folkes" had in fact perpetrated the much-talked-about violence.[64]

Image-breakers did not randomly attack the artworks they pulled from portal niches. One observer noted how they broke off noses and heads, and "hammer[ed] away mainly at the faces."[65] The literal "figuring" agent of the work—the face, working like the "*figuer*" of the Utrecht panel—became the object of attack. As the most expressive and artful part of the human body, the face posed the most danger, and needed most to be neutralized—this was the face of God of Exodus 33, which Moses "shall not see and live."[66] In 1569, Philips Galle published a suite of engravings by Marten van Heemskerck on Old Testament iconoclasms, describing both the breaking of statues and the wide-scale razing of buildings. In *The Destruction of the Temple of Ashtoreth, Chemosh, and Milcolm* (Figure 0.7), for example, Heemskerck shows a figure standing over a fallen torso at the far left of a besieged idol. His hammer poised, the image breaker looks directly into the face of the sculpture, about to de-figure it as an echo of a second, high up in the temple's coffered dome, who lustily hacks apart the roof. In the

0.7
Phillips Galle after Marten van Heemskerck, *The Destruction of the Temple of Ashtoreth, Chemosh, and Milcolm (2 Kings 23:13)*, c.1569. Engraving, H.45.
Prentenkabinet, Leiden.

1560s, present-day resonances with such actions, and printed images of pagan ruins, would have been clear to Heemskerck's viewers. The godly visage was problematic because it gave a countenance to the sacred, imparting specificity, as it were, to something omniscient. Indeed, as Joseph Koerner has noted, iconoclasts disavowed the true idea of the image, the idea of *representation*—they scorned the idea that any poetic *figura* points away from itself to some exterior value. By dis-"figuring" a sculpture's face, then, iconoclasts in Vredeman's milieu exposed the gap between image and prototype, which the faithful had, in fact, always acknowledged. In this they returned the artwork, perhaps, to a truly early Christian aesthetic—one of effacement and difference rather than resemblance and similarity.[67] But of course this effacement, in the cool white walls and text panels of Calvinist churches, quickly could become an aesthetic itself. When this aesthetic became the subject of independent panel paintings, as we shall see in Chapter 4, the obdurateness of the fashioned thing became the very theme of the artwork.

Iconoclasm always retained an architectural quality in the Netherlands. Reformers relied upon an insistent metaphorics of razing and re-building: around 1560, the preacher Hermann Moded compared the Roman church to the shell of a snail which needed to be crushed;[68] in 1540, a Flemish rhetorician decried sculpted images "stand[ing] in the temple like old house beams."[69] Visual propaganda consistently likened the old Roman Church to a ruin in need of clearance, as when the Onzelievevrouw cathedral in Antwerp was emptied in August 1566. Netherlandish iconoclasts saw their actions as the restructuring of a wrong world. Image breaking, as Heemskerck's straining chiselers showed it, was moral work. But at least one Protestant observer saw the removal of images as breeding a new kind of enchantment: "it was the marveylest piece of work that was ever done in so short a time . . . being more like a dreme . . . that yt is to be marveled at," exclaimed Richard Clough after he witnessed the 1566 Antwerp destruction.[70]

Artists without commissions under such circumstances often looked back to just those modes of art which did not "figure" as, say, altarpieces had, or figured in different ways—intarsia, ornament, or pattern. This is where Vredeman began his career. The painter Heinrich Vogtherr, an author Vredeman read, illustrated a model-book in 1538, republished in 1543, 1551, 1572, and 1587, explaining his own motivation in Reformation events:

> . . . God has brought about a noticeable decline and arrest of all these subtle and liberal arts [*subtilen und freyen Kunsten*], whereby numbers of men have been obliged to withdraw from these arts and to return to other kinds of handicraft [*hantwerckt*] . . .[71]

Vogtherr sketches the scenario facing artists in Vredeman's day. His book's woodcuts present heads, coulisses, armor shields, even hands for copying and re-use (Figure 3.7)—hands literally cut off from specific tasks. They float and gesture on the blank page awaiting deployment. Turning away from images of holy personages, then, such an art was often forced to deal in pictures which were not only simple and overtly *wrought* in themselves, but which went even further, to become patterns for conspicuously produced *things*. Vredeman modeled chairs, footstools, and tables (Figure 0.8). Arranged symmetrically on a page, these were offered as the pleasing "results" of craft, a spatial arrangement to be used by other artists. These *handwerken*, complete with strap- and roll-work, were luxury items that could shape other luxury items, "from" *het leven*, as well as "to" it. Particularly in terms of "applied" art, such self-reflectivity has not proven easy to reconcile in art history with the notion of purely artful style. Like Vogtherr, Vredeman turned out of choice or circumstance to new venues for his skill (*techne*) in art and architecture.

Iconoclasm, then, does not so much "explain" Vredeman's work as mark a moment when crafted objects were gradually alerted to their relations to *other* kinds of images, rather than simply to ritual or divinistic import. The Lutheran image controversy was several generations old by the time Vredeman began practice. The more interesting issue in the air in Antwerp during the later sixteenth century (and surely in Prague when Vredeman visited in the late 1590s, as we shall see) was how the image itself

0.8
Hans Vredeman de Vries, *Differents Pourtraicts de Menuiserie*, no. 6, 1583. Etching, H.497. Rijksprentenkabinet, Amsterdam.

could acquire a theory, a theory that could account for the idea of art as something increasingly reproducible.

Any attempt to come to grips with Vredeman's prints will have to reckon with a growing awareness that early modern "copies" can be regarded as more than gestures *back* towards a singular prototype.[72] Works like Vredeman's might be considered, conversely, as moves *outward*; forms assuming re-use and redefinition, and forms which were often appreciated precisely because of their resonances with other versions of themselves. This, we shall see, is how Vredeman's works were often understood in the late sixteenth century. The theater historian Richard Schechner has indicated this facility with the idea of *rehearsal*: ". . . rehearsal is a way of selecting from possible actions those to be performed,"[73] he writes. Indeed, the term *repetitie* was used by Dutch rhetoricians in the sixteenth century to describe both practices and re-stagings of single plays:[74] the repetition of the dramatic form did not presage the work, it *was* the work. In one 1587 Dutch dictionary *verhalen* (recount) meant both to imitate and recite; children "rehearsed" their school lessons when they read back to a master.[75] The word's place in present-day Dutch shades the idea of performance repeated, not just a performance prepared. Yet unlike "performance," rehearsal assumes a kind of reciprocity between different instantiations of similar phenomena straying from their origins, to chains of activities which, like Vredeman's own patterns, could be characterized by precisely Schechner's words: "repetition, simplification, exaggeration, rhythmic action, the transformation of 'natural sequences' of behavior into 'composed sequences.'" These summarize the processes of rehearsal at work in certain sixteenth-century artworks, and name the actions this book will explore.

Save for the opening chapter, the sections that follow correspond to the main undertakings of Vredeman's career. Chapter 1 introduces the ideas "*schilder-architect*" and of invention, as they were understood in the sixteenth-century Netherlands. Chapter 2 considers Vredeman's early designs in Antwerp and his work for the print publisher Hieronymus Cock in the 1560s. These prints introduced into the market an entirely new graphic product: the "ideal" cityscape in perspective. Rather than providing a description of urban space as a collection of architectural features, Vredeman, like his contemporary William Shakespeare, instead seems to have understood the civic street as a potential stage for human drama. Such works appeared at a time when authorities (both Catholic and Reformed) in Antwerp demonstrated increasing sensitivity to maintaining urban order and beauty through the promulgation of ordinances and edicts.

The same chapter discusses Vredeman's career as a *rederijker*, and the designs he created for joyous entries, or *blijde inkomsten*. Like many contemporaries (such as Cornelis Floris and Pieter Bruegel), Vredeman belonged to a rhetorical chamber that occupied a key position in the social life of the city; competitions held by the rhetoricians took place in Antwerp's physical center, the Groote Markt. Such events informed Vredeman's later architectural and perspective theory, not just in terms of built homologies but also in regard to the actual mechanisms of address. They were influential for Vredeman's pedagogical method. The very public (and indigenously urban) character of rhetoric competitions, I maintain, provided the basis for many of Vredeman's textless images.

Ornament and "grotesques"—the intransigent and vexed genres of graphic and literary imagery Vredeman explored throughout his career—are the subject of Chapter 3. The historiographic controversies played out in our own time and in his regarding the propriety and function of "ornament," are discussed in light of his column book prints. It is Vredeman's first systematic "book," the *Architectura* of 1577, which proves to be these controversies' most dynamic grounds for experiment. Here, his early ornament series seem to inflect his writings on painting, a theory that becomes essayed in a startling manner in his biography in Van Mander's *Schilderboeck*, which is the focus of Chapter 4.

Chapter 5 is devoted to Vredeman's *Perspective* of 1604–05. Intended chiefly as a guidebook for artists, the *Perspective* adopted the connection between vision, architecture, and the evocation of depth as intrinsic. In the treatise urban structures themselves provided the means for the process of sight to be expressed. Unlike treatises such as Leon Battista Alberti's *Della Pittura* (c. 1435–36) which, unillustrated, couched its explanations largely in terms of abstractions, Vredeman's work instead emphasized the instrumentality of pictorial/rhetorical demonstration. One of its most celebrated features is its supposed insistence that multiple viewpoints—something that can easily be imagined as a part of the life of the early-modern city—can be accommodated on paper or panel. Yet the *Perspective*'s plates, existing on something of a border between purely conceptualized and realized structures, evince an understanding of perspective rooted wholly in objects. As we shall see, Vredeman's perspective both underscored and effaced the boundaries between the built world and the simulated one; on the one hand, the book used geometry to create fantastic, overtly hermetic architectural utopias, on the other, it deployed perspective illusionistically to mark those utopias as fictions. The tension between these twinned roles of scaffold and mirror, always at the heart of perspective itself, became in the sixteenth century a source of pictorial anxiety out of which Vredeman was able to fashion his whole reputation.

Framing history

In a well-known passage from the *Critique of Judgment*, Immanuel Kant listed three examples of what he viewed as *Parerga*, or "ornamentation," that is, ". . . what is only an adjunct, and not an intrinsic constituent in the complete representation of the object."[76] These examples were: the frames of pictures, the clothes of statues, "the colonnades around sumptuous buildings" (*Säulengang um Prachtgebäude*). By being purely supplementary, Kant claimed, such features contrastingly indicated what was intrinsic to the aesthetic object. The adornments existed "merely to win approval by means of [their] charm," and, "as *finery*, take away from the genuine beauty." This genuine beauty, and, in it, the core art work itself, resides in forms appealing to taste alone—everything else (such as the column, frame, garment) was through its sensory allure purely supplementary, and, for Kant, wholly separate. For Kant, the division between work and by-work was quite fixed.

Yet, as Derrida showed, Kant's architectural example was problematic from its inception. In structural terms, of course, columns are anything but accessory to the functioning of a building. Among other things, they keep up the roof, and in this respect differ significantly from the other two *parerga*: the garment and the frame. Yet, most importantly, Kant's positing of a marginal entity as the sole determinant of what is essential in *all* art placed him in the awkward position of requiring a clear distinction between the two. What exactly is supplemental about a *Säulengang* (Figure 0.3) if it is the very means by which a building is defined? Derrida demonstrated how as framers of the aesthetic object Kant's supposed *parerga* are, in fact, one and the same, with the essential in the art work itself: "the frame is not at all an adornment," he wrote, "and one cannot do without it."[77] Derrida's now-canonical exposing of Kant's flaw forcefully pointed to the mutual dependency of object and supplement, and undermined the tantalizing notion—resurgent in early twenty-first-century discourse on building—of a free-floating, purely autonomous architecture.[78] As Rebecca Zorach has noted in her elegant study of art and Renaissance excess, what is most crucial about Derrida's critique for early modern studies is its emphasis upon *detachment*.[79] We could go on to say that

Derrida's model suggests the intrinsic *worth* of the ostensibly surplus in art and architecture, a worth that was defined by an *activity*—the performative designation of the aesthetic object. "Work" in Kant's sense, is, above all, a function of duration, not just of essence: if *ergon* is the amount of time needed to finish a task, *parergon* is the remainder, the pastime which lets art arise dialectically.[80]

We might ask, then, just why Vredeman de Vries—for many years a "supplement" to art- and architectural history, and still little known outside of the Netherlands and Belgium—matters today, and why he has lately become famous again: the subject of two dissertations, three exhibitions, six symposia, four books, and three dozen articles and reviews since 1994.[81] As *parergon*, Vredeman himself might offer less a corrective to art history's "traditional" exclusivities than, along the lines outlined by Derrida, a questioning of the category of "art" in the Renaissance itself. More specifically, he complicates the idea of art viewed as distinct from craft, and the idea of the "designer" standing in opposition to that of the artist or architect. These have never been particularly stable distinctions when one considers the overlaps of media and production techniques in early modern Europe, particularly after the Reformation. Today Vredeman might supply a history for some much-touted aspects of contemporary architectural practice—for example, the idea, whatever its merits may be, of architecture as "image building," wherein design itself becomes a collection of signature motifs applicable to sculpture, furniture, even jewelry, rather than a site- or medium-specific task.[82] It is not too difficult to see in Vredeman the seeds of a purely autonomous architecture, one of modernism's more chimerical totems.[83]

Yet if a categorical distinction between early modern "art" and "craft" objects becomes harder to sustain, a more dynamic notion of multiple cultural "renaissances" has arisen in the study of culture around 1600—one where Italy is a vibrant epicenter among many, with artists and objects moving freely among diffuse geographical milieus. Vredeman's paintings and prints are themselves examples of such phenomena, and his peripatetic biography—which ranged across borders long riven, until recent decades, into Cold-war geographies—forges a useful link into global histories de-motivating fixed sites, authors, and epochs. Vredeman folds nicely into an interest in "nomadic" modes of representation—nomadism, after Deleuze and Guattari, becoming an attractive metaphor for a kind of freedom. Yet souls who find themselves truly dispossessed tend to regard the romanticization of the nomad as a modish affectation; real exile tends to be calamitous for those who withstand it.[84] In the 1604 Leiden application that began this Introduction, Vredeman hoped to end his own banishment by casting his authorial skills apart from others. The following chapters will argue, however, this was not via a distancing from older, late-medieval models of collective artifact production, but through an engagement with and deepening of them. We can see Vredeman's desperate citation of his "numerous copper engravings" in the Leiden letter not just as a gesture to past ideas, but as a mark of his interest in making the replication of architecture *itself* a specific authorial gesture.

One final note: although this book is about a single artist, Hans Vredeman de Vries, it is intended as something other than a life-and-work monograph. Sophie-Petra

Zimmermann and Heiner Borggrefe have already made crucial inroads towards that task in their indispensable publications. This book, however, published on the 400th anniversary of Vredeman's death, deals quite heavily with issues of—and alternatives to—biography, in the belief that Vredeman was not so much "reflected" in his work as fashioned by it. Vredeman lived in the era not just of Calvin and Erasmus, but also of Castiglione and Montaigne, of the idea that the notion of "self" was mutable and aesthetic, an artwork subject to reshaping. There might therefore be a certain irony inherent in much recent research on Vredeman, which tends (often rightly) to be wary of imposing "theory" on phenomena of the past.[85] In fact, artists from Vredeman's sphere were obsessed with how their own historical specificity constructed a view of lost cultures, particularly antiquity: the dispute over the proper use of the architectural orders, which will be an interwoven theme of Chapter 3, is just one example of how these debates played out.

Erik Forssman once wrote that Vredeman's work stemmed from a late sixteenth-century crisis of architectural norms, from the "mannerist" realization that Rome could never be recovered, and that, when perceived, antiquity would be known only in fragments.[86] Early twentieth-century art historians were obsessed with mannerist art because it obdurately refused to gloss over the disjunction between its relation to antiquity and its embroilment in its own here-and-now. If ideas like "crisis" or "mannerism" remain useful today, they might be understood less as stylistic designations than as impetuses to experiential criticism, that is, as modes of interpretation which promise to engage the *tension* inherent in present-day access to past objects and sources.[87] Vredeman's mannerism, appearing at the strange moment of 1600, might therefore introduce an idea sunk deep into history: a recognition that art's confrontation with its various pasts was—relentlessly and fascinatingly—mediated anew by its presents.

Part One

PERFORMANCES OF ORDER

Chapter 1

Unbuilt architecture in the world of things

For all invention, Sir,
Comes by degrees, and on the view of nature;
A world of things, concurre to the designe
Which make it feasible, if Art conduce.
Ben Jonson[1]

Fertile and even prodigal as nature may be, it has not invented everything.
Paul Valéry, "Address to the Society of Engravers"[2]

1.1
Hans Vredeman de Vries and Gillis Mostaert, *Christ in the House of Mary and Martha*, 1566. Oil on panel, 86 × 114.3.
Hampton Court Palace. Reproduced by permission of Her Majesty Queen Elizabeth II.

When Vredeman cited "copper engravings" as testament to his architectural qualifications, he was not myopically overestimating his own ability. Rather, he summarized the changing role printed images had come to play in the practice of building over the course of the sixteenth century. Print was not the only kind of repeatable image in Vredeman's day. Yet print publishers were unique in the energy they devoted to the charting of different futures for their author's initial designs. In the Netherlands the interests of engravers, draughtsmen, and even dealers frequently clashed. This was particularly problematic for images of the built environment, the kind of work this chapter will examine. On the one hand, "independent" architecture appeared to early modern viewers to have many potential subjects (perspective, ornament, printmaking itself), and, on the other, no subject at all.

In the Middle Ages, architectural instruction relied upon a very private corpus of visual templates. Building techniques remained shrouded in guild conditions of secrecy, and, more significantly, of anonymity. As Mario Carpo has suggested, it was the mnemonic facility of the medieval architect that was most threatened by the effusion of print. Guilds banned sketch-making for journeymen traveling far from home, insuring that, before woodcut illustration, models of famous buildings existed chiefly in the minds of those who had seen structures firsthand.[3] Oral description remained the basis of design transmission for most medieval masons. Thus, when one of the first original vernacular architectural treatises was published in 1537—Sebastiano Serlio's epoch-defining *Fourth Book*—its most lasting effect was not just to render this memory function obsolete, but to subsume guild arcana under a banner of single authorship, supplying visual models seemingly useful to anybody. Books like Serlio's seemed to demystify the inventive act of architecture. By 1582, the Milanese theorist Giovanni Lomazzo could lament that Serlio's prints "turned more dog catchers into architects than [I] have hairs on my beard," while three centuries later, John Ruskin lamented that architectural manuals "made plagiarists of its architects, and slaves of its workmen."[4] If they differed in their view of the heroic (or pitiable) status of the craftsman transformed, both Ruskin and Lomazzo agreed that a mysterious link between original idea and architectural product had been severed by the initial appearance of print. The work of design had been democratized, for better or for worse. If not of dog catchers and plagiarists, central to both critics was the assumption that the onset of reproducible templates changed the notion of invention completely.

The collaboration of architects and printmaking in early modern Europe has, of late, attracted considerable interest, with the most important result being that Antwerp publishers like Philips Galle and Hieronymus Cock have come to be recognized as crucial for shaping the themes, as well as the distribution, of reproducible art on paper.[5] Thanks both to new trends in publishing and to Reformation debates over the status of images as a whole, the use of prints by the architect and visual artist—first defined in Italy and transmitted to the Netherlands—was changing in the sixteenth century. Many traditional benchmarks of achievement, of professional failure, and success, were undermined. To see precisely how this took place we need to begin not with a print or a building however, but with a painting.

Rhetorics of choice

A *Christ in the House of Mary and Martha*, now in Hampton Court (Figure 1.1, Color Plate II), is Hans Vredeman's earliest signed panel. It is the first of a series of paintings executed around 1566.[6] Based on an etching designed for Hieronymus Cock in 1560 (Figure 1.2), the painting shows the figure of Mary demurely reading at the feet of Christ. Three disciples converse at a table in a shaded corner. Martha, far away from this main scene, appears through a doorway on the extreme right, speaking to an old man near a kitchen fireplace. Outside, on the immediate right, at the stoop of a long colonnade, a youth draws water from a well. A deeply recessed vault reveals an arched pavilion in the middle right; here, a turbaned man slowly plods towards the foreground. Ebullient grotesque decoration splays over the ceiling and walls, covering the windows, the shutters, and even the hearth, interrupted only by a painted roundel; this tiny oval describes a sunny landscape with a single tree and a Sacrifice of Isaac. The heavy overhead beams echo the floor's diagonals. In effect, they vie with the New Testament story for spatial hegemony; the Gospel tale seems merely an afterthought, overwhelmed by the ornamental gush.

1.2
Hans Vredeman de Vries, *Scenographiae, sive perspectivae*, no. 10, 1560. Etching, H.40.
Albertina, Vienna.

Vredeman's architecture threatens to usurp the narrative, a story which was conventionally about choosing between alternate means of devotion. Mary, who welcomed Christ into her home by listening to his teachings, was contrasted with Martha, who busied herself with preparation for the house—the word, the gospel of Christ, as chosen by Mary, becomes "the good part," while works, the path chosen by Martha, is chastised by God. Vredeman's image envisions the dilemma outlined by the fable, fixing visual attention not on one of the sisters, but on the spaces between them, scattering ornament, line, color, and recession across the picture surface.

As a sequence of frames and surfaces—doorway, colonnade, window, hearth—the composition vigorously denies any central focus, drawing us instead into fictive corners, across elaborate thresholds, out through mullioned, painted glass windows. In contrast to Joachim Beuckelaer's roughly contemporary version of the same narrative (Figure 1.3), Vredeman's *House* draws its trappings away, remaining no push and all pull—attention does not flit between foodstuffs and vertiginous floors, but in the Hampton Court picture slinks outward into the painting's recesses.[7] Like Beuckelaer's kitchen, however, Vredeman's room relies upon multiple views—views splayed outward, overtaking the staffage. This is the kind of picture Max Dvořák first called a "mannerist inversion," in which the stuff of ordinary life, a signal for an emergent genre painting, does not crowd out some moral, but circulates and structures it.[8] Through the separation of the figures of Mary and Martha to twin extremes of the picture,

1.3
Joachim Beuckelaer, *Kitchen Scene with Christ in the House of Mary and Martha (The Four Elements: Fire)*, 1570. Oil on canvas, 157.5 × 214.5.
National Gallery, London.

Vredeman opts for a different kind of designatory function for his architecture, however: rather than splitting the scene into "secular" or "spiritual" realms of study, it frames the relation between the two as fluctuating and tense; if anything, it is the architecture which has become the "the better part" of the Gospel story, not the seated figures. One nineteenth-century observer of the picture put this in moral tones: ". . . there is great impropriety, in rendering the decorations of [Mary and Martha's] palace more important than the personages of the scene."[9] Vredeman's version of the Luke story is itself thrust into the present, becoming the "better" part of the work—the theme as one apprehension of the New Testament in the here-and-now.

In Van Mander's account, the Martha painting figures as a particular specialty of Vredeman, a "perspective," a species of image equivalent to an effect known as *deursiende*, or "seeing-into," or "seeing-through." For the Antwerp banker Gillis Hooftman, we learn Vredeman "made a large perspective [*Perspect*] looking like a view into a court [*als een doorsien in eenen hof*]."[10] The label of "perspective" was not just a term for empty, or empty-seeming paintings—panels constructed for triumphal entries were also known by the term.[11] That contemporaries regarded the religious subject as often secondary to its actual arrangement in pictures is suggested by designations in early inventories;[12] the Hampton Court painting itself, for example, was described as "A small prospective" when it was cataloged in 1619.[13] In the collection of Henry Frederick, Prince of Wales, the work sat among other "perspectives;" a visitor to Henry's collection also described "a vaulted house . . . perspectivally painted."[14] In fact, it is as a "perspectivist" that Vredeman was best known; in the Saxon courtier Gabriel Kaltmarkt's 1587 list of "Famous Living Painters from the Netherlands," he urged collectors to seek out works by one "*Johann Fridman Freiß,*" who was described as "*ein guter perspectivus.*"[15]

In the sixteenth century, the story of Mary and Martha (Luke 10: 38–42) was frequently framed as a narrative of doctrinal choices; Christ, visiting the house of two sisters, chastised his hostess Martha for preoccupying herself with the preparation of food in the kitchen, when she should have followed the example of her sister, Mary, who sat listening to his teachings. Protestants found in this story an easy allegory of ideal Christian behavior—the Word (Mary), not church works (Martha), legitimized as the path to salvation.[16] Late versions of the story from the Netherlands posited related inequivalency to the pairs, insisting upon each figure's significance as a varied form of worship, not one or the other.[17]

In the painting by Vredeman, Mary's choice is seemingly upheld as the wise one, yet not just through the capacious space she occupies. Rather, Vredeman splits the panel between the vault at right and the figures seated at left, so that the space is united by the box-like composition of the room and the tunneling archway at center. At its heart, the picture is empty; Jantzen marveled at how this painting managed to look deserted, even as it stayed ornamentally abuzz.[18] The tunnel is one destination for a viewing, the seated party another. We are accustomed in Italian paintings to follow perspective to the site of action or history at a vanishing point. But in the Hampton Court picture there is none, we find only a turbaned, indecipherable human blotch. The dynamic switching of attention prompted by the disjointed spaces posits the "choosing" itself—rather than its results—as the drama of the picture. In moving among the different spaces—foreground, background, ceiling, floor—the viewer faces not just the didactic outcome of the decision making of the Biblical story, but the tension inherent in *making* that decision. Yet, if such an image of choices made regarding the apprehension of God had clear resonances with both Protestant and Counter-Reformation sides of theological debates, the protagonists could be interchangeable: X-ray photography has shown that an earlier state of the painting put Martha's body in a center doorway carrying a basket. This figure was obliterated sometime in the late-sixteenth century.[19] Vredeman's picture was thus confessionally mutated, moved away from a celebration of "good" work towards the architecture itself.

When the *Martha* painting was signed by Vredeman in 1566 it was marked in two separate places along the architecture, once atop a Moses bust at right in Latin, and a second time, in Greek script, below the roundel landscape at the center. If we consider this kind of painting not simply as a pictorial translation of a Bible passage, as Sergiusz Michalski does,[20] but as a specific pictorial statement, the *Mary and Martha* becomes less about conflicts between "earthly" or "divine," or, say, direct versus mediated apprehension of Christian teachings. Rather, it evinces the way an artist effects a beholder's imbrication in such conflicts. Viewed from afar, the fable now becomes a shard of Christian teaching conveyed into the present by Vredeman's work. If not for us, the scene thematizes one translation of a history thrust awkwardly into the setting of the present, into a world crafted (perhaps not entirely successfully) by Vredeman's specific hands. The figures sit awkwardly, immaterial, and tenuous. We have the distinct feeling we are looking not at Vredeman's symbolism of Mary and Martha, but at somebody else's. The apostles, the kitchen, the two sisters seem not to belong here, and, it seems, perhaps neither do we.

In his 1516 edition of the New Testament published in Basel, Erasmus retranslated the Mary and Martha passage from the Book of Luke. The Latin Vulgate had rendered Luke's words as the following: "One thing is needful: Mary has chosen the better part, which shall not be taken away from her." Based on the Greek Septaguint, Erasmus amended the verse to read simply: "Mary has chosen a good part." This alteration, which shocked early humanists,[21] had the effect of reconfiguring the story's didacticism altogether; gone was a clear hierarchy between work and word, between praxis and theory, between busy-ness and leisure assigned to Martha and Mary at Christ's feet. Suddenly, the two personifications were roughly equivalent—Mary was one "good" among two. Erasmus's substitution was a philological thunderclap, one that had the effect of posing the sisters as dual aspects of the single soul; faith *and* works, the Basel edition seemed to imply, were not only coincident but unriven elements of a Christian life.

Vredeman's painting, with its Greek and Latin signatures, and its colossal arch cleaving the middle, seems to be about both Mary and Martha and about the translator's act. The Hampton Court picture is slashed by calligraphic ornament and lines, but is, in a sense, dominated by only one: the tunneling arch which vanishes into nothing.

Off-center as it is, the view heralds the painting as emanating from a particular point of view, a view that bridges the paired realms of Martha and Mary. Now, the tension *between* these separate realms is what is delivered to the viewer, a tension that is the very subject of the inventoried "*Perspect.*" The painting's basis in a specific engraving meant that other versions—not-quite replicas—could and did exist: identically sized versions after the Hampton Court picture, for example, are now in Bremen and London.[22] Ultimately, the allusion of the painting is not just to Luke or to Vredeman, but to the awkwardness of choosing in a translation from word to image.

The work of print in the age of architectural reproducibility

Vredeman's initial involvement with "perspective," and, secondarily, the architecture it constructed, was first through drawings. In the 1550s, while still living in Mechelen, Vredeman began to design prints for painters and tapestry makers. The drawing eventually used for the *Martha* panel, now in Vienna, formed part of a series of 24 architectural views, accompanied only by a title page with a dedication to Antoine Perrenot de Granvelle, then cardinal of Mechelen.[23] Granvelle was an ardent bibliophile, antiquarian, and art collector, who, in 1558, had underwritten the massive drawing expedition to Rome by the military engineer, Sebastian van Noyen; this trip resulted in the series of engravings describing elevations and plans of the Baths of Diocletian (Figure 0.5.). Hieronymus Cock's firm, *Aux Quatre Vents* (at the Four Winds), often took the subject of perspective as something akin to ruined architecture—something whose efficacy derived from its formal adaptability, its suitability to other media.[24]

By the 1560s, Hieronymus Cock (c.1510–70) had established himself as the most innovative printmaker in north Europe. He had introduced an entirely new set of themes into the Antwerp print market and taken subjects pioneered in Italy and southern Germany—sophisticated sheets of ornament, Roman ruins, landscape—and put them before the eyes of an unprecedentedly vast public. A former painter, Cock was listed in Antwerp's St Lucasgild by 1546, and traveled to Italy in 1549 and 1550.[25] Employing a filial team of etchers—Lucas and Jan van Doetecum—Cock offered the Antwerp market reproductions of Vatican frescoes as well as "vernacular" subjects like Pieter Bruegel's peasant scenes. Between 1551 and his death in 1570, Cock maintained a stable of Italian engravers such as the Mantuan expatriate Giorgio Ghisi, who furnished him with reproductions of antique sculpture.[26] Between 1557 and 1565, it was Cock who published Vredeman's series exclusively, and for whom he would go on to produce nearly 200 individual images.[27] Vredeman was ideal for a house eager to take on unorthodox subjects, and to adapt recognizably "antique" motifs into a Netherlandish milieu. *Aux Quatre Vents* was distinguished from other firms in Antwerp, like those run by Hans Lefrinck and Gerard de Jode, for its savvy estimation of the heterogeneity of the audience for prints—"let the cock cook what the people (*volcx*) want," the punning motto of the *Vents* firm, was etched into a 1560 street scene designed by Vredeman in the same *Scenographiae* series (Figure 1.4)—*volcx* a play on the name of Cock's wife, Volcken, who for a time operated his shop.[28] If what the people wanted certainly changed from year to year, it seems Cock's reputation as an adventurous chooser of subjects granted Vredeman's work an imprimatur and marketability it might not otherwise have seen. Vredeman's setting of Cock's shop into such a plunging sceneography—a street with Netherlandish features but ultimately fantastic—allegorized the reach of *Aux Quatre Vents*' products, of which it was one. The firm's building in Vredeman's print is presented as anchoring a world that could be anywhere, at any of the "four winds" marked on the cartouche adorning the upper floor of the facade.

By the 1560s, the real Antwerp of Vredeman's youth, as we shall see in Chapter 2, had come to rival cities like Paris, Basel, Nuremberg, Strasbourg, and Venice in sheer volume of printed output. Close proximity to a deep-sea port, a relatively large supply of local labor, and, perhaps most importantly, a high concentration of interested and wealthy art buyers attached to the city's spice trade and banking industry, insured that demand for luxury goods and books was constant. The nearby university of Leuven

1.4
Hans Vredeman de Vries, *Scenographiae, sive perspectivae,* no. 1, 1560. Etching, H.31.
Albertina, Vienna.

provided an eager market for theological texts, and, at least initially, church authorities in charge of monitoring doctrinal content rarely interfered. Although paper, typically one of the largest costs in book production, remained particularly expensive in Antwerp,[29] print publishers were often quite bold in the nature and scale of their undertakings. By 1560, the printing firm headed by French expatriate Christoffel Plantin was turning out texts on no less than 22 presses—books devoted to everything from philology, horticulture, and astronomy, to mythology, travel descriptions, and law.[30]

In the Netherlands the print trade retained professional associations with woodcutting, glass painting, goldsmithing, and metalwork. "*Prenters*" were listed as members of the St Lucasgild in Antwerp as early as 1492.[31] As in Germany, the production of prints there was legislated by the same rules overseeing other replicated objects: floor tiles, clay figurines, wax seals, even ensigns and badges (Figure 1.5). The professionalization of these small industries remained a model for early engravers and printers.[32] Associations between print and, say, pilgrimage tokens were not new: Gutenberg, an early innovator (if not the inventor) of the printing press, had himself started out as a fashioner of *Spiegelzeichen* (mirror-badges) in Strasbourg before he experimented with movable type.[33] Forms and repeatable media in Antwerp were likewise intermixed.

1.5
Netherlandish, Pilgrimage Badge of St. Ursula, c.1300–50. Lead-tin alloy, 9.1 × 7.1.
Collection Amsterdams Historisch Museum.

Hieronymus Cock's and, later, Christoffel Plantin's operations in Antwerp were in many ways grandiose streamlinings of late-medieval serial-object production. Albrecht Dürer's *Life of the Virgin* series, printed in Nuremberg in 1500, was perhaps the earliest instance of a new, singularly bound "fine art print" dominating complementary text, an example followed in the Netherlands by Lucas van Leyden around 1520. Lucas and Dürer, in an extension of the painter's craft, effectively consolidated control over print production under one roof.[34] Through the adoption of copper and iron engraving—more precise and often quicker to execute than woodcutting—publishers' intaglio processes allowed a visual precision that was perfectly suited to new print subjects like cartography. Engraved images had, of course, long elevated the selling price of books. But by the 1550s, those "independent" subjects of engraving which had traditionally been subservient to a text—ornament prints, for example—became, for many publishers, high-end, independent items. Cock, as discussed in Chapter 3, issued designs such as cartouches in elaborate, autographed suites. In this manner, the *Aux Quatre Vents* firm was able to carve out a niche in an Antwerp awash with printed images: not just by issuing new types and formats for prints (which appealed to collectors), but by nourishing and updating the print medium's traditional imbrication with older kinds of craft.

In general, the print process in which Vredeman participated, even when under the support and control of a single patron like Granvelle and a publisher like Cock, remained a diffuse and largely businesslike affair. Following the examples of Roman firms like the houses of Antonio Salamanca and Antoine Lafrery, Antwerp printmakers seem to have doled out work on what are now called "reproductive" prints—works that translated paintings or sculpture into line—to separate workshops and sites. In the mid-sixteenth century, demand for Biblical histories quickly eclipsed that of mythology, and Counter-Reformation bans on overly "artful" images, particularly after the Council of Trent (1563), sent publishers scurrying to find non-controversial subject matter. Architecture, perspective, and landscape filled this need. Cock's firm, for its part, was later able to maintain distribution contracts with Christoffel Plantin's firm (which also dabbled in the publication of banned texts),[35] which allowed his sheets to circulate throughout Europe and, in several cases, to Spanish dominions overseas—inventories record crates of *kunstprenten* being shipped to Mexico alongside dictionaries and missals as early as 1568.[36] Additionally, the audiences for Cock's materials appear to have matched that for Plantin's books. Not only did both items travel along the same distribution networks ("history" prints, architectural books, and theological texts are listed in Plantin's entries for the catalog of the Frankfurt Book Fair between 1582 and 1589),[37] but there was also little difference in price—loose engravings of Biblical subjects fetched consistently high sums, at two and three guilders. One must recall that Cock's publications (among them, Vredeman's etchings), in contrast to their state today, did not always appear in sets; we know that, particularly for craftsmen, ornament sheets were often offered independently, and more affordably. In some cases materials from a variety of different series would be brought together in a single luxury artifact, bound in calfskin or fabric.

1.6
Hans Vredeman de Vries, preliminary drawing for *Scenographiae, sive perspectivae,* no. 19, 1556–60. Pen and wash on paper, 20.8 × 26.0.
Albertina, Vienna.

But how were the prints actually produced? A drawing like Vredeman's early Vienna sheet (Figure 1.6) showing an Italianate colonnade in wash, was, in an establishment such as Cock's, the first stage in a sophisticated system of manufacture. In Antwerp the idea of a single artist exerting a firm hold over his entire publication, copyright, and sale remained quite rare, since guild regulations insisted upon firm separations between the tasks of *figurschnyder* and *drukker*.[38] Put simply, the process of making a print did nothing more than farm out the processes that artists like Lucas van Leyden and Albrecht Dürer had controlled. First, an initial design would be produced, usually by a painter. This composition, in ink or chalk on paper, would be engraved, etched, or carved into copper or wood by another craftsman. Next, a printer would press the resulting onto wet paper, and leave it to dry. Finally, a publisher, who often financed all of these activities, would collate and distribute the image to local sellers and dealers abroad.[39] Cock's and Plantin's firms published *and* dealt prints. These tasks were not, it seems, generally conducted under one roof. Around mid-century, Antwerp publishing firms probably resembled offices rather than workshops, closer to hushed libraries than bustling places of craft. In Cock's case the actual presses were kept in his shop's basement, while the upper floors were reserved for engravers to take advantage of the good light.[40]

Dutch printmaking remained a business undertaking precisely by refashioning, rather than replacing, older divisions of labor and responsibility. Van Mander described Cock as a "merchant" rather than an artist, despite Cock's long tenure in Italy and his training as a painter; in turning to print publishing Cock seems to have abandoned "true" art.[41] Yet Van Mander reports that Cock "gave up art in order to deal in it," indicating an implied worth to the paper products of the *Aux Quatre Vents*. Cock's invention subsisted in his management of the firm. In Antwerp the various activities connected with printing were scattered among the small shops of the Lombardenvest, a neighborhood known for the sale of paintings and textiles.[42] In Cock's case large stocks of finished prints were kept on hand for sale on his premises, while preliminary materials (sketches) were stored offsite. In the inventory of Cock's widow, Volcken, drawn up in 1601, it was revealed that the headquarters of "*de vier winden*" did not even keep copperplates on its immediate site, and contracted out the act of printing to a master printer named Sander Janssen some blocks away. Several of the copperplates in the same inventory, etched by the van Doetecums, survive today reused as painting supports.[43] In such an organization the job of print design would have remained relatively insular in comparison to other tasks tied more closely (both spatially and conceptually in the city) to the production sites of paintings.

Vredeman, for his part, joined Pieter Bruegel, Cornelis Floris, and Lambert Lombard in having his designs etched by the brothers Lucas and Jan van Doetecum. Initially engravers of maps, the van Doetecums occupied a shop near the Arenbergstraat,[44] where they developed a mysterious technique of engraving. This mixed the trace of the needle with that of the burin, which in itself attracted comment: "a completely new and ingenious manner," the German traveler Matthias Quod called it in 1609, "that was not considered etching but pure engraving."[45] The allure of the van Doetecums' technique was its capacity to evoke the effects of quick drawing and even wash, using scraped and hatched lines. Their etchings mimicked the appearance of engravings—much more time-consuming to make (and accordingly priced). Connoisseurs were evidently delighted by the Van Doetecums' cross-medium subterfuge, which Cock promoted himself in unexpected ways; on surviving early impressions of Vredeman's first *Sceneographiae* print (Figure 1.4) a thin contour of acid residue was left visible in the right-hand sky where the plate was bitten with acid. Seemingly engraved, this plate was, in fact, etched, a subtlety early collectors would have adored.

As engravers the van Doetecums would have received double the pay normally allotted to draughtsmen.[46] This may appear surprising today, but from a business point of view such high value hardly seems strange: etching, in its materials and meticulousness, remained largely an extension of metalsmithing; the van Doetecums, of course, used the more expensive materials (copper), and produced the tangible objects from which impressions would ultimately be pulled (plates). In doing so, they supplied the tangible stuff that permitted print production to occur. Plates, once etched, often became the most highly valued assets of a publishing firm: we know that in October 1561, Cock was able to pay more than half the deposit on a new house with a collection of his copperplates and other works of art.[47]

The etchers were also granted relative freedom in their interpretation of designs. Unlike preliminary drawings, engraved plates were protected by guild price standards, since plates without presses remained relatively worthless. The large numbers of Antwerp metalworkers who were employed as engravers suggests that a very different kind of expertise than sheer draughtsmanship was called for at the stage of print engraving, and Quod's comments on the van Doetecums indicate that the specialty was not without its own opportunities for creativity and distinction. Hendrick Goltzius, for example, saw his asking prices rise in the 1590s, after he developed a way to simulate etched line with a pen and paper rather than vice versa.[48]

Yet even though Antwerp prints were valued highly, and etchers paid more, the very survival of so many designs originally destined for transferral suggests that drawings retained a valued financial role in print publishing around 1560. Aesthetically, drawings underpinned any collaborative print project, and it was the "inventor" who showed ultimate responsibility for their contents. Countless intellectual property disputes raged as prints became more profitable, as well as doctrinally inflammatory. In May 1558, the Guild of St. Luke hived off an entire sub-section for printers in order to shield members from potential Inquisition charges. In a court case from 1567, meanwhile, the block cutter Willem van Parys was charged with heresy for several anti-Inquisition prints he had produced. When interrogated, van Parys, like any good employee under duress, passed the buck, in this case to his boss, a minor publisher named Hans van Bauhuysen. As van Parys claimed, it was van Bauhuysen the Inquisition wanted, since van Parys had merely *cut* the images, not designed them. Why then should he be held accountable for what they described? The two processes of drawing and engraving were categorically separate, he argued, and responsibility for the invention of the image lay squarely with the former. Apparently the Inquisition agreed. Van Bauhuysen, the publisher, was arrested and sentenced to six years of civic exile, while van Parys—like the van Doetecums, an engraver—was released on bail.[49]

Even given this woodcutter's very understandable desire to minimize his own importance under interrogation, design remained a collaborative (if not solitary) process behind printmaking. It was a cognitive act, wherein drawing contributed to a repository of compositional ideas. The florid signatures Vredeman added to his early preparatory drawings are explicit acknowledgments of his role (Figure 1.6). They denoted not just the name of the author, but his exact function as "inventor." Even the most accomplished of Cock's draughtsmen was not as consistent as Vredeman in appending this information to his designs.[50] In a preliminary print drawing now in the Albertina, however, the syncretic role that Vredeman served was relocated and abbreviated when the drawing was transferred to print (Figure 1.7), lodged into one of two upper-story windows near the margins of the page. Here, it quietly affirmed Vredeman's secondary status beside the publisher's, looking out from the building, in keeping with standard practice. Raphael had first drawn a corporeal division between *inventit* and *execudit* when he entrusted Marcantonio Raimondi with the cutting of his designs in the 1520s, and Giorgio Ghisi carried it to Antwerp while in Cock's employ. For the *Aux Quatre Vents*—and by association Vredeman—this division of labor became conspicuously established as

1.7
Hans Vredeman de Vries, *Scenographiae, sive perspectivae,* no. 19, 1560. Etching, H.49.
Albertina, Vienna.

the dominant schema for Antwerp. Virtually no documents have survived regarding payments or commissions for prints to Vredeman before 1575. But it appears (with one exception)[51] that, much like other draughtsmen, he never engraved his own designs in these early years.

Instead, Vredeman entered into a very collaborative enterprise in which his reputation was contingent upon the coordinated skills of others.[52] At the most basic level, the appellation "inventor" labeled the cognitive actor in print design, literally the creator of drawing, who may or may not have been the same as the etcher or engraver. "To invent" seems, in sixteenth-century painting theory, to have designated an imaginative faculty desirable in young artists and architects. In a marginal note to his poem, "On Foundation of the Free and Noble Art of Painting" (the "*Grondt*"), Van Mander claimed that for painters "*inventy*" could only be developed by drawing from memory, not after nature.[53] It was crucial, he claimed, to learn to make art "*uyt zijn selve*" (from one's self) before turning to any copying of sculpture or figures. Primacy was placed upon the notion of invention as the transference of an "idea" located in the artist's own head. Rhetoric, meanwhile, equated invention with the unveiling of the *res*, the subject, of courtroom oratory, or as Cicero put it, "the devising of matter, true or plausible, that would make a case convincing."[54] Vitruvius borrowed this definition of invention for his *First Book*, infusing invention with an even more vigorous mathematical overtone: ". . . *invention* is the unraveling of obscure problems, arriving, through energetic flexibility, at a new set of principles."[55] Adapting a design to fit an extant site or situation became the architect's challenge, as it had been the orator's task and the printmaker's charge. Inflected to a medium *between* drawing and building, as in Vredeman's prints, the domain of invention lay at the literal periphery of the scene.

Books and building

On folio 266 of the *Schilderboeck* Van Mander was very specific about an episode from Vredeman's youth:

> . . . in Kollum, while painting a panel in oils [Vredeman] came across a joiner or cabinetmaker who owned the books of Sebastiano Serlio or Vitruvius published by Pieter Koeck. Vries assiduously copied these out (*schreef nacht en dagh vlijtich uyt*), the large one as well as the small one. From thereafter he returned again to Mechelen, to a painter . . . who had him make various works which incorporated architecture.[56]

Vredeman's discovery of these books probably occurred sometime around 1550. The works Van Mander mentions in the joiners' keep are both identifiable: the "large" one was a Dutch translation of Serlio's *Fourth Book* (Figure 1.8), the "small one," undoubtedly, was *De Inventie der Colommen* (Figure 1.9), a little quarto, which also appeared in 1539.[57] Both were by the same author, the polymath Pieter Coecke van Aelst (1502–50). Coecke van Aelst was a tapestry designer and antiquarian, as well as, briefly, a court painter to Emperor Charles V. He had traveled to Constantinople on diplomatic missions and become famous for designing festival decorations in Antwerp. Coecke may also have been, for a short period, the master of Pieter Bruegel the Elder (the painter married his daughter, Mayeken), overseeing a large workshop in Brussels in the 1540s which specialized in replicas of his own works, alongside painted versions of Italian prints.[58]

Coecke van Aelst's work on Serlio brought about an (unauthorized) Dutch translation of one of the first illustrated architectural treatises in Europe. The original Italian edition had appeared in Venice a mere two years earlier, in 1537 Van Aelst's edition itself served as the basis for the first English translation of Serlio. Although the first of van Aelst's works was initially printed in fairly large runs (probably around 1000–1200 copies), the little book appeared in an edition of 650, or perhaps less. Exemplars of *Die Inventie der Colommen* are extremely rare today; only two complete copies survive, in Ghent and Wolfenbüttel, and of the first edition of the *Regelen*, less than a dozen.[59] They seem to have been relatively affordable and interesting to craftsmen, and sold well;[60] in fact, their modern scarcity testifies to the wide use they may have seen in workshops. Clearly, seeing the books, if Van Mander is to be believed, was a revelatory experience for

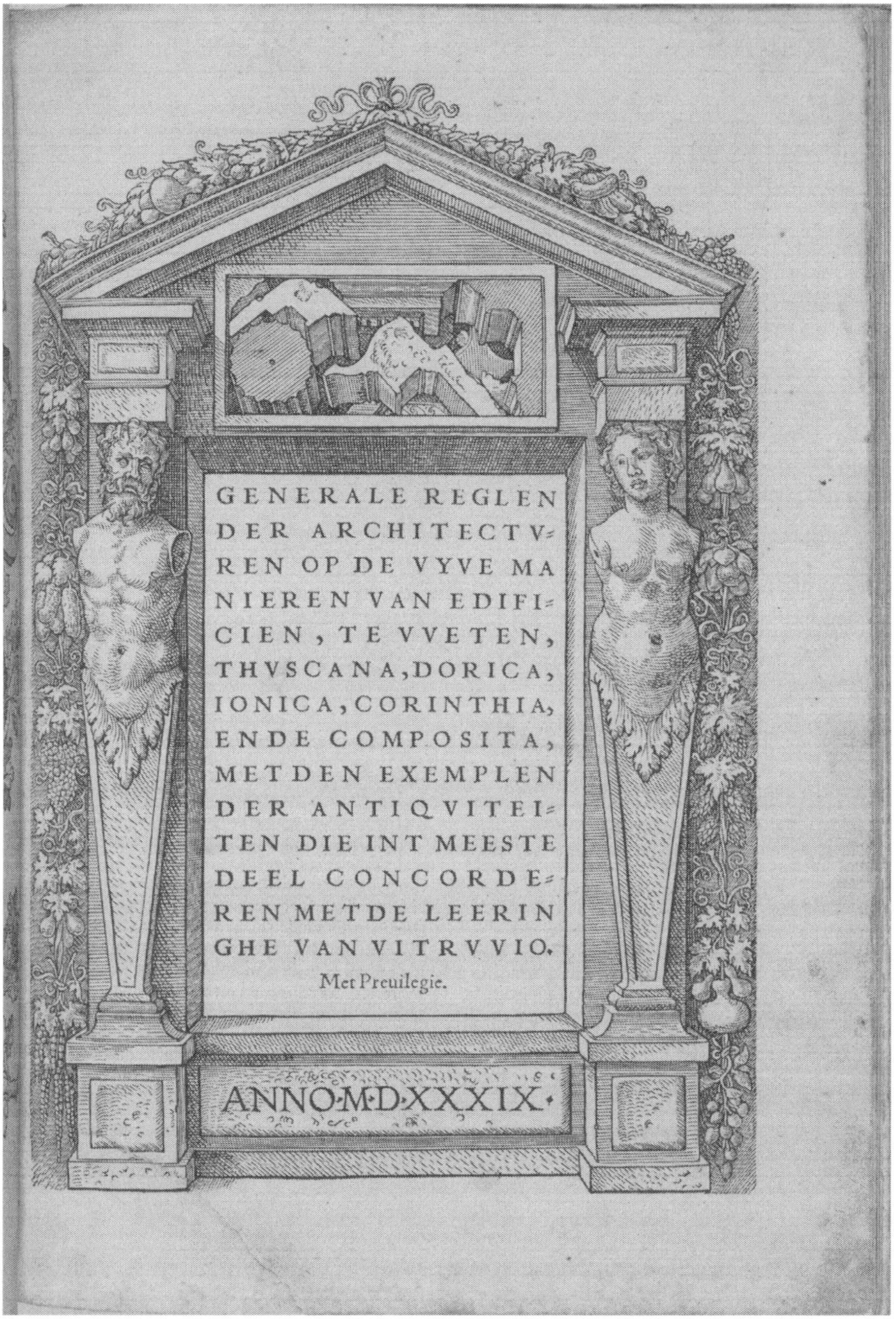
GENERALE REGLEN DER ARCHITECTV= REN OP DE VYVE MA NIEREN VAN EDIFI= CIEN, TE VVETEN, THVSCANA, DORICA, IONICA, CORINTHIA, ENDE COMPOSITA, METDEN EXEMPLEN DER ANTIQVITEI= TEN DIE INT MEESTE DEEL CONCORDE= REN METDE LEERIN GHE VAN VITRVVIO.

Met Preuilegie.

ANNO·M·D·XXXIX·

1.8
Pieter Coecke van Aelst, *Generale Regelen der architecturen* . . . (Antwerp, 1539), title page. Universiteitsbibliotheek, Amsterdam.

Vredeman. In Van Mander's retelling it is only after this exposure in Kollum that the young artist devoted himself entirely to architecture, first in paint and then, as we have seen, in print.

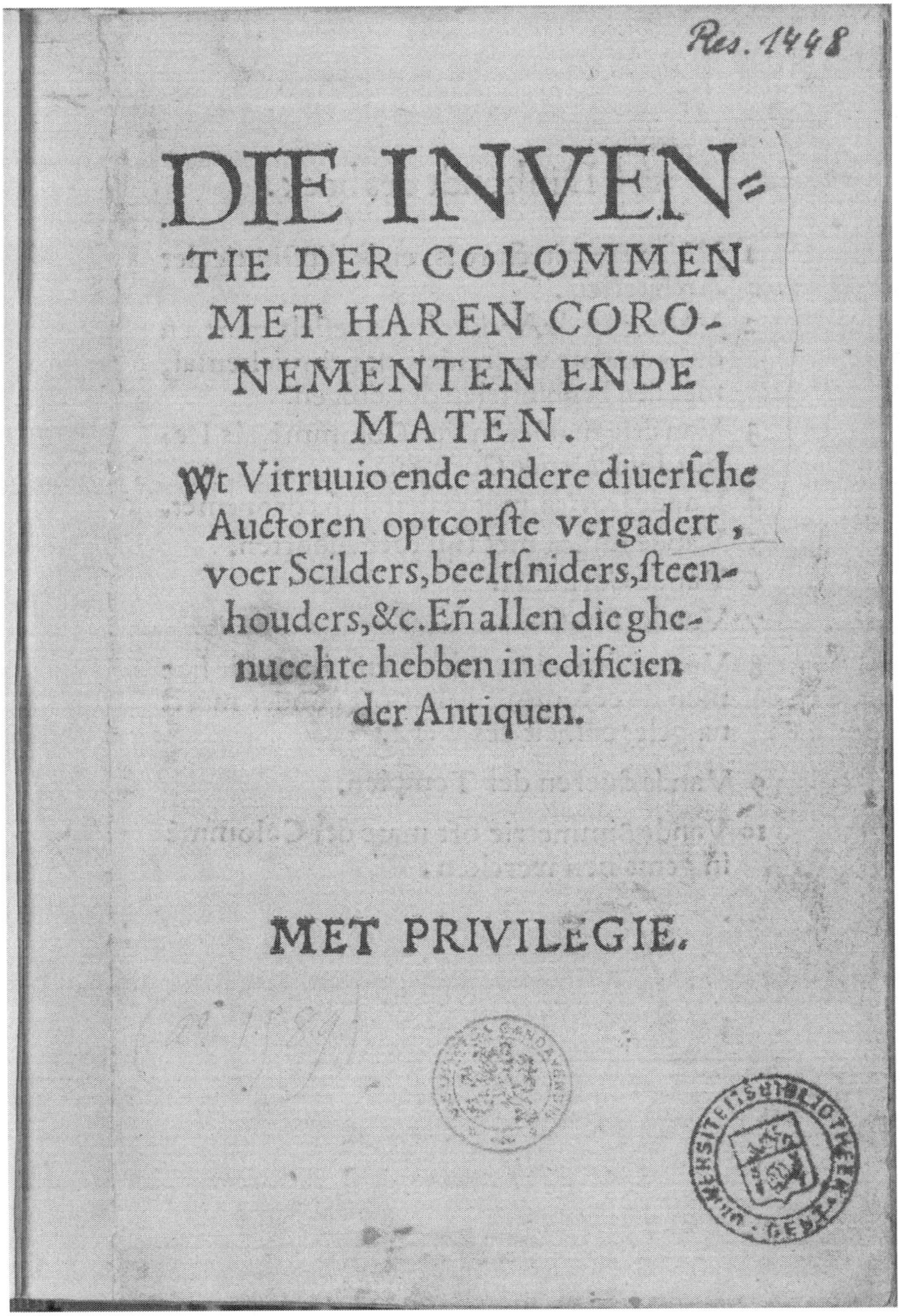
Res. 1448

DIE INVEN=
TIE DER COLOMMEN
MET HAREN CORO-
NEMENTEN ENDE
MATEN.
Wt Vitruuio ende andere diuerſche
Auctoren optcorſte vergadert,
voer Scilders,beeltſniders,ſteen-
houders,&c.Eñ allen die ghe-
nuechte hebben in edificien
der Antiquen.

MET PRIVILEGIE.

1.9
Pieter Coecke van Aelst, *Die Inventie der Colommen* (Antwerp, 1539), title page.
Universiteitsbibliotheek, Ghent.

Coecke van Aelst's *Die Inventie* was a remarkable pamphlet. Van Mander claimed "it brought the light to our Netherlands and helped the lost art of architecture onto the right path," while the humanist Lampsonius named it as the only Dutch book to discuss the building styles of other countries.[61] A pocket-size translation of Vitruvian fragments, *Die Inventie* was not an entirely original composition. In 1511, Fra Giancondo had famously published a "complete" version of Vitruvius's manuscript, which became the first illustrated architectural treatise to appear in print.[62] Containing rather crude woodcuts that showed schematic diagrams of structures like the Colosseum and the Pantheon, this version, too, appeared in a "pocket" edition in 1513, but was overhauled in a folio version of 1522 by Cesare Cesarino, which soon became one of the most widely copied books of the sixteenth century. Van Aelst's *Die Inventie* was one of a flurry of imitators and, like them, contained content that was only partly new.[63]

Pieter Coecke van Aelst turned to a specifically Netherlandish tongue to discuss column types, volute design, and geometric ratios. Like Serlio, he afforded woodcut illustrations relative predominance in the tract (Figure 1.10), and used columns to distinguish, as Serlio had done (Figure 1.11), the difference between three kinds of architectural representation: plan, elevation, and view. The few printed treatises on architecture available in the Low Countries hitherto eschewed this kind of visual exegesis; Leon Battista Alberti had famously refused to illustrate his own (manuscript) treatise on building, *De re aedificatoria*, insisting that architectural principles could be more effectively understood when read aloud, in the form of a dialogue;[64] in this, he followed the original format of Vitruvius, who omitted diagrams, it was thought, in order to keep his audience more select, to keep architecture a discourse between enlightened practitioners and patrons.

Coecke van Aelst's illustrated version of Serlio, aware of this tradition, was thus to include an important—and quite beautiful—acknowledgment of its novel approach towards printed illustration. It explained how the Vitruvian dialogue was thrown open to anyone viewing its pages:

> . . . in the following Book we may read not only what the Romans had built, but also [what] authors have described to us in figure (as you may see them here) piece by piece, not only how many rods, ells, feet, & palms, but also the minutes thereof, and what compass they contained, all perfectly described.[65]

Coecke van Aelst showed elevations, cross-sections, and diagrams of the architectural orders, and offered a saleable summary of antique plinths, columns, and capitals based on composite ratios. These were drawn less on visual experience of specific Roman monuments than on older printed images. Most Dutch readers would not have known original marble structures from Italy; what they would have been familiar with, Coecke intimated, were images of "antique" structures from prints and altarpieces. *Die Inventie* served as a book of patterns more than an explication of theory. In fact, Coecke van Aelst admitted that he was not exactly clear what Vitruvius is describing at times.[66] His work contained not just the paper templates for the model forms of building, but the implicit argument that printed images themselves were valid, even vital, tools for making buildings.

Vitruvius's goal had been to justify the idea of architecture as a chiefly intellectual activity. Coecke van Aelst sought to bring this notion to a body of intellectuals and

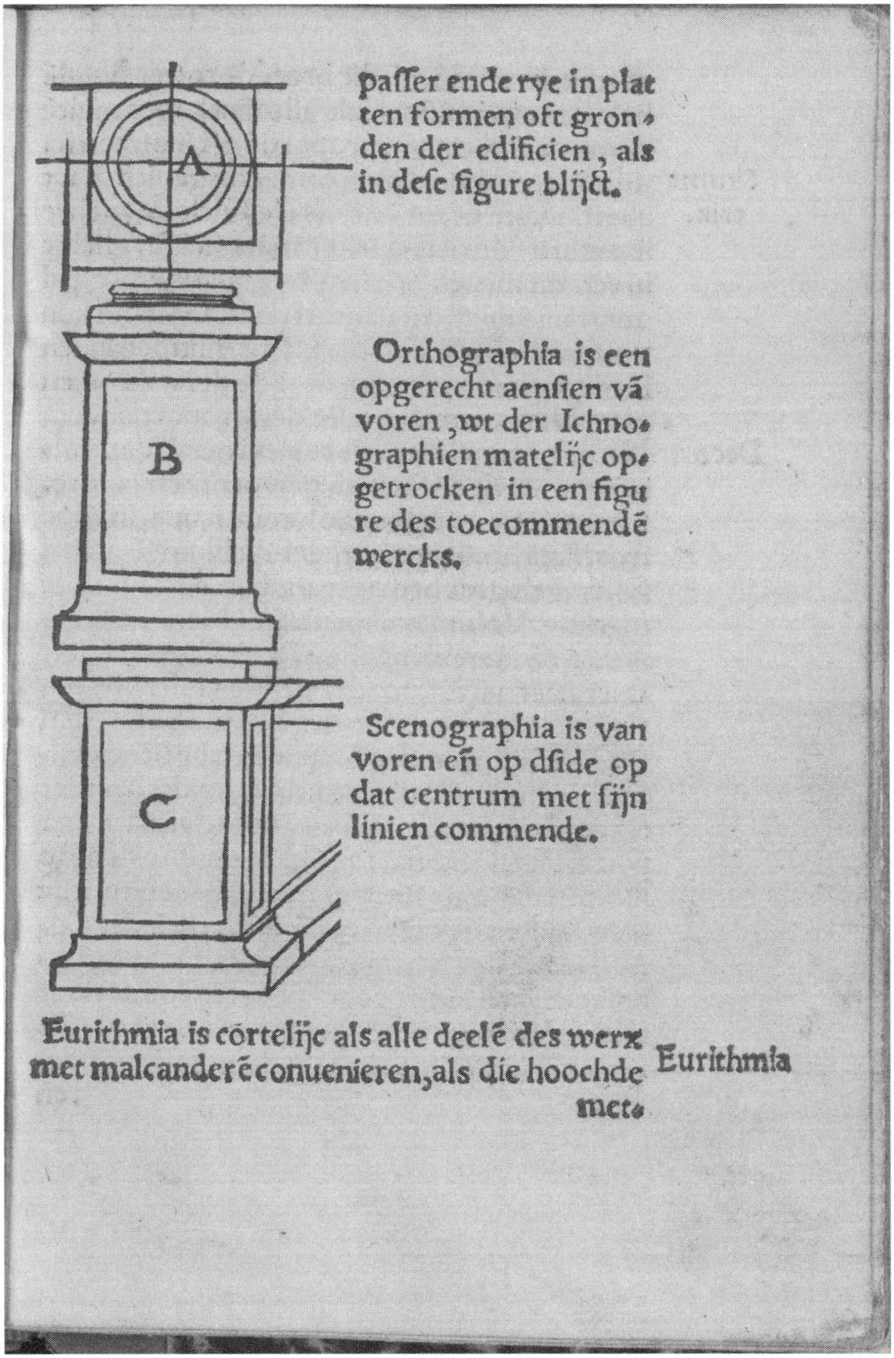
A

B

C

paſſer ende rye in plat
ten formen oft gron-
den der edificien, als
in deſe figure blijct.

Orthographia is een
opgerecht aenſien vā
voren, wt der Ichno-
graphien matelijc op-
getrocken in een figu
re des toecommendē
wercks.

Scenographia is van
voren ē op dſide op
dat centrum met ſijn
linien commende.

Eurithmia is cortelijc als alle deelē des werx
met malcanderē conuenieren, als die hoochde
met.

Eurithmia

1.10
Pieter Coecke van Aelst, *Die Inventie der Colommen* (Antwerp, 1539), fol. a8r.
Universiteitsbibliotheek, Ghent.

guild-based practitioners without disavowing craft altogether; on the cover page he described his audience as "painters, sculptors, and stonecutters, and anyone who takes pleasure from antique buildings." Written in Flemish, *Die Inventie* sought to vernacularize Vitruvius's dichotomous notion of "*Wat Architectura is*":

> Architecture, that is to say, *overbouwmeesterie*[67] depends upon many other arts and fields of training, which furnish the rules to make all works come about. These consist in two aspects: carpentry, and explanation [or deliberation]. Carpentry is itself traditional and familiar practise of using the hands to bring forth works, using whatever materials are necessary. Explanation is a faculty whereby built things are set out, a knowledge of the correct proportions which they contain.[68]

The rhetorical division between theory and practice was entirely new in Netherlandish building, and the isolated activity of "setting out" (*uytleggen*)—a mental pursuit—was clearly quite strange. Coecke van Aelst was thus forced to, in effect, introduce an occupation ("the architect") into a Dutch vernacular that literally had no word for it.[69] As Hessel Miedema has shown, Vitruvius's terms of *fabrica* (crafting) and *ratiocinatio* (reasoning out) left Coecke at a loss in terms of Dutch equivalents. His difficulty lay not so much in providing a direct translation for the antique words as in establishing a distinction between the acts of planning and executing a building. Previously, both acts had been seen as essentially practical pursuits under the domain of masons' guilds.[70] Vitruvian theory clearly mandated that theory and technique were vastly different concepts, and

1.11
Sebastiano Serlio, *Il Secondo libro di architettura* (Paris, 1545), fol. 46v.
Special Collections, Getty Research Institute, Los Angeles.

hierarchically related—the former was by far the more important. "The architect ought to be practiced in all accomplishments,"[71] wrote Vitruvius, and Coecke van Aelst dutifully transcribed how the new practice of *overlegginge* (planning out, prefatory drawing) was something perfectible via training in the liberal, not the industrial, arts: arithmetic, geometry, music, history, astronomy, optics, and rhetoric. On-site experience was still required, but it was valuable only in when coupled with an artistic sensitivity that allowed builders to "take hold of" (*betrekken*) architectural ideas in their mind.

But if the apprehension of mental images was the prerequisite for any architect's ability to "design" new structures himself, Coecke van Aelst seemed to imply, than a different section of the artesian population (that is, those who simply produced drawings) seemed eligible for the appellation "architect."[72] In the 1540s, divisions were quite new in the Netherlands between the people who conceived buildings and those who constructed them. In Antwerp in August 1542, for example, a carpenter from Utrecht named William van Noordt was accused of making designs for capitals in the city cathedrals without being a stonemason. In his defense, he called a series of witnesses from the local guilds: Philips Lammekens and Pieter Teels, master masons at the Onzelievevrouw cathedral; Rombout de Drijvere, a *clynsteker*, or carver of foliage for capitals, Rombout van den Loocke, a carpenter and stone cutter, and Pieter Frans, a younger Antwerp mason. These individuals cited examples of local work by non-craftsmen: an Italian painter named Tommasso Vincidor, who had designed the Buren castle, and a goldsmith, Jan van Nijmegen, who had *geordonneert* (laid out, designed) several different houses in Antwerp.[73] Quite stunningly, van Noordt even produced quotations from Alberti and Vitruvius, which were recorded by the court notary: ". . . architecture is an art," he apparently testified, "which embraces all of the other arts."[74] The sum conclusion of the witnesses was that construction was indeed the domain of masons and sculptors, but design remained the responsibility of the architect; the latter's task could not be subsumed under the heading of any one art, in a manner akin to painting, woodcarving, and carpentry. Rather, architecture consisted in an understanding of all of these practices.[75]

Whether or not Coecke van Aelst's publications of 1539 were solely responsible for the professional legitimization of this more theoretically oriented occupation, their theory certainly provided a textual basis for differentiation between tasks in the Netherlands. The "emancipation" of the builder, like the artist, from guild restrictions was quite sporadic in the southern Netherlands, and even more so in the north. The prints, however, suggested that the domain of the Dutch architect might be the domain of the image, or more precisely, the domain of *images*. Indeed, in a second court case from 1565, the sculptor Willem van den Broeke was sued by the city of Antwerp for producing drawn designs (*patronen*), which could not be built. In his defense, van den Broeke—who was cited in 1577 by Vredeman as a model "architect"[76]—stated that architects were "the schoolmasters of the masons," and need not be troubled about the executability of their plans. Masons, van den Broeke explained, "brought the designs to life," but "would not be able to lay one single stone without the oversight of architects." The city council, however, disagreed. The masons were paid to redraw Broeke's plan and take over the practical matters of laying foundations and installing staircases for the design.[77]

The old idea—never hegemonic—that painters or even goldsmiths could be the effective creators of buildings granted a new independence and primacy to preliminary designs, just as it imputed social distinctions to a craft where previously there had been few. As the Antwerp cases suggest, designs most often took the form of drawing—discrete manual utterances. Again, from Coecke van Aelst's Vitruvius:

> In general, and particularly in architecture, there exist two things: that which is signified [*het gene dat beteekent*], and that which signifies [*datter beteeket*]. That which is signified is the thing proposed; that which signifies is the demonstration, expressed through professional precepts.[78]

Such a schematic breakdown, which sounds not a little like contemporary semiotic theory, speaks to a division between form and matter, theory and practice. But it instates no aesthetic hierarchy *per se*. "That which signifies" is not just the architectural sketch, but the act of making the sketch itself. Coecke van Aelst's translation singles out the formal obdurateness of *datter beteeket*—that which signifies—rather than run beyond it to images. Within the pre-Socratic notion of the signifier–signified, cognates of *significare* meant to "show by signs"—through drawings, effigies, or ritual practice.[79] As Coecke van Aelst goes on to explain, drawing transmitted invention to craftsmen or patrons whole, who then rendered physical the form of the building. The 1565 court case in Antwerp saw Willem van den Bloecke rely on precisely this distinction in drafting his worthless design for the new town hall.

Drawing had remained the chief form of building design among Italian theorists since antiquity—both Alberti and Serlio reiterated draughtsmanship's function as a nexus of painting and building.[80] But it had never been upheld as an autonomous task of the architect in the Netherlands. Coecke van Aelst—a translator and a designer of engravings—thus introduced a new division of labor between invention and building, much like that imputed to printmaking. He sharply honed the idea of what the architect actually *does*; that is, he *onderwerpt*, he designs. This was a resolutely modern distinction: architects today rarely make buildings—they make *pictures* of buildings.[81] Yet this is no less distinct a practice than the carving of a porphyry capital or the cementing a brick wall—it involves its own set of physical materials (ink, paper, compass) and knowledge of craft methods (perspective, proportion), and, above all (as today), the sponsorship of a wealthy patron on its behalf. Yet as Coecke van Aelst's title metaphorically suggested, *Die Inventie van Colummen* sought to explain the cognitive aspect of architecture (*inventio*) as one that literally propped up (*Colummen* = columns) all its other aspects.

In his *Architectura* (1577) Vredeman wrote that Serlio and van Aelst, along with Vitruvius himself, made architecture "an excellent art, which garners praise for its masters."[82] Even more than Vredeman's citations and visual liftings from these authors, two borrowings from Coecke van Aelst's theory stand out in Vredeman. First, there is the fundamental contribution of van Aelst and Serlio towards making *books* a vector for architectural discourse in the Netherlands. Particularly through the dissemination of illustrations, both authors introduced the notion that architecture was not just about marble and stone, but also ink and paper.[83] This was done in different ways: Coecke's Vitruvius was a book of theory aimed at craftsmen in the tradition of earlier German books, like Hermann Ryff's *Vitruvius Teutsch*, which insisted on the intellectual sophistication of the architect interwoven with the skill of the mason. Second, Serlio's books were practical guides, concerned not only with the status of a building's practitioners but with the technical know-how of creating drawings—images of architecture that could be used by painters or sculptors as well.[84] Serlio had supplied a repertory of visual forms that were meant to be transferred within the context of the book—dominating the adjacent text and offering the reader the opportunity to "select" premade patterns for use.[85] As books, such materials exemplified the idea that architecture could be a recombination of refashioned parts, not just a rote grasping of rules. We will return to this point in Chapter 3.

Vredeman's declared capacity as "inventor" articulates a discourse of architectural design conceived of as *translation* from form to form, of culling and rendering from parts. In making his images Vredeman is not preparing to build, he is really building; the image is the project.[86] C. H. Peters saw Vredeman's worth in this, his vernacularizing of columns transmitting a typology of architecture.[87] Far from systematizing a set of precepts, however, as we shall see, Vredeman's own chains of visual translations instated new loci for old forms of creativity, ones still rooted in serial production, still reliant on resonances between different versions rather than on one version's fidelity to a single prototype. "One should do best to follow the *simulacrum* of perfect form," the humanist Pietro Bembo wrote of translation, asserting the primacy of the sign itself—as opposed to the signified—as the grounds for emulation.[88] Vredeman's works, like the translations he worked from, can be understood as multiples conditioned by and for an aesthetic of re-use. They are specific kinds of results, which, again like Zeuxis's Helen, were used (and praised) for their citation and refashioning of known things.[89]

We can recall Van Mander's anecdote wherein Vredeman is said to have "assiduously copied out" Coecke van Aelst's two books he discovered in Kollum, over and over.[90] The processes of repetition, long vital to the training of any young artist, is here installed at the font of Vredeman's historiography; in spite of (and in fact because of) the technological advances of print, a young artist's replication of a named type (Vitruvius), as much as the prototype itself, marks his skill and judgement. To repeat (*practiseren, ritrarre)* in the sixteenth century was to do much more than what today means simply to "copy;" indeed, prints often tightened some still-loose processes of translation, but often remained uncommitted to semblance or even visual similarity. In fact, William Ivins once suggested that it was specifically the technique of cross-hatching that prevented sixteenth-century print from ever imitating the world entirely.[91] Without color, prints always carried connotations of a building's loss or lack; Vasari lamented that engravings tended to "rob the image of something."[92] Print publishing sped up and spread out an older aesthetic of artistic copying, but it did not make architectural theory, at least in the Netherlands, clearer, "scientific," or more standardized than before.

Perspective roles

André Chastel suggested that Renaissance painters became interested in architecture purely as a conveyance for perspective, a nod to certain antique means of structuring surfaces.[93] To be sure, the focus in many "architectural" paintings (Figure 1.1) was indeed less architecture than architecture in perspective. By the sixteenth century, this apparent coupling had a long history. In 1537, Serlio quipped "perspective would be nothing without architecture and the architect nothing without perspective,"[94] a comment that is interesting for its insinuation that perspective was literally invisible without application to physical objects. Brunelleschi, a goldsmith, had begun to experiment with perspective chiefly as a means of surface decoration.[95] Serlio's application of perspective to stage design (Figure 1.11) was chiefly a result of his study of the antique, though it had seen limited use in drawing as a form of architectural practice. For architects, perspective was one of the three modes described by Vitruvius for describing a building. *Scenographia* joined *ichnographia* (plan) and *orthographia* (elevation) as a vehicle through which architectural inventions were given form. Although *scenographia* could be used in the planning of a building or theatre, Vitruvius claimed, it differed from the other types of projection in that it could also designate a subject unto itself—in fact, in Book II of his manuscript Vitruvius deemed perspective of use not for built architecture, but chiefly for its representation.

Indeed, early modern architecture had very little use for perspective in the construction of buildings. Alberti was explicit about its place in architectural practice:

> . . . whereas the painter takes pains to emphasize the relief of objects in paintings with shading and diminishing lines and angles, the architect rejects shading, but takes his projections from the ground plan and, without altering the lines and by maintaining the true angles, reveals the extent and the shape of each elevation and side—he is one who desires his work to be judged not by deceptive appearances but according to certain calculated standards.[96]

Perspective—or "shading"—co-opts painting's ability to evoke an object's appearance, but not to describe it precisely. The use of perspective by painters, Alberti states, is categorically different from the architect's in that it deals with impressions ("deceptive appearances"): that is, it provides a vivid means of representation, but one that is inherently inexact. Most Netherlandish layouts that survive today from the sixteenth century are ichnographic, in ground plan, since *scenographia* was notoriously prone to inaccuracies. While perspectival images could describe the appearance of a built (or potential) building, they famously lacked the structural precision needed to guide on-site work.[97] Raphael wrote that perspective's utility lay solely in paintings of architectural features; at the close of his famous 1519 letter to Pope Leo X about the construction of St. Peter's in Rome, perspective was rejected as too capricious a means to record monuments; "with perspective it would be impossible—or at least exceedingly difficult—to resolve things to their original form," he concluded.[98]

Early perspective drawings by architects were therefore most often taken *from* buildings rather than *to* them. Only rarely would such scenographic representation prescribe a building's shape. On the whole, perspective images were for the purpose of personal record or study, and in at least one case they were even responses to texts; sometime after 1530, the architect Giovanni Battista da Sangallo annotated his first-edition Vitruvius with tiny pen drawings in the margins, copying Serlio's three categories of stage designs—Comic, Tragic, and Satyric (Figure 1.12) out to the side.[99] Perspective here formed a literal response, not a premonition; the scenographic mode sacrificed any pretenses to pure instrumentality. Representations of perspective—inherently "deceptive"—dwelt in this cognitive realm of copying out.

In the Netherlands the relation between architecture and perspective acquired theoretical backing in Coecke van Aelst's translations. An (unauthorized) French translation of Serlio's second *Libro* appeared in Paris in 1545, before the Dutch version (Antwerp, 1550), and its woodblock illustrations were immediately taken up by painters and designers, including Coecke van Aelst in triumphal arches for Charles V and Philip II's 1549 entry into Antwerp (Figure 2.17); moreover, Pieter Aertsen and his pupil Beuckelaer, as we have already encountered, used Serlian elevations to structure interior scenes.[100] Serlio's Italian and "modern" connotations were exploited by northern copyists, who put forward new, "Italianate" architectonics (and not just the *istoriae* they staged) as a kind of picture lifted (consciously) from engravings in books.[101]

Hubert Damisch has noted that as a designation of picture type, "perspective" is different from landscape, still life, or portrait: it "seems to imply an emphasis on the *form* of representation" rather than content, where "the monstration takes the form of a demonstration."[102] That is to say, with perspective a painting's structure becomes uniquely declared as a subject when named as such, or, as one reviewer of Damisch claimed, "it overflows the particular epoch that invented it".[103] Indeed, for art history, perspective remains a transhistorical phenomenon. Much of the literature devoted to perspective, and Vredeman's place in its history, has been directed towards surveys of its origins, and, rightly enough, to its proximity to writings in early science. Perspective compositions in the Quattrocento are traditionally paired with an epochal point of modernity—the beholder as determinant of the "world picture" rather than guild or Church, the rationalization of space and the reorganization of the picture surface as the potential subject of a painting.[104] Art-historical recuperations of these moments have

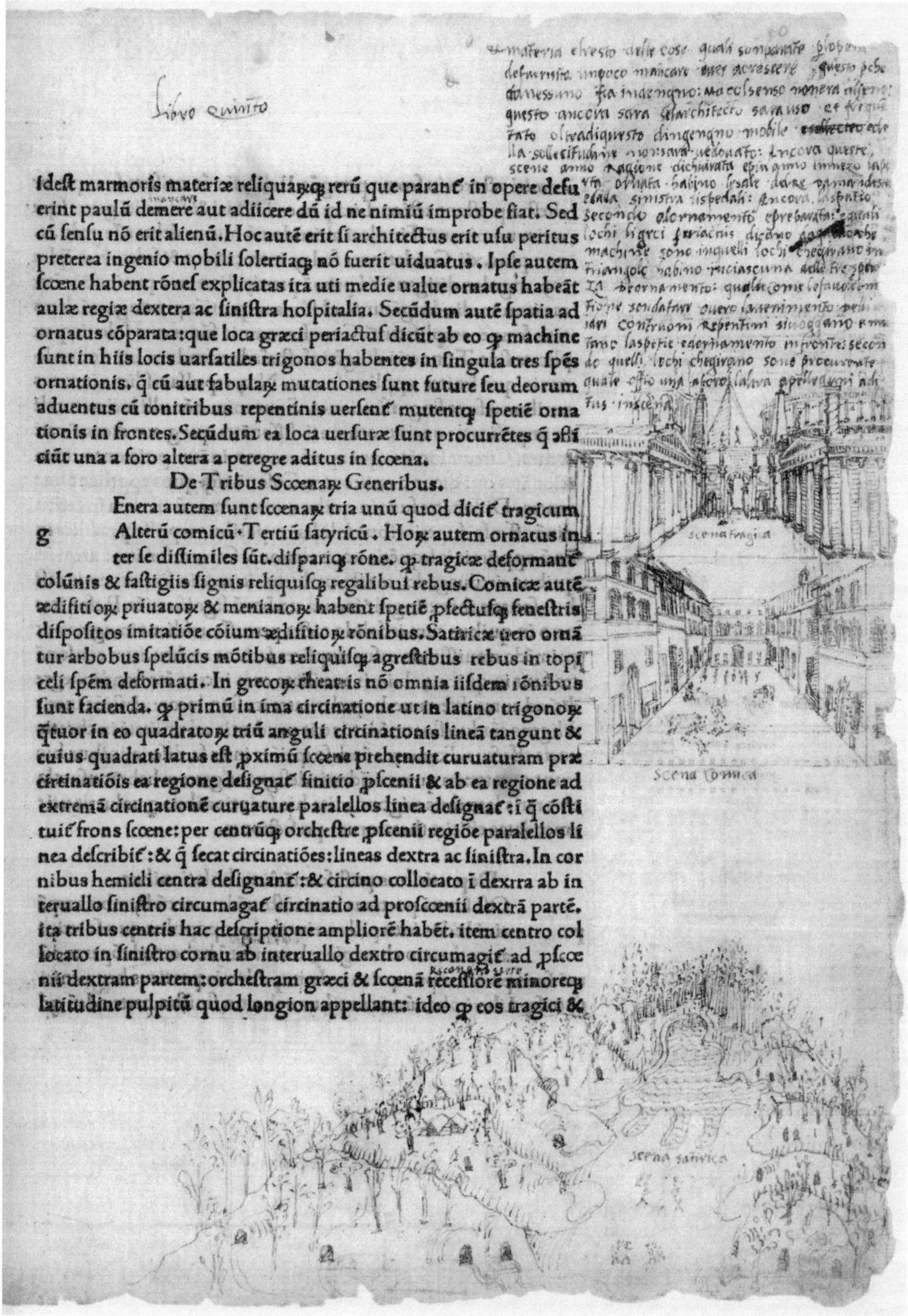

Idest marmoris materiæ reliquaꝝq; rerũ que parant̃ in opere desu erint paulũ demere aut adiicere dũ id ne nimiũ improbe fiat. Sed cũ sensu nõ erit alienũ. Hoc autẽ erit si architectus erit usu peritus preterea ingenio mobili solertiaq; nõ fuerit uiduatus. Ipse autem scœne habent rõnes explicatas ita uti medie ualue ornatus habeãt aulæ regiæ dextera ac sinistra hospitalia. Secũdum autẽ spatia ad ornatus cõparata: que loca græci periactus dicũt ab eo ꝙ machine sunt in hiis locis uarsatiles trigonos habentes in singula tres spẽs ornationis. q̃ cũ aut fabulaꝝ mutationes sunt future seu deorum aduentus cũ tonitribus repentinis uersent̃ mutentq; spetiẽ orna tionis in frontes. Secũdum ea loca uersuræ sunt procurrẽtes q̃ effi ciũt una a foro altera a peregre aditus in scœna.

De Tribus Scœnaꝝ Generibus.

G Enera autem sunt scœnaꝝ tria unũ quod dicit̃ tragicum Alterũ comicũ. Tertiũ satyricũ. Hoꝝ autem ornatus in ter se dissimiles sũt. dispariq; rõne. ꝙ tragicæ deformant̃ colũnis & fastigiis signis reliquisq; regalibus rebus. Comicæ autẽ ædifitioꝝ priuatoꝝ & menianoꝝ habent spetiẽ ꝓspectusq; fenestris dispositos imitatiõe cõium ædifitioꝝ rõnibus. Satiricæ uero ornã tur arbobus spelũcis mõtibus reliquisq; agrestibus rebus in topi celi spẽm deformati. In grecoꝝ theatris nõ omnia iisdem rõnibus sunt facienda. ꝙ primũ in ima circinatione ut in latino trigonoꝝ q̃tuor in eo quadratoꝝ triũ anguli circinationis lineã tangunt & cuius quadrati latus est ꝓximũ scœne prihẽdit curuaturam præ circinatiõis ea regione designat̃ finitio ꝓscenii & ab ea regione ad extremã circinationẽ curuature paralellos linea designat̃: i q̃ cõsti tuit̃ frons scœne: per centrũq; orchestre ꝓscenii regiõe paralellos li nea describit̃: & q̃ secat circinatiões: lineas dextra ac sinistra. In cor nibus hemicli centra designant̃: & circino collocato ĩ dextra ab in teruallo sinistro circumagat̃ circinatio ad proscœnii dextrã partẽ. ita tribus centris hac descriptione ampliorẽ habẽt. item centro col locato in sinistro cornu ab interuallo dextro circumagit̃ ad ꝓscœ nii dextram partem; orchestram græci & scœnã recessiorẽ minoreq; latitudine pulpitũ quod longion appellant: ideo ꝙ eos tragici &

followed the model of a perspectival picture itself, looking back to a stable and visible point. But by the sixteenth century, as we will see in Chapter 5, perspective had become a myriad of pictorial practices, characterized largely by an unexpected materiality. By Vredeman's time perspective was increasingly arcane and obfuscatory, and architecture, or more specifically architectural representation, remained the key vehicle for its expression. Just as Sartre once said of color, there can be no perspective, except that *of* something.[105]

In a series of prints from 1560 Vredeman's perspective became its own theme. In the 20 etchings published by Cock, narrow basilicas and whimsical loggia level themselves at the viewer. The vanishing points are off-center; the architecture, encrusted with queer forms, repudiates any claims to clarity in order to foreground the partiality of a single viewpoint. In one sheet (Figure 1.13, H.46), devilish caryatids scowl atop a raised platform above a garden courtyard, supporting three vaults beneath an elaborate dwelling seen from below. The print's frame allows only an oblique view of the structure and a squat topiary at the far right. Very few specifics about the settings are provided that would help build the structures depicted. It is the perspective itself, tunneling into the page ("like a railroad track," wrote Janzten), that provides the drama.[106]

Unlike Cock's Roman ruins (Figure 0.6), Vredeman's etchings describe an architecture hardly decaying and mottled, but freshly completed. The flinty outcrops and bushy sprigs of Cock's sheets are replaced by smooth floors and trapezoidal marquetry receding quickly into the background. Vredeman promotes "antique" architecture (the orders and rustication of the structures are clearly described) as a new vehicle for displays of perspectival expertise. Perspective, for Vredeman, becomes the component of a pattern book, an attenuated species of ornament.

It is precisely the contingent aspect of architecture in perspective—its dependence on the caprices of vision—that made Alberti so upset, and what Vredeman's prints engage. The play of "deceptive appearances" Alberti decried in scenographic images of buildings was fickle and unreliable; it sprung not from disinterested and measured qualities in a structure, but from a singular viewing experience. Vredeman's jarring, distended composition lends credence to Alberti's gripe about perspective's impracticality for building. But it also points to the main difference between Vredeman's works and those of his Italian, German, and French forebears. In the 1560s, Vredeman's prints did not form part of an architectural or perspectival tract intending to aid technique (that task would wait until 1577 and 1604, respectively)[107], nor did they evoke some wistful piecemeal antiquity: they were patterns. It was their seriality that remained vital: the *Scenographiae* sheets exploded the single viewpoint of perspective, relentlessly repeating it as a plurality, page after page. As prints, objects of private contemplation,[108] the etchings wilfully diffused their origins in the Vitriuvius translation. As Roland Barthes has said of texts, their "vanishing point is ceaselessly pushed back."[109] The drama of Vredeman's early sheets, like the Mary and Martha painting (Fig. 1.1), subsists in their imaginative deferral, across translations, of a single pictorial source.

1.12
Giovanni Battista da Sangallo, *Sketches of Dramatic, Satyric, and Comic Scenes* (in fol. 11 of 1486 edition of Vitruvius). Pen on paper.
Biblioteca Corsiniana, Rome.

1.13
Hans Vredeman de Vries, *Scenographiae, sive perspectivae*, no. 16, 1560. Etching, H.46.
Albertina, Vienna.

Collaboration in perspective: Mary and Martha once again

Sixteenth-century painting, Alois Riegl argued, depended at its most rudimentary level on the internal articulation of motifs, and only secondarily upon the functioning of these motifs vis-à-vis a beholder.[110] Like architecture, ornament uncluttered by figuration bore the potential to lay bare the internal structure of a work—not to make it legible, but to dramatize its confrontation with the spectator. As we shall explore in Chapter 3, Vredeman's ornament prints magnificently disrupt the contiguity of frame and world on spatial terms—as flat and two dimensional, they seemingly turn in on themselves, trapping elements at the surface. Yet at the same time, the ornament print in Vredeman's day entered the world as handleable, bodily thing.

Perspectival compositions, by contrast, allegedly define a contiguity with the viewer through the fictional extension of space. They ask for conversation. Indeed, Serlio stressed that perspective was "better taught orally, face to face."[111] While Van Mander inveighed against the overbearing *doorsien*, the looking-through, "too much of which," he claimed, "is a hindrance."[112] Riegl saw Netherlandish art as a crucial and unrecognized juncture between these twin poles of "object-emphasis" (ornament) and "subject-emphasis" (perspective). If modern art wholly privileged the viewing subject, he claimed, early Dutch painting still clung to the "medieval" integrity of the object. It preserved a sense of separateness in an era when perspective's entreaty to the single beholder via a functional "window" threatened to lie about what was actually there.[113]

In the Hampton Court *Mary and Martha* (Figure 1.1, Color Plate II) Vredeman signs his name twice. Yet the *staffage*, the figures of Christ, Mary, Martha, and the disciples, were not painted by Vredeman. As with most of his panels from the 1560s, they were probably the work of another artist, in this case Gillis Mostaert, an artist from the village of Hulst.[114] Like Jacob Grimmer and other contemporaries, Vredeman frequently collaborated with Mostaert in the 1560s ("a good master at figures, especially when they were somewhat small,"[115] claimed Van Mander). Mostaert added figures to several Vredeman paintings, to the grisly *Massacre of the Roman Triumvirate* in Tarbes, and a painting now in Bückeberg (Figure 1.14), and a tiny panel recently discovered in a German private collection.[116] Like the *Martha*, these paintings all derive from spatial templates in Vredeman's prints, and they nestle their fable within an elaborately architectural format.

The practice of collaboration was not just a division of labor. Vredeman relied upon it throughout his career as a painter, and it would come to dominate the architectural specialty he established, whether at the behest of dealers or of particular patrons. By the 1560s, Antwerp's art scene had begun to make collaboration both aesthetically attractive and economically viable for painters, and the role of second (or third) hands in the making of "perspective" pictures, specifically, had a long pedigree.

1.14
Hans Vredeman de Vries and Gillis Mostaert, *Trajan and the Widow*, 1572. Oil on panel, 75 × 106.
Schloss Bückeberg.

Vasari, for example, attributed "*una Venizia in prospettiva e S Marco*" to Alberti, "with figures executed by other masters."[117] And Edward Norgate, after viewing a series of architectural *vedute*, concluded that anyone could (and did) finish a perspective work.[118] In Antwerp the often-formulaic character of architectural subjects surely contributed to a kind of assembly-line technique, and in a Netherlandish milieu, workshop production, as with other genres like still-life and landscape, insured that perspective pictures were churned out with astonishing speed and efficiency.[119] Market demand was not everything, however. Vredeman's *Court* paintings, commissioned in Prague by Rudolf II in 1596–98, for example, were "figured" by Dirck de Quade van Ravensteyn (Fig. 4.8), while Vredeman's son Paul, a lifelong collaborator, appears to have added staffage to at least two of his father's paintings from the same series.[120]

Dealers' inventories reveal similar examples; in 1615, the Amsterdam wine merchant Albert Martsz sold "*een stuck perspectieff gedean bij den Ouden de Vries waaring Pieter Isaacx de beelden gedaen heft,*"[121] while decades later the Antwerp firm of Forschoudt sold "*1 perspectief van de Vries, de figuren van Martinus van Cleef,*"[122] and, in 1669, the same house bought a *Calling of St. Matthew* which purported to be "*van de Vries, de figuren van langen Peer* [Pieter Aertsen]."[123] The city of Antwerp even paid one Peter Leys "*te voyeren* [to bring out] *ende stofferen van kleyne figuren,*" a Vredeman perspective in 1583.[124] Even when the exact identity of a collaborator was known and revered, it was clear that the human figures were often secondary to the architecture within the context of the picture; a lost canvas by Vredeman "*met prachtige Gebouwen pronkt*" was described as "*gestoffered* [adorned]" by Sebastian Vrancx, apparently some years after the initial composition.[125] In an architectural piece, the human figures, and any *istoriae*, were, in effect, the ornament. These embellishments increased the marketability of the paintings; there is little to suggest that relatively "unstaffed" paintings by Vredeman were necessarily incomplete or less valuable.

Vredeman's frequent assertion of authorship over the perspective view itself, alluded to in the familiar "*Vries inv.*" appended to his panels, as to his prints (Figure 1.7), suggests his awareness of the possibility for collaboration on the works at a later stage. Like printmaking, he often intimated that his hegemony over the "conception" of a work was fundamental, but all the same a preliminary in a larger process of production, one which in no way precluded the additions, alterations, and effacements of other hands and brushes. A lost painting from Wörlitz, for example, once bore the rare inscription "*Vredeman Vries fec. Inven.*" in Vredeman's hand,[126] a case of the artist distinguishing between—and at the same time subsuming into his own personality—the twin acts of picture-making. The architectural specialty *relied* upon a division of labor to impart both financial worth and narrative sense.

The presence of other hands in Vredeman's paintings has prompted scholars to set aside the figures as marginal to the works, or to overextend implausible evidence suggesting their authorship by Vredeman himself.[127] To do so might be to forsake the larger summative operations of works like *Mary and Martha* as a whole, and to overlook a historically grounded method dealers and artists used for attaching value to art, particularly in the Netherlands.[128] Mikhail Bakhtin famously described the ways that narrative in literature is generated through an intertwining of different voices, a polyphony in which all sources compete and interact within a work. In Vredeman's panels such voices, as different hands, conflict as well as coexist, to produce an object whose every detail cannot be accounted for by a single explanatory rubric.[129] With *Mary and Martha*, for example, the shearing of attention prompted by the myriad spaces, surfaces, and figures is far from ludic, and is paralleled by the profusion of hands at work in the original painting, and its ceaseless, multilayered re-iteration of visual and textual sources.[130] This seems not Bakhtin's dream of a pure dialogism, but what Walter Benjamin called "distraction."

No less than Vredeman's print series, which as we saw earlier were collaborative enterprises, the painting, a physical thing, assumes a reception that is as de-centered as its production. The visual elements of the Hampton Court picture (vault, doorway, Christ) stand, like the artists who painted them (Vredeman, Mostaert), not as alternative poles, but as amplifications of one another; exchange between them mirrors the beholder doing the same. The result of this polyphony, however, is not simply some happy pluralism of viewing for the single viewer. If anything, the perspective insists upon the work's elusiveness as a visual totality; in tandem with the decoration and the dual Greek and Latin signatures, Vredeman's architecture furnishes a visual alternative to the seated figures of Christ and Mary. And although perspective supplies a container, that tableau, like Vitruvius's scenography, is upheld blatantly as fiction. In perspective the architecture sheds all claims to be a functional window. A viewer's experience might be anchored very securely to separate elements of the work—the barrel vault, the kitchen doorway, the figures of Mary and Christ; all are embedded within the place of the painting itself. Yet the narrative of the work—indeed the subject—resides not within the isolated personifications, but in the *tensions* Vredeman's architecture articulates between its different parts. The composition depends upon this tension to relate; the aggregate of different hands, planes, surfaces, colors, depths, even signatures, ultimately models the viewer's confrontation with the narrative. Vredeman's painting *enacts*—as well as describes—a perspective of multiple views. *Mary and Martha* declares itself a contemporary translation of a Biblical event, but one torn between the past and present: a stranger in the house of the here-and-now.

*

To *invent*, in early modern Europe, meant to discover as well as to create. Cicero considered *inventio* the first stage in the preparation of a rhetorical discourse, important not simply as an imaginative activity, but as the process of unearthing worthy topics to explore. "*Inventio est excogitatio rerum verarum aut verisimilium*," he wrote—invention is the discovery of things true or probable.[131] Both Plato and Aristotle associated invention with discovery, while the German version of humanist Polydore Vergil's *De inventoribus rerum* (Of Inventors) of 1533 rendered *invenire* as synonymous with *Erfindung*—making, discovering, and finding.[132] In the *Grondt*, Van Mander named *inventy* as work "of one's self" (*uyt zijn selve*). It was this selecting of subject which preceded *ordinatie*, or arrangement.

This chapter has attempted to trace how a dichotomy between invention and execution was applied to architectural theory in the sixteenth century, and how a parallel distinction was in place for printmaking and often for panel painting. Invention was in both cases wholly imbricated with execution and rhetorical flourish. Indeed, Van Mander related how Hendrick Goltzius once "invented and engraved some little histories of Lucretia himself."[133] Goltzius, in this story, did not conceive of the tale (Livy did), but his choosing was a subset of *inventy*. The achievements of selecting and giving form to an invention intimates the kind of dynamism at stake when trying to isolate artistic originality in early modern *architecture*.[134]

With his euphuistic signature on the Vienna drawing (Figure 1.6), Hans Vredeman at once cites and restages the building theory he read as a youth. Vredeman's prints represent ends in themselves, functioning not simply as models for further works, but willful statements of an expressive encounter with past theory and past traditions. These were traditions recoupable only in versions—Italian as well as ostensibly Dutch. Vredeman's "architectural" designs, perhaps, thus abet the paradoxical project of a printmaking medium newly professionalized in early modern Europe, wherein authorship is certified by the very act of being diffused, among new hands and eyes. Few sites were to be as nurturing of such maneuvers as Antwerp, to which Vredeman now turned.

Chapter 2

Antwerp: the city rehearsed

The festival apparatus, the improvised scaffolding with all the special splendor and thrills . . . this is the motive of the permanent monument.

Gottfried Semper[1]

Antwerp was like a world, one could lie concealed there without going outside it.

Antoon Verdickt, 1558[2]

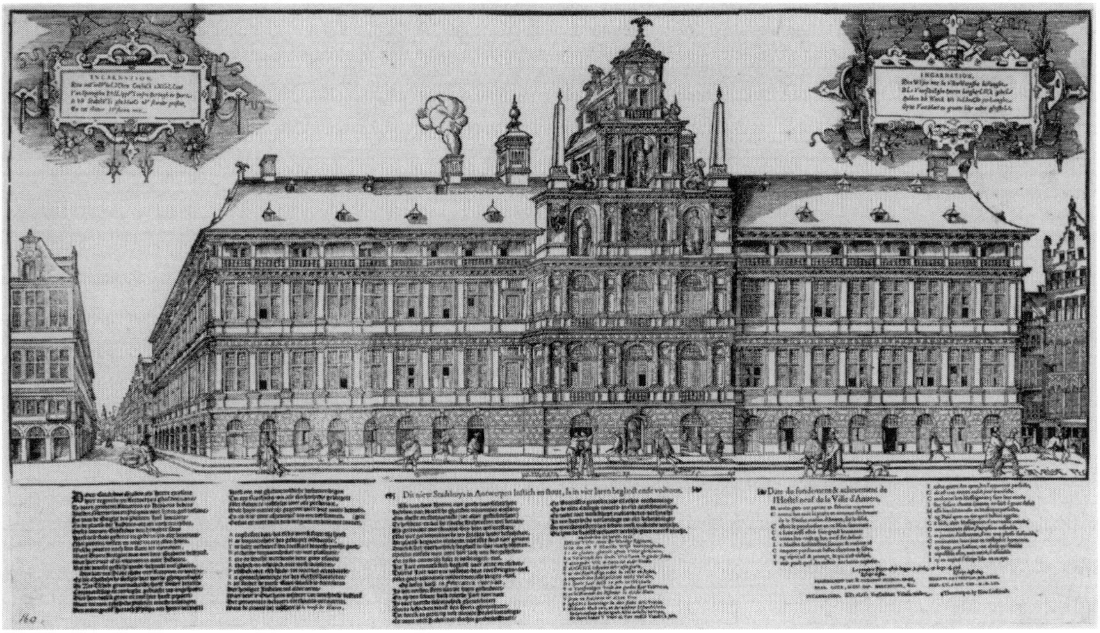

2.1
Hans Vredeman de Vries, *The Town Hall of Antwerp*, 1564–65. Woodcut, H.181.
Kungliga Biblioteket, Stockholm.

"A new town hall is needed," pleaded the magistrates of Antwerp to the Spanish crown in August 1560, ". . . the present one is too small, too narrow, and too old. The decrepit ruin is a danger to its users, far more than one would expect."[3] Writing to the regent of the Netherlands, Margaret of Parma, the city governors thus proposed a colossal replacement building for the Groote Markt, the city's main square. This building was to be constructed according to designs (*patronen*) the city had commissioned from local artists years before. In order that royal representatives in Brussels could better understand the proposal, the magistrates even included copies of the plan with their complaint.[4] Within a month the Spanish crown had allotted 100,000 *livres* for a new *stadhuys*, and in her reply Margaret even cited the measurements the enclosed drawing had described.[5] An astonishing four years later the new town hall of Antwerp was nearly complete.

When Hans Vredeman de Vries depicted the building around 1565 (Figure 2.1) accolades for its size and the swiftness of its construction had already begun to stream in. "Unparalleled in Europe . . . a wonder of the whole earth," wrote the Italian mapmaker Virgilius Bononiensis.[6] In Vredeman's giant three-block woodcut, known today only through a unique impression in Stockholm, the building is shown dwarfing groups of human passersby, its splendid Serlian facade juxtaposed sharply with a recessed avenue to its south. Twin obelisks atop its central elevation bear the tiny inscription "SPQA"—Senatus Populusque Antwerpensia—a boastful nod to the example of Republican Rome. Unlike other contemporary images of the town hall, Vredeman's sheet refused to isolate the building as a frontal stage, but instead framed it within the urban fabric, nestling it among other *pakhuysen*, or warehouses, on the central square. The woodcut included verses eulogizing the winning project, fusing visual and textual entreaties:

> Voy donc, amy Lecteur, une chose qui semble Impossible estre, mais verite, si assemble.[7]
>
> [Come look then, dear reader, upon something which seemed to have been impossible, but indeed was constructed].

Apart from the architecture itself, the town hall's assertion of civic autonomy was indeed quite incredible, even in a place such as Antwerp, traditionally afforded great latitude by central authorities. Antwerp, for all its affluence, remained a city in the Holy Roman Empire, and few viewers would have regarded the brashness of its architecture (along with its representations) as ideologically inert. Not long after the print appeared, civic authorities stepped up the suppression of increasingly frequent civic revolts, and the vicar-general of Mechelen, Maximilian Morillion, wrote: "It would be a good thing to make [the Antwerpeners] erase their SPQA which they inscribe everywhere, on their buildings and edifices, pretending to be a free republic."[8] What Vredeman's audience might visually infer from even pictures of buildings—a kind of small-scale architectural propaganda—could be cause for concern, if not outright censure.

The previous chapter examined how independent images of architecture, their conception, execution, and reception, responded to new print technologies to articulate ideas of invention in the Netherlands. We must now attend to the artistic and social realities of a specific urban landscape—Antwerp—where Vredeman's work engaged these issues most visibly. The following chapter will survey the historical coordinates of Vredeman's art and its strategies in and for the *Scheldtstadt* of Antwerp, a city where he worked on and off from 1561 to 1585, a city which, "for an intoxicating few years," as Simon Schama put it, "*was* European civilization."[9]

It was not just in the town hall print that Vredeman located himself at the center of Antwerp's dynamic town fabric. As early as 1577 he was involved with the physical refashioning of Antwerp's infrastructure as an engineer, re-designing a fortress on the city's south flank. Vredeman belonged to a chamber of rhetoric in Antwerp in the 1560s, and of course, worked as a print designer and painter for Hieronymus Cock and Gerard de Jode between short trips away after 1570 and 1585. His multiple appellations in the Antwerp archives reflect diverse services for the city: In 1581, he is "*ingenieur*" (engineer), in 1583 "*schilder*" (painter), in 1585 simply "*onderwerper*" (designer).[10] None of these faculties, of course, was without confessional and political charge. When Vredeman's town hall woodcut (Figure 2.1) was republished as a copper engraving in 1565, for example, the insolent "SPQA" was effaced from the facade—evidence of how seriously printmakers, as well as authorities, considered architectural utterances imputed to the public sphere.[11]

Vredeman's work in and for Antwerp was concerned with no less than the question of how certain visual complexities of urban life could be addressed, suspended, or constructed by architectural and rhetorical representations. His rhetorical performances, which have hitherto received little scholarly attention, offer clues to the ways his architectures were designed. In terms of civic space, as Michel de Certeau once argued, the seemingly mundane practices of everyday urban life—repetitive, bodily, patterned—while increasingly subject to centralized control in early modern capitalism, remained under market conditions the sole places for creative appropriation of space—fugitive sites for the making of individual meaning, potential resistance, and unpredictability.[12] Yet in Antwerp, those activities which have, in the past, come to be seen as creating utopian, carnivalesque sites of "discursive" interactions with the urban fabric—places of poetic freedom and "exchange"—increasingly seem to have been less so; indeed, civic and imperial authorities actively promoted social "exchange" as an extension of their power. "Public" was a murky concept in early modern Antwerp.[13] I will argue along such lines that Vredeman's practices and—not insignificantly—his chosen medium of print, actively and repetitively engaged the *alledag* of the early metropolis. His designs were not a reflection, an escape from, or outright resistance to, Antwerp's architectural reality, but a means to architecturally transform it. As in his town hall woodcut, Vredeman saw the city as a landscape, not a model for a place but a place unto itself.

Expansion, wane, and social pragmatics

Before the fifteenth century, Antwerp had little to distinguish it from Northern inland ports apart from a brisk trade in peat, and a biannual fair. Around 1400, however, English cloth merchants, banned from rival markets in Bruges and Ghent, became attracted to these fairs for the contacts they allowed with bankers from the Rhineland and southern Germany. By 1450, these bankers, and the precious metals they controlled, attracted a third group of individuals—Portuguese merchants, eager to obtain the silver and copper needed to maintain their spice trade in West Africa and southern Asia.[14] In 1501, Antwerp's position at the center of these activities was formalized when the king of Portugal recognized the city as the central distribution point for spices for all of Europe, a move which made Antwerp suddenly attractive to shipping, finance, and commerce representatives throughout the world.[15] Thanks to such triangulation, by 1520 the city began to occupy a position in international trade rivaled only by Italian centers such as Venice and Genoa. Like those cities, Antwerp rapidly developed an independent banking industry, eventually lending money to Emperor Charles V and lesser heads of state at staggering rates of interest.[16] Combined with the increasing volume of international trade, this financial industry fueled a virtually unmitigated period of economic growth in Antwerp until 1560. The presence of Antwerp's almost perpetual trading fairs was crucial in this development. It was not just merchants from England, Portugal, and German lands who settled in the city to take part in these soon-permanent markets, but local craftsmen from smaller towns who supplied the retail, transport, and service infrastructure they required. This infrastructure, in turn, provided an impetus for broadening extant trade fairs dealing in textiles and handcrafts, which, finally, led to an increasingly sophisticated commerce in high-end luxury goods aimed at the New World and the European hinterlands—paintings, jewelry, clothing, books, and prints.[17] Antwerp's population soared. In 1526, there were around 55,000 people living inside the city walls, where a century earlier there had been less than 20,000. By 1568, the number of citizens reached 104,000, a number paralleled north of the Alps only by Paris.[18] Jaw-dropping accounts of visiting foreigners testified to the city's prosperity and pace: in 1550, the English humanist Roger Ascham exclaimed: "Good God! Antwerp is not just the richest emporium in Brabant but in the whole world!," while, in 1567, Guicciardini suggested that Antwerp should serve as the economic exemplar for any European city.[19]

Antwerp's economic and cultural prosperity in Vredeman's day was dependent upon its location, its access to new technology in banking and shipping, and above all, its immigrants. The city magistrates, or *wethouders*, went to great lengths to insure that merchants and financiers of any national or religious stripe were not harassed by the Spanish authorities, and that civic privileges were respected at all costs. This was a key reason why the city became so attractive to legions of wealthy English, Italians, Germans, Danes, and Poles who settled there, and it surely influenced the decision of less-prosperous, skilled men and women from the Flemish countryside to emigrate as

2.2
Virgilius Bononiensis, Map of Antwerp, 1565. Woodcut, 120 × 165. Prentenkabinet, Antwerp.

well. Lutheranism had arrived in the city through German merchants in the 1530s, and Calvinism spread to Antwerp via France starting in 1545. Thus, before the abdication of Charles V in 1555, Antwerp's relative freedom resulted in a tense, but fairly peaceful situation between the city and central government representatives in Brussels and Madrid.[20] Charles V was able to borrow funds from Antwerp's bankers to finance his numerous wars, while the *wet*, guarding the interests of merchants themselves, quietly guaranteed the city a degree of urban autonomy otherwise unthinkable: more than six Antwerp militia companies and a civic guard were tolerated in the city itself.[21] And although Charles was ostensibly dedicated to Roman Catholicism, most Calvinists within Antwerp's business community remained unmolested in his reign.[22] Much of this changed when Philip II succeeded Charles V as emperor in 1555.

During the initial years of Vredeman's stay in Antwerp (c.1562–65) religious tensions prompted by Philip's policies, as well as inflation, resulted in periodic rioting. Evangelicals often took advantage of the disorder to preach political resistance rooted in scripture. Banishments, imprisonments, and executions were increasingly directed against openly practicing Protestants. At the same time, beginning in the 1560s, political and economic factors colluded to gradually stem the city's demographic explosion; by 1591, Antwerp's population had fallen from a high of over 100,000 to just 46,100.[23] The causes and extent of this downturn have become the subject of considerable debate,[24] but what is clear is that iconoclastic riots of 1566, along with their subsequent quelling by the Duke of Alva in 1567, made Antwerp a less desirable place to do business. Throughout the 1560s the government launched initiatives to centralize government in the Netherlands and to suppress heresy, founding new dioceses and outlawing any dissident faiths altogether. Cardinal Granvelle, the enthusiastic art collector (and a dedicatee of one of Vredeman's print series),[25] sought to quell disturbances through church teaching rather than military action, and was a vocal advocate for the establishment of a new bishopric in Antwerp. While initially Philip's regent, Margaret of Parma, succeeded in protecting

Antwerp's rights and the cherished privilege to try (or dismiss) its own heretics,[26] this privilege was ultimately forfeited by 1562—the same year that Vredeman moved from Mechelen. In 1576, the town hall was burned by rampaging unpaid Spanish troops, a blatant symbol of the compromised state of civic security that had developed over the course of mere decades.

Even after the confessionally aligned destruction and political violence, immigrants continued to be attracted to Antwerp in droves. Any walled city, even a chaotic one, seems to have been preferable to a countryside riddled with bandits and rogue soldiers.[27] After Vredeman moved to Antwerp from Mechelen he married a second wife, Sara van der Elsmaer, on February 10, 1562, in the Onzelievevrouw cathedral.[28] In 1567, his first of three sons, Pauwels, was born. Vredeman was occupying a house on the Everdijstraat by the 1570s, but, interestingly, he does not appear anywhere in the records of the St Lucasgild.[29] Archives reveal that Vredeman was paid (handsomely) to design a triumphal arch for the Antwerp entry of Anna of Austria, daughter of Emperor Maximilian II, in 1570, but the artist fled the city suddenly to Aachen in 1572.[30] His exit was likely spurred by the so-called "General Amnesty" of 1570, an edict which, while touted as an extension of tolerance to minority groups, in effect forbade Calvinists, Lutherans, and Anabaptists from practicing their faiths in the city.[31] Vredeman returned to Antwerp with his wife and son only in 1577.

Antwerp sided with the Protestant North in the rebellion against Spain, and instated a Calvinist government between 1578 and 1585. It was during this time that Vredeman appears to have enjoyed his most productive period of work as both a printmaker and architect, designing fortifications in the southern part of the city and mural designs for the "palace" of William of Orange within the converted Antwerp citadel.[32] In 1581, Vredeman complained to the *wet* that he was shouldering a disproportionate amount of work on the city's walls as a secondary engineer, and that his tasks were, in fact, far more burdensome ("*lastig*") than those allotted to one of the chief architects, Hans van Schille.[33] The same year, Vredeman personally petitioned the town council requesting back pay for drawing plans, in a document that has survived.[34] Vredeman was taxed as a resident of the sixth district (*wijk*) of the city in 1584, a modest neighborhood that was home to several Antwerp painters. He even served as a member of that *wijk*'s civil guard (*burgerlijke wacht*) in 1585.[35] On the Everdijstraat his next-door neighbor was Cornelis Floris, the painter and designer of grotesques, who had won the competition to design the city hall. After Floris quit the city in 1584, the painters Hendrick van Steenwyck the Elder and Maarten van Valkenborch, one-time pupils of Vredeman and specialists in architectural painting, moved briefly into his vacant house, before they, too, took flight for religious reasons and went to Frankfurt.[36]

Vredeman left Antwerp by 1586, but the year before his departure he painted the stilted *Allegory of Antwerp's Second Flowering* (Figure 2.3) for the town hall.[37] In the canvas, structured like a rhetorician's stage, the conquering Spanish general, Alexander Farnese, hands the shield of Antwerp to Philip II, as female personifications marked "Faith," "Truth," "Prosperity," "Reason," "Understanding," and "Clemency" crown the pair with laurel wreaths. On a stairway to the right, a fisherman and hunter,

2.3
Hans Vredeman de Vries, *Allegory of Antwerp's Second Flowering,* 1586. Oil on canvas, 152 × 214.
Formerly Stadsarchief, Antwerp.

in caps, carrying fish, game, and mussels, climb towards this union as symbols of Antwerp's economic rebirth, while figures of *Proprium Commodum* ("Self-Interest"), and *Tyrannis* ("Tyranny") are driven aside at the lower left. Behind the tableau a chronogram is inscribed in a panel, wherein the figures of "Peace" and "Righteousness" embrace, illuminating a verse referenced simply as "PSAL[M] 85." The passage is an entreaty to God, which, in the context of the painting, wordlessly forms a plea from Antwerp to Philip II: "Wilt thou be angry with us forever? Wilt thou draw out thine anger to all generations? Wilt thou not revive us again, that thy people may rejoice in thee?" The painting deftly appropriates the visual language of triumphal entries and *rederijker* presentations to commemorate, significantly, via a question format, the arrival of an as-yet undetermined future for the city. Yet in 1585, the panel's rosy, rebus-like allegory of restored Spanish rule begetting economic prosperity occluded real conditions in the beleaguered city; Vredeman's fellow architect, Francesco Marchi, had offered a somewhat darker, perhaps more authentic view earlier: ". . . whoever sees the city must inevitably think of a place where a fair has been held, and all the goods removed and the shops left empty."[38] Peter Paul Rubens expressed a similar sentiment 50 years later, comparing Antwerp to "a consumptive body, declining little by little."[39]

The ideal view

Was escapism possible in art? In 1562, Hieronymus Cock published 28 engravings of fantastic cities by Vredeman de Vries (Figures 2.3a, 2.4, 2.5, H.85, 89, 88). They were transferred by the van Doetecums, who applied their mixed process of etching and engraving to cut shallowly into the plates. In one print (Figure 2.4) a broad, stony avenue plunges through a dense patchwork of roofs. An open shop window in the foreground at right is manned by a single figure in a large house beneath a crenellated attic. Faceless human figures, dogs, horses, and soldiers with spears and pantaloons scurry across the central space and into the darkened doorways of gabled houses which line the wide street, itself of a width and straightness that was not unknown, but quite rare, in Antwerp.[40] Italianate rustication textures the two palaces in the immediate front, with light falling from the left, casting a group of soldiers emerging from one house into dark shadow. All of these falling shadows are set off from the cobbled street surface by the van Doetecums' diagonal strokes, which impart a sinister, grayish luminosity to the left side of the street. This contrasts with the flat black of Vredeman's windows and doorways, more than 60 of them, which open up like facades and masks.

Beyond this city's boundaries, the landscape opens up to clouds and earth. The view roams over trees and a rumpled field, which passes a windmill and gives way at right, alarmingly, to a denuded *paysage* of knolls, three torture wheels, and a gallows.

2.3a
Hans Vredeman de Vries, *Architectural Perspective View,* 1562. Etching, H.85.
Avery Architectural and Fine Arts Library, Columbia University.

2.4
Hans Vredeman de Vries, *Architectural Perspective View*, 1562. Etching, H.89. Avery Architectural and Fine Arts Library, Columbia University.

The wheels—a punishment reserved for thieves, murderers, and civil miscreants in Brabant[41]—are stabbed into the tranquil countryside, their stalky points rhyming with the upturned spears of the soldiers in the print's left foreground. Such "gallows-fields," or *galgevelden*, were very real places outside Netherlandish cities in the 1560s, marked on contemporary maps and reserved exclusively for the public execution of common citizens;[42] only military criminals could be executed in town, burned, or beheaded like heretics and witches. The sense of future violence which emerges from the print's vertiginous collapsing of near and far stems from an air of surveillance. Vredeman hides the left-hand city figures in shadow. The great print historian Hans Mielke once likened the work to a "claustrophobic, nightmare world," and, seen today, its juxtapositions of black and white rectangles (Figure 2.5) educe the key effects of a hallucination, a bad dream.[43]

Vredeman's print is small enough to hold in one hand, and was usually pasted into albums alongside landscapes. It appears to have been used as an intarsia model, and its copper plate, along with others in the series, was sold in the seventeenth century as an image from "a small Perspective book" (*een cleyn Perspectiffboecxken*).[44] Placing the viewer *within* the street, and at the same time above it, the print marks off the city from the country with a slicing medieval wall. The views echo Bruegel's contemporaneous vision of pandemic dread in *The Triumph of Death*. It is with Bruegel, whose

2.5
Hans Vredeman de Vries, *Architectural Perspective View*, 1562. Etching, H.88.
Avery Architectural and Fine Arts Library, Colombia University.

Large Landscape engraving series of 1555–56 (Figure 2.6) was being re-published in the early 1560s by Hieronymus Cock, that Vredeman's city views have historically been associated. Bruegel purportedly collaborated with Vredeman on an architectural mural in the summer house of Aert Molckemann sometime around 1559, but this, if it ever existed, is now lost.[45] Cock knew both artists, however, and likely saw Vredeman's prints (much smaller in size, but like Bruegel's *Large Landscapes*, etched by the van Doetecums) as variants of an interest in topographies. Mielke first suggested that Vredeman's "city" images (Figure 2.3a) were products intended to capitalize on the popularity of Bruegel's Alpine Landscapes (which are, indeed, larger) in both format and subject.[46] And, in fact, the drawings Vredeman submitted for the 1562 series are chiefly dated from before 1561, the precise year the *Quatre Vents* republished a separate set of Bruegel's landscapes, and a suite of Cock's own spriggy Roman views (Figure 0.6).[47] While Vredeman's buildings are stylistically indebted to vernacular Flemish stone-masonry (particularly with the stone gables, Figure 2.7, H.90), they fail to show the architectural reality of sixteenth-century Netherlands, where most grand houses continued to be built chiefly of wood.[48] The perspective thrust, however, completely unprecedented in the Netherlands, was the series's determining feature; when Philips Galle bought the original plates for the series from Cock's widow in the 1580s, they were inventoried as "*parspectiven van Vries.*"[49]

2.6
Peter Bruegel the Elder, *Milites Requiescentes*, c.1555–56. Engraving and etching, H.58.
Rijksprentenkabinet, Amsterdam.

Eleven pen-and-wash preliminary drawings for the prints survive in Paris and Berlin (Figure 2.11). The plates were eventually republished under the heading *Variae Architecturae Formae* in small, oblong folios, with Johannes Galle issuing a fourth and final edition in 1636.[50] Inventories show that dealers and buyers referred to the sheets as architectural capriccios, and *Stadtslandschaften*. In contemporary print collections, such as that amassed by Philip II of Spain at the Escorial, they appear to have been bound and categorized as everything from landscapes to grotesques.[51] Surviving impressions in Ambras and Wolfenbüttel document their appeal to wealthy amateurs;[52] Van Mander spoke of "twenty-six pieces [showing] palaces with views into and from above, exterior and interior,"[53] and the Antwerp tax collector Gerard Gramaye owned a folio devoted specifically to different editions of Vredeman's city designs.[54]

In Antwerp, Vredeman came into contact with Abraham Ortelius, the famed maker of maps. With maps and landscapes Vredeman's cities share a certain aesthetic of ocular travel, of viewing the world from afar.[55] Vredeman's vistas (Figure 2.5, H.88) position the viewer high above the ground, or looking up from it (Figure 2.7, H.90), encountering successive hills and doors which diminish. This gradation effect was the result of the van Doetecums' wondrous transferal process. Even less so than in Bruegel's landscapes, in Vredeman's cities, humans are present, but nominal. The few figures one sees flit among the shadowy architectures (preliminary drawings reveal that

2.7
Hans Vredeman de Vries, *Architectural Perspective View,* 1562. Etching, H.90.
Avery Architectural and Fine Arts Library, Columbia University.

such staffage was often added in separate brown ink, by another hand)[56]. Groups of soldiers march up hills, dogs follow lansquenets, men accompany horses leading prisoners away. Vredeman seems to transform the city into a grouping of objects, an arrangement of shapes—his perspective casts views *onto* the urban fabric rather than taking them from it; indeed, for Mielke, the engravings disclosed "the possibility not of showing streets but of imagining them."[57] Largely denuded of people, the prints show not the lived street but the dead space of the speculator.[58]

What *did* the streets of early modern Antwerp look like? The demographic explosion in the first part of the century wrought a threefold increase in average house prices between 1500 and 1567. During that time, property values rose even when an average of 115 new dwellings were being constructed a year; between 1480 and 1526 this number had been only 66.[59] This meant that between 1542 and 1567 more than 3,000 houses were built within the city walls, and rents still soared, an indication that the influx of immigrants kept demand high and the city space increasingly dense. While Antwerp's walls were expanded in the 1540s, the lived-in area of the center remained medieval in layout—a warren-like patchwork of small streets and alleys. In 1526, about 42,000 inhabitants were living in 8,479 buildings, while in 1580, there were 80,000 inhabitants for 11,000 buildings. The crowding was unprecedented: ". . . the greater part of the inhabitants are so straightly lodged because of the dearth of houses," wrote the Antwerp city magistrates to Margaret of Parma in the later 1560s, ". . . ordinarily there are several households in one house, and very few rooms or places empty."[60] By the time of Vredeman's return to Antwerp around 1577, more than 1,700 houses were left empty, with an additional 2,520 demolished, partitioned, or burned.

As Hugo Soly has argued, this revamping was often the result of the construction of dozens of new street thoroughfares. More than 85 streets and four new market squares were created *ex nihilo* between 1502 and 1583, 51 between 1540 and 1553 alone.[61] A large part of this development took place in the carefully orchestrated *Nieuwstad* on Antwerp's northern flank, a project initiated by the banker-turned-land-speculator, Gilbert van Schoonbeke (1519–56). Schoonbeke had won commissions earlier to overhaul and expand Antwerp's fortifications, and when the city extended him the offer to develop the marshy northern section of the town (ostensibly to augment the harbor's mooring space) he developed a lucrative new source of rentable land.[62] The project failed as a commercial enterprise, but his speculation reconfigured the city's morphology deleteriously, adding almost a third of surface area to the city within the walls. The new streets laid out by Schoonbeke adhered to a grid plan (Figure 2.8), with straight vistas and buildings of uniform height, justified, in his communications to the town council, as elements of *venustas*, or beauty, a concept (the town council claimed) derived from Alberti.[63] An aesthetic of urban magnificence linked, in essence, to painting, thus drove one of the first urban planning projects in North Europe.

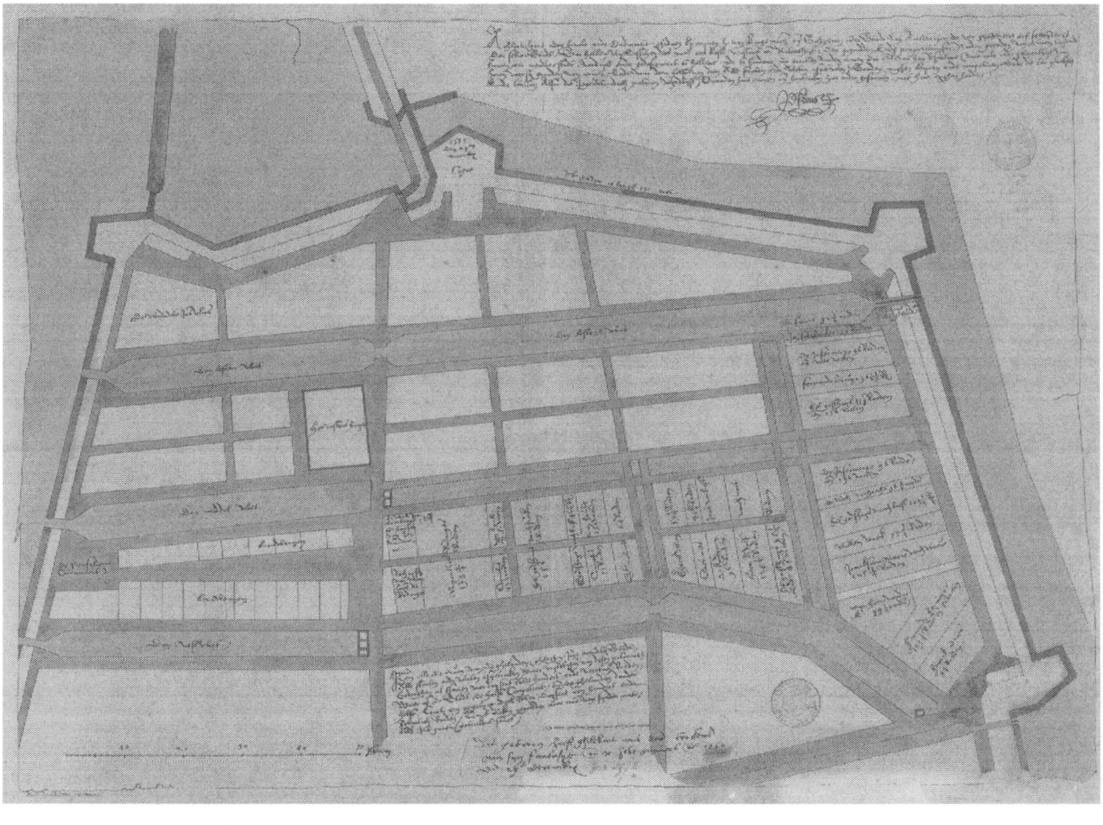

2.8
After Peter Frans, Street map of Antwerp Nieuwstad designed by Gilbert van Schoonbeke, c.1550 (copy). Stadsarchief, Antwerp.

In the interior of the old city the *wethouders* actively sponsored Schoonbeke's plans to clear new avenues, or improve older neighborhoods like the Vrijdagmaarkt. For one 12-year period a new street was added to Antwerp's fabric every six months.[64] After 1577, the Calvinist council proposed similar measures; in 1578, it seized all ecclesiastical properties, with the result that new streets were plowed straight through former monasteries and cloisters.[65] A remarkable drawing of the Predikherenklooster from July 1582 (Figure 2.9) shows the design for a street, stretched across the top third of the sheet through a former abbey complex. A kind of architectural iconoclasm (or an early modern Hausmannization), the plan was one of dozens.

The construction of a citadel in the south of the city, for example, evicted many citizens from neighborhoods of Antwerp, and plowed access roads through otherwise untouched *wijken*, or districts. More insidiously, its construction called for mercilessly high taxes on the population itself.[66] Throughout most of Antwerp, dirt, stench, and darkness continued to reign, and most private buildings and their surroundings, unlike the grand new public ones, remained largely unchanged architecturally; ". . . the houses are poorly arranged, built in an ugly manner and usually of timber and earth," wrote one Italian visitor in 1557, adding ". . . however, the public buildings are of brick and very large and beautiful."[67] Near the Schelde wharf dwellings remained small, cramped, and blighted by vermin, and disease was rife. Pigs and wild dogs seem to have been a constant problem in the streets, and, as the books of civic edicts (*Gebodsboeken*) reveal, the public dumping of dung, blood, and animal entrails onto public passageways occurred

2.9
Sebastian van Uffelen, Plan for a new street extension through former Predikerenklooster, 1582.
Stadsarchief, Antwerp.

with startling frequency well into the 1580s.[68] Christoffel Plantin complained twice that decade about rubbish pile-ups near his print shop.[69] Indeed, industry impacted on the quality of civic life for many, by dispersing noisy and smelly trades throughout the city. When the French merchant Frans de Carter visited the Groote Markt in the 1570s, he noted how the density "of people, carts, and horses" [*van volke, wagens, ende peerden*] stopped Antwerp traffic for half-hours at a time.[70] In the Nieuwstad the original plans for a brewing industry had to be scrapped when the canal water became too polluted in the 1570s.[71] And although the city authorities eventually developed a rather sophisticated service for refuse collection—even distinguishing between three different classes of garbage, picked up by workers at night—such measures failed to keep pace with Antwerp's increasingly packed neighborhoods, and the ever-growing number of streets.[72] The emergence of a hegemonic middle-class in Antwerp was to direct all city spaces towards the smooth functioning of the market; yet despite Soly's assertion, this class seems simply to have amplified, rather than overturned, long-held medieval definitions of street spaces in Antwerp itself.

The overall design of both Schoonbeke's Nieuwstad and over 20 new streets in the city core were touted as elements of urban beautification: the importation of light and air to the city center were aimed at improving traffic through the overcrowded city. The Groenplaats, an open square dedicated to shrubbery (which is very different today) was one of the first public parks in Europe. Vredeman's own designs for perspectival gardens and fountains published in Antwerp (Figure 2.10, H 283) were frequently set in urban contexts, but, more often, they were used to model private gardens at court and country houses. Much to the surprise of visitors, trees grew along Antwerp's ramparts as well.[73] Civic ordinances from 1585 reveal that the public was even called upon to plant these trees, and urged the harvesting of herbs and even spices on the walls during winter.[74] John Evelyn witnessed these bushy improvements decades after they had matured: ". . . there was nothing about this city which more refreshed one that those delicious shades and walks of stately trees, which render the fortified walls of the town one of the sweetest places in Europe," he wrote. Records indicate these were probably lime trees.[75]

Vredeman's images appeared at a time when these civic improvements, in the wake of the new town hall, were being intensely debated, and when the "public" spaces of the city were becoming sites of what now look like official restriction and policing.[76] Particularly through their sharp perspective, Vredeman's prints echo many constructive methods deployed in Antwerp streets in the second half of the century. Their emptiness also foretells specific dictates; a civic injunction of 1567, for example, mandated that Antwerp houses burned in riots the previous year should be rebuilt in brick with uniform facades, and, whenever possible, avenues laid without undue curves.[77] And, at least once, Antwerp authorities concerned themselves overtly with the optical effects of civic buildings: when the Vrijdagmaarkt, an open square created by van Schoonbeke, was constructed, the surrounding houses were to be "built on pillars, in order that one can see through them, and at the same time oversee the entire market," indicating an interest if not in surveillance then in what must have been a novel

2.10
Hans Vredeman de Vries, *Artis Perspectivae*, 1568. Etching, H.283.
Avery Architectural and Fine Arts Library, Columbia University.

architectural transparency.[78] Vredeman's colleague Hans van Schille made straight streets a part of his fortification-cities in a tract published in 1573.[79]

Vredeman's cities could indeed model these proposals, but their tiny size, ornamental character, and self-ascribed status as pattern prints make their connection to architectural occurrences circumspect. Purchased by the same propertied amateurs like Gramaye, who benefited from the freer movement of goods the new Antwerp streets permitted, Vredeman's prints more likely pictured the idea of city space as a quilt of possessable patches, a new form of transferable good. The cities in the prints are "neutral"—sites akin to the speculators purview, which, as patterns, are useful insofar as they could be made into something else. Unstamped by any specific, lived, or historical traits, Vredeman's little worlds show scenes a merchant elite would recognize, wherein a real-estate parcel—like a print—awaits valuation by and for use and exchange. Only outside the city walls (Figure 2.4) does Vredeman's perspective keel upward and disperse, to deliniate a rugged background with trees and torture wheels. The ordered city stops at the wall, and with it the urban speculator's gaze.

The order of the street

The anthropologist Clifford Geertz describes how representations, as of cities, can "localize" apprehension of the public sphere:

> . . . any art form . . . renders ordinary, everyday experience comprehensible by presenting it in terms of acts and objects which have had their practical consequences removed and been reduced (or, if you prefer, raised) to the level of sheer appearances, where their meaning can be more powerfully articulated and more exactly perceived.[80]

In one etching of 1568 (Figure 2.10, H.283) Vredeman described the ornate facade of an imaginary public structure, traversed by exterior staircases; in a rare inclusion, human figures are accorded visual prominence—a woman and a child process towards a fountain. Explaining a similar work in his *Architectura* of 1577, Vredeman wrote:

> In this piece, unlike my others, no special or exact measurements have been followed; instead just some regular forms and lines are included . . . The distances and placements are arranged so that anyone may appropriate from it for their own needs [*chascun a son comandement usurper*], respecting the particular appropriateness of each thing it describes.[81]

With its violent recession, the image might be prescriptive not of a particular palace, but of the deliberate siting of that palace according to scenographic dictates. The immaterial *process* of clearing such perspective spaces, what Spiro Kostof termed the architectural *Freilungen* (disencumbering) of early town planning, overlaps with the making of Vredeman's images.[82] Of the more than 200 new Antwerp streets designed by van Schoonbeke in the sixteenth century, many were architectural manifestations of older civic ordinances that had passively regulated Antwerp street life for years. The Antwerp *Gebodsboeken* reveal fascinating evidence of these regulations, addressing perpetual urban nuisances like filth, noise, and smell in tandem with the architectural appearance of the city. The books also dictated everything from rules against drinking or dancing in public, to restrictions on the length and width of doorsteps, to prohibitions against the throwing of snowballs (fine, as dictated in 1535: 3 guilders).[83]

Civic order in Antwerp increasingly embraced tactics of deletion on both social and architectural terms: clearing old buildings and relocating industry. An important function of published civic edicts had long been to regulate where and when groups of the population could potentially live and work; in 1530, the council ordered all brothels off the "*schone*" Steenbergstraat, a then newly constructed and straight street near the St Joriskerk. Employees and patrons were relocated to the Blyenhoek area.[84] After the crackdown on Reformed activity around 1566, the number of exclusionary edicts increased; civic authorities wrestled with the problem of who, exactly, were supposed to be serving as police; on September 3, 1568, for example, a Spanish soldier was shot "*met pistoletten*" near the Mier.[85] Corporal punishments and taxes affected Catholics as well as Protestants. The Calvinist government of 1577–85 was hardly different in many of its restrictions; in 1580, for example, the singing of "seditious and scandalous songs" ("*sediteuse en scandaleuse liedekens*") was banned from the streets, while the same year children were barred altogether from playing outside.[86] Such rules dated to the Middle Ages, but their expanded scale affected the physical character of the entire city.[87] Soly has claimed that labor unrest was not uncommon during Antwerp's large engineering projects, that the *wet* specifically targeted law-breakers on the newly built streets.[88] Civic authorities were forced to step up surveillance and regulation of many previously unmolested social groups, not just Protestants. In June 1569, a rule mandated that all lepers and widows must register with the *wijk* authorities.[89] Meanwhile, in an attempt to combat Spanish edicts on billeting, the city required the registration of all foreign lodgers with the authorities, and explicitly forbade the housing of soldiers outside specific neighborhoods.[90]

The process of Vredeman's sketch becoming a print forms a parallel to these edicts' apotheosis (Figure 2.11, Color Plate III). In four of Vredeman's drawings in Berlin for the 1562 *Views*, undesirable or incongruous human and architectural elements have been altered or deleted. In a rare surviving example of the actual correcting process in printmaking, Cock (or the van Doetecums, or Vredeman himself), as

2.11
Hans Vredeman de Vries, preliminary drawing for *Untitled Architectural View*, 1560–62. Brown ink, wash, and corrective red pencil on paper. 15.7 × 21.4.
Kupferstichkabinett, Staatliche Museen zu Berlin.

2.12
Hans Vredeman de Vries, *Architectural Perspective View*, 1562. Etching, H.91.
Avery Architectural and Fine Arts Library, Columbia University.

if rectifying a proof, has taken an editor's red pencil and slashed through certain parts of the sheet with an "X". The corrections, sometimes executed and sometimes not in the final print (Figure 2.12), mark out figures clumsily drawn or awkward to the composition.[91] Clearly, Cock was interested in the appearance of his merchandise. But in tandem with the subject matter of the finished print series—the city viewed—the deletions echo not just the results of the edicts but the expunging processes at work in Antwerp streets, wherein undesirables have mysteriously vanished; the street is cleared, ready for use. Vredeman's etching dreams the city street as an artwork, a locus for speculation.

A woodcut from the jurist Jan de Damhouder's 1555 *Practical Book on Criminal Affairs* (Figure 2.13) reveals another take on these edicts. It demonstrates, as an inscription at the top suggests, the harm cased by "*uytworpinghe*" (throwing out) human waste from windows.[92] In the woodcut two unsuspecting house-dwellers nonchalantly empty their chamber-buckets into the streets below, as a pair of well-to-do citizens unsuccessfully flee the twin showers of filth. The idea that the practice of *uytvvorpinghe* is contrary to the appearance, and correspondingly the character, of a clean, orderly city is intimated through the woodcutter's structure of the design—the street pattern conceptualized as an unblemished perspectival grid.

2.13
Joost de Damhouder, *Praktyck ende handboeck in criminale zaeken* (Leuven, 1555), fol. 266r.
Universiteitsbibliotheek, Amsterdam.

Governance of Antwerp, always a "question of privileges," could turn any such regulation into a combination of conflict and compromise between the sovereign and the city. In Antwerp dictates for housing specifications on a dwelling-to-dwelling scale can be found as early as the 1530s. These laws often drew upon an older tradition of admonitory publications, which adopted the guise of *moralia*. Once designated, certain physical or social elements were inimical to a regular, orderly city.

But they pronounce this order overtly as artifice, as ostentatiously *fashioned* as if in perspective.

Composing and questioning: triumphal procession, a Brussels *refereyn*

In the Stockholm woodcut (Figure 2.1) Vredeman referred to himself as a member of an Antwerp chamber of rhetoric, or *rederijkerskamer*, although his name appears nowhere on their records.[93] His rhetorical career has not been considered of great interest to scholars, which is particularly strange given Vredeman's dealings with Pieter Bruegel.[94] Two extant written sources testify to Vredeman's rhetorical activity. The first is the verses appended to the 1565 print; the second is the text of a *refrein*, or balladic poem, Vredeman delivered at a Brussels literary festival in 1562. An obscure quarto edition of the competition's poems was published in 1563 (Figure 2.14).[95] In the book Vredeman identified himself as a brother of the *Peone*, one of Mechelen's three chambers. Significantly, Van Mander makes no mention of Vredeman's oratorical activities in the *Lives*, as he did for other artists involved with rhetoric, such as Hans Baltens or Jan van Scorel.[96] All that survives is the printed text of his oration.

Like printmaking, *rederijkerij* was a collaborative and inherently urban pursuit in Flanders and Brabant. Originally founded to produce religious plays, Netherlandish *gheselscepen, broederscepen*, or *camersen "vander rhetoricken"* were the descendants of French dramatic societies and poetry clubs from the Middle Ages.[97] *Rederijkerkamers* were imbricated with the social and often with the physical context of cities and large towns. Confraternities decorated buildings and streets for processions, gave public performances of religious dramas on temporary stages, and organized competitions, plays, and civic pageants on feast days and religious holidays. *Rederijkers* frequently worked in tandem with civic militia, pilgrimage brotherhoods, and guilds. Even small cities in the Netherlands boasted at least one chamber of rhetoric by the middle of the sixteenth century. Leuven had two; Mechelen, Amsterdam, and Brussels each had three, and, at one point, Antwerp had four.[98]

In Antwerp the *Violieren* chamber of rhetoric had formally merged with the artists guild of St. Luke in 1480, so that contemporaries spoke of the "*rhetorijcklicke Schilder-Gildt van Antwerpen.*"[99] In fact, Van Mander detailed the rhetorical activities of several painters; Jan van Scorel was described as "a good musician, poet, and rhetorician," while the landscapist Jacques Grimmer was "an asset to the rederijkers and actors in their plays."[100] The painter and print designer William van Haecht, for example, authored several poems for competitions. Artists Pieter Baltens, Marten de Vos, and Hieronymus Cock were all registered members of the *Violieren* in the 1560s, where, along with Vredeman, they would have encountered the cartographer/publisher, Ortelius, the banker and art-collector, Hans Frankert, and the city treasurer, Gillis Hooftman.[101] The secretary of the *Violieren*, meanwhile, was, Vredeman's fellow engineer Hans van Schille.[102]

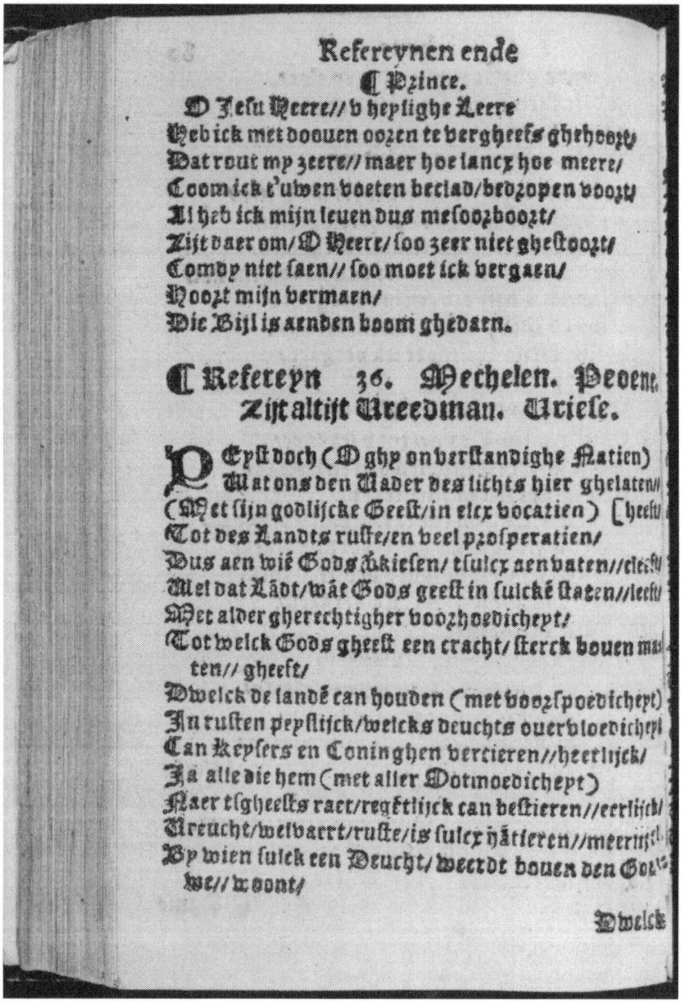
Referepnen ende
Prince.
O Jesu Heere// v heylighe Leere
Heb ick met dooven ooren te verghheefs ghehoort/
Dat rout my zeere// maer hoe lancx hoe meere/
Coom ick t'uwen voeten beclad/bedropen voort/
Al heb ick mijn leuen dus mesoorboort/
Zijt daer om/ O Heere/ soo zeer niet ghestoort/
Comdy niet saen// soo moet ick vergaen/
Hoort mijn vermaen/
Die Bijl is aenden boom ghedaen.

Referepn 36. Mechelen. Peoene.
Zijt altijt Vreedman. Vriese.

P Eyst doch (O ghy onverstandighe Natien)
Wat ons den Vader des lichts hier ghelaten//
(Met sijn godlijcke Geest/in elcx vocatien) [heeft//
Tot des Landts ruste/en veel prosperatien/
Dus aen wie Gods ghekiesen/ tsulcx aenvaten//
Wel dat Lādt/wāt Gods geest in sulckē staten//leeft/
Met alder gherechtigher voorhoedichept/
Tot welck Gods gheest een cracht/ sterck bouen ma-
ten// gheeft/
Dwelck de landē can houden (met voorspoedichept)
In rusten peysllijck/welcks deuchts ouervloedichept
Can keysers en Coninghen vercieren//heerlijck/
Ja alle die hem (met aller Ootmoedichept)
Maer tsgheelts raet/regētlijck can bestieren//eerlijck/
Vreucht/welvaert/ruste/is sulcx hātieren//
By wien sulck een Deucht/ weerdt bouen den
we// woont/
Dwelck

2.14
Michael van Hamont, *Refereynen ende Liedekens* (Brussels, 1563), fol. 80v.
Universiteitsbibliotheek, Amsterdam.

The relationship between the practises of vernacular rhetoric and the visual arts in sixteenth-century Brabant and Flanders was intimate and complex, extending not just to shared themes and practitioners but to common strategies of composition and address.[103] We have seen how rhetorical categories of organization, borrowed from the writings of Cicero and Quintilian, structured much of the art and architectural theory in the Low Countries in the sixteenth century, shaping Coecke van Aelst's translations of Vitruvius and Serlio, and the painting theory later essayed by Van Mander in the *Grondt*.[104] Informed by antique tenets, architects and artists, like poets, increasingly relied upon standardized forms and "places" for composition, reviving an interest in architecture's role in communication and persuasion. Theorists such as Serlio advocated a language of compositional models which could be deployed in different contexts, not just for functionality, but also to impress and/or instruct beholders.[105] A phenomenon like the *doorsien* (a view or vista), for example, was presented by Van Mander as a painterly device based on rhetoric; the active "seeing through" worked like a rhetorical gambit, to draw the beholder into a composition. In his discussion of the *doorsien*, Van Mander, who was a *rederijker* himself in Haarlem, was simply carrying over rhetorical structures, such as antithesis, into the realm of the visual arts.

Rederijker presentations in the Flemish vernacular were hardly classical in style. Orators continued to deal with topics as varied as war, food, art, and politics. This placed them at odds, sometimes violently, with the civic authorities. *Rederijkers* were frequently accused of nourishing Reformed ideas and fomenting civic dissent. When the citizens of Ghent rioted over tax increases in 1539, Spanish authorities blamed a rhetorical festival held that year for farming insurrection; the observer Richard Clough wrote that "those plays was [*sic*] one of the prynsypall occasyons of the dystrouccyon of the towne of Gannt."[106] The following year, an imperial decree even forbade the possession of the Ghent poems published after the event. Meanwhile, in 1558, Spanish authorities actually beheaded the *facteur* (playwright) of the Antwerp *violieren*, one Frans Fraet, declaring him guilty of pronouncing heretical poems.[107]

Like executions, presentations of rhetoric were well-attended spectacles, staged in the most public sites in town. *Landjuwelen*—large group competitions between entire chambers—were elaborate pageants that included processions, tournaments, and feasts that could last for weeks. The smaller cousins of the *landjuwelen, refreinfeesten*, usually brought together single entrants of chambers, who each represented a single *kamer. Refreinfeests* are recorded in Antwerp in 1556, 1559, 1561, 1562, and 1564, in Brussels in 1559, 1561, 1562, in Breda in 1564, and in Lier in 1564.[108]

The main attractions at such events were dramatic responses to a question, a predetermined *vraghe*, prepared weeks in advance. Before the iconoclastic riots of 1566, these *vraghen* often revealed a surprising degree of latitude with regard to controversial subject matter; the fraught question of "*Wie in sheeren Tabernakel woonen sall?*" (Who shall dwell in the house of the Lord?), for example, was freely debated at a *refreinfeest* at s'Hertogenbosch on March 16, 1547. However, after 1560, when an edict of January 26 outlawed the performance of chamber plays and ballads without prior censorship,[109] topics became more subdued. In 1562, a s'Hertogenbosch competition debated "*Waer in smensen victorie meest gelegen is?*" (Where does human victory most strongly manifest itself?)—a relatively non-religious topic by comparison.[110]

While the *spele evan sinne*—a kind of morality drama, literally "a play of meaning,"—was the most common form of reply to the *vraghe*, chambers had two other alternatives at a *landjuweel*. They could stage a disputation between two people (*arguacie*), or an explanation (*presentatie*).[111] Whereas at a *refreinfeest* a single orator would generally speak as a representative of a single chamber, at a *landjuweel* the *spele* would necessitate collaboration of many participants, on stage and off. Sets and costumes had to be designed, songs composed and memorized, attendant festivities arranged. Awards would finally have been granted, but prize categories were not limited to the oratory performance itself; best entry decoration, best delivery, best prologue, even best celebratory *feest* were appropriately recognized as well, suggesting that the visual aspects of the rhetorical presentations were in many cases just as valued as the purely oral ones. In fact, the great literary competitions that were documented in publications, the two *landjuweels* of 1561 in Antwerp and 1562 in Rotterdam, were remarkable for their lavish stage designs, as much as their conscious skirting of potentially controversial topics in the city. The *Violeren's vraghe* for the 1561 event "*Wat de mensch aldermeest tot conste verwaect?*" (What best awakens man to the arts?), for example, stimulated replies that were decidedly non-confrontational: "love" (Diest), "Truth" (Mechelen's *Lisbloeme*), "God's spirit" (Leuven), and "Utility and Profit" (Brussels's *D'Maris Crosten*).[112] As was customary, the participating *kamers* would have received word of the *vraghe* in advance.

Nina Serebrennikov has suggested that the *spele van sinne* produced by the Mechelen *Peone*, in Antwerp in 1561, had some input from Vredeman.[113] Vredeman was living in Mechelen at the time and had worked previously on festival decorations, a task allotted specifically to the town's *rederijkerkamers*. The *Peone* had won first prize (a silver chalice) at a competition held in Herenthals in 1510, and took second prize at the 1561 event, for their *prologhe*.[114] The main *spele* at the latter produced by the *Peone* proposed "*Dbevoedsaem aenmercken van d'exellencie der consten*" (Understanding of the excellence of the arts) as reply to the invitation's *vraghe*.[115] In the play, an allegorical figure of man begins a conversation with personification of "Wisdom" and "Understanding," who is introduced to the figures of "Portraiture" and "Sculpture." Two female figures representing *Pictura* and *Statuaria* emerge from behind a curtain. "*Wie is datte?*" asks mankind; to which Understanding replies:

> That is noble portraiture
> The build and shape of every creature
> Calmly done after life
> Rendered and adherent to it
> She is to be learned among the liberal arts
> Since she is silent poetry.

Reason then adds:

> And she can be seen presently
> As founded upon Geometry,
> Perspective, and other new discoveries [*vonden*]
> Which render works artful and ornamental.[116]

Even within the turgid style of the play, the "new discoveries" of perspective and geometry, two of Vredeman's concerns, stand out; no other chamber mentioned the two arts so explicitly. The concept of "*stomme Poetrije*" likens the art of the *rederijker* to that of the painter, an ancient trope indeed.[117] Horace's famed simile *ut pictura poesis* fueled visualizations of the relation between the arts in painting and in print, and in both Antwerp and Mechelen painters, stonemasons, and goldsmiths were frequently among the members of the chambers. In Antwerp authors of the *Peone's* 1561 *spel*, Philips Ghysmans and one Frans de Coster,[118] would, as was customary, have conferred with their brothers before the play was produced; Vredeman's explicit involvement in the production can therefore hardly be discounted. Perspective, in the *Peone's* presentation, became a bestower of both order and ornament.

The actual stages erected by *rederijkers* concretized this perspective within the city street. Painters were generally entrusted with constructing the stage structures for rhetorical competitions.[119] The double-arched facade for the 1561 Antwerp *landjuweel* (Figure 2.15) was designed—like the Antwerp town hall—by *Violeren* brother Cornelis Floris, based on the prints of Serlio's *Second Book*.[120] The image is known today through a woodcut in Silvius's account. Placed on the Groote Markt, its stylistic rhyming with the in-process *Stadhuis* must have been impressive. In his account Silvius connects this elaborate *toneel* to the amphitheatres of the ancients.[121] The apparent novelty of a kind of permanent stage was underlined in a historiated description:

> . . . and so desirous was the community [*ghemeynte*] of seeing poetic productions and plays, that the city of Athens ordained a beautiful structure be built, called a *theatre* in Greek, which took the form of a semi-circle . . . So beautifully constructed was this building that all the citizens and inhabitants of Athens had sufficient space to sit, from which they all could easy see, perfectly hear, and thus fully understand the plays [. . .].[122]

Silvius goes on to urge the construction of a similar structure in Antwerp. An enclosed woodcut of the "Greek" amphitheatre, lifted from Cock's 1551 prints of ruins, paralleled the form of Floris's *landjuweel* stage.

Most commonly, the *rederijker* platform was a humble affair: a flat wooden stage and curtain placed in the middle of the street. A painting by Frans Floris, known today through a 1565 engraving by Cornelis Cort (Figure 2.16) reveals a sharpened view of a stage during a performance, witnessed by scattered observers.[123] The temporary character of such stages emphasized the street setting as a clear backdrop, in complete contrast to the woodcut of the disembodied floating *toneel* by Cornelis Floris (Figure 2.15). Indeed, most rhetorical performances in Vredeman's time adopted the urban setting as an intrinsic, even potentially dangerous element of the production. One Antwerp edict from the days before the 1561 *landjuweel*, for example, prohibited spectators from climbing on the town hall's scaffolding and on the stage itself during performances.[124] In Ghent regulations were issued against carrying knives, torches, and halberds near a rhetorical stage. And a fascinating edict of 1539 forbade "anyone to carry, cover, or disguise himself in order to enter the play";[125]—urban masquerade literally impinging upon the traditional *rederijker* structure.

An important sub-species of the *landjuweels* were the smaller festivals known as *refreynfeesten*. These brought together members of chambers for the presentation of individually written poems. The entrants could choose to compose

2.15
***Spelen van Sinne van scone moralisacien . . .* (Antwerp, 1562), fol. Aiiiv.**
Universiteitsbibliotheek, Amsterdam.

verses around a *stok*, a particular phrase or subject, or to answer one of several *vraghen*. The *Violeren* hosted the first recorded festival in 1480, and the large rhetoric festival in Ghent in April 1539, sponsored by the *Fontaine* chamber, included a *refereyn* competition as well.[126] Like the *landjuweels*, the *referynefeest* gradually backed off from socio-religious flashpoints as topics; whereas the *vraghe* at s'Hertogenbosch on March 16,

2.16
Cornelis Cort after Frans Floris, *Rhetorica*, 1565. Engraving, H.200.
Rijksprentenkabinet, Amsterdam.

1547, was the touchy "*Wie in sheeren Tabernakel woonen sall?*" (Who shall dwell in the house of the Lord?), in 1562, contestants had to ponder the lighter issue of "*Waer in smensen victorie meest gelegen is?*" (Where does human victory most strongly manifest itself?).[127]

It was at a *refereynfeest* hosted by the Brussels *Corenbloem* that Vredeman de Vries delivered an oration on July 24, 1562. The *vrage* was "*Wat dat de Landen can houden in Rusten?*" (What best keeps the land at peace?).[128] Vredeman's answer ("*Wysheyt*"—Wisdom) was couched in a long poem extolling the virtues of inner revelation:

> Wisdom, full of zeal
> It is a power of God to be looked upon as the font
> Of all artful eminences;
> Because Wisdom spies all, because she is discreet
> And above all skilled in the attainment of triumph.
> She lays unwise follies bare
> For she is prudent, full of love, and understanding.[129]

The somewhat turgid language of triumph and unveiling is descended from the traditional form of the refrain *in 't vroed*, that is, a lyric pertaining to didactic matters. There is also a faintly Protestant character to Vredeman's entry: he celebrates the internal abidance of God's law, divine scripture, and direct communion with the spirit, unmediated by church teaching. In fact, the phrase "prudent, full of love, and understanding" appears to have been lifted straight from a 1553 book by the spiritualist sect-leader, Hendrik Niclaes, as we will see in Chapter 4. Radical spiritualists were commonly among the elites attracted to—and often punished for—rhetorical activities.

Vredeman opted to direct his composition towards an elaboration of a given theme ("Wisdom") rather than towards any argument. As Dirk Coigneau has shown, the *referyn* or *refereyn* or *refrein* form among the *rederijkers* was a peculiar invention of the fifteenth century, rooted in "imitation" of a particular poetic model rather than in composition of new subject matter.[130] Before it became a competitive vehicle, the *refrein* would be a conversational meeting-point for members of individual Flemish chambers, who would gather to elect a member to compose a poem on a given theme; other members would then be judged simply on their ability to amplify and repeat this topic, that is, on the eloquence of their enunciation.[131] The textual "theme" of the *refrein* was therefore of secondary importance, and it became execution by the participant that provided the grounds for real excellence and, indeed, invention. The situation approaches Vredeman's *Scenographiae* (1560), or the *Architectural Views* (1562), which repeated manifestations of a similar architectural "place". At *refreinfeests* speakers consciously abandoned the deliberative academicism humanists like Erasmus had hoped to revive, in favor of more vernacular verse rooted in poetry and even song; here, the visual functions of actors, their gestures, facial expressions, and bodily movements, were far more important than "content" alone.[132]

In the sixteenth century, orators assumed a dramatically different stance towards their audiences than in antiquity. Classical rhetoric took for granted the idea of a shared cultural heritage among speakers and listeners, one it was the orator's task to acknowledge and praise. By Vredeman's day, no such coherent cultural tradition existed. In fractious Antwerp, rhetoric became predicated instead on the creation and explanation of individual, realms; as Michael Halloran has put it, "rhetoric's task became not the inhabitation of the listener and speaker's shared world, but the creation of a world from the self."[133] Accordingly, it was during the sixteenth century that the word "rhetoric" accrued its modern-day connotations of pedantry and hermeticism.

An increasingly popular strategy for the *refrein* form was the use of "places." Mark Meadow has argued that under the influence of the Liège-born orator Petrus Ramus, North European rhetoric underwent a so-called aural-to-visual shift in the early sixteenth century, wherein tropes and propositions of a presentation would increasingly resort to metaphors of space.[134] "Shapes," "lines," and "rooms" became the things constituting speakers' presentations, rather than a linear sequence of terms or arguments in a speaker's mind. Erasmus, for instance (who loathed *rederijkers*), sang the praises of visual example and "living symbols," which, he claimed, "brightened" speech on any topic.[135] Orators would increasingly aim to show rather than tell, exhorting listeners to "see," or "view" points rather than aurally intuit them.[136]

While hardly reliant on such strictly antique modes or oration, Vredeman's address was, in effect, demonstrative rather than argumentative; his poem was *epideictic*, its roots lay in oration aimed at praise, blame, and the evocation of pleasing effects.[137] The resulting style is anything but pure Ciceronian. Ornate, flowery, abstruse, even grotesque. The verses adhere to the fanciful style outlined in contemporary textbooks like Matthijs de Castelijn's *Const van Rhetoriken*, published in Brussels six times between 1555 and 1616.[138] Elocution, Castelijn stressed, rather than *inventie*, was the main point of speech. To be avoided, Castelijn wrote, were "exordiums, positions, division, narrations, argumentations, egressions . . .,"[139] such as antique Roman doctrines of deliberative rhetoric. The *refrein* style, which Vredeman's verses exemplified, privileged delivery, performance, and display at an individual level. The play, as it were, was intended not to prove but to demonstrate through a deliberately arcane enumeration of wisdom's attributes. The Greek orator Hermogenes described this ekphrastic sheen as a function of individual repetition: "the style must contrive to bring about seeing through hearing."[140] In his 1562 Brussels composition Vredeman repeated a single line at the end of each verse: "*de Wijsheyt, want zij brengt in praktijk: Vrede, Liefde, en Trouw*") (Wisdom brings forth tranquility, love, and faithfulness). This so-called *stokregel*, repeated four times, reiterates a celebration of God's law, divine scripture, and direct communion with the "spirit." However, the structure of the poem winds almost circuitously through a sequence of Wisdom's attributes (she is "free/devoid of hypocrisy, amiable/brave and kind/just, merciful, gallant and helpful"). The epideictic nodes of the poem form a wandering, itinerant parallel to the last kind of urban performance Vredeman staged in Antwerp, the ceremonial entry.

Festive objects

Vredeman's *refrein*, aimed at the passionate disclosure of a world, speaks to his earlier participation in the *blijde inkomst* tradition. We know from a short passage in Van Mander that Vredeman, along with 1,726 other Antwerp artisans (233 of which were painters), took part in the preparations for the ceremonial entry of Philip II and Charles V into Antwerp on September 11–14, 1549. Vredeman appears to have worked specifically on arches.[141] It is probable that in these tasks Vredeman was introduced to the idea of large-scale festival tableaux for the first time, as well as to the intricacies of presenting immaterial themes (such as *Wijsheyt*) in visual terms. Charles and Philip's entry necessitated the construction of elaborate temporary stages in Antwerp's streets and periphery, including a wood and pasteboard town hall.[142] This *Aula Temporalia*, designed by the painter Lambert van Noordt, would have stood on the Groote Markt, where it housed banqueting chambers and a large viewing tribunal, all arranged on three sides of the Markt. Here, poems were presented to the sovereigns and to Antwerp's body politic during the festivities themselves.[143]

In his 1550 publication on the Antwerp entry Cornelis Grapheus illustrated the *Aula* with a large two-block woodcut that folded out of his quarto edition (Figure 2.17); the extended format cleverly matched the manner in which van Noordt's Italianate tribunal angled around three sides of the Groote Markt. The sham structure, claims Grapheus, was made of

> . . . painted architecture and many Doric columns, arranged on the ground and so artfully constructed that it appeared to be made not of painted wood but of living stone.[144]

The woodcut illustration not only illustrated this structure but, falling out of the book, emphasized the building's disruption of the flow of the city. Of course, citizens could not attend the banquet that took place inside this fake Stadhuis, although they could, Grapheus reports, pass through the great arch constructed beneath its tribunal.[145] The resulting effect, redoubled by the book, supplied the veneer of a dialogue. Citizens regarded Charles and Philip (ensconced in royal viewing boxes at the center of the "square"), while the sovereigns, in turn, regarded them from atop the central archway. Greeted by carefully scripted songs and speeches, the royals would have arrived after processing along streets artificially straightened by decoration, to stop at *tableaux vivants*, and watch—and be watched by—the population, as actors and rhetoricians delivered addresses from stages. Ostensibly, the "dialogic" character of the entry was its key, as was its reliance upon a dynamic of repetition and pattern.[146] At several nodes on the itinerary, Philip's cortège would be obliged to respond to prepared chants read by the populace itself—promises of respect for civic rights exchanged for oaths of fealty.

Yet the formalities of who was to stand where, what decorations to look at, and in which order they were to be viewed, both on stage and off, were all carefully

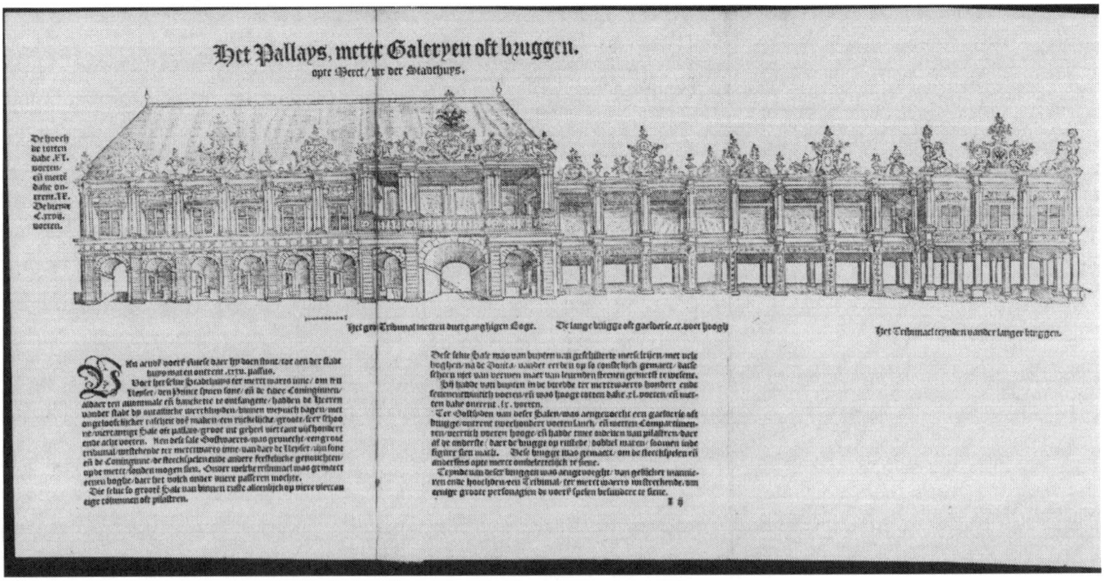

2.17
Cornelis Grapheus, *De seer wonderlijcke, schoone, triumphelijcke inkomst . . .* (Antwerp, 1550), fol. Lir.
Universiteitsbibliotheek, Amsterdam.

scripted by the civic organizers under Grapheus; indeed, prizes of food and drink were offered to the neighborhood that could lure the most spectators to the parade route.[147] That the design of the pieces recalled Serlio's woodcuts is hardly coincidental—Coecke van Aelst, who designed the stages, had copied Serlio's woodcuts in 1539 for his own book of architecture. As Meadow has noted, the form of the Roman arch allowed for the simultaneous presence of both concrete threshold and fictive tableau.[148] Serlian architecture was resolutely "modern" to many Netherlandish artists in the mid-sixteenth century, and, even shorn of inscriptions or tableaux, it would have bodied forth sufficiently "antique" connotations for viewers.[149] Indeed, the Porta Caesara, a heavy permanent gate at Antwerp's eastern edge, built in the Tuscan style, was one of the few permanent structures left unadorned for Philip's entry, since it alone seems to have manifested a suitably antique architectural vocabulary. Yet the festival architecture in Antwerp would have been most extraordinary for its temporary nature; Grapheus's book emphasized the decoration as a once-only affair. Its task was not so much an obliteration of the everyday, as a juxtaposition of the mundane with the splendid.[150]

Vredeman's city prints echo the utopian endeavors of the festival organizers, transplanting a spacious, facade-driven vision of rhetorical "place" onto a web of extant streets. In Antwerp the ceremonial preparations called for more than just tableaux; civic ordinances mandated increased street maintenance, suspension of trade activity producing offensive noises and smells (such as tannery and smithing), and the rounding up of potential human troublemakers, during the weeks before the spectacles.[151] For a temporary period, the festival transformed the city into a visual and social utopia. But this ideal, recognized as ephemeral, was contingent upon the proximity of commonplace buildings and structures. The *inkomst* adhered to the form of an allegorical poem. Its efficacy derived not just from a glib transmission of symbols, but from an awareness of the materiality of that symbolization's bearers—stone, paper pasteboard, or wood. In fact the scenery of *rederijker* competitions and royal entries was valued in quite physical terms. An edict of September 23, 1549, two weeks after the entry of Philip and Charles, ordered Antwerp citizens who still kept "fragments" of the festival architecture in their houses to return them to city authorities at once.[152]

Possession of remnants of the civic performances was one motive behind a new type of publication in the sixteenth century: festival books. Triumphal entry rites were not, in and of themselves, new in northern Europe. Yet the complex architectural vocabulary deployed to host them was, and publications like that of Grapheus in 1550 explained the iconography and enabled the legal rites of the entry to take a handleable form. Vredeman's own ceremonial designs appeared in the lavish *La Joyeuse & Magnifique Entrée de Monseigneor Francoys*, a folio published by Christoffel Plantin in 1582[153] (Fig. 2.18.) This work described decorations crafted to welcome Anjou, brother of the king of France, to Antwerp in 1581. Anjou was invited to lead the States General of the Netherlands in 1577, when the Antwerp city council—then officially Protestant—became increasingly displeased with the demands of the Hapsburg representatives in Brussels. In 1576, William of Orange, Stadhouder of Holland and Zeeland, expelled

Spanish troops from Antwerp. After months of negotiations with England and France trying to recruit a new regent, Orange settled on Anjou, a second-rate military leader, who, penniless and Catholic, was popular neither with the States General nor with Antwerp's Protestant city leaders. However, as brother of Henri III of France, Anjou retained the lukewarm support of England (he had, in fact, been vainly wooing Elizabeth I in London when he received Orange's call). Anjou sailed to Antwerp from Flushing in early February 1581, leaving less than six days of advance notification for artists to prepare for an official ceremony to crown him Duke of Brabant.

The entry took place on February 17. The author of its written descriptions is unknown, although Frances Yates suggested that Lucas de Gheere, the rhetorician who had designed Anjou's entry into Ghent six months later, oversaw its textual program.[154] We know that iconography of Anjou's tableaux was devised by Vredeman himself, and he is recorded as being paid by the city council to "layout, oversee, and organize" ephemeral stages and direct young male actors.[155] Like Charles and Philip's entry in 1549, the 1581 program relied heavily on imagery of a "Burgundian" renaissance; one float, described on folios A1r-B3v of Plantin's book, shows an effigy of Anjou beside those of his ancestors, Philip the Good (b.1419) and Francis I (b.1515), both great patrons of French letters. Yet unlike the 1549 entry, which had emphasized the monarchs' symbolic conquest of Antwerp in 1581, Anjou was confronted with imagery thematizing the limitations on his royal power. One stage contained a personification of Antwerp addressing the Duke's cortège directly:

> Feerce furie, moodie rage, unbridled ire
> Stout foirce, hot violence, cruel tyrannie
> Nought booted me, ne furthered my desire
> In keeping of my wished soverignity
> The surest waie for kings to govern by
> Is mildness matched with a prudent mind. [156]

The sum effect of such pronouncements, in tandem with the décor, was the equating of peace and temperance with a kind of Flemish cultural rebirth. A ceremonial car crowned with a *fleur de lys* presented Anjou as an Apollo driving out the "hellhounds" of Discord, Violence, and Tyranny. The expulsion of despotism—in effect, Antwerp's concern after its break with Spain—resurfaced throughout the printed book: Vredeman's arch in Plate XVIII showed Anjou dispersing pasteboard clouds of "Envy" and "Slander."[157] It was important, warned the actors and the prints, that Anjou did not repeat the mistakes of predecessors like Philip, in neglecting his obligations to the city. Legally, this was audacious: Anjou's *inkomst* struck down the same succession of Hapsburg power that the 1549 book, and Philip and Charles's entry, had intended to ratify. A long colonnade of 12-foot-tall painted pillars on the St Michalestraat, designed by Vredeman (Figure 2.18, H.469), appeared as well. Plantin shows this stage as a vista, read at horseback height. Within the book the effect of this print is a jolt: suddenly, Anjou's view slides into that of the reader. This was precisely the political equivalence the *inkomst* hoped to secure:

while the entry assured Anjou a symbolic wealth that he, an itinerant duke constantly strapped for cash, did not know in reality, the book rendered his "acqusition" of the city something witnessed, instead of simply told.

The panoramic view of Antwerp that opens the book reveals the rickety wooden stage designed by Vredeman upon which Anjou had been crowned. It is almost hidden, at center right, on the city's outskirts (Figure. 2.19). In the following plate (Figure 2.20) the same structure suddenly appears again, this time facing the viewer as a formidable classical edifice. Plantin lowers us from the cartographic space of the map into the extraordinary setting of the entry: by permitting us to see the flimsy backboard of Vredeman's stage *first*, he recapitulates—for viewers, and sovereigns—the juxtaposition of the real and ideal worlds. Presenting Anjou as Apollo, and staging the Burgundian Renaissance in Brabant, he achieves a spectacular suspension of belief. Grapheus even hand-colored versions of his entry book, which sold for nearly double the price of black-and-white editions (in May 1581, 24 copies of a similar book were purchased by the members of the Antwerp city council).[158] The allure of this type of project to the merchant classes of Antwerp seems obvious: in underwriting, designing, and promoting the coronation spectacles, the urban elites increasingly saw themselves as co-contractors in a royal agreement, rather than, as with Philip's entry of 1549, its humble bindees. The book permitted these elites mastery, even possession, of the aristocratically ephemeral.

As dealers in the still-new world of financial notes, property speculation, and securities,[159] the festival-book consumers would have readily understood simulacra-based transactions. Ownership of a ceremony's likenesses (*contrafeyten*) functioned as an extension and legitimization of the ritual itself. The prints after Vredeman were part of the event; they reified the festival's status as an occurrence that crossed all media, yet are lodged in a particular place and time.[160] William McClung has described

2.18
***La Joyeuse & Magnifique entrée* (Antwerp, Christoffel Plantin, 1582), no. XVII.**
Rijksprentenkabinet, Amsterdam.

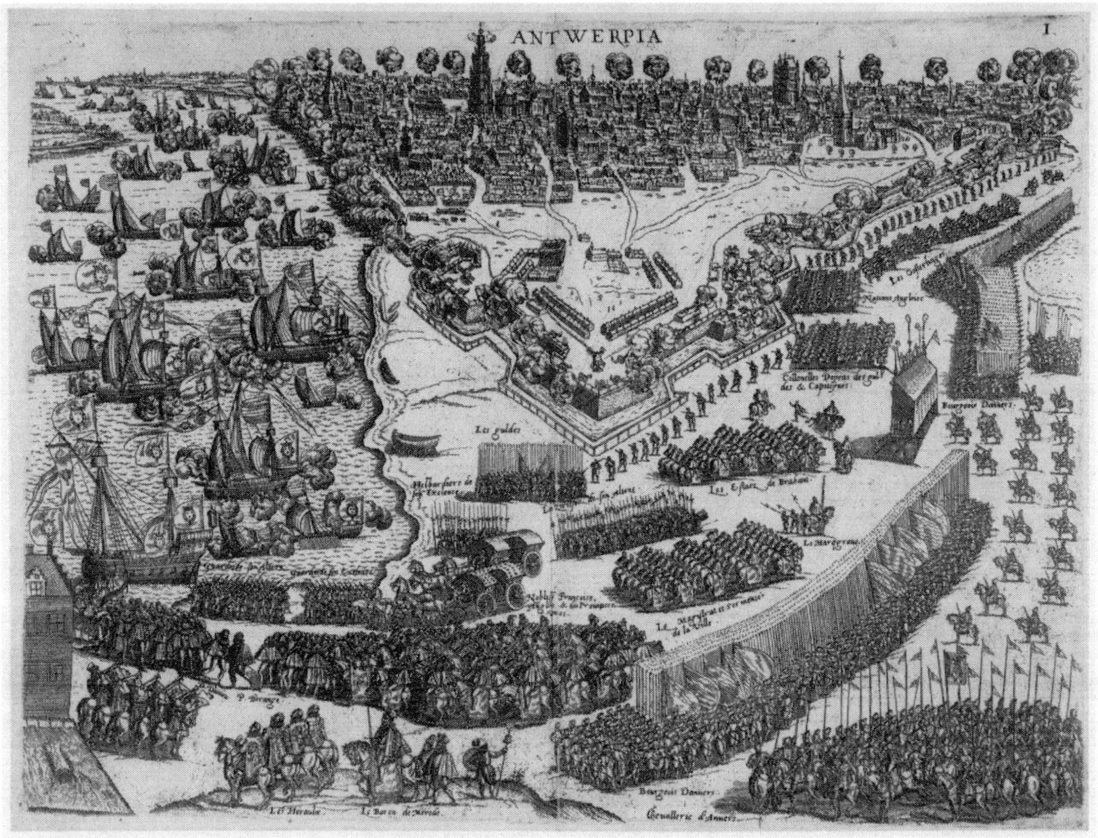

2.19
***La Joyeuse & Magnifique entrée* (Antwerp, Christoffel Plantin, 1582), no. I. Etching.**
Rijksprentenkabinet, Amsterdam.

this process elegantly: "... festival books are both acts of homage and salvage operations, testimony to the fact that epiphanic moments will not permanently transfer the celebrant to a dimension beyond the clock."[161] The early modern entry book, like the architecture it described, attempted to put these moments—and an awareness of their disappearance—into the hands of the urban elite.

Recounting how great theatre, seeking truth, should vaunt its own artificiality, Berthold Brecht claimed that "what is 'natural' must have the force of what is startling."[162] The refashioning of familiar streets and themes, which was part of both Vredeman's rhetoric and his ceremonial décor, relied upon an Antwerp just visible beneath its scaffoldings, cloaking but not obscuring the native with the new. The underpinnings of Vredeman's printed townscapes too, it seems, lie not within the fragile category of slavish "realism" or its opposites. If anything, it is the *distance* that they, as ostensible fictions, posit between the actual and an ideal of Antwerp that was crucial; as Louis Marin has suggested of utopias, such distance imparts to the works a necessary instability which mandates the bridging action of beholders.[163] In Vredeman's engravings sprawling new streets are cleared of trash, malcontents, and disease, but also scoured of any fixed set of players, like the *toneel* of the *rederijkers*. Nowhere within Vredeman's cityscapes does one encounter a church. One looks in vain even for a non-signatory

2.20
***La Joyeuse & Magnifique entrée* (Antwerp, Christoffel Plantin, 1582), no. II. Etching.**
Rijksprentenkabinet, Amsterdam.

inscription—we recall the Mechelen vicar's complaint about Antwerp's "SPQA." This reconfiguration of clear reference, while echoing an experience not unknown to émigrés like Vredeman (think of his bowdlerized city hall print), also parallels the evacuation of conventional values and relationships from the city under pressure of market-based realities.[164] Like a stage set or royal entry route, with house doors and windows transformed into rows of shadowy masks,[165] the city in Vredeman's engravings is a black-and-white backdrop for civic performances. Vredeman's empty cities challenge viewers—in serving as patterns for other artists—to literally fill the streets themselves.

Walks in the city, walks in the country

Urban itineraries exist only by contrast with the world *extra muros*. The woolly countryside, barely visible at the periphery of Vredeman's walled cities (Figure 2.4), is a foil and frame for the empty architectural spaces at his composition's heart. Windmills, cliffs, and hillocks appear often in his preliminary drawings (Figure 2.11). Although in the ten Berlin drawings and single Paris sheet for the series of 1560 and 1562 Vredeman was largely responsible for the architecture, Cock, or someone in his workshop (or both), occasionally made small additions and modifications to the human staffage, as we have seen. The skeletal groupings of figures in the sheets appear in black ink, as opposed to the brown wash and pencil of the main compositions.[166] These correspond almost exactly with the forms added to other sheets associated with Cock's circle, such as a pen-drawing now in Amsterdam by Frederick van Valkenborch, and with another, different set of drawings and prints produced by the so-called Master of the Small Landscapes (Figure 2.21).[167]

In 1559 and 1561, Cock published 44 etchings after these anonymous landscape designs. The resulting sheets, republished in 1601 and in 1612, remain an attributional quagmire.[168] Variously ascribed to Hans Bol, Cornelis Cort, Joos van Liere, Gillis von Coninxloo, Pieter Bruegel, Jan or Lucas van Doetecum, and, at one point, Vredeman himself, the works are unsigned and unlabeled. The small pages depict villages, farmers, and languid cattle among thin trees and thatched houses. Some show shepherds at work, or the outsides of barns and inns. When published, the scenes were touted by Cock as recognizably local sites of recreation; a title page described them as "various cottages and attractive places . . . all portrayed from life (*ad vivum*), (Figure 2.21) mostly situated in the countryside near Antwerp."[169] As in Vredeman's city prints, the faceless calligraphic staffage of the *Landscapes* has been hastily inserted to adorn (or, as Cock's opening text claims, *verciert*) otherwise self-sufficient compositions. Yet localization of the scenes outside Antwerp, alluded to in Cock's title, imparts them an intelligibility Vredeman's ideal cities lack. As Peter Parshall has pointed out, within the landscape prints, a *naer d'leven* character of the Flemish rustic idyll obviates the viewer's expectation of a clear *istoria*—the works are to be valued less for their hosting of a particular narrative than for their evocation of a real, habitable place.[170] Yet as images *ad vivum*, they are also useful "to" the life, as well as from it—that is, useful in engendering other kinds of art. This was precisely the function served by Vredeman's cityscapes.

The formal relationship between the Small Landscapes and Vredeman's cityscapes was noted as early as 1977, again by Hans Mielke, who assumed that the landscape setting of the former series was aimed as a deliberate contrast to the nebulous

2.21
Master of the Small Landscapes, *Village Scene*, c.1559–61. Etching, H.137.
Albertina, Vienna.

"urban-ness" of the city views.[171] It was during the sixteenth century that real landscape became defined by a *conjunction* of, not a contrast between, city and country.[172] Indeed, contemporary images of Antwerp often pictured this symbiosis in prints documenting the city and its urban outskirts, or in *plein air* sketches made from atop far hills. In a sketchbook from around 1540, now in Berlin, an anonymous draughtsman pictured the exterior of Antwerp from various angles, describing the masonry walls and the steeple of the recently completed Onzelievevrouw cathedral (Figure 2.22). Years later, Joris Hoefnagel may have established a similar, more macabre contrast in a sketch of the village of St Polten, outside Vienna (Figure 2.23). As Vredeman had done, Hoefnagel drew, from the inside *out*, the surrounds of the city from a hillock lined with execution victims, their corpses swelling in various stages of decay.[173] Such sheets relocated once-marginal features of the landscape to a picture's center.

During the 1560s, travel through the countryside, as through the city, was becoming increasingly dangerous, and it is simulated wanderings that both the *Landscapes* and Vredeman's series idealize. The rustic *plaetsen* advertised on the introductory page to Cock's landscapes are not so much houses and cottages but roads between them, just as Vredeman's city views show less fantastic architectures than their flanking boulevards and canals. In both the *Landscape* etchings (Figure 2.21) and Vredeman's city views (such as Figure 2.5) the place of *passage* is the focus of the compositions—muddy, perspectival, hilly, or claustrophobic. In fact, this harkens back to a previous generation of Italian landscape prints depicting the act of traveling, as well

2.22
View of Antwerp from the Southwest, c.1530–43, from the "Berlin Sketchbook," fols. 76v–77r. Pen, wash, black and brown ink, 19.1 × 26.3. Kupferstichkabinett, Staatliche Museen zu Berlin.

as the more local example of prints after Bruegel by the van Doetecums. In Bruegel's print of 1555–56, for example (Figure 2.6), onlookers are placed on a hilltop before a sprawling Alpine landscape crossed by serpentine rivers and roads. The viewpoint lingers high above the plunging valley, yet is offset by the intimate tree and the two peasants in the immediate foreground, along with a third figure who begins a descent with a horse and cart. These peasants mediate not just between the city viewer's experience of the print and the expansiveness of the rustic countryside, but between the twin realms of rest and travel; to look into Bruegel's landscape is to be confronted by the potential for either tranquillity or action. Viewing it, like an atlas, enables travel without toil. Our glance ceaselessly travels from rock to crevasse, treetop to church spire, ocean to river.[174] As Joseph Koerner has noted, the sum effect of the print is to present us, as viewers outside, with the lived process of a journey rather than with the simple product of that journey itself.

Cityscapes, too, entertained a history of this passage, as, for example, in German illustrations from perspective handbooks. The *modelbüch* associated with the printer Hieronymus Rodler, published in 1531 and 1546 (Figure 2.24),[175] used the city to juxtapose urban flatland with hilly foil. Cock's staffage from both the Small Landscapes and Vredeman's prints are (more often than not) *mobile*—soldiers charging forward on horseback, peasants strolling dolefully on foot. It was common enough in Vredeman's

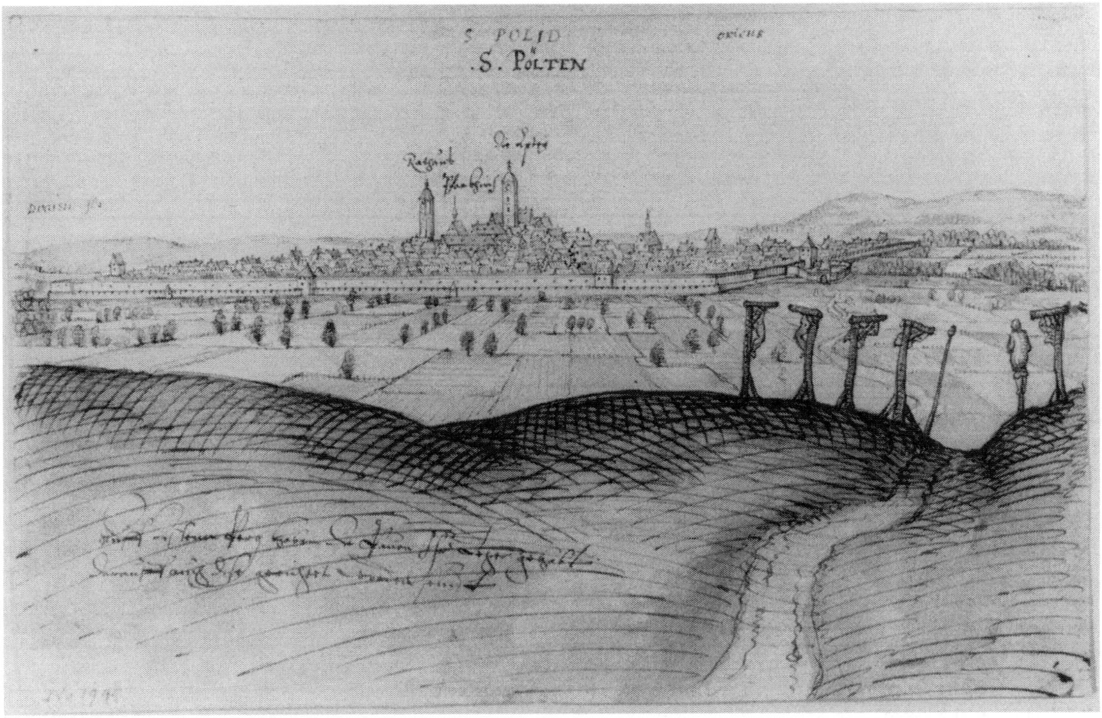

2.23
Attributed to Joris Hoefnagel, *St. Polten outside Vienna, with Gallows. c. 1590.* Brown pen and wash, 20.8 × 31.4. Universitätsbibliothek, Erlangen.

Antwerp to speak of the rejuvenative properties of movement through open spaces; "We must go for walks out of doors," Seneca had written, in a passage once cited by Abraham Ortelius, "so that the mind can be strengthened and invigorated by a clear sky and plenty of fresh air."[176] Later in the *Grondt* Van Mander likened the workings of perspective to that of a natural panorama:

> Work enjoys a fine arrangement, delighting the senses, if we allow there a view into a vista [*doorsien*] with small background figures and a distant landscape into which the eyes can plunge. We should take care sometimes to place our figure in the middle of the foreground, and let one see over them for many miles.[177]

It was important that this vista be lived, however: "make your landscape, your town, your water cultivated," writes Van Mander, "your houses inhabited and your ways trod."[178] Later Van Mander described Vredeman's prints as using the "*doorsien*," a device to draw the beholder into and through a framed composition, as if walking. If De Certeau has described the way moving through a place inscribes in it an alternative, subversive species of ownership,[179] Netherlandish views tended to be aimed towards the opposite: conjoining the sequential experience of viewing rural villages or city streets as a stamp of official possession. In the southern Netherlands it was usually at the behest of property owners—large and small—that maps, for example, were made.

2.24
Hieronymus Rodler, *Eyn schön nützlich Büchlin* (Simmern, 1531), fol. Ciiv. Germanisches Museum, Nuremberg.

In 1561, for example, the painter Jan de Hervy was paid by the city of Bruges to make a map of a newly commissioned canal.[180] And when the Small Landscapes were reprinted in 1600, the title page, which had described the subject matter as "Various cottages," was discarded for one labeling them as "the country-houses of the Duke of Brabant." Map-making involved the same skills (and hands) that designed tapestry, or published prints. Lucas van Doetecum, Vredeman's etcher, was commissioned in 1567 by the Deventer town council to make a survey of the marshy land south of the city. His watercolor-and-ink map (Figure 2.25) traced the flow of the Ijssel south to Zutphen, combining profiles of the adjacent towns with a plan of the river's width.[181] A map of 1583 by Vredeman, now lost, could have looked like this.[182] Known only through the record of a payment made to the artist for "*een sekere caerte van Brabant*," the work apparently depicted the road from Antwerp to Maastricht, running southeasterly through the region of Kampen. The map hung briefly in the Antwerp *Stadhuis*.[183] Like the triumphal entries, here such a work inscribed upon a space—by the act of picturing

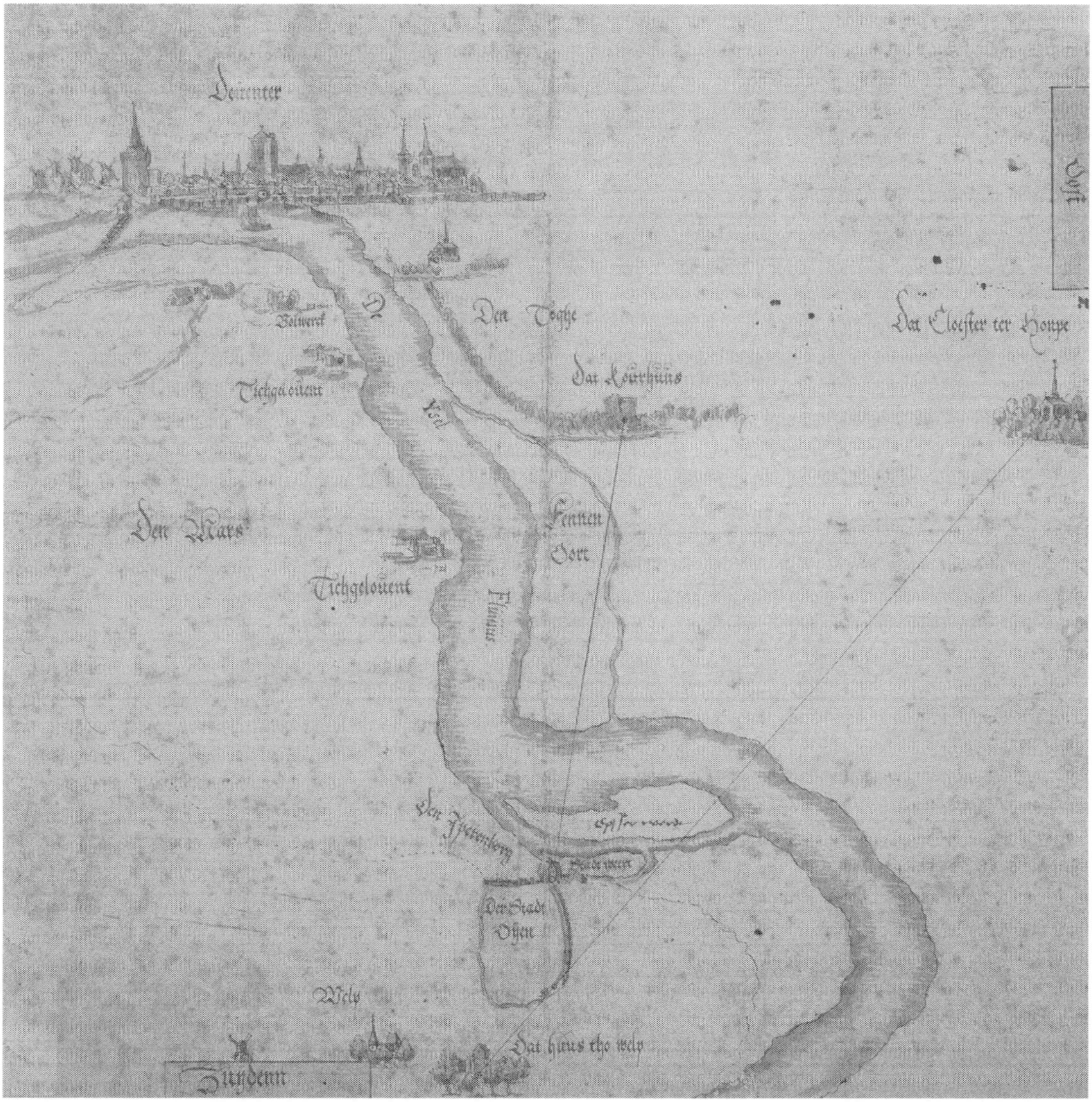

2.25
Jan van Doetecum, *Map of the Esperwaard,* 1567. Watercolor, black wash, and brown ink.
Historisches Museum, Deventer.

it—testimony to ownership. It became the product of a rural itinerary sprung from a decidedly urban perspective.

*

We conclude, then, where this chapter began, at the center of town, at the Antwerp town hall (Figure 2.1). The jagged, foreshortened signature at the far lower right of the Stockholm sheet published by Hans Lefrinck, "VRIESE FEC," refers to Vredeman's act of cutting. The print seems the only one Vredeman incised as well as designed himself.[184] The woodcut was executed in the years before the town hall would be burned by Spanish troops, and the city would begin its slide towards economic and cultural parochialism. In signing the woodcut as "Vredeman Vriese, *violiere,*" Vredeman conjoins his activity as a maker of visual and verbal fictions, likening his audience to that which would have observed the same building—under construction—behind Floris's sham town hall in the *landjuweel* of 1561. Rather than modeling a future project, the print was a lavish project itself, necessitating three separate blocks.[185] "We hope that you will help it forward, rather than let it fall behind," Vredeman later urged his audience in a print.[186] It is precisely this language of transit, of moving forward in order to stay put, of—ultimately—making the city strange in order to keep it familiar, that constituted the aesthetic of urban spectacle. So too was the motivation of Vredeman's uncanny city prints, in which repetition dissolved all "meaning" into form.

1

North Netherlandish. ***Four Members of the Brotherhood of Jerusalem before the Grotto of the Nativity*****, c.1520. Oil on panel, 99 × 230.**

Museum Catharijneconvent, Utrecht.

II

Hans Vredeman de Vries and Gillis Mostaert, *Christ in the House of Mary and Martha*, 1566. Oil on panel, 86 × 114.3.

Reproduced by permission of Her Majesty Queen Elizabeth II.

Hampton Court Palace.

III

Hans Vredeman de Vries, preliminary drawing for *Untitled Architectural View*, 1560–62. Brown ink, wash, and corrective red pencil on paper. 15.7 × 21.4.

Kupferstichkabinett, Staatliche Museen zu Berlin.

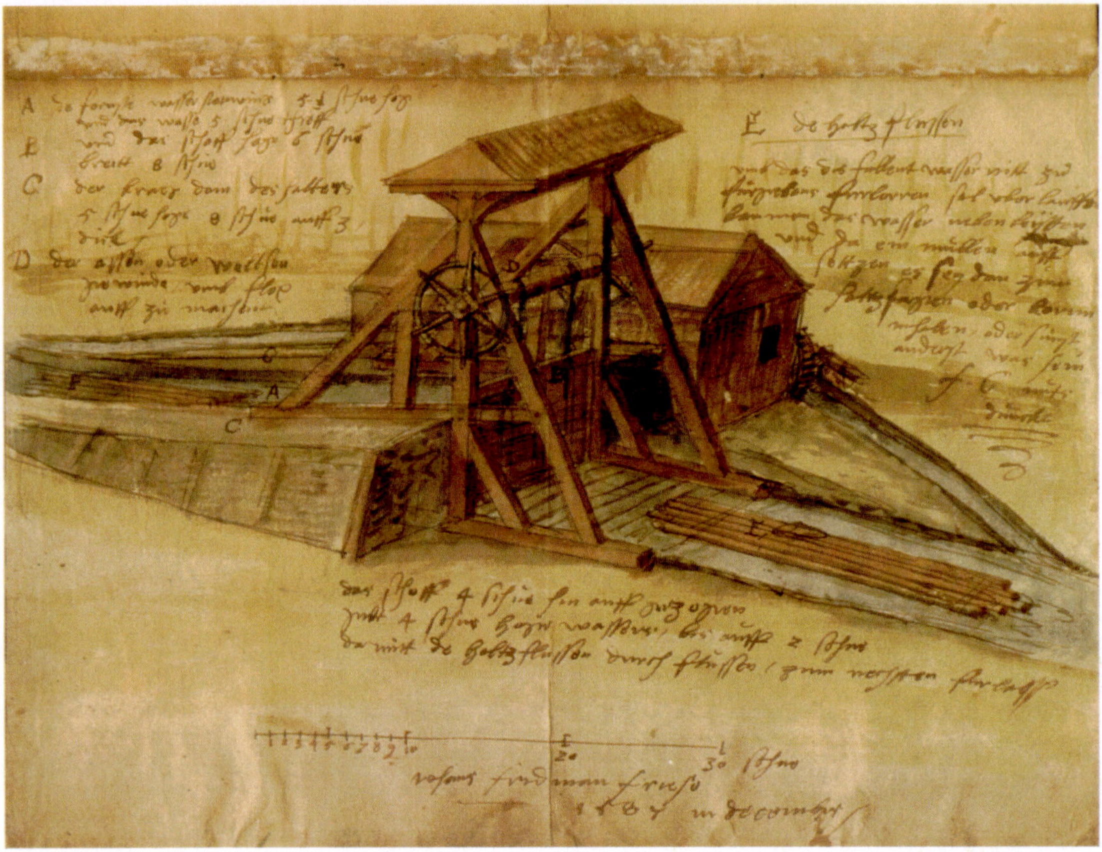

IV

Hans Vredeman de Vries, *Design for Lock and Water-mill,* 1587. Watercolor, 25.3 × 35.3.

Niedersächsisches Staatsarchiv, Wolfenbüttel.

Chapter 3

Guidebooks to chaos

Albrecht Dürer paused in his 1525 book on measurement to assuage readers' fears about his patterns: "I do not put these things down for you to follow exactly," he said, "but so that you can take away from them [*genumen*] what you require, and use them as a starting point."[1] Personal selection, Dürer implied, was always part of using his examples. Decades later, this advice was pictured by a fellow Nuremberger named Christoph Jamnitzer (Figure 3.1). The etched cover of Jamnitzer's *Grottesken Buch*, a

3.1
Christoph Jamnitzer, *Neuw Grottesken Buch* (Nuremberg, 1609), title page.
Herzog-August Bibliothek, Wolfenbüttel.

suite of ornament engravings, showed a market stall roofed with masks, where a merchant stood patting a large folio on its side. Craftsmen and cavaliers crowd around the stall, dressed in cloaks and bearing swords. They point at the merchant's bug-like, winged grotesques with drooping bodies and antennae, which bounce on shelves and flutter around the landscape, some flapping just beyond eager buyers' grasps. As three men depart into the background with their new purchases, other patrons rummage through a large basket filled with still more fantastic bodies. Jamnitzer's title page labels the scene with a couplet: "The *schnacken Markt* [literally, 'snail' or 'scroll market'] is now open/Take from it as you please."

Dürer's process of acquiring *fantasia* is here imagined, nearly one century later, as a mode of personal selection, culling from a suite of prints. The merchant-ornamentalist, supplied by a gigantic pattern book, purveys insectile grotesques, which seem to change shape before their users' very eyes.[2] As Dürer went on to declaim in an unpublished manuscript: "I wish to set free for everyone all the various things I've described—which I've also myself varied, so that, if one so desires, one can leave nothing be as it is shown here."[3] Jamnitzer's ornaments, as if heeding Dürer's injunction, acquire transformed lives of their own once they leave their sheltered stall.

Like Jamnitzer, Vredeman struggled to make a living supplying "ornament" designs to other craftsmen throughout his life.[4] These designs are the subject of this chapter. Starting in 1555, Vredeman created drawings of tendrils, brackets, volutes, garlands, cartouches, caryatids, strapworks, entablatures, and grotesques, which he submitted first to Gerard de Jode's firm (Figure 3.2, H.25), and then, beginning in 1562, to Hieronymus Cock. By the 1580s, these books of florid, bulbous designs could be found as far afield as Riga, and cut out and pasted into print albums in Sicily and Spain.[5] While ornament prints have played a large, if curious role in the reception of Vredeman and of sixteenth-century Netherlandish art in general, the precise function of these materials has proven difficult to historicize. Early modern writings on the use of ornamental motifs said very little about print. The unprecedented portability, tactility, and multiplicity of architectural engravings, as we have seen, stunned contemporaries like Lomazzo, who often saw them breeding a decline in artistic quality. Ornament prints supplied a vocabulary of designs that could be used to make and adorn other things: woodwork, furniture, buildings. For collectors, ornament engravings meant a new species of possessible object, one which made visible—as Vasari marveled in 1550, "the *maniere* of all artists who have ever lived."[6]

The category that Vasari installed at the core of art history—*style*—has long seen ornament as an index to cultural investigation. Heinrich Wölfflin, in his 1886 dissertation, was an ardent advocate of the notion that an organic, almost bodily sense of history was detectable in the minutiae of visual production. "The pulse of the age has to be felt," he wrote, ". . . in the minor or decorative arts, in the lines of ornament, of lettering, and so on . . ."[7] Indeed, during the formative years of a critical art history, the idea of style *in* things provided a bulwark against the rootlessness and disorientation of capitalist modernity, supplying a "kernel" (Wölfflin's word) of a vanished, once-communal *Gemeinschaft*, now supplanted by fragmented, technological

3.2
after Hans Vredeman de Vries, *Grotesque Cartouche,* from *Variarum Protractionum,* no. 9 1555. Etching, H.25.
Centre Canadien d'Architecture, Montréal.

Zivilization.[8] In Wölfflin's nostalgic view, ornament became a totem of creative spirit—a primitivist *Formkraft* (force), which could be apprehended ("felt") but not consciously detected. Ornament thus required a history scoured of mass-production's taint, predicated as it was on an almost cultic sense of social collectivity. Print technology, in such a history, was the first symptom of modern loss, wherein instrumentation obviated old ways of making art. Indeed, when Adolf Loos published his ironic *Ornament und Verbrechen* (Ornament and Crime) in 1908, he assailed machine-produced decor specifically, claiming it betrayed the *Trieb*, or impulse, of handicraft.[9]

But there is a reverse to this idea of ornament as a cipher for (collective) identity, a reverse that Wölfflin himself later observed.[10] This was the idea of ornament as a marker of individualism, of anomaly and difference—a role it often played in the late Renaissance. Grotesques, strapworks, hybrid monsters, vegetal homunculi, animalian nudes—this was the stuff of *ornamentum*, "of strangeness and variety," wrote Montaigne, "filling empty space."[11] In court circles ornamental décor could speak a visual patois of secrecy and deviation. At the same time, architecture, embroidered with forms, relied upon ornament to supply an index to antiquity. In fact, Alina Payne has argued that ornament was possibly the *main* concern of Renaissance art and architectural theorists: "ornament," Payne writes, ". . . stood as a claim of artistic independence, a claim to *licentia*," while at the same time declaring "immediately and directly the successful appropriation and *imitatio* of antiquity."[12] Ornament in the

Netherlands, repeatedly a subject of prints, incessantly invited comparisons with other versions of itself from the past and present—forms in paper, wood, gold, or marble, those very same "variations" pressed by Dürer upon his pupils.

Although a handful of art-historical studies have addressed Vredeman's role as a purveyor of forms for craftsmen, architects, and *constbeminders* ("enthusiasts of art," as he put it in 1565), no systematic attempt has been made to locate any theoretical armature behind his type of sixteenth-century "decorative" printed engravings.[13] Vredeman offers an explicit discourse on decoration in his illustrated tract of 1577, the *Architectura*. Though Vredeman never visited Italy, he became one of the most influential sources for Northern artists interested in "Italianate" forms. Like Jamnitzer's bugs (Figure 3.1), Vredeman's prints thrived on an aesthetic of recombination, one where printed forms were not so much copied as metamorphosed into new kinds of objects.

Origins and fragments

In 1565, Vredeman designed two sets of prints on the architectural orders. These were both published by Hieronymus Cock, one with a Dutch title, the other in German: *Den Eersten Boeck Ghemaect opde Twee Columnen Dorica En Ionica* (The first book, on the subject of the Doric and Ionic Columns),[14] and *Das ander buech Gemacht auff die zway Colonnen, Corinthia und Composita* (The other book treating the two Corinthian and Composite Columns). A book on the Tuscan order, entitled *Architectura 3e stuck de Oorden Tuschana* (A Third Part on Architecture, on the Tuscan Order), appeared in 1578, after the first two had gone into second editions.[15]

The first versions of the sets of 1565 were published with 18 and 22 plates of etchings, respectively, illustrating pedestals, volutes, and shaft capitals (Figure 3.3). Scrollworks were shown encrusting gables with dormer windows (*lucarnes*), split side-by-side into variants (Figure 3.4), or hovering, collage-like, around sheathed entablatures cast in shadow (Figure 3.5). This page-assembly stratagem, while indebted to Serlio's *Third Book*, was entirely new in the Netherlands.[16] Vredeman used etching instead of woodcut, and probably looked to the more local example of column-books like Hans Blüm's *Von den fünff Saülen* for his source, a beautiful compendium of elevations, available in Dutch translations in Antwerp by 1551.[17] Yet in a letterpress poem at the beginning of the *Eersten Boeck* Vredeman named Vitruvius as the immediate example for his designs:

> Since my youth I have occupied myself
> With the teachings of Vitruvius and other books
> From them I copied [*gechopieert*] the buildings of antiquity
> As well as the five Columns, which I investigated and explored
> [. . .]

3.3
Hans Vredeman de Vries, *Den Eersten Boeck*, 1565, fol. Q. Etching, H.198.
Avery Architectural and Fine Arts Library, Columbia University.

Because Vitruvius' teachings are so correct and subtle
Nothing among them can be improved (such would be ignorance!)
Yet their demonstrations are at times rather difficult
While knowing painters, sculptors, and carvers
Are inclined towards things easy and pleasant . . .[18]

Vitruvius, or more precisely copies *after* Vitruvius, become the wellspring of the book. Vredeman intimates that his act is one of translation. He goes on to name Serlio and the architect Jacques Androuet du Cerceau, but refrains from stating that his work will better their teachings; rather, his prints shall render them more approachable to craftsmen. Ornament, Vredeman went on, is the key area in which it will do so:

Here one may seek, find, and use
Various isolated ornaments [*cieraten*]
They can be used in paintings, or without difficulty
To make things of wood; although anyone may draw from and employ [them],
According to whatever he deems best . . .[19]

3.4
Hans Vredeman de Vries, *Den Eersten Boeck*, 1565, fol. R. Etching, H.199.
Avery Architectural and Fine Arts Library, Columbia University.

These entreaties are part sales-pitch, part explanatory program, but they repeatedly insist upon application across media. The verses go on to list the columns as useful "in paintings," or "if made out of wood." At the outset of the book, the architectural features are introduced as patterns.

Beginning with the cornices (Figure 3.3), for example, Vredeman's etchings show parts of columns on separate pages, as detachable parts. He moves on to upper entablatures and friezes, to top gables and pinnacles. Vredeman lays out these separate elements symmetrically, using bodily oppositions: fluted Ionic bases are contrasted with squat Doric ones (Figure 3.5), obelisks are set against flagpoles, round transoms against square (Figure 3.13). This kind of asymmetrical relationship cast ornamental elements against one another. The minute differences imply how the components are to interact with other versions of themselves.[20] While stressing the antique "correctness" of Vitruvius, Vredeman here urges readers to extract and deploy forms according to their own whims, for "with what one finds here one may do with what one sees fit."[21] Thus, as with Dürer and Jamnitzer, choosing becomes a key function of *inventie*. Vredeman's very refusal to explicitly prescribe one use or another aligns his works with those Italian tracts on building that were gradually percolating to the North. In *De re aedificatoria*, Alberti put it thus: "To contravene established customs often detracts

3.5
Hans Vredeman de Vries, *Den Eersten Boeck*, 1565, fol. H. Etching, H.190.
Avery Architectural and Fine Arts Library, Columbia University.

from the general elegance of a building, while . . . there is no reason why we should follow their design in our work as though legally obliged."[22] Judicious navigation of both tradition and invention, echoed by Vredeman, was the mark of an accomplished talent in design.

Pattern—ornament

In the late Middle Ages, the word "ornament" could be synonymous with "equipment," much as any type of appliqué work. In England sixteenth-century dictionaries referred to "the ornaments of a ship" when describing rope and, around 1495, the Cornish poet John Treviso named the human hand "a grete helpe and ornament to the body."[23] Along with the five stages in the preparation of a discourse: *inventio*, *dispositio* (disposition), *actio* (execution), *memoria* (memory) and *elocutio* (enunciation), ornament was one of the buttresses of a rhetorical presentation. Quintilian describes it in specifically visual terms:

> Ornament brightens lucidity and acceptability. Its first two stages consist in conceiving and carrying out your intention; the third is the stage that puts the

> polish on, and may properly be called "finish" [. . .] Underpinning all this is the virtue of bringing the object before our eyes not only plainly but also concisely and rapidly.

Ornament, writes Quintilian further, also alludes to its own presence: "it somehow shows itself off, for it is a great virtue to express our subject clearly and in such a way that it seems to be actually seen."[24] Cicero, meanwhile, had been uniquely architectonic in his description, speaking of the way ornamented ideas "stand out from the others . . . like those objects . . . in the embellishments of a stage or of a forum."[25] Only later was ornament's definition extended to the idea of excess or praise (*laus*): Petrus Ramus, for example, spoke of being "ornamented" with a stipend from the French crown in the 1540s.[26]

For artists and printmakers, ornament was never a particularly circumscribed category of thing.[27] In fifteenth-century pattern manuscripts floral and acanthus motifs appeared alongside studies of heads, columns, and animals, and, as early as the 1440s, German artists were using a form of wood engraving to represent intertwined leaves and nymphs on playing cards and small papers.[28] In fact, the first etchings ever seem to have been acanthus ornaments scratched into iron in the workshop of Daniel Hopfer around 1500 (Figure 3.6).[29] If the early history of woodblock printing was linked to devotional images, ornament was a genre associated with the history of intaglio processes proper.

Albrecht Dürer, for example, made ornament drawings for sword sheathing while in the Netherlands.[30] In Antwerp decorative etchings were pasted onto the exterior of furniture and keepsake boxes.[31] Flemish wallpapers have even been preserved from the early sixteenth century, and fragments of uncut playing cards used as colored ceiling paper from c.1520 have been discovered in a former Portuguese merchant's house in Antwerp.[32] Other wallpapers survive from the early sixteenth century made up of printed interlace. It seems that publishers sold ornament prints as both individual pictures and covering tools: one Anthony de Leest, documented in Antwerp in 1582 as a "cutter of figures and a printer," dealt in decorative papers for ceilings in his shop near the *Pand*, Antwerp's central art-market area.[33]

Proliferation of ornamental pattern books, or *modelbücher*, in Antwerp, while ultimately tied to earlier explosions of metalworking around Nuremberg, answered a post-Reformation turn to less-narrative motifs, and soon found appeal far abroad.[34] Heinrich Vogtherr's *Büchlin*, issued with Dutch, French, Italian, and Spanish preambles before 1556,[35] included woodcuts of heads, feet, helmets, cuirasses, quivers, swords, column capitals, and even hands (Figure 3.7). These were all culled from larger compositions and, arranged artfully on separate pages, forming discrete patterns of their own.[36]

The Nuremberg firm of Virgil Solis issued thousands of pattern prints. Jost Amman, a Swiss woodcutter in Solis's employ, lifted entire figures from paintings by Hans Baldung, Urs Graf, and Albrecht Altdorfer. Amman's designs broke down the large works into components, excerpting details such as fighting horses and drunken peasants which could be re-used by artists and small-time publishers.[37] Fractious notions of copyright and intellectual property in the German lands troubled this kind of appropriation:

3.6
Daniel Hopfer, *Gothic thistle design*, c.1505. Iron engraving, H.104.
Kupferstichkabinett, Staatliche Museen zu Berlin.

Solis was frequently sued, although rarely successfully.[38] Amman's editor, Sigmund Feyerbend, attached a preamble to one pattern suite which justified this borrowing, using germinative imagery: "One ought to be able to emulate the bee, who visits only those blooms where the honey may be most easily extracted,"[39] he opined. The allegory of

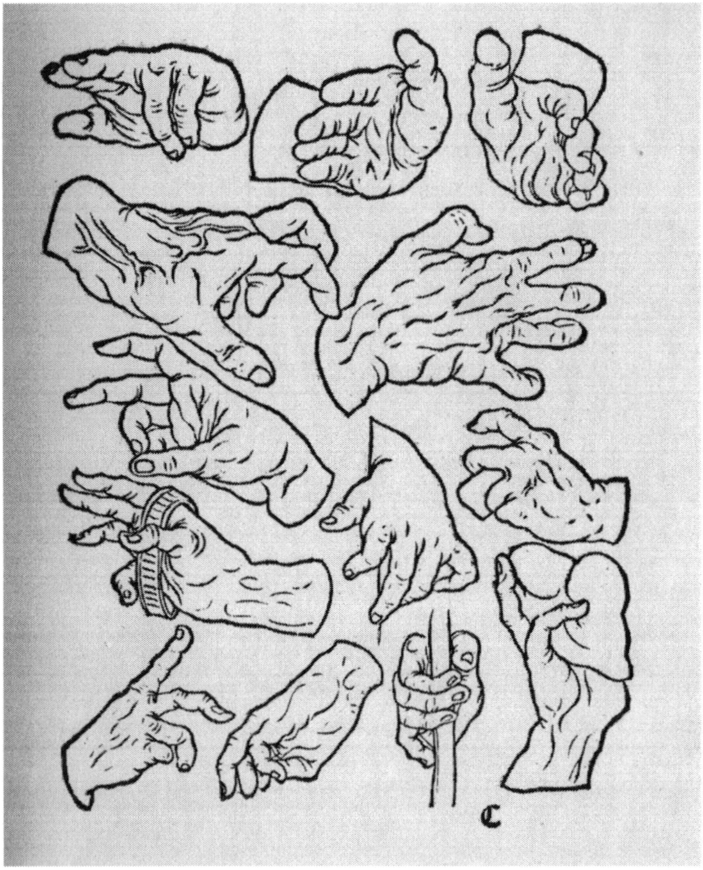

3.7
Heinrich Vogtherr the Elder, *Ein frembdes und wunderbares kunstbüchlein,* (Strasbourg, 1538), fol. C1r.
Metropolitan Museum of Art, New York.

the nimble, selective bee was itself a humanist trope (from Plato's *Ion*) for judicious scholarship, and Feyerbend invoked it, apparently, both to tout his pattern books and take advantage of their role within a newly mechanized atmosphere of citation.

Feyerbend and Solis understood—in much the same way as Cock would in Antwerp—that in the wake of the Reformation, artistic patronage trends were changing. Princely courts had always been centers for stylistic innovation, but the emergence in Germany and Flanders of a large merchant class interested in luxury goods, but less (or differently) interested in church commissions, meant that "secular" objects in decorative styles took up an increased share of craft production. Engravings and etchings permitted the cheap and rapid transmission of styles and motifs for everything from chairs to ceremonial floats. And in the case of prints used, say, as wallpaper or box wrapping, they permitted the literal grafting of new styles onto old objects. Ornament prints also appealed to collectors: the Frankfurt lawyer Paul Freher (1571–1625) amassed a sprawling collection of grotesque engravings, wherein eight series of cartouches by Vredeman were pasted into folio albums alongside other Cock prints, including title pages by Marcus Gheeraerts and Jacob Floris.[40]

Prints, after all, transmitted the crucial aspect that marked furniture, jewelry, clothing, and interior design as *new*: style. Using prints, craftsmen could supply bourgeois patrons with relatively quick approximations of recent aristocratic fashion. Michael Snodin has noted how from the sixteenth century through the nineteenth, great bursts of ornament prints tended to appear "after, rather than during, the birth of a style in a court centre."[41] This "delay" effect often resulted from printmakers and designers' gradual assimilation of motifs cribbed from paintings or objects in aristocratic collections; in Paris the designer Jean Mignon made etchings in 1552 and 1556 based on molding executed by Italian artists at Fontainebleau in the 1530s, belatedly disseminating motifs two decades after their courtly artistic flowering.[42] Later, Aegidius Sadeler's engravings transmitted Hans von Aachen and Bartholomeus Spranger's corpus of "Prague Mannerism" throughout Europe, a generation after the fact.[43] A renewed interest in Albrecht Dürer's work in the Netherlands around 1600, which will be examined in Chapter 5, was indebted largely to engravings of the 1580s issued by Hans and Jerome Wierix—both, incidentally, trained as goldsmiths—in Antwerp.

How much did time matter in these developments? In Vredeman's Netherlands there was little idea of "new" as a marketing tool on the modern scale, to be sure, but certainly one of "fashion," or "manner." The "Flemish" ornamental patterns in Coecke van Aelst's *Generale Regelen*, as we saw in Chapter 1, touted themselves as contemporary versions of Sebastiano Serlio's manner of building, just as Vredeman himself distinguished between "antique" and "modern" architecture—equating a modern type with what would today be called the Gothic.[44] Yet in the interest of a "local" fashion, Coecke van Aelst's book altered Serlio's significantly,[45] inserting 24 Latin block-letter patterns (Figure 3.8) where Serlio's had placed woodcuts of shields. Coecke van Aelst wrote about the change:

> I will not uphold these letters to be the best, but every one should take from them as they see fit; it is also not necessary to take pains with every one . . .[46]

Coecke van Aelst's alterations have been described as a Dutch "vernacularization" of Serlio's theory on ceiling carving.[47] But the *Generale Regelen*'s intention, like Serlio's, was "to enrich with inventions those who may be poor in them." Coecke van Aelst's book was itself an embroidering on Serlio. The recombinatory facility of prints licensed, indeed mandated, a book on building which *itself* fused old and new traditions. Such an aesthetic of ornamental admixture, of what Serlio called *mescolanza*, derived from another concept in sixteenth-century art theory: the grotesque.

The Netherlandish grotesque

In the *Grondt*, basing himself on Pliny's account of Protogenes, Karel Van Mander referred to a quixotic body of forms he called "*grotissen*," "side-pieces," or "by-werks"—The artist Pieter Vlerick painted "an entire room of grotesques . . . worth a great deal of money," in Tournai.[48] The forms Van Mander described were images

3.8
Pieter Coecke van Aelst, *Generale Regelen der Architecturen . . .* (Antwerp, 1539), fol. Siiiv.
Universiteitsbibliotheek, Amsterdam.

of hybrid plants, animals, and sculptures, the lost ornament species bequeathed by a vanished Rome. The Domus Aurea, the golden palace of Nero, had been excavated haphazardly in the latter part of the fifteenth century, and the strange paintings found in its treacherous underground *grotte*, or caves, quickly attracted artists.[49] Frescoes of griffins, centaurs, fantastic vegetables and foliages became rediscovered by torchlight; painters lowered themselves by rope to collect fragments and make sketches. Raphael used grotesques in decorating the Vatican loggia in 1518–19. French and Netherlandish artists made pilgrimages to the Rome catacombs themselves—Van Mander and Bartholomeus Spranger scratched their names on the Domus Aurea vaults in 1570–73, leaving graffiti that are still visible today. Frans Floris probably saw similar paintings in the 1530s, before his own experiments in Antwerp with ornamental engraving.[50] The prints

Floris—and soon after, Vredeman—began to design for Gerard de Jode introduced this new fashion for grotesques to the Netherlands, using it chiefly for cartouches, a tradition adapted from scribal marginalia.

Vredeman's early frames from 1555 (Figure 3.2) were distinguished from previous grotesqueries by their use of "strapwork," an imitation of curling leather or parchment. The great print historian Rudolf Berliner regarded strapwork as one of the first "modern" ornaments insofar as no precedents could be found in either antiquity or in medieval manuscripts.[51] In the early cartouche, Vredeman's border work encloses Latin type, still a novelty in the Netherlandish printing at mid-century.[52] The text is from the Book of Romans: "Let us not therefore judge one another any more: but judge this rather, that no man put a stumbling block or an occasion to fall in his brother's way" (14:10–13). Horizontal black lines push the etched tablet off the page, as a tiny human figure trapped within the unfurling scrolls glares outward, arms crossed, as if to underscore the seriousness of this admonishment.

The monstrous heads and strange vegetal forms of Vredeman's image appear in a ornament drawing in St. Petersburg (Figure 3.9), where they play out a resignedly quieter form of carnivalesque didactic. Frogs, goats, satyrs, and sphinxes ring a drawing illustrating an obscure episode from Livy: Marcus Curtius, the Roman hero, drives his horse into a chasm that appeared in the Forum in AD 342, in order to save the city.[53] To the drawing Vredeman appended the cryptic phrase "*Doet*" in the upper right of the compartment. Alexi Larinov as suggested this might be a reference to the van Doetecums.[54]

In Classical art theory the "grotesque" was both a specific kind of art and a recipe for how it should be fashioned. In writings on art, *grottesco* found cognates in *fantasia* (fantasy) or even *imaginativa* (imagination), and bore connotations of the subterranean, the deathly, and the unseen (*grotesque* = grotto-like, from Vulgar Latin *grupta*, crypt = hidden, from Greek *kruptos*). It also bespoke the licentious and the hybridic. Horace supplied the most famous definition:

> If a painter chooses to join a horse's neck to a human head and to make multicolored feathers grow everywhere over a medley of limbs, so that what at the top is a beautiful woman ends below in an ugly dark fish—friends, at such a show, try not to laugh.[55]

Vitruvius, a century later, left no room for gaiety, lamenting the efflorescence of grotesques in his own day's painting, around AD 70:

> Monsters are now painted in frescoes rather than reliable images of definite things. Reeds are set up in place of columns, as pediments, little scrolls, striped with curly leaves and volutes, candelabra hold up the figures of *aediculae*, and above the pediments of these, several tender shoots, sprouting in coils from roots, have little statues nestled in them for no reason . . . these things do not exist nor can they exist nor have they ever existed . . .[56]

3.9
Hans Vredeman de Vries, preliminary drawing for *Grottesco*, c.1565. Pen and blue wash on paper with pen and white highlights, 15.6 × 21.
State Hermitage Museum, St. Petersburg.

Vitruvius and Horace dismayed at such images less for their fantastic appearance than for their inappropriate assemblage of isolated things. The forms were all the more threatening for what they presumed about mankind's bestial side, humanity's interconnectedness to all levels of living beings.[57] Along such lines, Vitruvius was invoked by both Reformed and Church opponents of dangerous art. Gabriele Paleotti's *On Sacred and Profane Images* (1582) thundered against grotesque painting, writing "who doubts that to give candelabra the shape of the faces of men with flames issuing from their heads, or shells that spout rivers of water, or trees emerging from serpents . . . is repugnant?"[58] Vredeman's fellow print designer, Cornelis Floris, was even fined by representatives of the Catholic King of Denmark for "departing from the canons of good taste in art" in adding grotesques to a funerary monument.[59]

Vitruvius had hit on an issue that vexed architects and painters of Vredeman's day: how to reconcile the "license" of grotesques (themselves sanctioned, so it seemed, by antiquity) while maintaining deference to standards of decorum. This was, again, not just a question of style but of epistemology. In his *Trattato* of 1584 Lomazzo pointed to the special challenge that *grotteschi* presented to Neoplatonic concepts of meaning. He compared grotesques to "hieroglyphics" which existed only to "feed the eye."[60] Measured against the viewed world, Lomazzo claimed, strapworks, flowers, human bodies, tendrils and roots were legitimate subjects, but, once conjoined, these made up a realm purely of art. After all, Vitruvius's opprobrium of "bastard forms of heads and flowers" was not leveled at individual parts, but at their indecorous mingling. Not just in formal terms were the hybrid, forms on *grotteschi* seen as an affront. More egregious than their artificiality, it seems, was the grotesques' potential to confuse.

What seemed most problematic for many commentators was the sheer profusion of grotesques, a facet that clearly resonated with print. The engraving medium, like grotesquery, bore a capacity for seemingly endless replication. Henri Focillon once claimed that the effect of print was to demystify the strangeness of the Roman grotesques: like the sealed antique grottoes poisoned by inrushes of Renaissance air, mass-market engravings neutralized the writhing energy of the original antique forms by exposing them to the world.[61] As prints, Vredeman's grotesques thus framed the precise quandary of license and decorum that earlier theorists had wrestled with, now twice removed from Rome. Netherlandish prints of grotesques suggested domestication and disclosure of far-off antique secrets; but they also alluded to the "strong ego" of the artist, or the publisher's will to transform and vary that tradition.[62]

By pointing, however faintly, to ancient Rome *and* to their designer's invention, Vredeman's early grotesque etchings posited a double intermediacy between local and distant bodies. Lomazzo implied that the omniscience of fantasy work was particularly galling in the sixteenth century, just as inventions like linear perspective were making huge strides in the goal of "realism." For, unlike perspective systems, grotesque ornament seemed not to work by connecting art to reality, to legible text or narrative, or to the beholder. Incapable of *re-presenting* something real, grotesques served only to point, frighteningly, inward to themselves, as liminal decorations and framing devices for "true" subjects nearby. The result, it was soon realized, was that the grotesque might simply signify an artist's own inventive ability, blurring the division between mimesis and imagination. Vasari labeled grotesquery "a type of free and farcical painting,"[63] and the Neapolitan garden designer Pirro Ligorio, around 1553, wrote that grotesque images "signified as much as possible the pregnancy and fullness of the intellect and its imaginings . . . to accommodate insatiability of various and strange concepts [*concetti*]."[64] Such were the issues Italian aesthetics exported to art theory in northern Europe: how to account for hybridic, self-enclosed elements of art that are not immediately legible, and that, like Jamnitzer's squirming *schnacken*, seem to thrive on resistance to quick interpretive capture?

In Lutheran Germany, in fact, grotesque decoration was prized for this facility for strangeness. Around 1568, the Wittenberg satirist Johann Fischart wrote that the goblins, heads, and gargoyles peering out from old choir stalls and column capitals in Strasbourg cathedral amounted to a secret language of ornament, one that hearkened back to early Christian cults (Figure 3.10). These grotesques, Fischart claimed, contrasted with the beautiful altarpieces and sculpture in naves and chapels through their simple rusticity, unadorned as they were with the lascivious colors and recessive effects. Grotesque reliefs, he implied, sniped at official Church dogma from the margins, returning true believers to, as Fischart said, "the old art/and what else [people] used to believe."[65] For certain evangelicals, grotesques signified not just secrecy but godly

opposition in the enemy's very midst. The Huguenot architect Bernard Palissy designed actual grottoes in Paris as part of landscape designs. Grotesques bespoke a subversion (*subvertere*—"to turn from beneath"), an image of the early humble church hidden beneath papist encrustations. It was mighty in its very shapelessness. As Calvin, repeatedly asked in the *Institutes*, "How many times since the coming of Christ has the church been hidden without form?"[66]

3.10
Strasbourg Cathedral, detail of nave capital, from *La Cathédrale de Strasbourg* (Paris: Alpina, 1929), pl. 35.

It is significant that these discussions of the grotesque in North Europe were so often couched in *architecture*. Vredeman's own copying, as we saw in Chapter 1, took place on the basis of a Flemish book of architectural prints—Coecke van Aelst's small books of 1539 (Figure 1.9). Coecke's book embroidered only a little on Serlio and

Vitruvius's text, but his addition was significant. Of ornamental invention, or *inventy*, van Aelst wrote this:

> Although Vitruvius spoke of four manners of Columns, the Doric, Ionic, Corinthian, and Tuscan, thus giving us the first and most simple ornaments of Architecture, I wanted to add to these four a kind of fifth manner of column, composed [*gemegt*] of the previous four simple ones . . . to be sure, the foresight of the Architect must be such that he is able to, on occasion, make a proper mixture [*een menghinge behoort te maken*] from the previous other four, according to the nature of the subject.[67]

This idea of *menghinge*, or mixing, was Coecke van Aelst's rendering of what Serlio called *mescolanza*. The bringing together of multiple disconnected things was at the very center of sixteenth-century debates about how to quote from, yet not copy, antique and natural idioms. The painter Antonio Doni described assemblages of "animals, men and heads" conjured from a splotch of paint, assemblages which existed only "in the *fantasia* and my *imaginativa*, in the chaos of my brain."[68] The mental form-giving that the grotesque symbolized was continuously explained in combinatory terms: in his essay on friendship Montaigne famously compared his writings to ". . . these things of mine, grotesques and monstrous bodies, pieced together from sundry limbs with not definite shape, with no order, sequence, or proportion except by chance."[69] In North Europe this combinatory tack was cultivated by the exceptionally fugitive status of antique texts and ruins, distant not just in time but in space.[70] Prints matched these conditions as a metaphor for the dispersal, profusion, and recombination of dislocated forms. The pattern engraving nourished an aesthetic in which craftsmen would take elements from all over and judiciously recombine.[71]

For Vredeman, the idea of architecture drew precisely upon this trait of *hybridity*, hybridity wrenched from the intellect. Vredeman laid out *menghinge* as an explicit pictorial strategy in the sheets of the 1565 *Ander Buech*. In sheet 13 of his Corinthian page, for example (Figure 3.11, H.213), fragments are dispersed to all areas of the etched page in a kind of jumpy, disordered flux. Loose arrangements of cornices, shafts, and friezes lie suspended, cast from different angles, in different groupings, on different scales. By the time the large sheets devoted to *Composita* appear (the order made up of the other four (Figure 3.12, H.220), *menghinge* appears as a specific pictorial end. Light falls across a vertical drum's fluting from left to right, which alternates with the scrollwork and calligraphic arabesques on the architrave at top. Smooth surfaces of the fascia clash with the interlace and modillions above it. These are parts presented *qua* parts, as Alina Payne has written of Serlio,[72] a maze-like collection of possibilities, an architecture of superabundance. Vredeman's Composite is *pictured* as an act of assemblage and recombination of the light and the dark, the vertical with the horizontal, the smooth and the roughened, the antique with the Netherlandish, the historical with the modern. As Vredeman wrote in the dedication to the 1565 *Ander Buech*: "It is no bad thing to adorn the old with the new, within reason." [73]

3.11
Hans Vredeman de Vries, *Das Ander Buech*, 1565, fol. 13. Etching, H.213.
Avery Architectural and Fine Arts Library, Columbia University.

By embedding the parts in a reprinted suite of etchings, Vredeman's book ingeniously reiterates the idea of *menghinge* as ongoing repeatable process. The print medium emphasizes the aggregate quality of his bits: these shafts and scrolls are not

3.12
Hans Vredeman de Vries, *Das Ander Buech*, 1565, fol. 20. Etching, H.220.
Avery Architectural and Fine Arts Library, Columbia University.

archeologically correct fragments, but local emulations of the antique, which drift and recombine across the pages of a etched suite, astride other variants of themselves. Architectural invention is here linked to precisely the cut-and-paste strategy that

Vredeman adduces in his text, their visual assemblage enacting the very principle of pictorial admixture Coecke van Aelst advocated. In Vredeman's prints from 1565, the process of *menghinge*—the undercurrent of the grotesque—emerges as a principle of architectural design.

Vredeman even recruits a printmaking credit towards this combinatory approach (Figure 3.3. H.198). Nestled in an architrave in an Ionic entablature on the left edge of folio Q, an inscribed cartouche names Vredeman as designer and Cock as publisher: "*Vriese Inventor Cock Excudebat.*" Vredeman deploys the past imperfect form of the verb (*excudebat*—was being published, or, more literally, was being fashioned or shaped) rather than the conventional *excudit* (published) or *fecit* (made). The disavowal of the strictly past tense, and the use of the imperfect to sign a work (such as *faciebat*—"was making") was an antique practice described by Pliny. Michelangelo used *faciebat* for his only signed sculpture, and Titian deployed it in three canvases.[74] Included by Vredeman here, the verb imparts the suite a suitably Italianate air. But it also addresses the compendium's status as a workable collection of parts; *excudebat* speaks to an active state of recombining, implying ornament yet to come. And, in fact, Hieronymus Cock and Volcken Diercx reissued Vredeman's print three more times before 1578.[75] Such re-pressing, a literal "re-making" of the image, parallels the act of the architect-viewer who *uses* the print. Just as the plates are restruck, the architectural fragments are potentially reassembled by each viewer of the page. Vredeman pictures ornament as an ongoing *activity* instead of a set of inviolable rules; the "making" of the print is not circumscribed off in the past as perfectly done, but presented as an ongoing gesture, an incomplete act.

And Vredeman's acts impacted the architectural world. In 1568, the Flemish architects Johann Kramer and Wilhelm van den Blocke used gable motifs from folio E of the 1565 *Eersten Boeck* (Figure 3.13) for the Green Gate (*Zieolna Brama*) in Danzig, and, later, it was used for the roof transoms of the Haarlem meat hall (Figure 3.14).[76] The south end of the latter's archway employed S-forms broken by colored keystones on the roof-lines, taken directly from Vredeman's Ionic and Doric models. English masons used Vredeman's prints for hearth décor in Oxfordshire,[77] and van den Blocke later lifted designs of Vredeman's "Tuscan" order from the 1577 *Architectura* for the Danzig Arsenal, in 1602–05. In 1569–70, one architect used gable tops from the *Architectura* to line the cornices of the *Schabbelhaus* in the Baltic port of Wismar, and in Riga, a guild house was renovated by two Dutch architects using Vredeman's engravings (Figure 3.15).[78] In mid-seventeenth-century Portugal masons used scrollworks for the facade of the Santarém seminary (Figure 3.16),[79] and in Spanish South America, loose variants on Vredeman's prints were applied to churches and specific portal sculptures in Bolivia, Ecuador, Peru, and, later, the doorway of a Jesuit cathedral in south-western Mexico (Figure 3.17).[80] Seventeenth-century gables based on Vredeman prints have been located in the Philippines.[81]

Craftsmen and architects tended not to follow Vredeman's patterns exactly. They fused them with local traditions. In the Riga guild house elements from the 1565 books were installed behind fifteenth-century sculptures in Gothic arches; archi-

3.13
Hans Vredeman de Vries, *Den Eersten Boeck*, 1565, fol. E. Etching, H.187. Etching.
Avery Architectural and Fine Arts Library, Columbia University.

tects interwove the new elements of ornament among older interior features piece by piece.[82] Similarly, in two Spanish-built Jesuit churches in southern Mexico from the early seventeenth century, Vredeman's decorations from *Das Ander Buech* covered pilasters inside local portal coverings. In frescoes from the palace of an unnamed

3.14
Vleeshuis, Haarlem, 1604, south dormer window.

Andalucian *conquistador* in the colonial capital of Tunja, Columbia, built after 1585, cartouches from Vredeman's series of grotesques were appended to pre-fashioned *sillerias*, or carved seats. As some of the earliest and most utilized patterns outside of Europe, the decor tended not occlude native forms, but became synonymous with them.[83] Even if Vredeman's gables always bore faint undertones of *notre Niderlandi*, they held different connotations in Wismar than they did in Oaxaca. Far from being somehow subversive, this architectural hybridity shored up, even constructed, the idea of a dominant "order."

In the two column books of 1565 Vredeman recognized that a rigid typology of architecture, while evocative, was about more than reference. Factors like location and use—as he would later explain in his *Architectura*, of 1577, made it clear that fixed associations were applicable to the antique canon of the orders. Like his exemplar Serlio, Vredeman eschewed strict patterns of architecture in favor of loosely articulated groupings of forms. The etchings therefore established a kind of decorative thesaurus to

3.15
Schwarzhaupterhaus, Riga, Latvia, façade, 1581–1621.

3.16
Jesuit seminary church (facade), Santarém, Portugal, before 1676.

be used in the creation of larger assemblages. It is important that in print Vredeman's pieces are not shown to crumble or crack (as Serlio's occasionally did), as if salvaged fragments of fallen Roman structures. They are insistently new, not deliberately unfinished.[84] Whatever Vredeman's religious loyalties (and we will turn to this issue in the next chapter), it is not difficult to map the architectural prints onto a Reformist world-view—the idea of dismantling a reigning "order" in order to refashion one afresh.[85] It is more likely, however, that Vredeman sought to scour architecture of *any* confessionalist nuance whatsoever, so that his works could be useful to Church and Reformed audiences. The overall gesture of using the patterns, as Vredeman wrote in 1577, was a granting of "*gutte ordinanz*," that is, the literal making of order where there was none.[86]

This was, ultimately, a capital-based model of architecture design, perfectly suited to the trade-based locales where Vredeman lived and worked. Such transformation of architecture itself into a fungible good, possible only with print, clearly appealed to a bourgeois culture; design now became little more than a kind of shopping trip (Figure 3.1). And if print allowed Vredeman to produce work that he was never able to build himself, it also allied his designs with a whole tradition of ornament prints as

3.17
Window of Morelia Cathedral, Michoacan, Mexico, c.1600.

a collector's item. Yet as mute images that do not narrate, in the sense of, say, a history print, they perhaps amplified the grotesque's nuance of *fantasia*, of the grotesque not just as creatural, but mobile and, above all, profuse—something similar to Jamnitzer's bugs, which also sprang from a large book: things endlessly mutable in medium and scale once they entered the realm of the market.

Excursus: allegorical orders

There is little to suggest that the viewer of a town hall in Leiden, or of a drinking fountain in Bückeburg, knew or cared that these objects derived from designs by Vredeman. But as much as permitting the dispersal of specific designs, print introduced the very *idea* of ornament to places that may not have known it, and naturalized as self-evident a model of ornament as a separate and transformable thing. Vredeman's books suggested that every reader understood architecture and the orders as different things, and that some readers didn't really need to understand them at all.

Images "made for reproducibility" changed the cultural value of art objects in early modern culture, for makers as well as users. As Walter Benjamin pointed out, print insisted not just on a new estimation of the artwork in the eyes of the viewer (a category famously termed "authenticity"), but also seemed to presage a new kind of viewer, the individual accustomed to art as image, not as object. Architecture, Benjamin went on to note, was the "prototype" of an artwork received in this distracted state.[87] Sixteenth-century print severed direct relations between designer and product in a different way.

With early modern print, form was no longer "worked-up" but created outright, if not as a complete *Bild* then as a syncretic image of pre-fashioned parts. For Vredeman's ornament etchings, this status meant cleaving the relationship between the maker and the supposedly "expressive" ornament an object bore. As Georg Simmel once pointed out, successful adornment (*Schmuck*) needs to be somewhat impersonal to function, for it is the public facet of a "wearer," a neutral plane that should not be too hermetic, lest it not be recognizable to all.[88] Unique ornament speaks to no 'typic form' apprehensible by the public, and thus runs the risk of letting its adornee be ignored. True ornament's function, in this reading, is to level rather than upraise.[89]

Yet Benjamin did not, in fact, mourn some auratic image deadened by replication. Ultimately, he was much more ambivalent. In a little-studied footnote to the "Artwork" essay, Benjamin explicitly claimed that reproduction not only fed originality, it preceded it: an art object "became authentic . . . during the succeeding centuries," not at the moment of its inception.[90] Reproduction, in this reading, spurs the art-historical yearning to recover an image's "original" context, at precisely the same moment that it occludes this context through a flurry of replicas. Benjamin's question as to who rightly "made" art—the expert art historian, the manipulator of images, or the cloistered genius in the workshop—has been eloquently answered by Roger Chartier, in a discussion of books from Vredeman's milieu:

> The book always aims at installing an order, whether it is the order in which it is deciphered, the order in which it is to be understood, or the order intended by the authority who commanded or permitted the work. This multi-faceted order is not all-powerful, however, when it comes to annulling the reader's liberty. Even when it is hemmed in by differences in competence and by conventions, liberty knows how to distort and reformulate the significations that were supposed to defeat it. The dialectic between imposition and appropriation, between constraints transgressed and freedoms bridled, is not the same in all places or all times or for all people.[91]

If Vredeman's books codified anything it was the idea that ornament was not subject to a definition. In this respect, Vredeman's situation recalls not "aura," but Benjamin's earlier idea of allegory, which he emphatically linked to the grotesque.[92] In the grotesque, form is placed forever at a distance from its meaning, and accrues signification not by matching up with fixed content, but by constantly deferring it. By failing to symbolize—indeed, by remaining imperfect—the allegory reveals the void between material and meaning, a chasm which is itself an ingenious expression of art's unbridgeable distance from what it strives to represent. Vredeman's parts bundle, stack, and disperse, thematizing their own drift from a fixed point of origin at the levels both of publication history and of interpretation. They do not recoup antiquity, but establish their own jumbled visual language in the space of antiquity's absence, on and across the white arena of the printed page.

Columns and the aesthetic of *Menghinge*

Sixteenth-century discussions of decorum and license in architecture, as in painting, centered on the debate between the ancients and the moderns.[93] In the 1540s, Giovanni Battista Sangallo proved himself one of the most vociferous opponents to unchecked *licenza* in architecture. In a long missive to Pope Paul III he chastised a cornice designed by Michelangelo: "here there is no *qualita* because the work should be done from good memory according to the rules of Vitruvius . . . This one of [his] is neither Doric, nor Ionic, nor Corinthian, it is willfully bastard." [94] As with the grotesque, there was a tendency for some theorists to lionize and at the same time vilify an artist's adeptness at *mescolanza*, or *menghinge*. The boundaries were never clearly drawn; as Christoph Thoenes noted, the architectural orders (Doric, Ionic, and so on) vexed study, since they seemed to cut some middle way between tradition and innovation: the orders remained antique models, but models intended to be transformed.[95] Vitruvius complicated the matter through his relative silence on the subject of architectural ornament.

Where does Vredeman come down in this debate? He was clearly worried about the dearth of homegrown Netherlandish models for architectural decoration. His full-fledged treaty on the orders, *Architectura, Oder Bauung der Antiquen*, was published in March 1577 by Gerard de Jode, in French and Dutch versions. Here Vredeman recognized that, while providing general outlines, the decorative precepts outlined in Italian and French sources could not be imported whole:

> We find in the books of these masters, and in the designs of still others, a kind of style, adornment, and manner [*mode, coustume, et façon*] of building perfectly suited to the particular country from which they derive . . . However in these Netherlands of ours [*notre Niderlandi*], things are different. In our great cities of business, where sites are small and very expensive, one must strive towards making tall buildings specific to their site in which men may conduct business up high, with the most light, yet always keeping in mind a building's situation and use.[96]

Vredeman thus outlines an awareness of the need for local license in certain aspects of construction, and the importance of heeding decorum whenever appropriate. In the Netherlands "things are different," and Vredeman's "antique" breaks down into separate uses:[97] Doric is for "palaces, town halls [*Rattheusser*] or the dwellings of great gentlemen," Ionic for interior chambers and hallways, Corinthian for "council halls," the Tuscan for citadels and fortresses.[98] At the time of writing the tract, Vredeman was back in Antwerp, courting the patronage of a newly restored Protestant town council. This is likely why unlike the earlier column books, the *Architectura* offers textual explanations on how the parts should be used. Agglomerations of décor that once floated around on pages now cling to the bases of columns, animated with variant shafts and strapwork (Figure 3.18, H.431).

3.18

Hans Vredeman de Vries, *Architectura* (Antwerp: de Jode, 1577, 1581), fol. 23. Etching, H.431.

Herzog-August Bibliothek, Wolfenbüttel.

The five orders of architecture, Alberti claimed, were themselves the originary species of ornament, and choosing between them, an act similar to the composition of an oration, was subject to the standards of decorum. Vitruvius had explicitly claimed the body as the traditional bestower of meaning on an architectural space,[99] and in Alberti's gloss this became a crucial point: "The building is entirely like a body composed of its parts . . . in the whole of the building the column is the principal ornament without any doubt."[100] The analogy of body-column was more than just metaphor. In the *Architectura* Vredeman's graded alternation of light and dark endowed the columns with a sense of depth, of texture, and, through the changing conditions of brightness and shadow, a sense of contingence.[101] In very concrete terms it represented the closest thing a building had to figural expression, to a literal *face*.[102] The orders, Serlio intimated, were how a building *expressed*—in Vredeman's *Architectura* they spoke of the occupation and social position of its dwellers.[103] What mattered was less a fixed use for each order than some differentiation between building types.

Dagobert Frey once wrote how such yearning for self-sustaining typologies represented a recoiling into medievalism, a wish for architectural stability at a moment of social crisis.[104] In the *Theatrum Vitae Humanae* series of 1577, first published by Pieter Baltens immediately after Vredeman returned to Antwerp from Aachen and Liege, six engravings linked the architectural orders to periods of earthly life.[105] The Composite allegorized childhood; the Corinthian, youth; Ionic, maturity for woman; Doric, maturity for man; and finally the Tuscan, universal old age. The orders now represented not just types of bodies, but different physical and mental states of a single soul.[106] They envisioned the orders as vast and complicated *spaces*, (Figure 3.19), which included not just architecture in action, but a narrative of building's physical generation. Latin verses were added to the sheets by Baltens. For Composita/childhood he wrote:

> Behold the humanity, that God and Creative nature
> Wrought from wombs of mothers, to fill a parent's cradle;
> Some are raised sweetly, beneath the soft shade
> Others are left to the vicissitudes of fate.[107]

In *Composita* Dawn breaks on a courtyard of vigorous youths, who clamber over walls and *parterres* around a cloistered lawn and courtyard. Their protectedness symbolizes good architecture. In a final sheet Vredeman depicted "Ruin," the *absence* of an order (Figure 3.20, H.441). Allegories of death and time accost a decrepit human figure in a shattered desert landscape. Fragments of sculpture and column entablatures lie strewn across a desiccated, burning hillside as flames leap from a crumbling building and storms lash a jagged cliff. The horror of the scene implies ethical consequences on a Biblical scale for the rejection of proper décor; naturalized as extensions of human existence, the columns are bodies which time will ravage and disassemble. The only order not explained by antiquity, the Composite, is in Baltens's series associated with childhood—Vredeman links it to a building's birth. Although referred to by Filarete in the

3.19
Hans Vredeman de Vries, *Theatrum Vitae Humanae, 1: Composita,* 1577. Engraving, H.436.
Avery Architectural and Fine Arts Library, Columbia University.

1450s,[108] the Composite order was basically an invention of the sixteenth century; morphologically it dated to the late Roman Imperial period, but was not distinguished from the Corinthian until far later. The Composite also differed from other orders in that it bore no originary myth, and was conventionally a "free" column, a template unto itself.[109] It came about precisely through a collaging of pre-extant traditions, a process of generative exuberance.

In his 1979 study, *The Sense of Order*, Ernst Gombrich described how ornament signaled ruptures and continuities in the stylistic appearance of things. "Ornament serves to facilitate the grasp of the object it decorates,"[110] he wrote. The repetitive decoration found in Renaissance pattern books, Gombrich claimed, affected viewers mainly by recalling perceptual norms. These permitted one to experience general feelings of repose, instability, or balance. Netherlandish ornament prints, however—and in his book Gombrich here illustrated an Antwerp grotesque by Vredeman's predecessor Cornelis Bos—worry such a schema by "outraging our 'sense of order' ":

> It may be argued that the very possibility of reproducing and spreading these designs through the medium of engraving changed the status and the function of the grotesque. There is something self-contradictory in a pattern

3.20
Hans Vredeman de Vries, *Theatrum Vitae Humanae, 6: Ruin*, 1577. Engraving, H.441. Avery Architectural and Fine Arts Library, Columbia University.

> for dreamwork, a guidebook to chaos . . . The grotesque has moved from the margin to the centre and offers its inconsequential riddles to focused vision . . .[111]

The moment of the autonomous ornament heralds the breakdown of borders between twin kinds of apprehension—conscious and unconscious, historical and now. Exasperated with details in revolt, this reading sees ornament in print as a flooding of the frame, an event that denies contemplative distance between subject and object, and presents simply the pictorial "chaos" that perspective (what Doni, too, had called "focused vision") hoped to restrain. Perched on the margins of "representative" art (here, seemingly, synonymous with "mimetic" art), Flemish ornament marks a betrayal of reference, a literal omission of "human" legibility at the cost of the inconsequential and unformed.

How distinct were these categories of "pure" design and illusion in the sixteenth century? Like many histories of décor, Gombrich's compelling account never really questions the idea of "internal" and "external" aspects of art. As Henri Zerner has shown, not only can printed decorative motifs acquire vastly different associations in different cultural contexts, but even the simplest arranging of shapes or patterns represents an intentional, artful act (Figure 3.7).[112] Indeed, the transformation from chaos to universe, the fundamental creative gesture, wrought the first definition of the term ornament in the West—*kosmos*. Heraclitus saw *kosmos* as a constantly recurring "kindling and extinguishing" of the world.[113] Greek architects later used *kosmos* to denote friezes and triglyphs—those parts of a building's entablature that, hosting sculpture, gave a building sense. As Pythagoras described it, *kosmos* was the agency by which animals and plants came into being; the Dutch scholar Franciscus Junius summarized the term in an early modern context:

> . . . the Good and great maker of this universe created the world after so glorious and beautiful a manner that the Greeks together with the Romans, a consent also, of the Nations perswading them thereonto, have called the universe by the name of an *Ornament.*[114]

Ornament, here, is the notion of chaos systematized, denoting not a by-work but the miasma of invention. Its danger subsists not in being pointless, but in saying too much, a danger that print puts in the hands of myriad makers.[115]

Vredeman's columns and cartouches—with their demons neatly bound, their grilli restrained by straps—enfold this chaos towards an aesthetic of judicious hybridity. They use the engraving medium to relentlessly and repetitively generate sheets that are both images *of* ornamented things and, by turns, ornaments themselves.[116] Frame grafted onto text, "Italianate" theorems affixed to Dutch practice, they humbly envision the grotesque scenario that was, perhaps, every truly artful gesture in the eyes of both the "ancients" and the "moderns" in the sixteenth century: the re-forming of the known.

Ortelius's intrinsic frame

As Vredeman de Vries's prints were used prodigiously by craftsmen throughout the world, dramatic shifts took place across scale, medium, and locale—from an Antwerp etching to a Danzig balustrade, from desk-size sheaf to public-scale monument. Just as frequently, however, Vredeman's prints would be used *as* prints, to make other graphic products. This often occurred with his early ornamental frames.

The grandest use of Vredeman's cartouches was within Abraham Ortelius's *Theatrum orbis terrarum*, "A Theatre of the Terrestrial World," the first modern atlas.[117] Vredeman designed 30 pencil frames for Ortelius's *Album Amicorum*, now in Cambridge, sometime before 1573,[118] and after this commission, seems to have been given extra work. Thirty-six different frames from Vredeman's sets of 1555 and 1560 were published as text holders in Ortelius's *editio princeps* of the atlas in 1570.[119] Inside the *Theatrum* Ortelius used grotesque cartouches to surround explanatory text or dedications. His map of New Spain, for example, used a plate from Vredeman's 1555 *Multarum* sheet, housing a scripted identification of what is now North America. Elsewhere Ortelius combined two cartouches on a page, as in the chart of Portugal (1570). In yet others he cropped sections astride ornamental borders. The same cartouches would be re-used for different countries' engravings in separate parts of the *Theatrum*; in a 1578 edition the same Vredeman grotesque appears in both maps of ancient Egypt and northern France.

Filling out voids left by sea, desert, or unmapped terrain, these additions allegorized the global reach of Vredeman's actual prints. The cartography of the *Theatrum* was largely the work of surveyors barely known to Ortelius, and many maps had been published earlier. As editor—or "expert"—Ortelius's role was largely limited to that of editor and decorator. Yet when the atlas was republished in 1579, it included a very curious section of maps of historical places, such as Troy, "Roman Gaul," and the Land of Abraham. This "supplement," entitled *Parergon*, (Figure 3.21) contained charts that were "in no way suitable to be integrated into our *Theatrum*," claimed Ortelius, "whose aim is to show the modern situation of localities."[120] Announcing its liminal status, the section was marked by a title-page with a bare frame. Charts in the *Parergon* depicted the world known by Ptolemy, Homer, and Strabo, Ulysses's wanderings in the Odyssey, the mythical paradises of Daphne and Tempe, the voyages of Jason and the Argonauts.

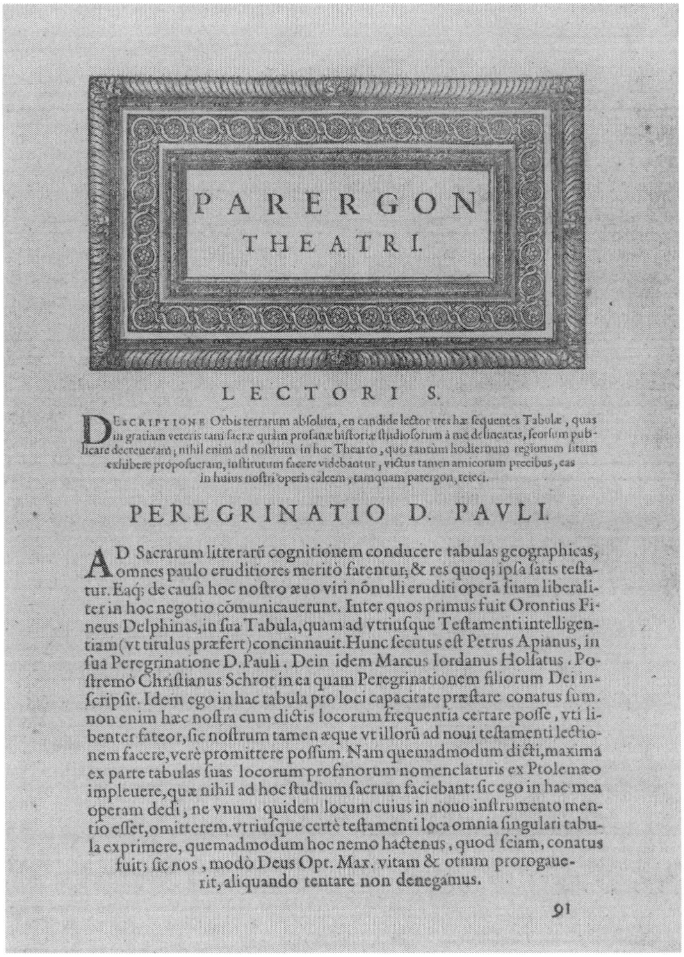

PARERGON THEATRI.

LECTORI S.

DESCRIPTIONE Orbis terrarum absoluta, en candide lector tres hæ sequentes Tabulæ, quas in gratiam veteris tam sacræ quàm profanæ historiæ studiosorum à me delineatas, seorsum publicare decreueram; nihil enim ad nostrum in hoc Theatro, quo tantùm hodiernum regionum situm exhibere proposueram, institutum facere videbantur, victus tamen amicorum precibus, eas in huius nostri operis calcem, tamquam parergon, reieci.

PEREGRINATIO D. PAVLI.

AD Sacrarum litterarũ cognitionem conducere tabulas geographicas, omnes paulo eruditiores meritò fatentur; & res quoq; ipsa satis testatur. Eaq; de causa hoc nostro æuo viri nõnulli eruditi operã suam liberaliter in hoc negotio cõmunicauerunt. Inter quos primus fuit Orontius Fineus Delphinas, in sua Tabula, quam ad vtriusque Testamenti intelligentiam (vt titulus præfert) concinnauit. Hunc secutus est Petrus Apianus, in sua Peregrinatione D. Pauli. Dein idem Marcus Iordanus Holsatus. Postremò Christianus Schrot in ea quam Peregrinationem filiorum Dei inscripsit. Idem ego in hac tabula pro loci capacitate præstare conatus sum. non enim hæc nostra cum dictis locorum frequentia certare posse, vti libenter fateor, sic nostrum tamen æque vt illorũ ad noui testamenti lectionem facere, verè promittere possum. Nam quemadmodum dicti, maxima ex parte tabulas suas locorum profanorum nomenclaturis ex Ptolemæo impleuere, quæ nihil ad hoc studium sacrum faciebant: sic ego in hac mea operam dedi, ne vnum quidem locum cuius in nouo instrumento mentio esset, omitterem. vtriusque certè testamenti loca omnia singulari tabula exprimere, quemadmodum hoc nemo hactenus, quod sciam, conatus fuit; sic nos, modò Deus Opt. Max. vitam & otium prorogauerit, aliquando tentare non denegamus.

91

3.21
Abraham Ortelius, *Parergon, Theatrum Orbis Terrarum*, 2nd ed. (Antwerp, 1579), p. 91.
Kaartenzaal, Universiteitsbibliotheek, Amsterdam.

Even among these fabulous places a particularly disjunctive site within the *Parergon* was Utopia, a chart that Ortelius seems to have drawn himself (Figure 3.22).[121] Names of cities and rivers not described by Thomas More's 1516 book were added by Ortelius's colleague, Mattheus Wackenfels, to whom the map is dedicated in a small cartouche in the lower left corner. That cartouche was itself based on a 1555 print by Vredeman (Figure 3.23, H.8). In the *Parergon*, Utopia was presented in the same format as the modern maps in the main body of the *Theatrum*; in a calligraphic annotation in a second half-cartouche at right Ortelius even named Raphael Hythlodorus, More's fictional narrator, as an eyewitness to attest the chart's reliability.

The *Parergon* section offset the scrupulously observed topographies of the atlas itself. In contrast to the main maps of the 1570 *Theatrum*, Ortelius signed all but three in the *Parergon* of 1578; the parergal elements are the most personal part of the atlas.[122] Ortelius states that whereas the main part of the *Theatrum* contained "completely new countries" shown by myriad discoverers, and assembled by assiduous observers, the *Parergon* was completely "drawn by me"—its far-off histories coming to light only through a subtle gesture of selection.

3.22
Abraham Ortelius, *Utopiae, Theatrum Orbis Terrarum*, 2nd ed. (Antwerp, 1579). Collection Marcel van den Broecke, Bithoven.

3.23 **Hans Vredeman de Vries, *Strapwork Cartouche*, from *Multarum Variarumque* (Antwerp, de Jode, 1555). Engraving and etching, H.8.** Rijksprentenkabinet, Amsterdam.

How auxiliary were such frames, such literal *parerga*, in a humanist milieu? Ortelius was fairly blunt about the extrinsic status of his supplement. Van Mander named "side-pieces" in antique wall paintings as "*parerga*," and later subsumed the grotesques in the Domus Aurea as a whole under this definition.[123] The ancient philologist Galen, meanwhile, translated in the early seventeenth century, was excerpted by Junius to offer a different view:

> Good workmen used to make some *Parergon*, or by-work for a document of their art [*specimen artis*], upon the bolts and shields, oftentimes also do they make upon the sword hilts and drinking pots, some little images over and above the use of the work.[124]

Here, quixotically, the *Parergon* serves as a personal signature, a mark of craft. This is consistent with one side of the sixteenth-century debate over *grotteschi*, viewed, for better or worse, as sites of pure licentiousness and artistic self-expression. Unlike *ornatus* per se, *parerga* seemed to work through a peculiar capacity for *contrast*, good or bad. Plutarch wrote of *parerga* in painting: "the Artificers hit the true force and facility of grace better in these sudden things (that is, *parerga*) than in the work itself."[125] There, the artistic flourish became synonymous with relief from ponderous decorum. Through such an autographical function the supplement reveals what is lacking or incomplete in the main work. The *Parergon* in Ortelius's atlas, like Vredeman's cartouches, brought new worlds into view, not just by ascribing them the status of seen places, but by bracketing their representations as craft.

*

Before ending his 1886 dissertation, Heinrich Wölfflin asked readers two questions:

> What is ornament? The answer to this has been clouded by those many critics who . . . inquired into the meaning of each part . . . I am in a more fortunate position as I only need to know one thing: what is the *effect* of ornament?[126]

As Wölfflin would go on to argue, the real function of ornament (and specifically, architectural ornament) lay in its capacity not to bejewel a structure, but to negotiate a relationship to history. The volutes, scrolls, and leaves atop Greek temples, the distended gargoyles scrabbling within Romanesque tympana, the pointed shoes of a Gothic figurine—these insured a relation between object and scholar. Wölfflin called this communicative bond empathy (*Einfühlung*), a psychological conjoining of mood, body, edifice, and (middle-class) spectator.

Wölfflin, however, was silent about the sixteenth century.[127] He seemed vexed by the strange excesses of strapworks, cartouches, caryatids, and foliages that proliferated after 1550, and which appeared, untethered to narrative, to at once nourish and destroy concepts that were again finding purchase in the nascent discipline of art history—style, perspective, periodization. Although useful measures of a period "spirit," ornament appeared to resist stabilization or absorption by a viewer. Simple and quotidian, it also seemed irresistibly tactile and direct. In these qualities Alois Riegl, in his early book on folk art, was to see the fundamental importance of ornament: its disavowal of purely visual address, and its aesthetics of *proliferation*.[128] Under Riegl's influence art history would reshape Wölfflin's empathy model to suit new, modern categories of spectatorship: abstraction, simultaneity, distraction. Ornament's *horror vacui*, its aversion to fixity and localization, would be for Riegl (as for his astute reader, Benjamin) a potent model for relating old art objects to the present as a whole.

As this chapter has tried to show, any ornament modeled and applied—at least in the case of one print designer, Vredeman—depends precisely on its embroilment with aesthetic processes, with a capacity to allow art and architectural design to refer to themselves in the midst of specific contexts. In early modern Europe this was not a decorative gesture towards aesthetic autonomy, but a marking of, say, architecture or sculpture's engagement with other kinds of art-making; to return to Wölfflin's terms one last time, ornament's main *effect* was to manifest the link between work and world, by probing the intermediary distance. The point, I have tried to suggest, is not to see Vredeman's source books as valuable only in terms of what gables, columns, or book plates they gave rise to in the end, but in terms of how their repeatability shaped habits of mind. In northern Europe the subject matter of ornament was never clearly defined. The unstable status of the "supplement," the frame, the periphery—the ancient phenomenon of the *parergon*—was bolted to any artistic utterance Vredeman and his publishers made.

Taken as *images*, then, Vredeman's prints essay art-making as a kind of grotesque. But what of art-beholding? Surely Vredeman said nothing outright in his ornament books about viewing. Yet rather than glorify and insure our relation to the work, as, say, a perspectival composition might do, the effect of his designs may be to disrupt easy contiguity with anything beyond surface, to transform the space of the page into an implicitly antagonistic field. This field seems to site us squarely, awkwardly, before the grotesque prospect of "endless variations," teeming like Jamnitzer's florid *schnacken* (Figure 3.1). And yet Vredeman also marks the way *all* art is set apart from the world, the way all art creates room for the mundane by contrast.[129] Isolated in print, Vredeman's curling designs overrun his borders and spindle outward, sheathing his floating entablatures, or entrapping text itself. Confronted with the impermeable screens of his variations, we are no longer the subject—*we* have become the supplement.

Part Two

PERSPECTIVE AND EXILE

Chapter 4

The vanishing self

Except among heretics, all Western metaphysics has been peephole metaphysics.

Theodor Adorno[1]

4.1
Hans Vredeman de Vries, *Trompe l'Oeil Doorway with Self Portrait*, 1595. Formerly Danzig, Rathaus, (destroyed.)

On September 8, 1585, the Antwerp town council endorsed a "General Pardon" for Protestant citizens living within the city walls. All non-adherents of "*de oude, Catholijcke, Apostolijcke, Roomische Religie*" (the Old Apostolic Roman Catholic Religion) were granted four years to leave Antwerp or convert.[2] Now 60 years old, Hans Vredeman de Vries did nothing. Soon afterwards, name was checked off as a practicing Catholic in a neighborhood census document.[3] He was paid the sum of eight stuivers and six *grosschen* for re-housing a guild altarpiece dismantled by iconoclasts, and, in August 1586, he successfully petitioned the town council—now actively promulgating the Inquisition—for back salary as a fortification engineer.[4] Yet that autumn Vredeman left Antwerp quietly and for good. That his flight may have been for religious reasons has been suggested by the fact that he was joined by two militantly Lutheran painters from his neighborhood, Lucas and Maarten van Valkenborch. The group left for Frankfurt am Main, where Vredeman stopped en route at the Protestant court of Duke Julius of Braunschweig-Lüneburg, moving on to Hamburg in October 1592, and then to the port of Danzig, an officially Protestant free city. Only two years before, Danzig had seen iconoclastic activity similar to that in Antwerp of 1566.[5] There, Vredeman was commissioned by the town council to decorate a meeting room in the town hall.

A *trompe l'oeil* from this Danzig period contains Vredeman's only self-portait (Figure 4.1).[6] Completed around 1596, the panel covered a large corner door in the town hall's summer meeting chambers. The building was deliberately destroyed in 1945.[7] Today, the work is known only from photographs. In it Vredeman appeared to paint himself standing behind a fictional doorway on a thin wedge of tiled floor. His face, compressed between a painted doorjamb and a stoop, stares outward from this false corridor. Vredeman's bulbous nose and bristled moustache catch the light from the front room, as his body is illuminated from the back—he is shown literally retiring from the front room and heading into an antechamber. A cartouche above the portal, first noted by the art historian Eugeniusz Iwanoyko, reads "DISPICE"—"look through with rigor"—an ingenious reference to the legal responsibilities of the Danzig *Rat*, who would have met to hear cases in the painting's very room.[8]

Self-portraits in Protestant spheres of Europe often pointed out the "madeness" of a devotional image. By inserting his face within a work, an artist rooted a picture within a particular time, illustrating the idea that any vision of the miraculous always sprang from a particular point of view.[9] Vredeman's Danzig inscription recalled a late medieval definition of *dispicio*—"to keep wide the eyes,"[10] even in the grainy reproduction, which we encounter now with our own knowledge of the painting's twentieth-century loss, Vredeman sees us first. Overturned is the visual hierarchy regarding who is inside and who is outside the door, or where and to whom thresholds apply.[11]

In the first part of this book we saw how Vredeman de Vries's engravings of the 1560s pictured a new way of seeing and knowing the city, a way in which Renaissance perspective came to eschew a role as simple container of narrative. Vredeman's most ambitious elaboration of this experiment, which this chapter and the next will explore, would be his *Perspective* treatise of 1604–05, written and conceived while Vredeman was away from Antwerp. The *Perspective* was published in The Hague and Leiden around 1604, where Vredeman settled after 13 years of wanderings to (apart from Danzig) Wolfenbüttel-Braunschweig (1586–91), Hamburg (1591–94, 1598–99), and Prague (1596–98).[12] Van Mander claimed this exile period shaped—indeed defined—the perspective book: Vredeman had "been busy with [it] (*hebbende daer een doende gheweest*) since the siege of Antwerp, that is, between times."[13] To make sense of how these interstitial travels affected his idiosyncratic take on what perspective was and did, we need first to bring these itinerant years into focus.

*

Confessional travel

Before Danzig, the first destination Vredeman reached in 1586 was Wolfenbüttel, the wealthy seat of the Duchy of Braunschweig-Lüneburg. He arrived in May 1587 bearing a gift of Seville oranges for the duchess Hedwig, herself a keen gardener and amateur botanist.[14] The Duchy of Braunschweig had become a prosperous entrepôt for credit and trade between the Baltic and the German hinterlands in the late fifteenth century. Enriched by traffic in silver, iron, copper, zinc, and salt from lodes in the nearby Harz mountains, it remained under the protection of the Schmalkaldic League, a loose federation of Protestant territories formed in 1550. In this respect, its wealth (as was formerly the situation in Antwerp) afforded it some socioeconomic latitude with regard to Imperial religious decrees; Duke Julius, who had studied in the Netherlands in Leuven, professed to be a Lutheran.[15] As sovereign, the Duke was an energetic patron of the arts, collecting books, manuscripts, and even authoring several plays in German himself.[16] Julius also employed numerous engineers and artists from the Netherlands. The carpenter Wouter van Elsmaer, Vredeman's father-in-law, was, in fact, invited to Wolfenbüttel in the 1570s, and the engineer William de Raedt, who helped with the new fortifications in Antwerp, was hired in 1574 to oversee Julius's new canals and bastions. Wolfenbüttel, along with the Saxon towns of Küstrin and Dömitz, was also one of the first planned cities in the region, and its expansion was in progress when Vredeman arrived. This expansion consisted of two activities: reinforcing outside walls, and laying out new sections of the town and gardens *ex nihilo*. On these tasks in Wolfenbüttel Vredeman worked directly with de Raedt, and with Duke Julius himself. Here he began to deploy the scenographic designs published by Hieronymus Cock as a way to lay out real streets.

But why, after all, did Vredeman emigrate from Antwerp? Nineteenth-century scholars assumed that his motivation was a devout Calvinism.[17] While there is indeed much in both Vredeman's earlier *rederijker* presentations and the iconography of certain paintings to suggest a certain Protestant sympathy (thus complicating the 1585 Antwerp *wijk* document listing Vredeman as Catholic),[18] his religious affiliation was probably more complex, and his peregrinations, as Hessel Miedema has rightly stressed, were more likely spurred by several factors in collusion rather than sheer confessional drive. A need for work, and compromised demand for services in Antwerp, all motivated his (like many of his fellow artists') decision to travel.[19] But based upon some imagery of his 1562 *refrein*, and archival evidence, it is not improbable that Vredeman may have been at least loosely affiliated with a Protestant sect known as the Family of Love, a mysterious group which attracted intellectuals from Antwerp's elite, including Christoffel Plantin, Justus Lipsius, and, again, Abraham Ortelius.[20]

The Familists flourished in Friesland, Brabant, and England between 1550 and 1600. They preached a brand of mystical natural philosophy, which called for the strict separation of mental and physical life. In the Netherlands Familist writings and commentary centered on the teachings of Hendrik Niclaes (c.1501–80), a Frisian preacher who was accused of everything from polygamy to theft, by Calvinists and Church officials alike. Niclaes, or "H. N." as he was known in his contraband publications (Figure 4.2), taught that Christ's life, rather than his crucifixion and resurrection, was the basis for all religious mediation. Believers should therefore seek only the inner apprehension of God, and give no regard to outward forms of worship: "the whole outward world is very great . . .," went one adage from Niclaes's *Dicta* of 1574, "but the inward world is, without comparison, much greater, inwardly, on us."[21]

Familists preached conformity to established religious practices while secretly adhering to one's true beliefs. This Nicodemism was both a survival tactic and an extension of Niclaes's own belief in the unique authority of inner spirit. Critics accused Niclaes of advocating a complete disregard for earthly laws, of preaching the impeccability (freedom from all sin) of all believers, and at one point charged him of espousing adultery and property disinheritance.[22] H. N.'s numerous books—many published by Christoffel Plantin using a false colophon from Paris—were consequently banned by both Reformed and Church authorities, and Niclaes, like many of his followers, was constantly moving from place to place. Artists, and in particular printmakers, seem to have been among groups who found Familist teachings attractive: Dirck Coornhert, who worked as an engraver for Cock in the 1550s, was a militant believer, and Cornelis Bos, who Vredeman knew, appears to have fled Antwerp in 1540 for his Familist sympathies. In fact Bos's unorthodox religious leanings have been used to explain his interest in grotesques.[23]

It is doubtful that one or another confessionalism legislated Vredeman's work uniformly. The teachings of Niclaes, laid out in flowery prose in works like the *Terra Pacis* (1562), urged, after all, a complete withdrawal from earthly pursuits. Godlike representations, "anything Figurely or Imagelike," were to be distrusted.[24] Niclaes's books, however, consisted of pages filled with poems on peace and spiritual concord in words which echo in some of Vredeman's own poetry. One of the eight steps Niclaes outlined towards knowing God in his 1553 *Spiegel der Richtigkeit* (The Glass of Righteousness) was an embrace of "a life full of love, peace and wisdom";[25] a line which Vredeman seems to have lifted for his 1562 *refrein* on "wisdom" itself, which, as he put it, was "full of love, peace, and understanding."[26] This gesture can be seen as of a piece with his earlier experience of architectural books: Vredeman might well have encountered Familist works as he encountered Vitruvius in translation—as a youth in Friesland.

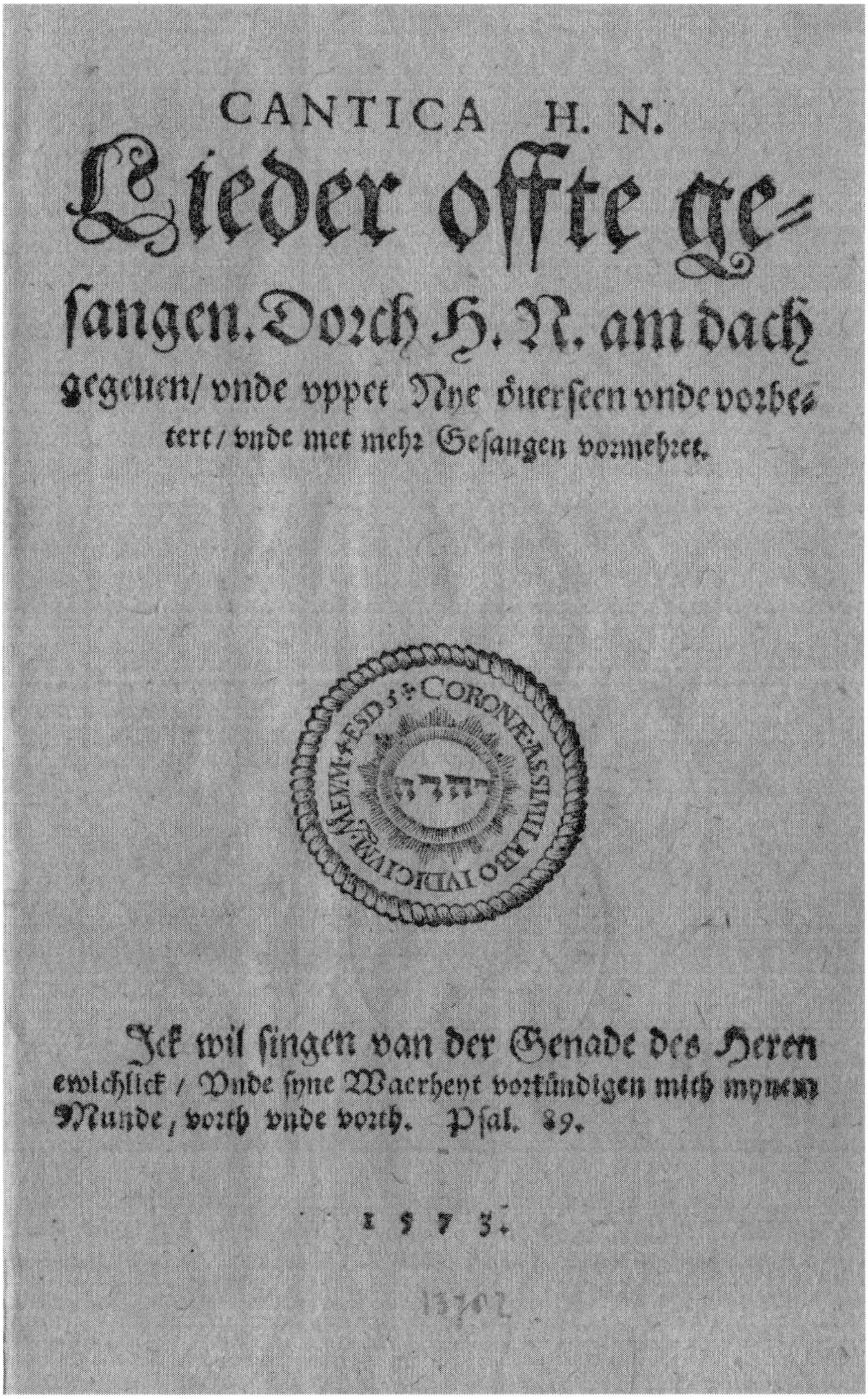

4.2

Hendrik Niclaes, *Cantica* (1573), title page.

Koninklijke Bibliotheek, The Hague.

Hendrick Niclaes was in fact living in Emden in the 1550s, around the time of Vredeman's apprenticeship in nearby Kollum.

While it is, of course, impossible to say anything about Vredeman's religious affiliation for certain, he likely had at least a passing knowledge of Familist tenets. At the very least, Vredeman probably found it exegetically convenient to subscribe to the same kind of Nicodemism espoused by the Familists as he moved, post-Antwerp, from city to city and court to court. Less an explanation for his work, the Family of Love's insistence on rigid separation between inner and outer lives, and between spiritual and bodily seeing, certainly complicates our understanding of his theory. Yet Niclaes's aversion to "anything figurely or Imagelike"—an attitude shared by certain Calvinists—may, as we shall shortly see, have factored in Vredeman's turn to architecture as an independent theme of painting.

For religious refugees in the late sixteenth century, there were four main destinations from Antwerp: the northern Netherlands, the Holy Roman Empire, and, to a lesser extent, England and France. Holland and Zeeland claimed independence as a Protestant polity in 1579 at the Union of Utrecht. Cities like Amsterdam and Middelburg quickly became attractive destinations for artists, since they hosted wealthy Protestant merchants who collected art. More than 375 foreign-born artists registered in guilds in the province of Holland between 1585 and 1630.[27] Like most immigrants, artists would often alight at one town before moving on; the painter Jacob Savery, for example, left Antwerp in 1585 and went to Haarlem, and then Amsterdam; Mechelen-born landscapist Hans Bol stopped at Bergen-op-Zoom before traveling to Delft, and then Dordrecht.[28] Many printers and publishers followed this course as well: in 1586 the well-connected William Silvius and Christoffel Plantin moved from s'Hertogenbosch and Lannoy, and then to Leiden and The Hague.[29]

German cities, linked to the Netherlands through trade, were equally receptive to many émigrés of Vredeman's stripe. From Antwerp, artists, architects, printers, and sculptors went first to locales like Alkmaar or Amsterdam, and then eastward to try to pay to join local guilds. The more fortunate artists found appointments at imperial residences around Munich, Vienna, and Prague. The Wittelsbach family of dukes in Bavaria recruited several Netherlanders to decorate their palace at Landshut, including Friedrich Sustris and Pieter de Witte.[30] Artists also went to Hanseatic free cities around the Baltic Sea, such as Danzig, Riga, and Tallinn. Some of Cornelis Floris's pupils—probably more for work than for any religious reasons—went to Königsberg.[31] Hamburg, in particular, became a large magnet for Protestant *Glaubensfluchten*. By 1585, the city was home to more than 2,000 refugees from the Netherlands, among them painters such as Gillis Coignet.[32]

Other artists went inland, or far abroad. Frans Hogenberg, another print designer, went to Cologne.[33] At least two Flemish painters went to the Viceroyalty of Peru in the 1580s.[34] The landscapists Gillis van Coninxloo and Anton Mirou settled in the Palatinate of Frankenthal, a protectorate for Calvinists founded around 1555.[35] Several of Cornelis Floris's other sculptor-pupils left Antwerp for Pomerania: Robert Coppens went to Schwerin, and Philip Brandin, who used Vredeman's ornament books, began working in Wismar. England was an attractive haven as well; Hans Eworth, a portrait painter from Antwerp, moved to London in the 1550s, and Cornelis Ketel, apparently a Mennonite, worked in and around Cambridge between 1573 and 1581.[36] When Vredeman and his son Paul stopped in Frankfurt in 1586 they would have been joined by émigrés from Antwerp like Hendrick van Steenwyck the Elder, who, under Vredeman's guidance, began to specialize in architectural painting.[37] On his return trip to Frankfurt, Vredeman may also have encountered Joris Hoefnagel and Jan Sadeler, who worked there in the 1590s as painters of naturalia.[38] All traces of Vredeman's work in Hamburg, however, have been lost.[39]

Wolfenbüttel-Braunschweig: cutting and pasting

In the Wolfenbüttel archives Vredeman is listed as *Bauwervalter* or *Bauwmeister* (building supervisor, engineer, or architect).[40] At the time of Vredeman's arrival, Duke Julius was overseeing work on a pentagonal fortification plan enclosing a new section to the north of the city. This had been drafted by the Brabant-trained Strasbourg architect, Daniel Specklin, who had also designed buildings at Zevenbergen and Utrecht. Like Vredeman, Specklin was trained as fortification engineer, and would later pen a treatise dealing with military architecture.[41] Specklin's *Architectura von Vestungen* (Figure 4.3) contained engravings of mountainous, fortified enclaves. His projects, like Vredeman's *Architectura*, were intended as designs not just for protection but for modernization, as the full title of Specklin's book implied.[42] Along with the architect de Raedt, Vredeman was entrusted with implementing a version of Specklin's models in Wolfenbüttel, and designing a new residential quarter known as the *Heinrichstadt*.[43]

There is reason to believe, as Barbara Uppenkamp has suggested, that Wolfenbüttel's still-extant geometric street design was based on Vredeman's 1560 and 1562 print series published by Cock.[44] Julius had been an avid collector of Netherlandish books on architecture, geometry, anatomy, and perspective, and the ducal library he helped found in 1572 (which would later become the Herzog-August Bibliothek) acquired first editions of Vredeman city etchings (such as the *Scenographiae*) as early as 1565. On April 16, 1574, the duke himself even presented his nine-year old son, Heinrich, with a set of Vredeman's etchings bound in vellum, which he inscribed as a birthday gift.[45] These etchings may have influenced Julius's vision of a new *Hofstadt*; in 1588, Vredeman was paid to create a sketch of a fortified gate akin to those near the terminus of his *Scenographiae* perspectives.[46] While the gate probably went unbuilt, Vredeman's involvement with the design of a chancellery building, dating to 1588 (which still stands today off the Marktplatz in Wolfenbüttel), cannot be completely dismissed.[47]

In Wolfenbüttel Vredeman was paid to design rows of trellises in Hedwig's garden in 1588.[48] He also worked on a rectangular design of a vanished *Lustgarten* near the castle, and later consulted the duchess personally on the selection of plantings. The gardens constituted one of the most extensive collections of flora in northern Europe, and Vredeman's *parterres*, ornamental configurations of plantings in rows, seem to have

4.3
Daniel Specklin, *Architectura von Vestungen* (Strasbourg, 1589), plate after fol. Yiiir. Herzog-August Bibliothek, Wolfenbüttel.

won compliments for permitting extensive displays.[49] Hedwig's garden contained local plants such as artichokes, laurel trees, and rosemary bushes, as well as *exotica* like cauliflower, maize, pepper and tulips; most of these were gifts from aristocratic neighbors, and the duchess even maintained a considerable budget for purchasing specimens from abroad.[50]

In the employ of the duke, Vredeman was commissioned to travel from Wolfenbüttel to Bremen and Hamburg to study local defenses in June 1587.[51] Upon his return he executed an astonishing two-sided watercolor (Figure 4.4, Color Plate IV), which described a project for a sluice and lock-system, intended to float timber.[52] On the recto of the Wolfenbüttel sheet Vredeman depicted a single mill for moving felled trees, along with a handwritten explanation of its parts; he keyed each point to a sequence of letters describing stages in the wood's movement through a gate. "A," for example, marked the place in the left center of the image where the wood approaches the sluice, "C" the stage where a side canal powered a water wheel opening a gate, while "E," at the far right, denoted the stage where, as Vredeman's inscription presents it, "*die holtz flussen*" (the wood floats on). The illustration format was derived from contemporary

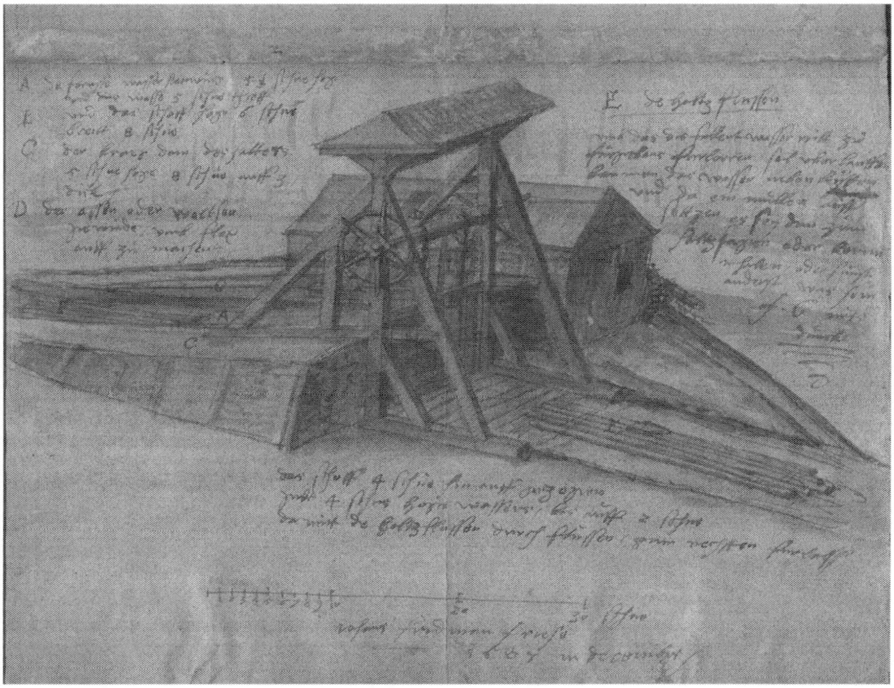

4.4
Hans Vredeman de Vries, *Design for Lock and Water-mill*, 1587. Watercolor, 25.3 × 35.3.
Niedersächsisches Staatsarchiv, Wolfenbüttel.

instrument books, and probably supplemented an oral presentation to the duke or fellow engineers; the sluice-mill at the time was a relatively new invention.[53]

Vredeman's small watercolor stuns today for its informality. The looseness of the mill's outline, the drawing's ruddy ochres and mute blues contrast starkly with the blacks and whites of his sketches for print. The calligraphic descriptions on the page were added in a separate ink,[54] and, overlaying the watercolor, offered Julius the possibility to use the design in several different ways. The verso of the sheet (Figure 4.5) depicts three alternative settings for the sluice's implementation in horizontal bands: the top incorporates an artificial lake, the middle a single canal, and the lower a second sluice which joins two waterways of separate heights. The elaboration of several alternatives on a single page, and the sheet's period appellation in the Wolfenbüttel archives as "*Apriss*" (sketch drawing or *prècis*) suggests the image was no definitive template, but part of a planning sequence, one that Vredeman oversaw.[55]

Multiple designs for single engineering projects—combined on the same page—were part of Vredeman's work while still in Antwerp. A large paper sheet now in the Stadsarchief, for example, used movable flaps to illustrate six different reconstruction possibilities of the town citadel, all viewable atop the same plan (Figure 4.6).[56] Vredeman combined older city documents with designs he had drawn up, in one case literally cutting up an old parchment and pasting in his drawn fragments.[57] On other parts of the plan, Vredeman collaged sheets, using them folded to set to scale the placement of potential bastions and waterways. In designing the citadel, Vredeman thus relied upon the same recombinatory aesthetic that characterized his column books. Similar to the

4.5
Hans Vredeman de Vries, *Three Scenarios for Implementation of Lock and Water-mill.* 1587. Watercolor, 25.3 × 35.3.
Niedersächsisches Staatsarchiv, Wolfenbüttel.

verso of the Wolfenbüttel drawing, the Antwerp plan juxtaposed a sequence of different designs with one another. The watercolors were not so much "solutions" to technical problems, however, as steps in the engineering process. But they were also about architectural drawing—exploring a way to lay out and infoliate multiple renderings of the same subject.

After Duke Julius died in 1589 in Wolfenbüttel, his son Heinrich dismissed many older court hires. Vredeman quickly left for Braunschweig, a mere seven kilometers away. He was apparently still in debt to his father-in-law, Wouter van Elsmaer, for several hundred *thalers*. Van Elsmaer brought a suit against Vredeman in May 1590, apparently forcing Vredeman to pay,[58] though this did not prevent van Elsmaer from collaborating with Vredeman on a Lutheran altarpiece painted in Braunschweig the next year.[59] Along with his son Paul, Hans Vredeman was in Hamburg by 1591. While where, according to Van Mander, he painted a *trompe l'oeil* mural in the Peterskirche for Jacob Moor, a wealthy jeweler. The painting was destroyed by fire in the nineteenth century, yet was referred to as a *doorsien*, a "seeing-through," in the *Schilderboeck*'s account.[60] The *doorsien*, a term Van Mander used in the *Grondt*, in this case described a life-sized painting of architecture or a fictional corridor, similar to the prints Vredeman had begun to produce in Antwerp. It is a term this chapter will return to shortly, as it quickly became a type of work Vredeman made synonymous with himself.

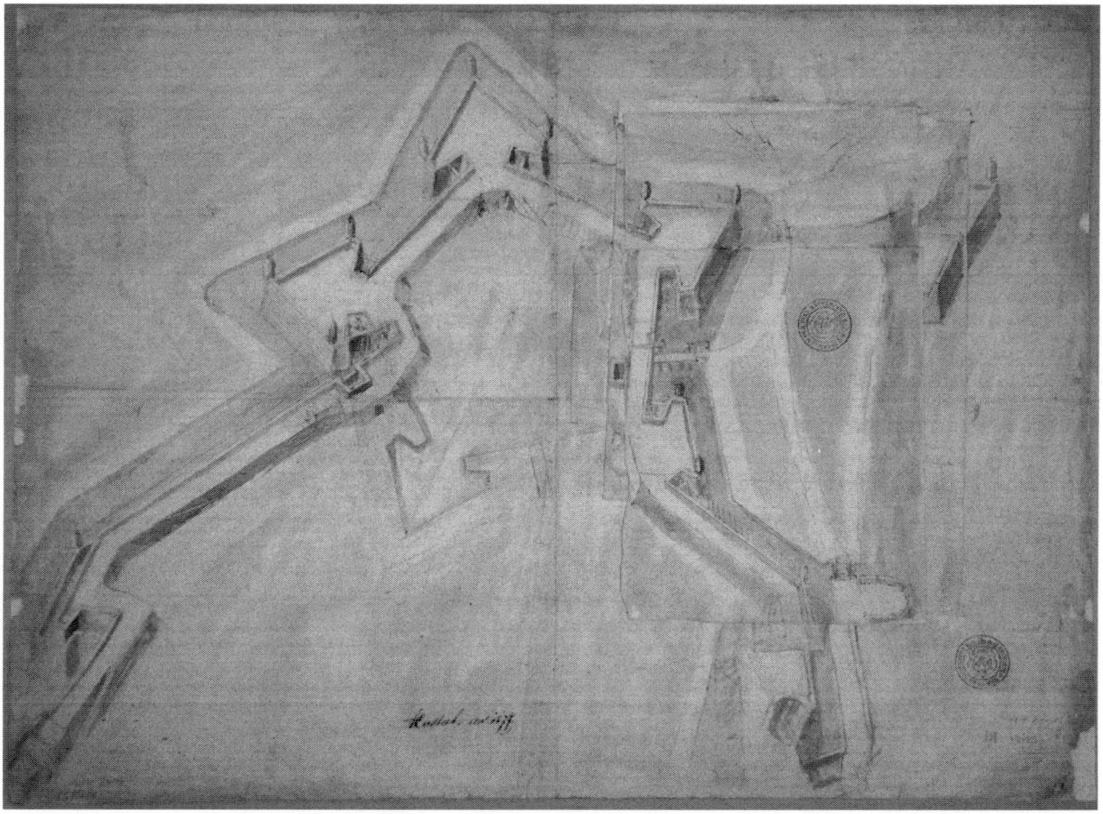

4.6
Hans Vredeman de Vries, *Five Designs for the Incorporation of the Spanish Citadel at Antwerp into the City Walls*, c. 1577–78. Ink and pencil with wash, 44.2 × 59.5.
Stadarchief, Antwerp.

Danzig: the visible church

In the summer of 1592, Vredeman accepted an invitation from the Danzig town council to serve as city *Festungbaumeister*.[61] Danzig was an officially Calvinist *Freistadt*, having paid the Prussian crown 100,000 zlotys in 1557 to guarantee religious freedom for a large population of bankers and shipbuilders.[62] As a Protestant bullwark against Swedish-Catholic forces on the Baltic coast, the prosperous Hanseatic city had been heavily bombarded as recently as 1577, and the city council was eager to expand and develop the city's defenses; as in Wolfenbüttel, numerous engineers from Italy and the Netherlands were recruited. Frederick Vroom, Peter Jansen, and the Bruges mathematician Simon Stevin (who, in 1605, would publish a textbook on perspective to rival Vredeman's) all worked in Danzig in the 1590s.[63] Although enlisted as fortification overseer for a year, Vredeman was apparently released, abruptly, on May 26, 1593.[64] Plans for new bastions designed by his fellow engineer Anton von Oppbergen were, after much discussion in the council, chosen over those Vredeman had produced, being "not as wide, tall, and elaborate" (*nichts so groß, hoch, und weitleuffig*) and hence cheaper to build.[65] In October, Vredeman demanded compensation for his trouble, which he received.[66] With his wife and son he stayed on, even signing a petition in May 1592, along with 28 local artists, asking the town council, unsuccessfully, to form a painters' guild.[67]

4.7
Hans Vredeman de Vries, *Interior of a Gothic Church*. 1594. Oil on panel, 24.5 × 40.
Private Collection, Germany.

Hans was given work as a painter in Danzig until around 1596. He produced a handful of church interior paintings for Protestant clients in the city, which, debatably, initiated the specialty of the whitewashed church nave as an independent pictorial subject. A signed panel by Vredeman from this period, formerly with a dealer in Münster, is dated 1594 (Figure 4.7).[68] The painting looks forward to the church interior theme Pieter Saenredam would adopt in the seventeenth-century Dutch Republic. The empty Gothic nave is scoured of all but the barest decoration, with arcades cleared and old wall decorations covered over, and hosts only a baptismal font, whitewashed tracery, and untouched stained glass. It is hardly coincidental that the space, bereft of any congregants, recalls the black and white properties of a print: based on Vredeman's *Scenographiae* engravings of 1560, the panel may itself have functioned as a *modello* to be copied by local students. We know that the mysterious Hendrick Aerts, for example, a native of Mechelen, apprenticed with Vredeman in Danzig, and later became a specialist in architectural pictures on the basis of such work. Three of Danzig's churches had, in fact, withstood Calvinist iconoclasm in 1590, just prior to Vredeman's arrival.[69]

Panels like the Münster piece have been associated with a specifically Calvinist aesthetic of visual purity, of an attempt—it has been argued—to eulogize the (unpictureable) Reformed idea of community.[70] Calvin's exordiums frequently invoked architectural imagery: ". . . the face of the church comes forth and becomes visible to our eyes," claimed Book IV of the *Institutes* (1536), ". . . wherever we see the Word of god preached and heard . . . there, it cannot be discounted, a church of God exists."[71] By teaching that the church was within the hearts of every true believer who heard the Word,

Calvin implied the importance of the church as an idea, just as he resisted the localizing effect of any site-specific religious architecture:

> . . . the days themselves, the hours, the structure of the places of worship . . . are matters of no importance . . . for it will never happen that the same thing will please all if matters are regarded as indifferent and left to individual choice.[72]

For iconoclasts, the holy image affixed divinity to some material, thereby marginalizing certain beholders. It was, they maintained, the bare church which became the means to apprehend the divine. Read this way, painted views of a church's emptiness—as in Vredeman's Danzig panel—come to symbolize, in effect, precisely that indeterminacy of reference many Protestant theologians associated with any fashioned image. Empty architectures can always communicate on their own; yet what they communicate, in an ostensibly Calvinist way, is a forceful *lack*, an indeterminacy of signification outside of themselves. Perhaps this is why the terms used by art historians to describe the Danzig picture—and Netherlandish architectural painting as a whole—often seem so unsatisfactory; terms like "clarity," "purity," "emptiness," and even "perspective" are deliberately accurate in their hollowness—they, quite literally, mean *nothing.*[73]

Michael Montias has demonstrated that church interiors from the Dutch Republic appeared in the collections of Calvinists more frequently than that of Catholics by a factor of four to one.[74] Given such a rubric, church interiors' abrogation of signs might itself take on signification. Vredeman's aestheticization of a bare nave in Danzig, painted under duress, seems to offer a new kind of religious picture, with Calvinist "austerity" now betokened by whitewashed walls. Perspective—which makes "visible to our eyes" the church view to which it is introduced—becomes a cipher for an inner knowledge that should not, and cannot, be given fixed representation. In a Reformed setting perspective becomes an emblem of the limitations, rather than the powers, of human sight alone.

Prague: passages at court

As recompense for the unused bastion plans in Danzig, in spring of 1594 both Hans and Paul Vredeman were put to work on decorations for the summer chamber of the town hall. There they completed a cycle of seven allegorical canvases, all of which survive, and an oval ceiling painting, which has been lost. The Danzig *Rat* seems not to have been exceptionally pleased with the latter work, and had it painted over as early as 1611.[75] During work on this large ceiling in 1594, Paul apparently fell from some scaffolding and was treated by the town's barber-surgeon; the civic council bore the cost.[76]

Both Hans and Paul were gone from Danzig by December 1596. Paul apparently went directly to Prague, while Hans returned to Hamburg once again, where he decorated the house of a wealthy Antwerp émigré, a confectioner named Hans

Lommel. Nineteenth-century accounts of the Hamburg works detail the paintings as frescoes of illusionistic vistas and grotesques.[77] Yet these frescoes, too, have been lost. With his move away from Danzig, Hans de Vredeman gave up fortification engineering once and for all to concentrate on a specific type of interior mural the previous town hall *trompe l'oeil* (Figure 4.1) had hinted at, and which Van Mander's account credited Vredeman and his son with inventing: the so-called *perspects*.

Rudolf II's glittering court in Prague, which emerged as the relatively tolerant seat of the Holy Roman Empire after 1583, became the end destination for many expatriate Netherlanders after the fall of Antwerp, whether by invitation or entreaties.[78] The draughtsman Aegidius Sadeler, for example, reached the Bohemian capital after short stays in Cologne, Mainz, and Frankfurt. Bartholomeus Spranger, Peter Stevens and Otto van Veen also won appointments by the late 1590s, and were in residence when Vredeman and his son arrived in 1596. Emperor Rudolf II (1552–1612), grandson of Charles V, had moved the court of the Holy Roman Empire to Prague from Vienna in 1576. The castle he expanded atop the Hradčany became an artistic colony, a site of scientific experiment, and an enormous repository of art: Van Mander described it housing "a remarkable number of outstanding and precious, unusual and priceless works."[79]

Prague had long been renowned for the small-scale production of painting, sculpture, woodwork, and scientific instruments. With Rudolf, it acquired a sprawling collection of books and prints, much in the tradition of other "Austrian" Hapsburg residences like Schloss Ambras in the Tyrol, decorated under Rudolf's uncle Archduke Ferdinand II.[80] The situation in the arts in Rudolf's Prague, however, differed from other court centers in two important respects; first, the scale on which collecting and patronage was carried out was infinitely larger, and, second, painting in particular was allotted special status. On April 27, 1595, the year before Vredeman's arrival, Rudolf had issued a Letter of Majesty (*Dekret*) asserting the exceptionality of the Prague painters' guild, claiming that "because [members'] art and mastery is different from other handicrafts . . . it shall no longer be regarded or described as a craft by anybody."[81] While ostensibly an elevation of painting's status as an art, on a more practical level the imperial decree's formation of an official "brotherhood" at the Hradčany, as Lubomír Komecký has argued, actually damaged the situation for most artists in the city.[82] Most high-ranking painters—Hans von Aachen, Bartholomeus Spranger, and Peter Stevens—were exempt from guild restrictions anyway, as employees of the court. Rudolf's gesture simply empowered the intellectual status of painting, and in essence made court art the *only* pursuit in which painters could actively compete without the protection of guilds. In 1603, guild representatives even complained to Rudolf that "emancipation" helped them little in terms of support, since they could in no way vie with court artists for large commissions on an open market.[83]

The court at Prague castle, professionally and topographically elevated from the rest of the city, thus became the real center for any innovation in painting or architecture. By the time of Vredeman's arrival, Hans Hoffman, Joris Hoefnagel, and Guiseppe Arcimboldo—the first great generation of artists supported by Rudolf—had either died or moved on, and a new group of painters and sculptors, among them many Netherlanders, now dominated the court: Hans van Aachen, Joseph Heintz, Adrien de Vries, Aegedis Sadeler, Bartholomeus Spranger, and Dirck Quade van Ravensteyn.[84] Spranger had been ennobled in 1588.[85]

Hans and Paul Vredeman collaborated directly with Spranger and Heintz on an altarpiece, and worked with van Ravensteyn on four large architectural canvases which survive today in Vienna, the first of which is signed and dated 1596 (Figure 4.8).[86] These works' production was reportedly overseen by the emperor; Van Mander writes that Rudolf actually "came to watch [Paul] painting," a nod to the legend of Alexander in Apelles's studio, but apparently a not-uncommon practice in Prague.[87] These architectural canvases were listed in an inventory of 1610–19 as "*4 stukh perspectiff von Pauln De Phyrss*,"[88] indicating that they were in imperial collections which had been moved back to Vienna after Rudolf's death. Three bear Hans's as well as Paul's monogram. The first canvas shows an elaborate terrace and colonnade leading to a garden and mountainous landscape. The central vault with a balustrade and two obelisks is almost an exact copy of the ephemeral arch forms of Vredeman's earlier Antwerp triumphal entry decorations and the *rederijker* stage (Figure 2.15). The latticework palace, in deep perspective, also hosts banquet tables, lute players, and an assortment of

4.8
Hans Vredeman de Vries, Paul Vredeman de Vries, and Dirck Quade van Ravensteyn, *Palace Courtyard*, 1596. Oil on canvas, 137 × 174.
Kunsthistorisches Museum, Vienna.

wildlife. Pelicans, peacocks, and turkeys roam throughout the palace amongst elaborately garbed courtiers, apparently added by Ravensteyn.

Lothar and Sigfried Dittrich have suggested that this painting's strangely encyclopedic combination of imagery articulated an imperial iconography of the world: nature and society collected, ordered and mingled under the aegis of the court.[89] In this light, the naturalia's cohabitation with human staffage becomes a model for an aristocratic utopia; by the late sixteenth century, this kind of specifically courtly imagery for peaceful gardens of love, and for the genre of so-called "merry-companies," increasingly enfolded Biblical didacticism into allegories drawn from all strata of human life.[90]

One telling inclusion in a painting from the Prague cycle (Figure 4.8), however, was a small monkey, a common court pet, which appears beneath the colonnades' inner archway at far left. The crouching ape, an antique emblem of *ars simia*, likely alluded here not just to mimesis, but also to the specific situation at Prague. Here Vredeman's representational skills would have jostled, unprotected by a guild, with others for status; as Martin Warnke has written of *hof* culture: "Probably the most important effect of moving to court was that the artist had to prove himself irreplaceable,"[91] In the Vienna work, one of the first paintings executed upon arrival in Prague, the Vredemans and Ravensteyn thus offered the emperor a quiet assertion of their own collaborative uniqueness among what must have been a stupefying array of competitors; their art, in a literal sense, is capable not just of aping *hof* life, but, more impressively, can "make" the court itself. Courtiers—like Vredeman's staffage—are completely interchangeable.

Prague would have supplied a daunting climate for any working artist. Rudolf's enormous royal collection and the separate *kunstkammer*, which by 1597 contained close to 3,000 objects, was probably the only large-scale repository of freestanding panel and canvas paintings Vredeman saw in his life. By the later 1590s, Rudolf's galleries contained works by Parmaginino, Titian, Correggio, and Dossi, as well as altarpieces by Dürer and Cranach, Pieter Bruegel the Elder's *Months* cycle and his large *Tower of Babel*. Eliška Fucíková has shown that one of the most important side functions of Rudolf's galleries was as a study collection,[92] and, to be sure, Vredeman, as Van Mander notes, painted his own *Tower of Babel* not long after leaving Prague in 1598.[93] Paul, for his part, seems to have worked directly with the paintings in Rudolf's galleries; by spring or early summer of 1596, he was completing decorations for a so-called "Spanish Room," a *Galeriesaal* on the north side of the castle where Rudolf eventually hung part of his paintings collection.[94] On the ceiling of this room Paul and Hans apparently stretched an enormous canvas showing illusory vaulting.[95] In February 1599, the officers of the Prague painters guild advised that Paul be paid 980 Bohemian *schocken* for the piece, "a work painted in oils and called a perspective," done in Rudolf's summer study adjacent to the new gallery.[96]

Vredeman *père* seems to have worked as a garden designer and an interior decorator in Prague. In 1598, Hans was paid for "inventing" drawings of seven water fountains, which earned him 85 *thalers* in total. Metal structures similar to these fountains were still standing in the Prague gardens in 1794.[97] Hans also appears to have designed a series of passageways in the south part of the Prague castle, "rooms which permitted [the emperor] to roam throughout the court concealed, without having to be seen,"[98] reported Van Mander. Interestingly, these corridors connected Rudolf's private apartments to the *kunstkammer* itself.[99] Although gone today, the mysterious structures were described by the French traveler, Jacques Esprinchard, on his visit to Prague in 1598:

> The emperor has great covered galleries in his castle through which he can go where he will, even into his gardens and the playing court, without being seen by anyone: to reach the gardens one passes over a large covered bridge which is above the deep moats of the castle . . .[100]

If the *trompe l'oeil* of Vredeman's earlier paintings was any indication, these tunnel structures, if they ever existed in any concrete sense, would have resembled small passageways embedded in the walls and the periphery of the castle; Rudolf's uncle Philip II, whom he visited in Spain as a youth around 1561, installed a system of secret tunnels in the Escorial, which a courtier once described as "a long twisting passage, somewhat dark" near Phillip's personal quarters.[101] Rudolf could have seen such a passageway during the Escorial's construction on his trip.

In Prague such passages' routing near the imperial collections is itself, perhaps, significant in light of the arguments Thomas da Costa Kaufmann has made regarding Prague patronage of the arts.[102] As Kaufmann convincingly suggests, Rudolf's magnificent collections of sculpture, books, scientific instruments, minerals, jewels, and paintings represented a microcosm of his rule; to privileged visitors these objects' arrangement in a *kunst-* and *wunderkammer* symbolized imperial power over the worldly sphere. It was a realm mastered and ordered through mediating entities, from different schemes of classification to alchemical symbolism and the writings of the ancients on art. Moving invisibly through Vredeman's hidden passages, then, Rudolf would have let assembled *curiosa*, and his art collection, express his symbolic power to visitors and keep his own body out of sight. His withdrawal from the fixed spaces of his castle foisted unprecedented responsibility upon art to express his reign. In this respect, Vredeman's tunnel designs may have abetted a quixotic program of imperial representation, concealing the emperor's "body" in order to permit his possessions alone to construct a royal image.

Sometime in 1598, Vredeman left Prague, stopping briefly again in Hamburg. Then, for the first time since his twenties, he returned to Amsterdam. By this time the city was the bustling commercial center of the Province of Holland, and home to many declaredly Protestant art collectors. Hans was listed in the Amsterdam archives as "*architekt*," and, in April 1601, attended his son Paul's marriage to Mayken Godelet. All three were residing in the Hoogstraat soon after.[103] It seems likely Hans Vredeman then spent the next three years designing illustrations and writing text for the large book of engravings that would appear in 1604–05, the *Perspective*, before launching the failed bid for a professorship at Leiden in February 1604. Around a dozen architectural paintings and some watercolors date from this Amsterdam period, usually made in collaboration with Paul Vredeman.[104] For these, Vredeman adhered to the Prague and Danzig formulas of court interior paintings, as in the strange, undated canvas now in Mönchengladbach (Figure 4.9)[105] The single recessive colonnade probably gives some indication of what the last *trompe l'oeils* at Hamburg and Prague may have looked like.[106] Whether or not Hans relied directly on paintings or sketches like this for the *Perspective* book remains unknown.[107] What seems clear, however, is that by 1600 the novel experiment of Vredeman's paintings, based on the counterfeiting of distance, and of space real and fictive, he worked on at Prague and Danzig, had established a painted specialty. Vredeman had solidified the way "perspectives" could effect more than illusion, and make concealment a signature style.

Vredeman in the *Schilderboeck*

Of Vredeman's days in Prague, Hamburg, Danzig, and Wolfenbüttel, many details remain uncertain. What is known relies to a large extent on Van Mander's *Schilderboeck*, published in 1603–04 (Figure 4.10). This biography of Vredeman has itself become a trope for the power of Dutch *mimesis* to attract and delight viewers of authority in cities

4.9
Hans Vredeman de Vries, *Palace Loggia*, c. 1601. Oil on canvas, 92.5 × 131.
Städisches Museum Schloss Rheydt, Mönchengladbach.

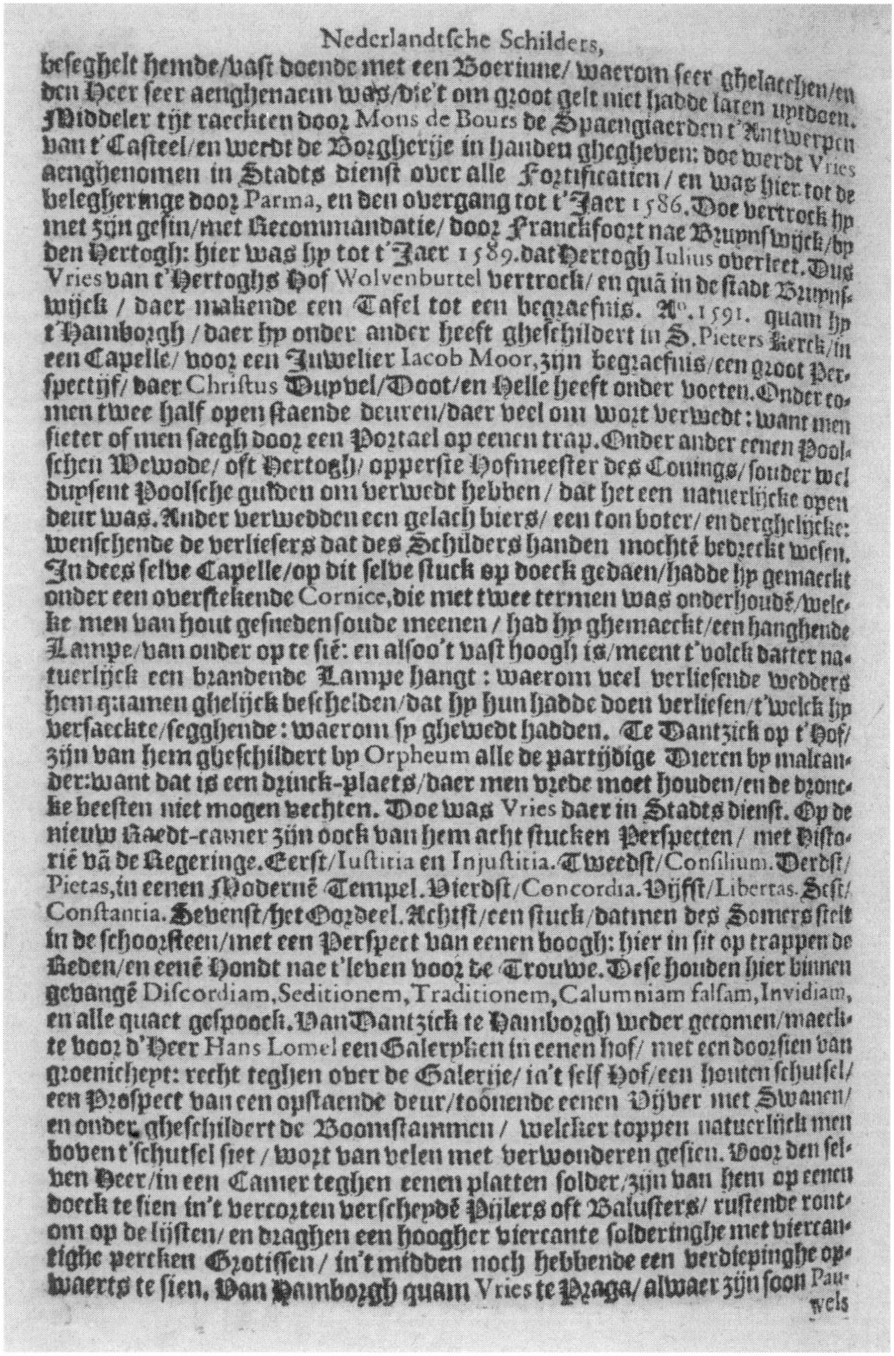

Nederlandtsche Schilders,
beseghelt hemde/vast doende met een Boerinne/ waerom seer ghelacchen/en
den Heer seer aenghenaem was/die't om groot gelt niet hadde laten uytdoen.
Middeler tijt raeckten door Mons de Bours de Spaengiaerden t'Antwerpen
van t'Casteel/en werdt de Borgherije in handen ghegheven: doe werdt Vries
aenghenomen in Stadts dienst over alle Fortificatien / en was hier tot de
beleghheringe door Parma, en den overgang tot t'Jaer 1586. Doe vertrock hy
met zijn gesin/met Recommandatie/ door Franckfoort nae Bruynswijck/by
den Hertogh: hier was hy tot t'Jaer 1589. dat Hertogh Iulius overleet. Dus
Vries van t'Hertoghs Hof Wolvenburtel vertrock/ en quã in de stadt Bruyns-
wijck / daer makende een Tafel tot een begraefnis. A°. 1591. quam hy
t'Hamborgh / daer hy onder ander heeft gheschildert in S. Pieters Kerck/in
een Capelle/ voor een Juwelier Iacob Moor, zijn begraefnis/een groot Per-
spectijf/ daer Christus Duyvel/Doot/en Helle heeft onder voeten. Onder co-
men twee half open staende deuren/daer veel om wort verwedt: want men
sieter of men saegh door een Portael op eenen trap. Onder ander eenen Pool-
schen Wewode/ oft Hertogh/ opperste Hofmeester des Conings/ souder wel
duysent Poolsche gulden om verwedt hebben / dat het een natuerlijcke open
deur was. Ander verwedden een gelach biers/ een ton boter/ en dergheliicke:
wenschende de verliesers dat des Schilders handen mochtẽ bedreckt wesen.
In dees selve Capelle/op dit selve stuck op doeck gedaen/hadde hy gemaeckt
onder een overstekende Cornice, die met twee termen was onderhoudẽ/welc-
ke men van hout gesneden soude meenen / had hy ghemaeckt/een hanghende
Lampe/van onder op te siẽ: en alsoo't vast hoogh is/meent t'volck datter na-
tuerlijck een brandende Lampe hangt : waerom veel verliesende wedders
hem gramen ghelijck beschelden/dat hy hun hadde doen verliesen/t'welck hy
versaeckte/segghende: waerom sy ghewedt hadden. Te Dantzick op t'Hof/
zijn van hem gheschildert by Orpheum alle de partijdige Dieren by malcan-
der: want dat is een drinck-plaets/daer men vrede moet houden/en de dronc-
ke beesten niet mogen vechten. Doe was Vries daer in Stadts dienst. Op de
nieuw Raedt-camer zijn oock van hem acht stucken Perspecten / met Histo-
riẽ vã de Regeringe. Eerst/Iustitia en Injustitia. Tweedst/Consilium. Derdst/
Pietas, in eenen Modernẽ Tempel. Vierdst/Concordia. Vijfst/Libertas. Sest/
Constantia. Sevenst/het Oordeel. Achtst/een stuck/datmen des Somers stelt
in de schoorsteen/met een Perspect van eenen boogh: hier in sit op trappen de
Reden/en eenẽ Hondt nae t'leven voor de Trouwe. Dese houden hier binnen
gevangẽ Discordiam, Seditionem, Traditionem, Calumniam falsam, Invidiam,
en alle quaet gespoock. Van Dantzick te Hamborgh weder gecomen/maeck-
te voor d'Heer Hans Lomel een Galerijken in eenen hof/ met een doorsien van
groenicheyt: recht teghen over de Galerije/ in't self Hof/een houten schutsel/
een Prospect van een opstaende deur/toonende eenen Vijver met Swanen/
en onder ghescbildert de Boomstammen / welcker toppen natuerlijck men
boven t'schutsel siet / wort van velen met verwonderen gesien. Voor den sel-
ven Heer/in een Camer teghen eenen platten solder/zijn van hem op eenen
doeck te sien in't vercorten verschedẽ Pijlers oft Balusters/ rustende ront-
om op de lijsten/ en draghen een hoogher viercante solderinghe met viercan-
tighe percken Grotissen / in't midden noch hebbende een verdiepinghe op-
waerts te sien. Van Hamborgh quam Vries te Praga/ alwaer zijn soon Pau-
wels

4.10
Karel Van Mander, *Het Schilderboeck*, 1604, fol. 266v.
Marquand Library of Art and Archaeology, Princeton University.

or at court.[108] Hessel Miedema has posed Vredeman's "Life" as part of Van Mander's project to align Netherlandish accomplishments in counterfeit architecture with Italian ones;[109] Celeste Brusati, on the other hand, has taken Vredeman's vita as a testament to the *Schilderboeck*'s specifically Dutch interest in "the illusionistic possibilities of painting."[110] Jürgen Müller has read Van Mander's account as a condemnation of brute illusionism, in which "perspective work," in its disavowal of narrative, represents the coarsest departure from Italian *historiae*.[111] Walter Melion, on the other hand, describes Van Mander's account as a self-referential meditation upon painting's uniqueness. In the *Lives*, Melion claims, "de Vries and his successors strive to elide representation into nature herself, eliminating the threshold between the image and its referent."[112]

To be sure, in Van Mander's text, as in the Danzig self-portrait from 1595 (Figure 4.1), the pictorial abrogation of thresholds becomes, paradoxically, the manner in which Vredeman distinguishes himself. In fact, it is in a preamble to Vredeman's *Life* that Van Mander likens the artist to a modern-day Parrhasius, who "had an astonishingly high opinion of his art, was immoderately ambitious and prided himself on his skill,"[113] manifesting this skill, as Parrhasius had done, through mimicry. The Parrhasius legend, wherein a curtain is feigned to fool Zeuxis, imagined an art so powerful it deceives not just nature but another outstanding artist. More broadly, the tale allegorized the capability of painting to overwrite its own boundaries. As Van Mander presents it in the *Schilderboeck*, Vredeman's apparent mastery of backgrounds, like Parrhasius's, pushes his craft forward from other artists. These illusionistic performances are recapitulated in Van Mander's own repetitive and excessive description of the counterfeiting practices themselves—as with myth, this retelling becomes in itself a conduit to art theory of the past.[114]

But what does the *Schilderboeck* say about Vredeman himself, about the role of his biography in his pictures? Van Mander describes several Vredeman mural paintings that have been lost. Of his Antwerp period, for example, the *Schilderboeck* details a work made in the palace of William the Silent, probably around 1580: "Vries made a large perspective [*Perspect*] looking like a view into [*doorsien*] a garden . . . later some German noblemen as well as the Prince of Orange were deceived, thinking it to be real building with a view [*doorsie*]."[115] Similar works appear elsewhere in Vredeman's *Life*. For example, Van Mander describes a commission executed for a chapel in the Hamburg cathedral:

> [Vredeman] went to Hamburg where, among other things, he painted an epitaph in a chapel of St. Peters church for a jeweler, Jacob Moor—a large perspective [*een groot Perspectijf*] in which Christ treads the Devil, Death, and Hell under foot. Underneath these are two half-open doors, about which many bets were made [*daer veel om wort werwedt*], for behind these one sees, or saw, a landing leading to a stairway. Among other men a Polish *Wewode*, or Duke, the loftiest steward to the king, is supposed to have bet a thousand Polish guilders that it was really an open door. Others bet a round of beer, a ton of butter, and the like; those who lost the bet cursed the painter's hands.[116]

Not only is the length, detail, and anecdotal scrutiny paid to this mythical painting remarkable within the context of the *Lives*, but the effects the paintings stimulated in viewers are relayed with unusual vivacity. In the Moor story there is wit, intrigue, gambling, the threat of violence, and above all, a rare appearance in the *Schilderboeck* of the term "*Perspectijf*" to denote a painting genre. The equally rare variant of it, the familiar "*doorsien*," appears soon after in an account of another lost Vredeman work. Again in Hamburg, Vredeman

> made a small gallery in a garden for Hans Lommel, with a view into [*doorsien*] greenery; directly opposite the gallery, in the same garden he painted upon a wooden fence a prospect of an open door showing a pond with swans . . . it was viewed with astonishment by many.[117]

The astonishment (*vewonderen*) aroused by the lost painting was again a function of its architectural effects. Notable, too, is the use of illusionistic painting to depict a view outside. Finally, in Prague, a third work described in the *Schilderboeck* elicited this response. Vredeman executed large oak shutters for a collaborative altarpiece made by three other artists: Bartholomeus Spranger, Hans van Aachen, and Joseph Heintz. Two wings of this work, the sole components executed by Vredeman, survive in Vienna (Figure 4.11), bearing a date of 1598 and Vredeman's signature, noting his age as 72.[118] A seam between the two doors of the altarpiece splits an architectural recession with an *Annunciation*, with figures of Gabriel and the Virgin by Hans van Aachen.[119] The scene's subject—Gabriel's act underscored by the "heralding" capacity of linear perspective itself[120]—unfolds across two wings, but is almost submerged in Vredeman's recessive architecture. Remarkably, the *Schilderboeck* details how the work was made:

> Vries painted a perspective [*Perspect*] onto the outside, to which end he first had the doors smoothed flat, then, next to the join where they closed, he placed a rectangular column so that the join is invisible; the emperor was much astonished with this.[121]

Indeed, the revelatory theme of the shutter's *istoriae* is complemented by Vredeman's own perspective structure, which "reveals" the subject to the viewers. The effect was still similar, in Van Mander's account, to one final work executed by Paul:

> . . . a perspective [*Perspect*] in [a] small hall showing an open gallery leading into a garden with a fountain; the Emperor, as if mistaken, often went to walk through it.[122]

There are different terms in all four passages to describe the paintings: "*doorsien*," "*perspect*," and "*Perspectief*,"[123] which allude collectively to a type of illusionistic canvas, as well as to a specific category of painted thing. All produce the effect of surprising—or winning sponsorship from—men of power: Rudolf II, William of Orange, Polish dukes, wealthy bourgeois like Moor and Hans Lommel. The accounts of the paintings,

4.11
Hans Vredeman de Vries and Hans van Aachen, Exterior Wings to an Altarpiece with the *Annunciation*, 1598. Oil on panel, 221 × 140.
Kunsthistorisches Museum, Vienna.

like many in the *Schilderboeck*, rely upon instances of secondary performance in beholders: paintings dupe (as in the betting of butter and beer), arouse good-natured astonishment or resentment ("cursed the painter's hands") or, in the case of Rudolf and the false passage, physically impede movement through space. Vredeman's paintings, that is, are activated through their revelation as fictions.[124] Pliny's dictum *ars adeo latet arte sua*—true art conceals art—thus emerges as the lesson of Vredeman's biography.

Yet if we consider where these descriptions from the *Schilderboeck* came from, a further mystery appears. Karel Van Mander, for one, never visited Prague.[125] As Henri Greve noted in his 1903 study of the *Schilderboeck*'s sources, the *Lives* were drafted on the basis of information gleaned through interviews, visits to collections, and, above all, letters.[126] Van Mander frequently referred to such correspondence in his work, particularly in cases where letters went unanswered: the painter Marcus Gheeraerts' son, to whom Van Mander sent inquiries, "did not think it his responsibility to write [*te schrijven*] anything honorable about his father."[127] Of Heinrich Aldegrever, Van Mander laments that he had little to report, since he had written to the town and to Aldegrever's descendants, yet "waited so long in vain, for full information . . ."[128] Still later, Van Mander, in the Netherlandish *Lives*, complains that he has not received written answers sent to the hometowns of Hans Holbein and Crispijn van den Broek.[129] However, Van Mander must have received letters that he eventually used. Indeed, in case of Cornelis Ketel, whose biography is inexplicably the second longest and most detailed life in the Netherlandish *Lives*, Van Mander seems to have copied from a letter directly.[130] The letter practice explains the presence of so much detailed information in the *Schilderboeck* about artists Van Mander could not have met, about artworks in cities he never visited, and the details rendered in a prose style—as Paul Taylor has suggested—that was not his own.[131]

The *Schilderboeck* texts were thus always authored by Van Mander alone.[132] Indeed, in his introduction Van Mander admits that he copied from an expanded version of Vasari's *Vite* for information about several older artists—most probably the 1568 edition that included a small section on Netherlandish painters.[133] And, like Vasari, Van Mander frequently manipulated established biographical conventions to champion local accomplishments in painting. A key element in this critical program, as with the Zeuxis and Parrhasius myth in Vredeman's *Life*, was the use of anecdote.[134] And yet classical *topoi* aside, there remains a scrupulousness about the factual details of many lives in the *Schilderboeck* which points beyond simple rhetorical overture, or a pat slotting of local hero into Italian modes of biography. Of the Danzig paintings by Vredeman, for example, Van Mander devotes more than 20 lines to specific iconographic details, even though he never visited the city. The same is true of Vredeman's paintings for Lommel and Moor in Hamburg. Van Mander seems to have taken his information from a second source.

More than likely, this source was a letter, one written by Hans Vredeman himself. There are, for example, flashes of unusual prose or diction elsewhere in the *Schilderboeck*, which, as in Vredeman's *Life*, suggest the presence of another hand. Describing a church interior by Hendrick Steenwyck the Elder, Van Mander deploys the conventional term "*Perspective,*"[135] yet in Vredeman's life the word "*Perspect*" suddenly appears, and then vanishes for the rest of the Netherlandish *Lives.*[136] In fact, "*Perspect*" occurs six times in Vredeman's own biography, yet in no other section of the Netherlandish painters.[137] Although Van Mander used "*Perspectief,*" for example, in the Italian section of the *Lives* to describe views of architecture by Piero della Francesca,[138] he adopts "*Perspect*" only to describe Vredeman's illusionistic paintings of architecture. Is this just because of the peculiar character of Vredeman's art? Similar interiors, or fictional views by other architectural painters like the Neffs, are mentioned, yet with different diction entirely—they are often "*metselrye*," or even "*architecktur*."

This switching occurs specifically with the term *doorsien*.[139] *Doorsien* is an exceptionally uncommon word in print before the early seventeenth century.[140] In the whole of the Netherlandish section of the *Schilderboeck* the term (derived loosely from *Durchsehung*—a seeing-through—a word used by Dürer and his copyists that we will examine in the next chapter) is used only twice: once to describe a Hans Vredeman painting for Lommel in Hamburg, and subsequently to describe a lost *Mercury and Psyche* by Bartholomeus Spranger from around 1587.[141] Whereas in the *Grondt* Van Mander used the term "*insien*" (a looking-into) as a synonym for *doorsien* (a looking-through), *insien* appears nowhere in Vredeman's *Life*. Vredeman's *Perspective* tract of 1604–05, which uses *doorsien* in its very title, was, in fact, published within months of the *Schilderboeck* (as Van Mander describes seeing the book). *Doorsien* then suddenly appears in two significant places around 1604: Chapter II of Van Mander's *Grondt*, published in July 1604, and Vredeman's *Perspective* treatise, published earlier that year.[142]

This matters, since the term *doorsien* is used only to describe two bodies of work in the Netherlandish section of the *Schilderboeck:* Bartholomeus Spranger's art and Vredeman's paintings; "*doorsiende*," a variant term is, in fact, unique to the life of Vredeman.[143] Why is this? Although Spranger and Karel Van Mander worked together in Vienna in 1577, Spranger went alone to Prague while Van Mander stayed in Vienna, and thus had to rely on secondary sources for information about Prague. Van Mander, as we have seen, praised Prague's art collections effusively. But of all the Prague paintings Van Mander mentions by name in his Netherlandish *Lives*, only a handful appear to have been hung in the imperial collection itself and not in the *Kunstkammer*, a chamber invisible to all but privileged guests like Spranger, who was officially a *valet de chambre*. Strangely enough, among the few works Van Mander mentions at Prague were a Dürer altarpiece, some Sprangers, and an architectural composition by Vredeman.[144] Spranger's life is among the longest in the Netherlandish *Levens*, but concentrates almost exclusively on his early career, focusing chiefly on works made before Van Mander and Spranger parted in Vienna. In fact, the only later works by Spranger Van Mander knows of at Prague are paintings that hung in public places, like a *Mercury and Psyche*. This suggests that Van Mander's information about Prague probably came not from Spranger himself (in which case he doubtless would have mentioned the dozens of paintings done for and treasured by Rudolf) but from another source who had only limited access to the galleries, and who was able to describe specific Spranger works in detail. This person could well have been Vredeman, who could have spoken to, or, as seems likely, written to Van Mander about Spranger, including information simultaneously about his own life and that of another artist. Since "*Doorsien*" was used in the *Schilderboeck* only to describe Vredeman's work and Spranger's *Mercury and Psyche*, information about Rudolf's court probably came from a single source. It could easily have been a communication by Vredeman that furnished Van Mander with his information about Spranger's time in Prague.

Hessel Miedema has noted that Van Mander "does not appear to have actually seen any painting by [Vredeman],"[145] and that he "does not seem to have been much interested in iconography."[146] Yet consider this description of the painting cycle at the Danzig *Rathaus*, where Vredeman installed his self-portrait (Figure 4.1) and which Van Mander, we recall, had never visited:

> In the new council chamber there are eight perspective pieces by [Hans] with representations of government. Firstly *Justicia* and *Injusticia*. Secondly *Consilium*. Thirdly *Pietas*, in a modern temple. Fourthly *Concordia*. Fifthly *Libertas*. Sixthly *Constantia*. Seventh the *Final Judgment*. The eighth is a piece which in summer is placed in a fireplace with a perspective [*Perspect*] of an arch upon which, on steps, sits Reason, with a dog from life representing Faith. These hold *Discordia, Seditio, Traditio, Calumnia Falsa, Invidia* and all evil ravings captive within . . .[147]

Even if such information was dictated to Van Mander, its detail suggests a relatively unedited version of Vredeman's own experience. The actual place the *Schilderboeck* seems to have been written was Zevenbergen castle, north of Haarlem, in 1603.[148] Since Vredeman was living in Amsterdam at this time, a mere seven kilometers away, a meeting between Van Mander and Vredeman almost certainly occurred. And while Van Mander could have obtained many details in conversation, there is a specificity elsewhere in the account ("a canvas two hundred feet long and eighty across"),[149] which gives the sense of a written account. More significant in Vredeman's *Life* is the sudden appearance (and disappearance) of words like *doorsien* and *Perspect*, which are found nowhere else in the *Schilderboeck*.[150] The unusual terms for such a significant subject point strongly to the presence of a writing hand that was not Van Mander's own.

I believe that, letter or not, there is much to support the idea that the bulk of Vredeman's biography in the *Schilderboeck* was written by Vredeman. While Greve's interview scenario explains for the wealth of detail in descriptions, it accounts awkwardly for the inclusion of strange terms like *doorsien* in Vredeman's life. Vredeman, we recall, had used the term in the title of his *Perspective* tract. The text we now recognize as Van Mander's biography of the artist in the *Schilderboeck* was most probably a collaborative autobiography, largely scripted by Hans Vredeman de Vries himself.

In the *Schilderboeck* account, to be sure, Van Mander appended the short preamble on Zeuxis and Parrhasius to Vredeman's *Life*. He may also have written the account of Vredeman's early career, as he elsewhere claims to have worked in the Antwerp guild records and demonstrates familiarity with engravings by Hieronymus Cock.[151] But I agree with Paul Taylor's reminder that "when Van Mander sat down to write a life . . . he sometimes had a letter before him; the letter could be long, with little need of editing."[152] If Vredeman did furnish such a document, it was not just via a wealth of detail of his travels throughout northern Europe that he distinguished himself. Rather—

significantly—it was through the particular uses of the terms *Perspect* and *doorsien*—types of pictures that he aligned with his whole output. Vredeman would have inserted into the *Schilderboeck* two words that made his specialty stand out as unique, on the basis of his extensive travels. The elderly Vredeman would have included the terms not just to isolate his work linguistically among the other lives, but to set his architectural paintings, as *Perspects*, apart from more conventional *perspectives* known to contemporaries.

Surely, the irony of using a term of dissimulation to distinguish oneself would have redoubled a project of self-promotion on Vredeman's part. Whatever his religious sympathies, Vredeman's gesture bespeaks a certain Nicodemist sensibility, where dissemblance becomes not just a means of survival, but a shrewd way to find work.[153] As with Rudolf's secret passages, or the lost *Self-Portrait* from Danzig with which this chapter began, the effect of Vredeman's autobiography would have been to insist upon a specific kind of relationship between his painting and beholders, a relationship steeped not just in tricksterism or wonder, but in the antique precedent of Parrhasius. Linguistically and biographically, Vredeman's *Perspect* functioned to set his work apart from that of his competitors, living and dead. Reversing the expectation of autobiography, Vredeman's vita in the *Schilderboeck* constructs a life, *post facto*, through art.

*

This was, of course, precisely the ingenuity of presenting one's portrait image as a *trompe l'oeil* (Figure 4.1). The vanished painting from Danzig was a signature of Vredeman's ability to restage his own form. The disappearance of the *Perspects* from Danzig and Prague in our own day, victims of various twentieth-century iconoclasms, may in some strange way be thus compensated for, even mandated by, Vredeman's own pictorial strategy—a strategy, this chapter has argued, which banks on a period idea of loss. So full of art as to seem actual, the *trompe l'oeil* image is nominally indistinguishable from surroundings as mundane as a wall, a door, or a hallway. Representation, intervening between copy and prototype, spills forth in the *Schilderboeck* as the "fictional" door is opened, the window shown to be wall, or, as with Pliny's Zeuxis, the curtain upheld as canvas. It was this not-entirely-unexpected unveiling of the illusion *as* illusion that marked the key gesture of Vredeman's biography, enacting the process Michael Leja has termed the "performance of deception."[154]

Nobody, not iconodules, and not even Zeuxis, really believed illusionistic images were "real." The self-reflexivity of Vredeman—a *Glaubensflüchtling* and the "Netherlandish Parrhasius" himself in his art and words—partakes of a belief which was never really limited to either Church or Reformed art theorists after the Reformation: a faith not in the image's perfection, but rather in its limited capacity to ever "depict" anything outside of itself. In Vredeman's world of exile a "perspective" can become a literal portrait, and a painter's absence a looming signature.[155] In much the same way the idea of the *Perspect* would figure in Vredeman's final book, where it would forge the artist's most eye-catching presentation of his own self.

Chapter 5

Hidden terrors: the *Perspective* (1604–05)

Nothing will come of nothing. Speak again.

King Lear I.i.92

Expansiveness, identified elsewhere with conquest . . . is here but a terrified escape.

Carl Einstein[1]

5.1
Hans Vredeman de Vries, *Perspective* I, no. 29, 1604. Engraving, H.548.
Centre Canadien d'Architecture, Montréal.

Alberti thought perspective revolutionary not because it was a rational way to make pictures, but because it was a *repeatable* one.[2] In the *Della Pittura* Alberti ascribed the term *prospettiva* a double meaning—it could designate a process for creating the illusion of depth on a flat surface, or, as we have seen in the case of Netherlandish architects, of ordering and controlling structural information from a single point of view.[3] In assuming a fixed relationship between an observer and sets of objects, a screen between work and world, *perspectiva artificialis*—as a drawing system, a symbol—has, since the Renaissance, been accused of collapsing the experience of lived space to geometric ends.

Yet from its inception perspective was a plural phenomenon, something predicated—in its many demonstration models and applications (Fig. 5.2)—upon discrete distances between viewers and viewed things. The most startling effects of Netherlandish perspective, Fritz Novotny once claimed, arise not from the duplication of optical experience, but in the tension perspective mapped between illusion and the materiality of support.[4] Indeed, distance, pressuring the idea of a correlation between perspective as a model for painting and for scientifically seeing the world, remains the framework for thinking about much post-Renaissance perspective in art, philosophy, and psychology. Since the early nineteenth century, rote linear perspective has been seen as a rough abstraction, incapable of accounting for the vagueness and volatility of individual bodies in space;[5] Bruno Taut called perspective a "corpse with one eye closed," while Hermann von Helmholtz saw it as biologically suspect, an oppressive compositional relic in art—anthropomorphic, conventional, tyrannical, confining, and leaden with metaphor.[6] It remained the optical burden photography and film were cursed to bear, and which avant-gardes of any stripe were bound to renounce.[7]

What is unusual now about much modernist criticism of perspective as a whole is how often it reprises the same complaints made by Renaissance detractors, towards completely different ends. Alberti, as we saw in Chapter 1, claimed perspective could be deceitful because it was based on "mere appearances" instead of geometric truths. Foucault likened perspective to a horse driver at the reigns, an example of modern visuality's infatuation with control over an image's visual and historical origins.[8] The two "foes" attack perspective for the same thing. Yet whereas, strangely, in the Renaissance perspective was criticized for being inexact, contemporary critics demonized it for being too exact; both sides assumed it bore a responsibility to connect work and world.[9] This assumption that perspective has some special claims to truth is actually a relatively new development; if anything, perspective's traditional power lay in its ability to lay bare art's separateness from the purely seen, to be anything but continuous with meaning, with the beholders' subjectivity. As Leonardo himself claimed in his notebooks, perspective banked on the interplay of near and far, not one or the other.[10]

Perspective has only recently become about reference. When it was described in treatises in the sixteenth and early seventeenth centuries, as in Vredeman de Vries's last, longest, and most startling tract of 1604–05, it retained a link to workshop traditions of goldsmithing, woodwork, even masonry. In Lutheran regions of Germany, for example, perspective prints became a quick professional outlet for craftsmen left commission-poor by doctrinal bans on images. Cheaper and more reproducible than paintings, prints could activate and apply perspective in signature ways, and by the year 1600 more than 450 different publications about perspective had appeared in western Europe.[11] Sometimes illustrated, most often not, these works compiled, annotated, abridged, expanded, and plagiarized an array of writings new and old, broaching theories dealing with perspective in relation to ballistics, military surveying, the proportions of the human body, and the structures of human sight (*perspectiva naturalis*). Perspective, like ornament, had always encompassed a myriad of practices and histories, but it remained tied to the methods, misunderstandings, and stubborn materiality of the crafted object. In print, however, it was as if perspective theory found a medium precisely attuned to its fundamental condition of axiality, of inversion: just as a cut block or copperplate, once pressed, makes a negative image positive, so did perspective, as a matrix, always strive to reverse the flat.[12]

Hans Vredeman's *Perspective* treatise, the subject of this chapter, was a lavish compilation of more than 70 etched and engraved illustrations. The book announced its subject as *deur-siende*—the praiseworthy art of "looking onto or through."[13] This was a term which offered a quiet nod to Dürer, but proffered an altogether different view of perspective. Karel Van Mander, who appears to have seen Vredeman's book just after its publication, called the *Perspective* not a treatise but "a very beautiful book of architecture."[14] Dutch, French, Latin, and German translations of the tract were among the most influential books on art in the seventeenth century: Rembrandt may have owned a copy, and Pieter Paul Rubens listed an edition in his library.[15] 1620s inventories from Haarlem and Amsterdam showed painters with Dutch translations. The workshop utility of Vredeman's book was, however, coextensive with its status as a

5.2
South Tyrol, writing cabinet with intarsia perspective designs, c. 1590. Resin, colored birch and pine, 58 × 88.5. Servitenkloster, Innsbruck.

luxury item, as an *objet d'art*; it was listed in ducal libraries in Wolfenbüttel, Madrid, and Paris in the early seventeenth century, and in the cabinets of mathematicians, art dealers, and botanists in Lithuania, Poland, Hungary, and even Mexico before 1740.[16]

Within the study of art history, Vredeman's work has come to occupy a position akin to Van Mander's *Grondt* (1603–04), or even Samuel van Hoogstraten's *Inleyding* (1678): it is a rare Netherlandish source on not just how to make pictures, but how to teach other people about them. Like Van Mander's and Hoogstraten's tracts, Vredeman's *Perspective* remains an aggregate source, made up of prolix, disparate, and unconnected texts. Vredeman drives his theory by illustrations, and, more precisely, printed illustrations. In so doing, the quixotic book, and its posthumous reception, offers not just a summation of Vredeman's career in exile, but reveals how perspective had diverged from its Quattrocento origins.

Since its original publication, Vredeman's book has been praised, ridiculed, dismembered, eulogized, excerpted and copied by artists. In *The Art of Limming* (c.1650) Edward Norgate described its "goed rules, and so easy method."[17] Michel Poudra's 1864 history of perspective, unable to decipher its instructions, deemed its plates "curieux."[18] Lawrence Wright's coffee-table *Perspective in Perspective* (1983), speaking for many scholars, scoffed at Vredeman's work as "the blind leading the blind,"[19] while a historian of philosophy recently touted it as "surrealism before the fact" (Figure 5.1, H.548).[20] Aside from a general assumption that the book is a kind of guide (or trap) for would-be artists, there remains little scholarly agreement on what Vredeman's tract actually *is*. This is a status that the impossibly hybridic quality of the work—a gallery of designs, texts, and half-hearted theorization—does little to assuage. Arthur Wheelock concluded that the *Perspective* "was far less a perspective treatise than an extensive source book for pattern," a capacity which accounts for the absolute befuddlement it has met with by historians of science.[21]

Van Mander remarked that Vredeman had labored on *Perspective* between commissions, "between times." Indeed, the interstitial aspect of the book within Vredeman's oeuvre, its place as a literal "*by-werk*," has been an overriding concern in the sporadic literature on the artist; fleeing from religious persecution in Antwerp, Vredeman composed the *Perspective* on the run, between courtly appointments in Prague, Danzig, and Wolfenbüttel. Recent scholarship has largely derided its geometrical accuracy (or lauded its precocious avant-gardism) precisely on the basis of its adherence to, or supposed critique of, "realism." The tract is incessantly cited by scholars of modernism, who have connected it variously to de Chirico's early canvases, to the kitsch of M. C. Escher (who was also born in Leeuwarden, coincidentally), and to 1960s photo essays by Robert Smithson.[22] Ironically, these latter scholars may have supplied the more historical takes on Vredeman's tract. Most seventeenth-century viewers approached the book not as a geometry problem, or a scientific treatise, but as an artwork.

The *Perspective* as treatise I: *"Elck sien een andere punct maect"*

Vredeman's book was made up of two sections: 11 folios of letterpress text followed by 48 plates for Book I (1604), and then 4 more folios of text followed by 24 plates for Book II (1605). The Dutch title names it as *Perspective, dat is de hoogh-gheroemde const een schijnenede in oft door-siende ooghen-ghesichtes punt* (Perspective, being the highly-praised art of a point looked upon or through). The first editions of the book were published with Dutch, Latin, French, and German commentary, and bound on oblong folio sheets; later pressings were folded and bound vertically, or broken up and sold as in loose sheets. The intended audience was listed on the title page: "artists, architects, tapestry-makers, cabinet-makers, engravers, goldsmiths, and other amateurs."[23] A bust of Vredeman, designed by the Amsterdam printer Hendrick Hondius (Figure 5.36), was included in the first folio, a relatively rare inclusion in a perspective treatise.[24] Vredeman's glowering visage at 77 years of age is topped by hair that curls and fluffs away, dissolving into bits of etched line. Vredeman is not pictured at work; unlike in his 1610 portrait (Figure 0.2), he now holds no compass or burin.[25]

What stands out in Vredeman's book is the *punt*, or seen point, which he includes in his title. Wolfgang Schäffner has recently shown that only in the late seventeenth century did Dutch mathematicians associate the concept of point with the notion of zero, that is, with absence rather than presence.[26] Previously it held a value. This matters, since Vredeman, like many sixteenth-century theorists, rooted his idea of perspective less in the act of seeing, than in the thing seen.

The *Perspective* was a typographic hybrid, requiring two different printing operations: the letterpress text was made by Beuckel Corneliszoon Nieulandt in The Hague, while the images were etched and published at Leiden, cut by Hondius himself. Bartholomeus Dolendo, a late pupil of Hendrick Goltzius, engraved four plates in Book II, and Vredeman's son Paul designed five of the later engravings from Book II, likely authoring some of the later texts as well.[27] The text at the beginning of both volumes presents annotations of the engravings in short paragraphs, each describing a "demonstration" which, headed with a numeral, was keyed to one of the engravings in the main body of the tract. These texts describe different aspects of the geometric bodies and architectural features in the sparse, etched "figures" of the subsequent pages. The plates themselves, uniquely, revolve around various instances of a "*orison*," or horizon, which is connected to the frame of the composition by dotted orthogonal lines. Over the dozens of plates, this horizon rises and falls, as denuded, geometric landscapes unfold. Stacked cube-forms (Figure 5.3, H.530) give way to fountains, colonnades and triumphal gates (Figure 5.4, H.544); corridors coalesce into spiral stairwells (Figure 5.5, H.554); full-grown architectural assemblages emerge within tunneling cisterns (Figure 5.6, H.559). Eventually, Gothic naves, and hallucinatory town squares arise (Figure 5.7, H.582). These all materialize as one moves through the tract, and Vredeman describes them only fleetingly in the text. Traces of human activity do appear among the prints'

5.3
Hans Vredeman de Vries, *Perspective* I, no. 12, 1604. Engraving, H.530.
Centre Canadien d'Architecture, Montréal.

shadowy recesses, but they are furtive, like the 1560 series from Antwerp: faceless men run away; a gondola, poled by an unseen driver, floats ominously on; an observer, smiling madly at nothing, looks down from an upper-floor window. At least one historian has seen Vredeman's engravings as preludes to Piranesi's *Carceri*.[28]

In his introduction Vredeman explains the novelty of his teaching program as a long-overdue relinquishing of secrets:

> One finds that many old, praiseworthy, and inventive masters have occupied themselves with the art of perspectives (*conste der Perspectiven*), and published numerous well-executed works expressing their opinions and the foundations of the art, with the help of illustrations of lines and circles. This has been done by authors of many nations—Italians, Frenchmen, and High-Germans; Albrecht Dürer is the most esteemed of these since, in my opinion, it is he who has studied nature's essence the best and made it visible [*bethoont*] in his works. Although rules, measurement, and bases for the same essence have been demonstrated in no less than nine books of perspective invented by me . . . there remains among them still no method; to be sure, no Dutchman in the Netherlands has devised or published such a method yet . . . for this reason we decided quickly upon the present work and published it.[29]

The book, Vredeman announces, will ally his own homegrown ingenuity with those of his continental forebears, "works by those of diverse nations: Italians, French, and

5.4
Hans Vredeman de Vries, *Perspective* I, no. 25, 1604. Engraving, H.544.
Centre Canadien d'Architecture, Montréal.

High-Germans."[30] Dürer is important, as we shall see below, as his 1525 tract on perspective seems to have been the immediate basis for Vredeman's own definitions. And yet the terminology of a "seeing-through" is older. It comes ultimately from Alberti's metaphor of the *aperta finestra*, the "open window," explained in the *Della Pittura*, first printed in 1540. This was the famous "veil" through which "the subject to be painted is seen."[31] The original metaphor (Alberti's manuscript was unillustrated) was intended to help craftsmen understand an artistic procedure based on optics. And although painters had achieved recessive effects similar to perspective well before the fifteenth century,[32] Alberti's work was crucial for naturalizing its foundations in the workings of vision, posing a "point of flight" *behind* the picture plane that anchored "what is seen" to the standing viewer's own sight lines. Alberti's feat was to codify the idea of a painting as an intersection between a viewed point and a beholder. Thus born, the notion of a transparent picture plane intimated that paintings could be constructed according to standardized positions, as if glimpsed through structured entities. Joel Snyder has pointed out that by reproducing the results of vision, Quattrocento perspective paintings in effect visualized the (Neoplatonic) idea that one paints not an object, but one's mental image of it.[33] In early modern Europe this meant a sought-after linking of art and optics. As a drawing system, perspective simply imported a model of sight into a model for making pictures.[34]

By 1600, the idea of the perspective tract as both a recipe *book* and an artwork itself meant that its content was buffered by new problematics.[35] Expense, marketability, the demands of engravers, editors, and authors frequently clashed;

5.5
Hans Vredeman de Vries, *Perspective* I, no. 36, 1604. Engraving, H.554. Centre Canadien d'Architecture, Montréal.

abstract theorization in the books was frequently just a pretext for authorial projects of self-promotion, for a guarding of copyright, for currying of princely favor, for the staging of professional attack, debasement, or praise, or even for a publisher's experimentation with new printing technologies. By the end of the sixteenth century, Alberti's original project and format (manuscript) had given way to a species of publication in which perspective's individual presentation, as much as the subject itself, had become a site of intellectual skirmishing, intensely distended and diffused.

Vredeman's work was unabashedly grounded in architecture, or more precisely, architectures. His scope, as he announces, consists of "churches, temples, palaces, rooms, chambers, galleries, city squares [*plaetsen*], hallways, hovels, marketplaces and streets."[36] We can recall that the architectural context for perspective was as old as the Trecento: Cennino Cennini urged artists to always use foreshortening "for buildings," and Filipo Brunelleschi's pinhole experiment in Florence deployed not just the Baptistery but the surrounding *piazza* as well.[37] Yet the exhaustiveness of architectural examples in Vredeman's book was completely unprecedented, save for one very particular source.

Jean Pélerin's extraordinary treatise, *De Artificiali Perspectiva*, printed in Toul in 1505, was the first tract to codify something called the *distance point* procedure of artificial perspective. Although this technique, too, had been known by artists since the late Middle Ages, it was popularized in northern Europe by Pélerin, whose book was sporadically issued in print in Germany and France until 1550.[38] Vredeman likely knew an edited pirated in Nuremberg in 1509 by the publisher Jörg Glockendon.[39]

5.6
Hans Vredeman de Vries, *Perspective* I, no. 41, 1604. Engraving, H.559. Centre Canadien d'Architecture, Montréal.

Pélerin—a priest, diplomat, Hebraicist, and antiquarian, wrote under the name "Viator" (traveler), and used a "principal point" to anchor his system, but focused on objects and rooms (Figure 5.8). Pélerin added to this point a pair of *tiers points* at the periphery of his constructions. These assumed, significantly, that the root of a perspective configuration resided in the picture plane itself, as opposed to a beholder's view through it, replacing Alberti's transcendent, imaginary rays (between scene and viewer) with hard orthogonals that intersected a horizon-line across the picture—lines drawn upon the surface itself.

But less than theory, Pélerin's real innovation was his use of woodcut demonstrations. These put the *tiers points* method vividly into action. Pélerin pictured tombs, church facades, fountains, furniture, and choir stalls. For, as Pélerin's title made clear, *De Artificiali Perspectiva* (On Artificial Perspective) was, like Vredeman's text, devoted to perspective as a construct, one that could—at best—approximate the effects of vision as a means towards crafting objects. Pélerin's book, too, used demonstrations and short instructions. These revolved—quite literally—around architecture. Pélerin:

> . . . one must always take account of the various views presented by objects including buildings. For one sees them straight on or at an angle, that is to say from in front or from a corner. And one may see them . . . from ground level or from above, and (as mentioned) from close and form afar.[40]

The mobility was a dramatic departure from Alberti's scheme, not least for its tolerance of visual whimsy. One of Pélerin's sixteenth-century followers, Jean Cousin, even

5.7
Hans Vredeman de Vries, *Perspective* II, no. 15, 1605. Engraving, H.582.
Centre Canadien d'Architecture, Montréal.

described his system as built upon "*points Accidentaux,*"[41] where a mobile viewpoint, flitting between scenes, became the essential format for explanation. In later Pélerin editions of 1509 and 1521, illustrations thematize this mobility by including sites that were geographically diffuse: cubicles, chateaux, even a woodcut of the bridge at Brioude (Figure 5.9),[42] the facade of Notre Dame in Paris and the cathedral at Angiers.[43] The images were captioned with staccato rhymed stanzas that reinforced a general thematic of itinerancy and flux.

If Pélerin's book codified a new method of perspective, it also outlined a new medium and context to discuss it. Rather than presenting perspective as the natural extension of—and corollary to—optics, the poet and traveler Pélerin rendered it as a sequence of mobile demonstrations, based on objects framed by the format of the printed book. Scenes lifted directly from local surroundings in France became examples. In defining perspective as an adding-on of viewed points, it engaged, ingeniously, the capacity of engraving not just to reproduce views of the world but to multiply and disseminate them.

Svetlana Alpers has made a very influential argument positing Pélerin and Vredeman as representative of a "northern" corollary to the perspective of Alberti.[44] Neither perspective method was entirely different from Alberti's, however; indeed, Vredeman's preface advised readers that he will not depart from an august tradition of perspective publications, but will, in fact, unabashedly amplify them. Yet Alpers is entirely correct in calling attention to Vredeman's reliance upon pictures rather than text for explanation. As he writes in the *Perspective*'s preface, engravings—more so than

5.8
Jean Pèlerin, *De artificiali perspectiva* (Toul, 1509), fol. b3r. Bibliothèque Nationale, Paris.

what he touts as his "clearly adumbrated descriptions" (*beschrijvinghe claerlijck uyt-geleyt*)—will be the focus of the work:

> It is not our intention to make the lovers of this art too melancholic or depressed *[zwaermoedich]* with a surfeit of reading matter, but rather to set

5.9
Jean Pèlerin, *De artificiali perspectiva* (Toul, 1509), fol. b4r. Bibliothèque Nationale, Paris.

out everything, as amply and sufficient as we feel necessary in as brief a form as possible through enlivening figures.[45]

Vredeman's figures, as Pélerin's, drive the treatise. One plate opens on a geometric square (Figure 5.10, H.518) glimpsed in groundplan from above. The beholder's

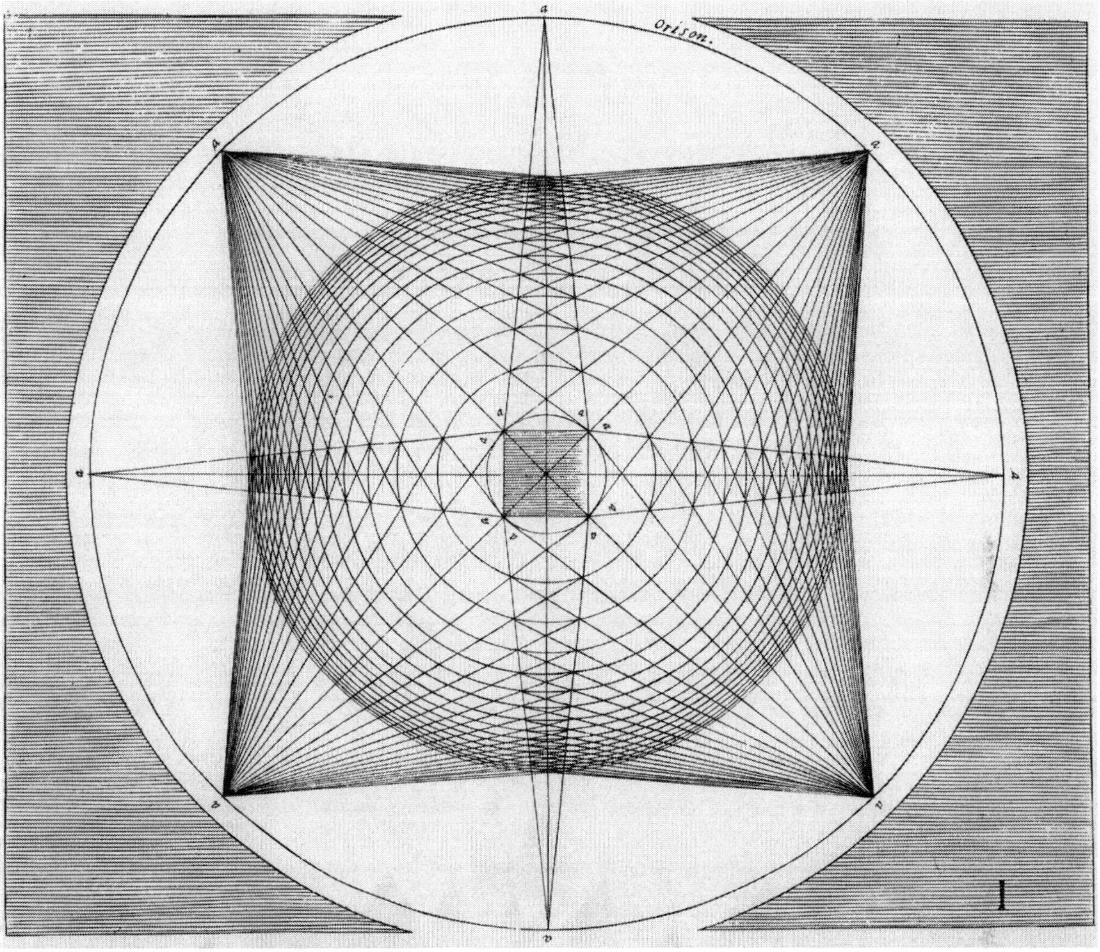

5.10
Hans Vredeman de Vries, *Perspective* I, no. 1, 1604. Engraving, H.518.
Centre Canadien d'Architecture, Montréal.

standpoint is at the center, at the intersection of the lines *aaaa*. Rays from beyond the circle, springing from points on a larger concentric one, correspond to the various "*oogh-punten*," which meet at the beholder's sight line: these points, arranged on a sweeping, 360-degree horizon, demarcate the field seen by the stationary viewer. While not depicted, the viewer is positioned at the crossing of this vortex of orthogonals, and sees them only as they meet the horizon, again marked clearly and overtly as a circling "*orison.*" Such different points, Vredeman's opening image shows, are recast anew by every glance over the sweeping radius: "If one turns . . . another point is formed, even if one looks up or down or sideways," he writes in the accompanying paragraph, ". . . every look . . . creates another point" (*elck sien een ander punct maect*).[46]

Other plates show this casting on a frontal level, against jumbles of still more geometric solids (Figure 5.11, H.521, Figure 5.12, H.538). Now presented with a baseline (Vredeman speaks of a "*baselinie*"), one looks across to that same horizon (again, "*ori-son*") which was formerly surveyed from above. The various points along the horizon (*e* and *c*) define the field presented to us across a distance. Rays circumscribe a tiled

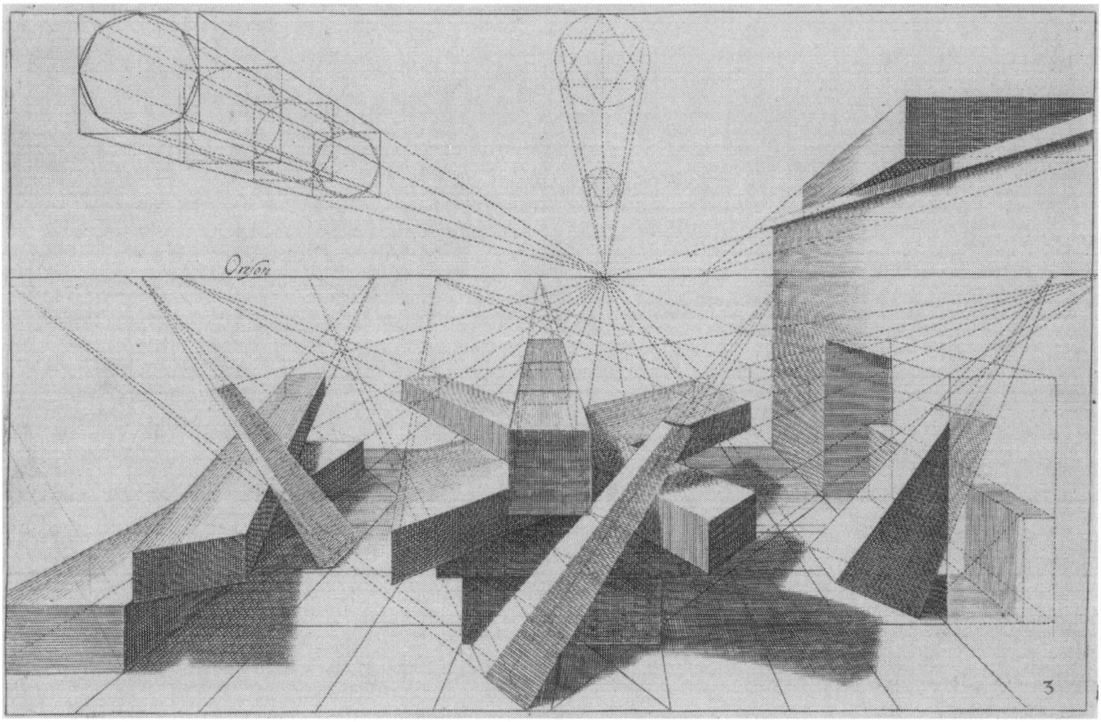

5.11
Hans Vredeman de Vries, *Perspective* II, no. 3, 1605. Engraving, H.570.
Centre Canadien d'Architecture, Montréal.

floor sweeping into the background, or a stacking of blocks. These rays withdraw from the horizon at measured points, creating a grid of quick recession. It is the *orison*, essentially a summation of an infinite number of possible viewpoints, which anchors the whole construction. Alberti never spoke of such a phenomenon,[47] mentioning only a line through a *punctus centrus*, which was used to mark the height of sitters' heads. But Vredeman stresses the horizon's fundamentality: it represents "*het grondt van perspective*," the foundation of perspective,[48] which delimits the visible field: "one cannot look down to things above the horizon or up to things below it."[49] Set along this *orison*, various nodes can be set far apart or close to one another, to expand or contract the picture and the solids described.

In later sections of Book I's plates, Vredeman's mobile *orison* initiates a complex sequence of architectures. Plate 3 confronts the viewer with a deserted room (Figure 5.13, H.520) in which five shelves rib the angles of planes. Concrete objects appear for the first time; a linen chest-door creaks open and four different "eye-points," marked by disembodied sockets, connect a center line. This multiple point schema continues in subsequent pages: a corridor with wooden beams, an arcade, a double archway, a rusticated barrel vault over a waterway, and, finally, a plummeting view through more sets of columns (Figure 5.4). Vredeman's texts describe the scenarios as different applications for the mobile, darting eye. Before long, the paragraphs simply list the architectural features described (Figure 0.3):

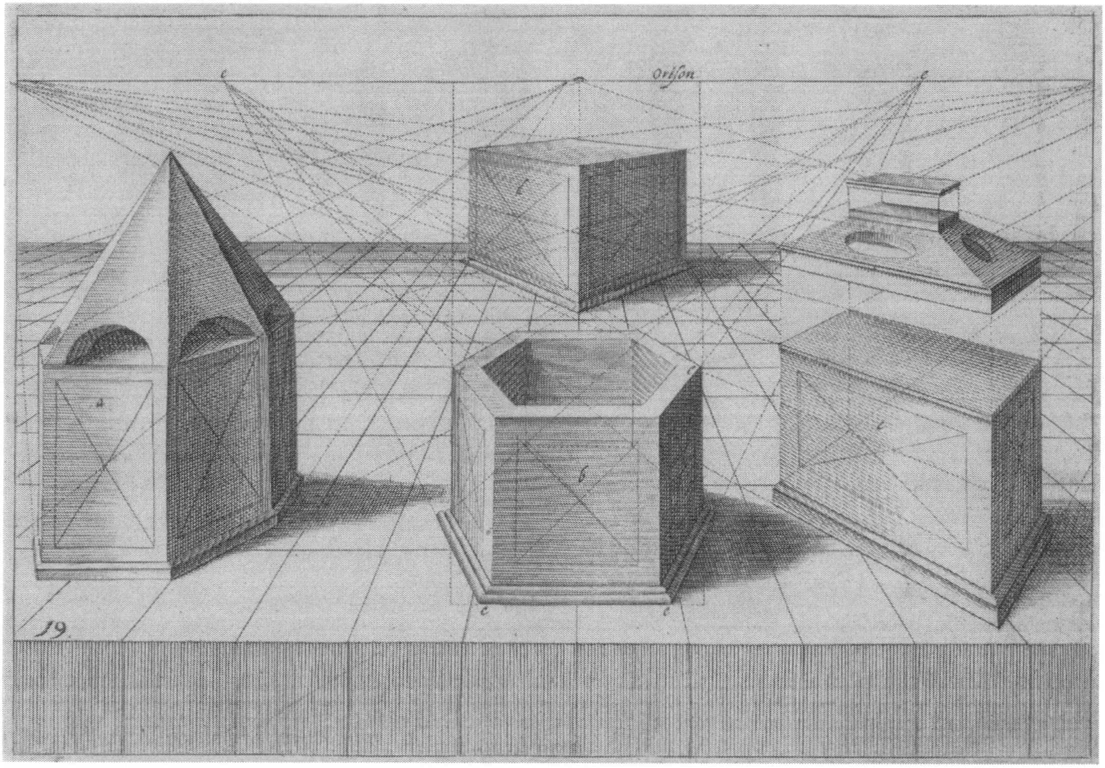

5.12
Hans Vredeman de Vries, *Perspective* II, no 19, 1605. Engraving, H.538.
Centre Canadien d'Architecture, Montréal.

> . . . in this figure, a view into a palace in the antique or old manner is represented . . . the piece of architecture marked "a" has been designed with fine architraves, friezes, and cornices, one on top of the other. In the view, four columns recede, each farther than the other, and join beneath a cross-vault . . .[50]

The imaginary structures themselves become the work's focus rather than any didactic arrangement in space, and Vredeman's refusal to ground the images in any explicit program makes their visual emptiness all the more disorienting, even as he is attempting to teach by example.

But in the final parts of Book I, human beholders have entered the scene. In plate 28 figures are lashed to the ground and awkwardly foreshortened (Figure 5.14). A box-like room is crossed by sight lines, hatched shadows, half-opened doors and windows. Two men step into the grid, while a third, immobilized, lies feet first on the ground, trussed by diagonals—a reference to the traditional perspectival problem of the foreshortened corpse.[51] Both entering figures' sight lines are, once again, concomitant with the marked "*orison.*" Yet their placement among the panoply of surfaces is too staggered to recall measurements, the kind of things Alberti called *braccia*. Rather, Vredeman's surfaces here evoke multiple moving planes, instead of a fixed cadre of objects. This specific plate was recently likened to the collage-effects of avant-garde film.[52]

5.13
Hans Vredeman de Vries, *Perspective* I, no. 3, 1604. Engraving, H.520.
Centre Canadien d'Architecture, Montréal.

All three of Vredeman's inhabitants in the engraving have their hands outstretched to the right or left. The palm itself of the figure in the far center background is bisected by the *orison*. Just as these models are seeing—and being seen—within Vredeman's diagram, they are also visibly touching the lines and grid that envelop them. Alternatively turning a doorknob, reaching against a threshold, or pressing palm-down on the floor, they engage the room as a tactile environment. Doors open and shut, figures beckon and fall, the separate hands activate the perspective's unfolding. Vredeman's lines and rectangles syncopate like the turning of pages. This is perspective rooted in the book as experience.

Dürer's long shadows

Where does this understanding of perspective in print come from? The pre-Vredeman history of the art-tract in northern Europe is characterized by opportunism, delay, and the bestriding influence of Albrecht Dürer. Vredeman made much of Dürer in his book's preface, and from Dürer's *Instruction in the Art of Measurement* (1525, and 2nd edition, 1538) he lifted the assumption that Italian treatises might frustrate unlettered apprentices. Dürer, like Viator, had depended on graphic woodcut illustrations; "to make bodies suitable for use in paintings,"[53] to picture the transcription of three-dimensional objects into two. Dürer intended his 1525 discussion as part of a larger, unrealized work, *Ein Spies der Malerknabe*, (Food for a Young Painter). He emphasized the idea of perspective as a fusion of rational knowledge (*Kunst*) and practical skill (*Brauch*). Further,

5.14
Hans Vredeman de Vries, *Perspective* I, no. 28, 1604. Engraving, H.547. Centre Canadien d'Architecture, Montréal.

Dürer addressed his audience as a master conversing with a pupil, frequently using the informal "*du*"; Alberti, the other great teacher of perspective, had couched his theory in a lecture format, using the gentlemanly "*lei*"—the second-person singular—to give his presentation the appearance of a chat among equals.

Put simply, Dürer's method established a means to compose rectangular space first, and then place projected solids onto it in light and shadow. This was an overtly mathematical version of what Pélerin had done. The specifics of Dürer's drawing machines, illustrated in the last two folios of the *Unterweyssung*, are well known.[54] But second editions of Dürer's book detailed a more "physical" method for rendering solids out of printed surfaces. Dealing with polyhedrons, Dürer described a way for "footprints" of solids to be illustrated in woodcut (Figure 5.15.), paper matrices Panofsky called "nets".[55] When cut out of paper, these nets were meant to be folded and assembled to form small paper objects, usually a three-dimensional model of the solid under discussion—in one case a cuboctahedron. With the nets Dürer imparted perspective a method coeval with the kinds of polyhedral shapes which would be used by some of the most influential writers on perspective in Germany—intarsia makers and goldsmiths. Wenzel Jamnitzer's *Perspectiva Corpus Regularium* of 1568, for example, dedicated to Emperor Maximilian, was one of the more high-end of these German publications, and included ornate illustrations of geometric solids, cast in shadow, and leaning precariously against one another (Figure 5.16).

These books focused on bodies—on perspective as a means "to treat solids," as Dürer put it, rather than spaces[56]—but readers were often perplexed. Abbess Eufemia Pirckheimer, sister of Dürer's great patron Willibald Pirckheimer, wrote to her brother in 1528 about the *Unterweyssung*'s instructions: "we have received a book by Albrecht Dürer dedicated to you . . . we are pleased with it, but our paintress thinks that she does not need it, and she can practice her art just as well without it."[57] In fact, the

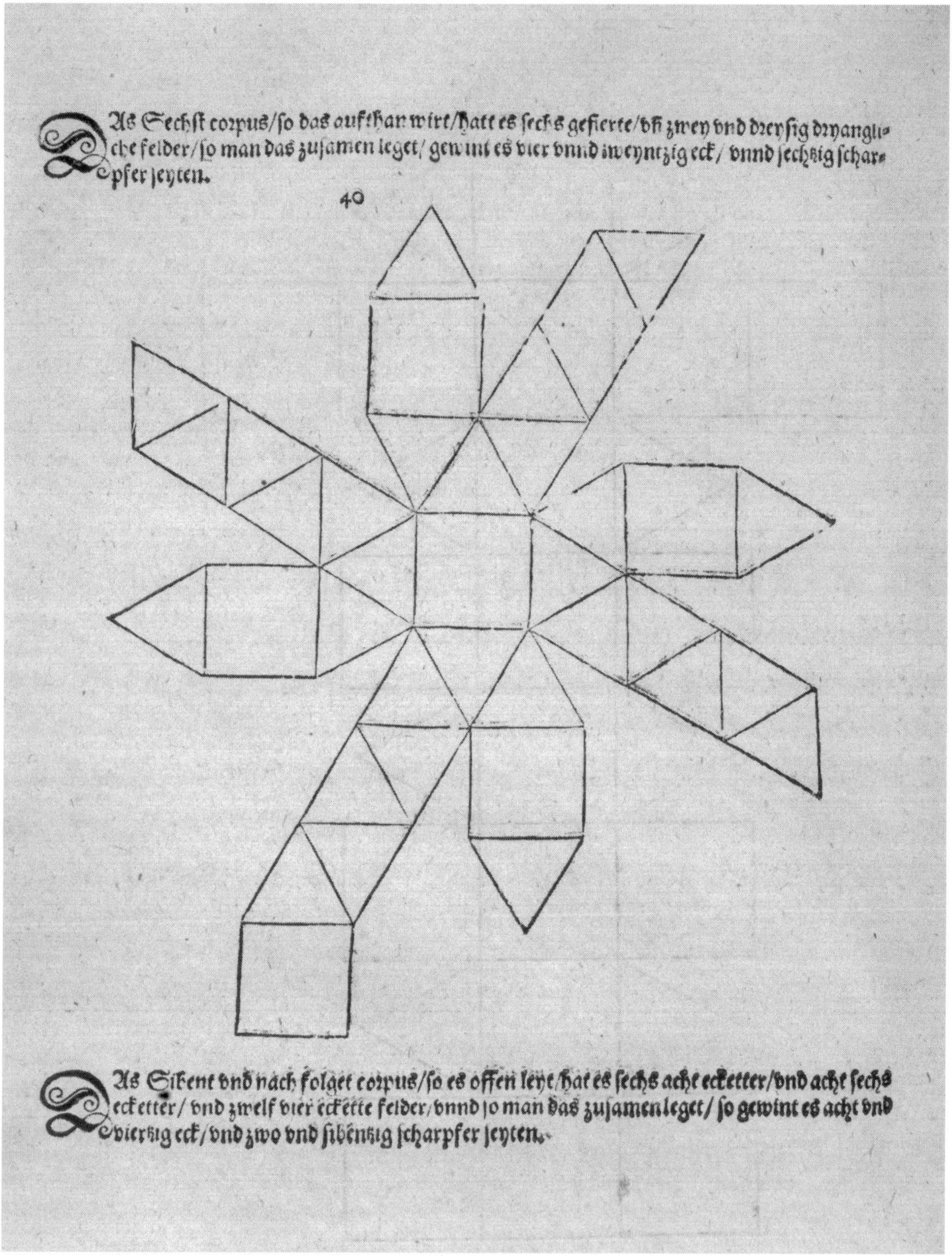

5.15

Albrecht Dürer, *Unterweyssung der Messung* (Nuremberg, 1525), fig. 40.

Marquand Library of Art and Archaeology, Princeton University.

5.16
Wenzel Jamnitzer, *Perspectiva Corpus Regularum* (Nuremberg, 1568), plate III.
Herzog-August Bibliothek, Wolfenbüttel.

dozens of perspective *kunstbuchleinen*, or little art books, which followed in Dürer's wake from presses in Nuremberg and Augsburg, exploited the *Unterweyssung*'s complexity, offering simplified versions as correctives. Jamnitzer's 1568 tract lamented the "errors" of earlier books in its preface, and avoided including any text.[58] Hans Lencker's *Perspectiva* (Nuremberg, 1571) claimed to distill Dürer's "troublesome and long-winded" (*mühselig und weitleufftig*) demonstrations. Heinrich Lautensack, in his 1564 book on proportion, sympathized with Dürer seeming "*zu schwer*" (too ponderous) for young apprentices.[59] And when Hieronymus Rodler published his 1531 study (most likely written by a local Wittelsbach duke, Johannes II), he claimed that Dürer's books were so "theoretical and incomprehensible [*uberkünstlich und unbegreifflich*] that only exceptionally learned people [*Hochuerstendigen*] might find them of use."[60]

Rodler's treatise also presented one of the first images of a perspectivist at work (Figure 5.17). In the last woodcut of the treatise—the same space Dürer devoted to his own drawing machines—a young master uses a drawing screen, squinting through a window while transferring a landscape beyond to a paper on a drawing board. Rodler's text names the window ("*rame*") posing it as a grid graphed into sections.[61] Legs askew, the apprentice cranes his neck and gazes out at the moutainside as he adds a final stroke to the top edge of a cliff. The scene recalls other images in Rodler's *buchlein* in its picturing of labor: stonemasons building walls, or carpenters shaving wood beams for joinery (Figure 5.18). Perspective is here nestled among the skills needed by a mason or woodworker as well as a painter. A panel painting in the style of Félix Chrétien, now in

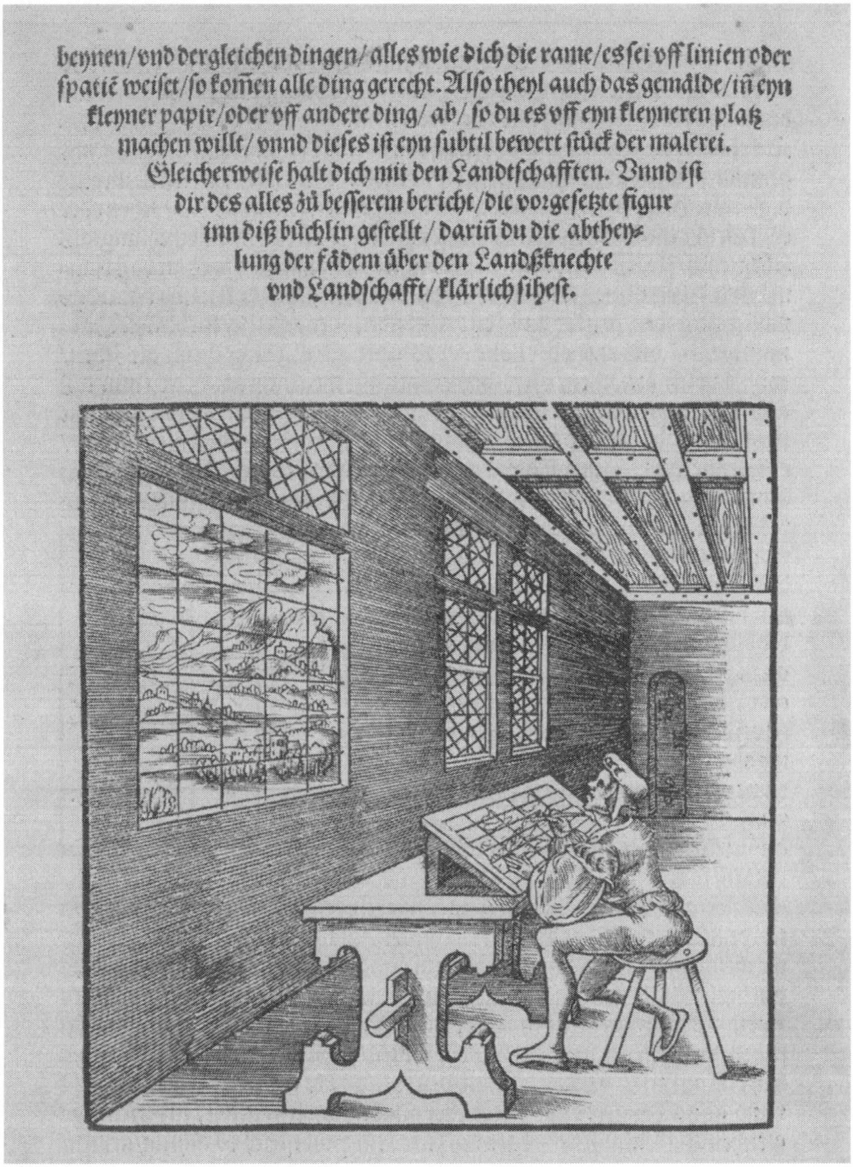
beynen/vnd dergleichen dingen/ alles wie dich die rame/es sei vff linien oder spatiẽ weiset/so kom̃en alle ding gerecht. Also theyl auch das gemälde/iñ eyn kleyner papir/oder vff andere ding/ ab/ so du es vff eyn kleyneren platz machen wilt/ vnnd dieses ist eyn subtil bewert stück der malerei. Gleicherweise halt dich mit den Landtschafften. Vnnd ist dir des alles zů besserem bericht/die vorgesetzte figur inn diß büchlin gestellt / dariñ du die abtheylung der fädem über den Landßknechte vnd Landschafft/ klärlich sihest.

5.17
Hieronymus Rodler, *Eyn schön nützlich Büchlin vnd Vnderweisung der Kunst des Messens . . .* (Simmern, 1531), fol. Hiiiv.
Germanisches Museum, Nuremberg.

Frankfurt, and probably by an anonymous Netherlandish artist working in France, reveals how Rodler's models could be used (Figure 5.19).[62] Three men strain and sweat in a basement, shifting barrels with ropes and ladders amidst doorways that splay and jut forcefully along angular planes. Just as for Rodler's carpenters, or for the assiduous young draughtsman at the window with his *rame*, in this painting, too, perspective is work, a tortuous practice of toil and effort.

Illustrated digests of "German" perspective like Rodler's envisaged perspective as a species of ornament explicitly tied to guild methods of woodwork.[63] Such books, humble but well illustrated, were often means by which Netherlandish artisans

5.18
Hieronymus Rodler, *Eyn schön nützlich Büchlin vnd Vnderweisung der Kunst des Messens . . .* (Simmern, 1531), fol. F5r.
Germanisches Museum, Nuremberg.

came into contact with Dürer's theory.[64] Printed perspective "*leerboecken*" were available on the Amsterdam book market around 1600.[65] Such books tended to identify their audience and subjects as widely and as internationally as possible, naming carpenters, and intarsia workers in their titles. Being less expensive and easier to understand than Dürer's *Unterweyussung*, these *Kunstbuchleinen*, with scant text, required no translation, and proved useful as patterns across media for designers in and of themselves. In fact, intarsia was the main application for perspective patterns in South Germany starting around 1560. In places where religious commissions, in the wake of Luther, had often dried up, artists often turned to perspective in books as an outlet for work, making (and using) designs that could be copied out as templates, and,

5.19
Pseudo-Félix Chrétien, *Laborers in a Wine Cellar,* c.1570. Oil on panel, 56.5 × 55.1.
Städelisches Museum, Frankfurt au Main.

as Jamnitzer's and later Vredeman's would do, simultaneously appeal to collectors. The Augsburg artist Erasmus Loy, for example, included pages of perspective intarsia alongside designs for ornamental grotesques in a 1557 book of chiaroscuro woodcuts.[66]

Within this tradition of South German tracts, perspective publications became attuned to applications outside of painting (Loy, for instance, was named as a wallpaper designer in documents, and at one point his woodcuts were used as decorative friezes). Results were exported to practical *handwerk*. Chests and cupboards from Zeeland survive which follow Jamnitzer's patterns exactly.[67] Tyrolean writing tables and coin chests from Augsburg and Innsbruck (Figure 5.20), dating to the 1560s and 1570s (many of which often found their way to the Netherlands), copied craft books as well, and seventeenth-century *Kasten* (chests) exist where perspective prints were glued directly onto wood surfaces, as a kind of *Flattenpapier*, or wallpaper.[68] An oak chest now in Leuven (Figure 5.21) represents one instance where a carpenter pasted and varnished one of Vredeman's plates from the second book of the *Perspective* onto a door.[69]

5.20
South Tyrol, two-winged coin chest, c.1570–80. Pine and walnut with ebony inlay, 130 × 183 × 90. Schloss Ambras, Innsbruck.

The idea of perspective as an aesthetic of surface decoration, as a species of ornament was far from new. In 1547, Walter Ryff published a treatise on the relations between mathematical and "practical" perspective. He noted how for craftsmen, perspective's realm was the sturdy world of objects, unlike that of "geometers":

> The mathematician involves himself in fashioning groups and forms of things only mentally (*im sinn und verstand*); he ignores their material reality: we shall present the subjects we treat as perceptible.[70]

Ryff goes on to remark, in a remarkable passage that has been isolated by Jeanne Peiffer, that for Ryff the purview of perspective was not limited to "*den gemehl*" (the picture), but to "whatever you would like to set in perspective" (*was du in die perspectiva bringen wilt*):[71] furniture, dead bodies, and buildings. This was the appeal of perspective to collectors of objects. Lencker's 1571 volume, for example, depicted rings, bronze pyramids, and Roman letters. Used variously to model door panels in Ulm, the book also won him an appointment teaching perspective to the elector of Saxony at Dresden.[72]

5.21
Anonymous Netherlandish, Four-chambered intarsia linen chest, c.1620. Oak, ebony, maple, rosewood, agate inlay. 139 × 168 × 68 cm.
Stedelijke Museum, Leuven.

The work of the German perspectivists after Dürer was, in fact, exceptionally popular at ducal courts, the destination of much of Vredeman's own travel. Lorenz Stoer's remarkable *Geometria et perspectiva* (Augsburg, 1567, Figures 5.22, 5.23) was a compendium of small, strange geometrical landscapes, and an exemplar was recorded in Duke Julius's library in Wolfenbüttel when Vredeman was there.[73] Stoer's stunning plates compressed strange rocks, vines, trees, and ruins into precipitously hilly landscapes. His title, for its part, addressed "cabinetmakers and amateurs [*Liebhaberen*]". In the sheets, strapwork shapes teeter in tight forest clearings, and pile onto rocky crags. As with Vredeman's tract, beams often lie fallen or precariously stacked against one another. Polygons tower over strange gardens, as crumbling architectures jut into the foreground. Stoer's prints cluttered the picture plane with jagged bodies, hybrids of geometrical decay that pushed up against the surface, and at times seemed to occlude the "perspective" recession altogether. Christopher Wood has demonstrated the numerous ways that Stoer, like Vredeman, furnished patterns for *real* intarsia surfaces (in Bavaria and the Tyrol), and that these patterns, as prints, were the subject of fiercely contested lawsuits over intellectual property.[74] Much of the legal trouble sprang from different ideas about what defined "appropriable" designs; far from neutral repositories

5.22
Lorenz Stoer, *Geometria et Perspectiva* (Augsburg, 1567), plate 4. Woodcut. Department of Printing and Graphic Arts, Houghton Library, Harvard University.

of viewed reality, intarsia perspective images were in many cases copyrighted performances of highly personal invention. They were the legal and aesthetic reverses of an "objective" view.

The German intarsists—even less than Pèlerin—were not interested in mathematical reconstructions of optical experience. Rather, in their adoption of perspective as a method for *pattern*, something used chiefly by craftsmen and painters, they—quite remarkably—forsook perspective's capacity for depth and accepted its power to con-

5.23
Lorenz Stoer, *Geometria et Perspectiva* (Augsburg, 1567), plate 10. Woodcut. Department of Printing and Graphic Arts, Houghton Library, Harvard University.

figure flat spaces. What the German works manifested was the idea that perspective was not simply a scientific procedure to extend the real world, but, alternatively—in a potentially post-Reformation sense—a means to create a new one; one that would engage craft traditions and, in a doctrinally-safe manuever, turn its glance inward rather than out.

Even second-hand, these German books carried with them a trace—however diluted—of Dürer's teachings and prestige. The "Dürer-Renaissance" of c.1600 was particularly marked in the Netherlands, where the artist's visit to Antwerp of 1520–21 was well remembered. The desultory character of much homegrown Netherlandish art from the late century cast the former moment in a posthumous glow. Hieronymus Wierix, for example, Vredeman's one-time neighbor in Antwerp, made a living repeatedly republishing Dürer's *Study of St Jerome* after 1566 (Figure 5.24), a design that Dürer distributed widely himself when he visited the Netherlands.[75] Particularly during Vredeman's tenure in Prague (1596–98), the lingering potency of Dürer's work was everywhere; Rudolf II owned several paintings, Hans Hoffmann was an overt imitator of Dürer's nature studies, and the Netherlandish engraver Aegidius Sadeler II copied the Marian engravings from imperial collections.[76] As went Dürer's reputation in Europe, so often did recognizably German prints as a whole.[77] Even materials like Stoer's *Perspectiva* would have been buoyed by the general reputation of Nuremberg art c.1600, the very moment at which Vredeman was composing his own perspective tract.

In fact, Dürer's most direct contribution to perspective for the majority of Dutch artists was less through his treatise than through independently copied prints, such as the *St Jerome*.[78] This image later became crucial to Dürer's greatest modern essayist, Erwin Panofsky. "We imagine that we ourselves have been admitted to it," he wrote in 1924, "because the floor seems to extend under our own feet . . . the representation [is] determined not by the objective lawfulness of the architecture, but by the subjective appearance of a beholder who has just appeared."[79] *St Jerome*, for the early Panofsky, pictured the specific capacity of the *printed* perspectival image to be viewed and scrutinized individually; the beholding that Panofsky describes as taking place at the level of the Renaissance viewer, is mirrored in Jerome's own hunched contemplation at his desk. Dürer's system, claimed Panofsky, thus marked the historical revision of an Albertian science, which took as its basis the vertically oriented, public surfaces of frescoes and walls.[80]

Seen around 1600, Vredeman's etchings would have brought the polyhedral exempla of Dürer and the crumbling strapwork of Stoer's craft-based perspective (Figure 5.23) violently into the present of the new century. Vredeman's book recalled and restaged for print collectors a perspective that had long since abandoned any pretense to mimesis. Indeed, whether aimed at simplifying older, often obscure techniques for rendering objects, or at the presentation of new arguments for or against Euclidian space, Vredeman's engravings—like the *kunsbuchleinen* themselves—were almost deliberately archaic.

Windows and opacities

Outside the forum of the treatise proper, what was referred to as perspective around 1600 was a large body of phenomena, dealing not only with goldsmithing and machines, but with alchemy and theology. It was also frequently imbricated with senses other than sight. For the Oxford occultist Robert Fludd (b.1574), perspective was one of the liberal arts, along with astronomy, geomancy, and music. In his colossal treatise, *De Naturae*

5.24
Hieronymus Wierix, *St Jerome in his Study* (after Dürer), c.1566. Engraving, H.1248.
Stedelijke Prentenkabinet, Antwerp.

Simia,[81] Fludd described perspective as a tactile process that allowed the eye to grasp objects (Figure 5.25), and, like Vredeman, stressed the centrality of the architectural horizon in arranging compositions. Wenzel Jamnitzer, meanwhile, writing in the preface to his 1568 tract, had likened perspective to an exhilarating array of objects, rather than the seeing of them: "we call perspective everything in the entire world . . . the terrestrial things—mountains valleys, buildings, castles, cities, villages, and other bodies [*Corpora*] . . ."[82] Seventeenth-century Dutch dictionaries define *perspectiva* specifically as a *konstwoord*.[83]

As a species of image, perspective often retained older associations with things deceptive, false, deceitful, or, in the years following the Reformation, idolatrous. In

5.25
Robert Fludd, *Utriusque cosmi maioris scilicet et minoris metaphysica, physica atqve technical historia* (Oppenheim, 1617–21), vol. 1, part IV, p. 293.
Department of Rare Books and Special Collections, Firestone Library, Princeton University.

the Middle Ages, "perspective" was often lumped in with *contrefeyt*, a trade category for any good "made to appear other than it is."[84] Contemporary with Vredeman's tract was the swindler-hero of Ben Jonson's *Alchemist* (1603), who used "perspectives" to lure wealthy gentlemen into financing his endeavors.[85] Most good-natured condemnations of perspective were folded into those of rhetorical dissimulation in general, of artists' and writers' cloaking of the real with ornamental, with needlessly showy and manipulative effects. "Too much perspective," Van Mander noted in the *Grondt*, "can be a hindrance to a painting."[86] In a remarkable Florentine carnival ballad from around 1518, unearthed by Claudio Gullién, revelers even sang of *prospettiva* as the false describer of the world:

> if wealth, wisdom, and faith are falsely rendered from the outside by color, then he who believes in the clothing of these errs more than the others . . . it all derives solely from the fact that the visible world is done in perspective [*che mondo e tutto fatto in prospettiva.*][87]

As with Baldassare Castiglione, who spoke of *prospettiva* in his advice to courtiers,[88] perspective could symbolize not sheer mendacity but the function of appearances *as* appearances in relating to society. Indeed, Lucien Febvre has shown that sight itself, as one matrix for perspective, ranked third in the sixteenth-century hierarchy of the senses, behind touch and hearing.[89] Calvinist doctrine, famously de-emphasized bodily vision as the means to apprehend the "true church."

The metaphor of perspective as image cleaved from essence was often reliant upon the conceit of an architectural inwardness. In describing the self in his essay "On Solitude," Montaigne deployed the image of the "*arrière boutique toute nostre*"—the room behind the shop all our own—to symbolize the individual, unexplored interior space that lurked beneath social facades.[90] Artists increasingly pictured perspective as a withdrawn, denatured condition. Paolo Uccello, ridiculed by Vasari for his soulless fanaticism for geometry, "shut himself up in his house and devoted all his time to perspective, which kept him poor and secluded until the day he died."[91] Perspective and intarsia, specifically shared a history of such associations with dolor and introspection. A writing cabinet of 1569 from Ulm bore an admonishing inscription: "If man were to reflect on who he is and when he arrived here he would become more pious on earth."[92] Indeed, the workshop exigencies of intarsia—slotting dissimilar, cut and burned wood pieces into craggy surface patterns—connoted a laborious hardening of theory. Around 1565, an Augsburg intarsist working in the Escorial placed Raphael's figure of Heraclitus, the philosopher of tumult and introspection, in a ruined perspective colonnade.[93] The flattened pattern substantiated a literal detachment from the world, in a doorway leading to the Philip II's private apartments. Finally, in 1561, Franz Brun, a metalworker and late Dürer copyist, published a tiny engraving Bartsch called simply "a sad-seeming room" ("*une chambre avec un air triste*")[94] enclosing a personification of melancholy in plunging recession (Figure 5.26).[95] In the tiny print, no more than 5 centimeters across, a grid extends below a seated figure who sits pensively in the foreground. Her eyes are cast downward, with attributes of sphere, cube, and ruler unused at her feet. Although her tools are within reach they sit forlorn, as the windows reveal a landscape outside; the figure indeed recalls the *zwarmoedich* (melancholic) reader Vredeman pondered in the opening of his tract. Erhard Schön later went on to staff his planes with weird cubic marionettes who, equally confined by perspective, struggle to stand, walk, and be seen (Figure 5.31).

Early in the sixteenth century, Lutheran teachings had problematized exactly how perspective might relate to tactile objects. Schön, in fact, issued an illustrated broadsheet in 1530 parodying the radical iconomachy advocated by Karlstadt and Zwingli, in the *Lament of the Persecuted Idols* (Figure 5.27). The same year Schön described what appeared to be the results of the earlier print's image cleansing (Figure 5.28), with a cleared courtyard of bricks and archways. When Vredeman's own intarsia designs *Formae* series from 1560 was republished in Antwerp by Philips Galle in 1601 (just three years before the *Perspective* appeared), its original front page with the coat of arms of Cardinal Mansveldt (Figure 5.29, H.51/I), was burnished out.[96] For the second state, Galle re-cut the same plate, dropping the oval to its side to use it as a title plaque with a Latin description of the series (Figure 5.30, H.51/II). Thus was ecclesiastic heraldry swapped for lines of text—a micro-iconoclasm in the context of perspective, where image was supplanted with the literal word.

Engravings and intarsia—media limited in their chromatic range—in fact

5.26
Franz Brun,
***Melancholia,* 1561.**
Engraving, H.87.
British Museum,
London.

spoke to a stubborn paradox of post-Reformation art, as to how perspective—a *Durchsehung* synonymous with art's claims to take the viewer imaginatively beyond an object itself—might function in a Protestant milieu. This was a milieu that was ostensibily suspicious of images' potential for enchantment. Thus, rather than "seeing through" the

5.27
Erhard Schön, *Lament of the Persecuted Idols*, c.1530. Woodcut, B.147.
Landesmuseum, Gotha.

things of this world, perspective, for Lutheran commentators like Karlstadt, often accomplished its opposite, embodying the "cold gaze" of pictures,[97] their status as dead matter. Karlstadt in fact praised Lucas Cranach's acuity at painting "perspectivally," exclaiming, "what a superb art! 'tis the only way to paint!"[98] Perspective appealed because it declared pictures to be images second, and crafted things first. What Vredeman, then, might ask his readers to "see through" with the *deursiende* of his title is not an imaginary window, but pictorial illusion itself. He asks them to alight on the *surfaces* making up its exquisite grids and spheres.

Plate 30 of Vredeman's *Perspective* (Figure 5.33), itself drawn from a German treatise by Schön (Figures 5.31, 5.32, H.549), went so far as to reconfigure what, exactly, this *deursiende* is. Here, the back of one viewer fronts a picture plane staffed with four onlookers. Centered on a recessed arch, he stands beneath a giant groin vault, viewing it, and being viewed, from without. What, precisely, is this *Rückenfigur* doing (Figure 5.33)? The inward-looking viewer had a long tradition in Netherlandish art; Jan van Eyck had placed two small back-turners at the center of his *Rolin Madonna*, Rogier van de Weyden bracketed a man and a woman gesturing towards a landscape in his *St. Luke Painting the Virgin*, and Pieter Bruegel set his two travelers gazing upon a road in the large *Miltes Requiescentes* (Figure 2.6). In these cases the *Rückenfigur* established pictorial scale and marked off a picture field rhetorically. Alberti had recommended that good painters deploy a supplementary figure in their compositions, "someone who admonishes and points out to us what is happening there."[99] In Vredeman's image, however, the *Rückenfigur* points to the *absence* of anything happening, and models the viewer's experience of the composition as limited by the bisecting *orison*. The work is not incompatible with the unpicturable, "turned-away God" of Protestant evangelicals and post-Tridentine theologians, the hidden deity of the Old Testament, present but without a face.[100]

Thomas Puttfarken has argued that the invention of perspective, long assumed to represent an art-historical break with the medieval image, in fact resuscitated an important function of the icon. Perspective, like the *Andachtsbild*, served first and foremost to position the viewer before an image.[101] This kind of faculty describes

5.28
Erhard Schön,
Empty Courtyard,
c.1532. Woodcut, B.308.
Universitätsibliothek, Erlangen.

precisely the dichotomous scenario at work with Vredeman's Plate 30, only in reverse. What the icon once accomplished in terms of God's visage, the perspectival composition does under the gaze of the artist. In both cases "I" as a viewer am interpolated as a subject only in relation to a greater ideology.[102]

Vredeman's scant texts, too, deny any real aesthetic of disclosure. The instructions in the *Perspective* tend to be extremely brief or elliptical, as in the blasé description of plate XXVII:

> Here is the twenty-seventh figure, showing a building designed using the same groundlines and orthogonals described before. It shows three arches made in the antique manner, the middle one being sectioned into five parts, and the two side archways each into three . . . as for the way of foreshortening

5.29

Hans Vredeman de Vries, *Oval Intarsia Designs, Title Page* (First State), c.1560. Etching, H.51.

Stedelijke Bibliotheek, Leeuwarden.

5.30
Hans Vredeman de Vries, *Oval Intarsia Designs, Title Page* (Second State), 1601. Etching, H.51/II.
Avery Architectural and Fine Arts Library, Columbia University.

> (*vercorten*) of the archway, this has been shown already; this figure is intended only to illustrate it for the lover of the art (*liefhebber*).[103]

The problem is that Vredeman has *not* in fact described the method before, at least not after his initial excursus. Vredeman, the *rederijker*, is interested chiefly in ekphrasis. His subsequent addresses are redundant and generally unforthcoming on how the "figures" should be drawn, yet full of copious detail as to what is within the engraving. The inadequacy of Vredeman's textual explanation was, in fact, a common complaint. In 1628, a Gouda mathematician named Isaac de Ville published a pamphlet detailing a hypothetical conversation between a carpenter, a painter, and a "painter-architect."[104] The latter mentioned Vredeman's *Perspective* as an example of the sources good artists should avoid: "it is about as easy to learn something from [de Vries's work] as to catch a bird from the sky," de Ville wrote, "I have never met anyone who has learned something from its prints."[105] Less of a dig at Vredeman's specific work, de Ville's comments probably speak of a seventeenth-century frustration with perspective books in general. Even as Vredeman's vistas open and appear co-extensive with our gaze, it is clearly Vredeman's—not our—ability to make views proliferate which is the theme of the book, to "*een andere punct maect*" with each cast of his eye. Vredeman's instructions waste

5.31
Erhard Schön, *Underweysung der Proportzion und Stellung der Bossen* (Nuremberg, 1538), fol. Ciir.
Metropolitan Museum of Art, New York, Harris Brisbane Dick Fund, 1946.

little time in describing steps: nowhere does the "learning" de Ville saw as the book's charge come to figure.

The *Perspective* as Treatise II: rivalries and users

For the art historians Theodor Hetzer and Hans Sedlmayr, later sixteenth-century perspective revealed a distended image of grander historical crises—crises of religion, epistemology, and of western culture's relation to the newly discovered exotic.[106] The clash of illusionistic yearnings with the picture plane's flatness became a symbol in and of itself, dissolving assumptions that classical homogenous perspective was necessarily a structure for enabling pictorial meaning. This, too, was latent in the reading that Erwin Panofsky would push (but in later writings, back away from) in the famous "Symbolic Form" essay cf 1923–4. As Panofsky knew, the leavening of perspective with modern-seeming connotations of subjectivity, of seeing things "from a point of view," was a process of metaphorization staged (if at all) chiefly in poetic or dramatic texts in the later sixteenth century. The Renaissance matched the early twentieth in disputes between

5.32
Erhard Schön,
Underweysung der Proportzion und Stellung der Bossen
(Nuremberg, 1538), fol. Dir.
Staatliche Graphische Sammlungen, Munich.

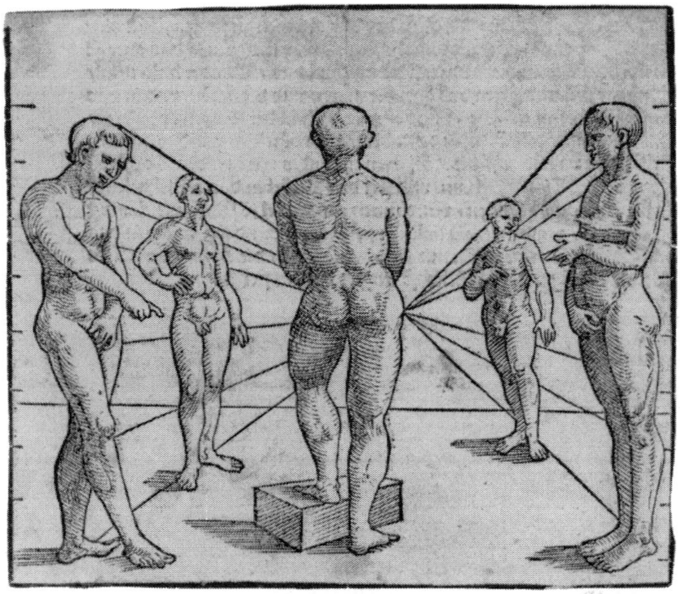

"allegorical" versus "mathematical" readings of perspective: the late fifteenth-century humanist Christoforo Landino sighed that perspective, from its inception had been "part philosophy and part geometry." [107]

What printed materials such as Vredeman's allowed, it seems, was the exploration of perspective *instruction* as a site for personal invention—a corollary to its use in painting and its discussion by humanists and poets. Philosophically, the perspective available to most early modern artists remained a fragmented and pluralized affair.[108] The printed perspective treatise—often riddled with misapprehensions, repetitions, and outright errors—vividly manifested this counter-idea in print; as James Elkins, echoing Landino, has pointed out, perspective's own background has always been discordant, poetic, interstitial, even hermaphroditic, "part convention and part invention."[109] By the year 1600, perspective in books no longer confined itself to the revelation of an outside view, but became the means for artists to actively construct one of their own.[110]

Pavel Florensky, a Russian theologian, mystic, art historian, and, like Vredeman, an exile,[111] wrote about this possibility in a little-known essay of 1920. Florensky claimed that linear perspective's aspirations towards pictorial transcendence, long associated with the Quattrocento, signaled not empirical promise but human egoism. Perspective's rise, and its subsequent unraveling in the sixteenth century, Florensky insisted, was symptomatic of the technological hubris of modern man and his spurning of spirituality. Instead, he claimed, the "reverse perspective," of late Russian icons was the more devotional pictorial scheme. In contrast to the boxed space of Western pictures, icons saw the far parts of a picture rushing forward rather than receding from the plane. Remarkably, Florensky's essay did not limit its analysis to Byzantine imagery, but cited relevant examples in sixteenth-century Italian and Netherlandish works. These, too, were marked by "an other, spiritual space" different to that of linear

5.33

Hans Vredeman de Vries, *Perspective* I, no. 30, 1604. Engraving, H.549.

Centre Canadien d'Architecture, Montréal.

perspective, one characterized by a "complete incommensurability" with the outside viewer. Florensky:

> This is reverse perspective. Examining it, especially when so consistently applied . . . we are not drawn into this space; on the contrary it repels us, as a mercury sea would repel our bodies . . .[112]

What amounts to mystical and "medieval" estrangement from the picture becomes, in Florensky's phrasing, the fate of the viewer of perspective. The structure of the artwork becomes an inviolable expanse, a space characterized not by welcome but by enmity. Florensky's model of picture beholding suggests a counter-history for the entire history of perspective, one taken, surprisingly, from Byzantine icons—the precise kind of objects Vredeman, for his part, seems to have seen in Prague in the 1590s.[113] In icons, reverse perspective derives its power from a chain of other versions of itself, diffusing and de-motivating the very possibility of a single viewpoint. The individual beholder is shunned in favor of omniscient and differenced divinity. Reverse perspective transcends the single beholder, aiming, Florensky claimed, at "a *suprapersonal metaphysics*.[114] Its origin, accordingly, lay not in painting but in textiles: "it was not in pure art perspective arose . . . [rather] it came out of the applied art sphere."[115]

Vredeman nowhere assumes as strongly as, say, Dürer or (indeed) Alberti had, that the picture plane represents a fictional window, a hypothetical negation of the stuff between a viewer and a depicted object. Alberti, as perspective's first modern discussant, established the metaphor of the "veil" in *Della Pittura*. Vredeman, one could say, overturns this lasting trope of transparency (so effectively taken up by the late Panofsky),[116] to coin a material one—the metaphor of the printed page. He sides ultimately with Schön, Stoer, and Walter Ryff's "material reality," and Dürer's foldout "nets." Vredeman's distance-point method impresses three points (not one) *on* the picture surface, not *through* it. His *doorsiende*, his seeing-through, legislates sight through the tactile, obsessively repeated surfaces named in his tract's title: "Paper, panels, or canvases." In the end, these entities constitute not just a metaphor, but Vredeman's idea of what perspective really is.

Just like the intarsia and tapestry Vredeman practiced in Mechelen, the 1604–05 book places perspective in the service of flat pattern as much as depth, a radical reversing of its expected functions in painting. We can recall Isaac de Ville's gripe about the *Perspective* experience being "like grabbing a bird from the sky." Yet a degree of opacity, one could say, is part of Vredeman's project. Vredeman fixes the *ooghpunt*, the "eye-point," but its architectural setting is always in flux; his "making" of perspective is a process rife with trial and error, false starts, and, above all, repetition, a process, in fact, not at all unlike a looping bird in flight. The multiplicity of Vredeman's illustrated examples is fundamental; every look literally creates another point (*"elck sien een andere punct maect"*), page after page after page. In fact, one of the few readers to explicitly praise the *Perspective* by name in the seventeenth century was neither a painter nor an architect but a poet, a theologian from Einkhuizen named Coreliszoon Biens. Biens listed Vredeman's books as sources helpful in "contemplating" the drawing of perspectives.[117] And, indeed, the tested reader who turns, scans, revisits, and actively peruses pages is part of Vredeman's system. Grounded in printed illustration, this system remains aggressively multiple. Where his earlier ornament sheets had staged *menghinge*, or mixture, with fragments, Vredeman's perspective engravings do it with views—perspective becomes not a pedagogical sequence but a commingling of handcrafted worlds.

After the publication of a second edition of *Perspective* in 1606, the tract was re-edited by Hendrick Hondius in 1614, and annotated by the French mathematician Samuel Marolois. The plates to Marolois's *Oeuvres mathématiques traitans de la géométrie*, published in Paris, revised dozens of Vredeman etchings, and proved to be wildly popular in the first part of the seventeenth century—12 more editions were published before 1651, first by Hondius in The Hague, and later by Johannes Janssonius in Amsterdam.[118] Even at the outrageously high price of seven guilders per book, Vredeman's *Perspective* sold five copies at a single sale in Amsterdam in 1610 (at the same sale, an edition of Livy fetched one to two guilders.)[119] The Leiden scholar Johannes Thysius purchased a first edition sometime before 1653,[120] and Marolois's edited version of the *Perspective* appears to have been sent all over Iberia and Scandinavia; one copy was in a Jesuit library in Portugal sometime in the late 1620s, and young architects were using it in Uppsala by 1640.[121] Inventories of the estates of the Amsterdam painters, Jan Jansz. (d.1621) and Adriaen van Neulandt (d.1627), indicate that they possessed "*perspectiefboeken*," authored by Vredeman specifically.[122] Throughout the seventeenth century, designs from *Perspective* provided the direct scaffolding for painters including Dirck van Delen, Sebastian Vrancx, and possibly Rembrandt.[123]

But even before Vredeman's death a new gap had begun to widen between books on perspective for artists and those for geometers and mathematicians. In the Netherlands, Simon Stevin's *Van de Deursichtighe* (1605, Figure 5.34) dealt, quite unlike Vredeman, in proofs of perspective (*bewijs*), offering a highly quantitative discourse against what it called the so-called "guesswork" (*gissing*) of painterly perspective.[124] Stevin was a bookkeeper, a mathematician, and, briefly, one of Vredeman's competing *baumeisters* in Danzig. He was also a highly influential advisor to Maurits of Nassau in The Hague, vying with Vredeman for royal patronage. Stevin's tract outlined a purely "mathematical" explanation for perspective drawing, born, it claimed, out of conversations with the prince himself, who had "wished to design exactly the perspective of any given figure, with knowledge of the causes and its mathematical proof."[125] Stevin's tract decried what he saw as a forsaking of exactitude within Dutch perspective praxis; Vredeman's *Perspective* was clearly among the culprits he had in mind. As Stevin wrote:

> Several experts [*meesters*] in practical perspective drawing consider that one should not follow the rules of this art quite perfectly, but sometimes give a more pleasant display, though it be contrary to the rule, they give an example thereof, saying that if a man stands in front and near the middle of a long façade with columns from one end to the other, the columns in the middle

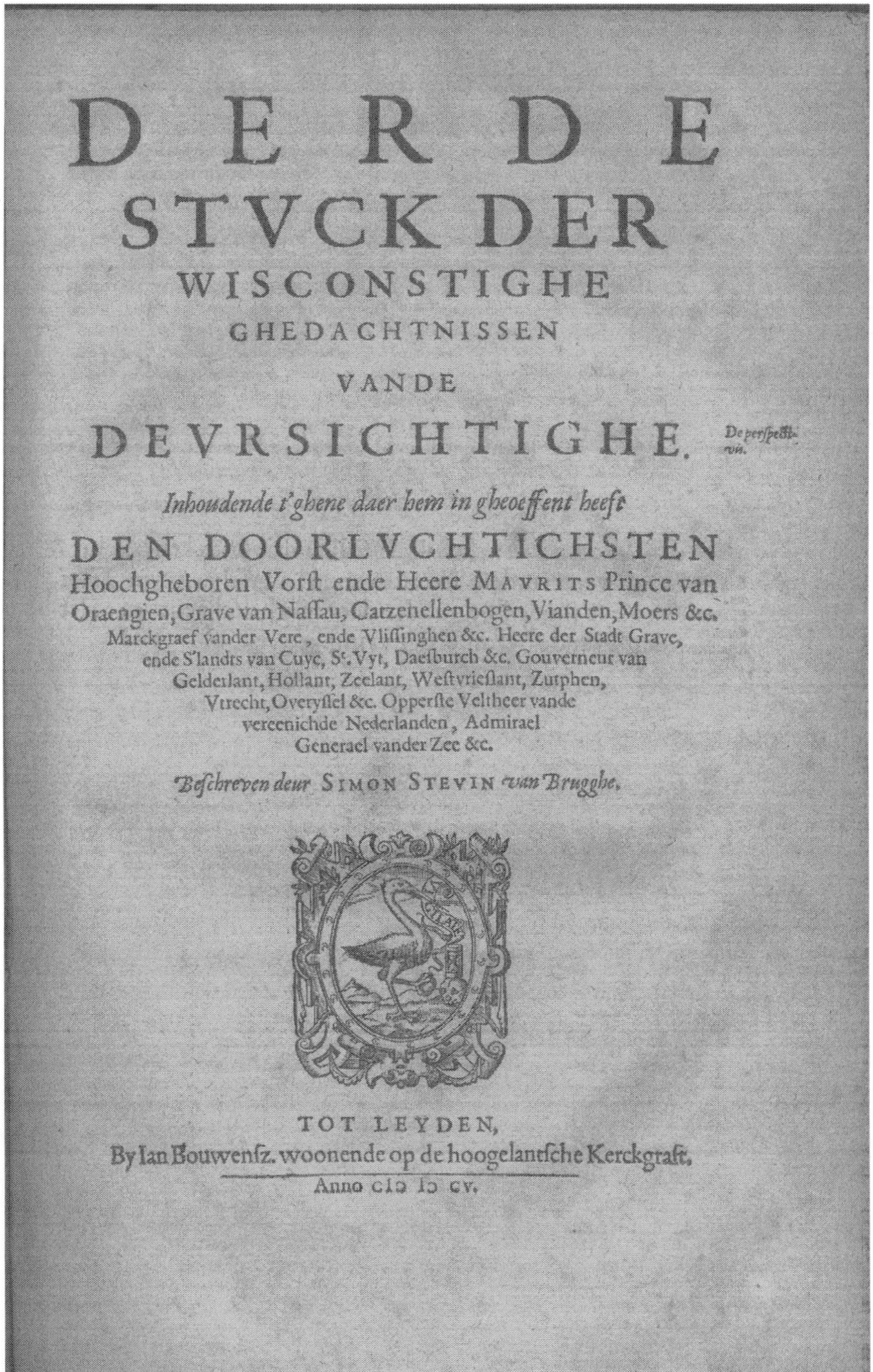

DERDE
STVCK DER
WISCONSTIGHE
GHEDACHTNISSEN
VANDE
DEVRSICHTIGHE. De perspecti-va.

Inhoudende t'ghene daer hem in gheoeffent heeft

DEN DOORLVCHTICHSTEN
Hoochgheboren Vorst ende Heere MAVRITS Prince van
Oraengien, Grave van Nassau, Catzenellenbogen, Vianden, Moers &c.
Marckgraef vander Vere, ende Vlissinghen &c. Heere der Stadt Grave,
ende S'landts van Cuyc, St. Vyt, Daesburch &c. Gouverneur van
Gelderlant, Hollant, Zeelant, Westvrieslant, Zutphen,
Vtrecht, Overyssel &c. Opperste Veltheer vande
vereenichde Nederlanden, Admirael
Generael vander Zee &c.

Beschreven deur SIMON STEVIN *van Brugghe.*

TOT LEYDEN,
By Ian Bouwensz. woonende op de hoogelantsche Kerckgraft.
Anno CIƆ IƆ CV.

5.34
Simon Stevin, *Van de Deursichtighe* (Leiden, 1605), title page.
Department of Rare Books, Butler Library, Columbia University.

> will appear to the eye to be much further apart than those near the ends; nevertheless, they will say, in drawing the perspective image [*vershaeuwing*] one should not imitate this appearance . . . but all this is wrong [. . .] in the drawing of buildings straight lines are drawn more accurately along a ruler than by a free stroke of the hand [*deur een vrye handttreck*] . . .[126]

Not only does Stevin appear to be attacking Vredeman's subjects directly (". . . a long façade with columns . . ."), but in his reliance on a dichotomy of right and "wrong," he enters into a mode of argument seemingly foreign to Vredeman's rhetorical tack. Stevin's treatise included scant illustrations,[127] and his book's appeal appears to have been limited to only the most rarified and patient of reader; royal secretary Christiaan Huygens, for example, named Stevin's *Deursichtighe* in his correspondence, and Pieter Saenredam, the patient transcriber of viewpoints, had a copy in his library, but no Vredeman.[128] If Stevin's interest lay with theoretical certainty, Vredeman was more interested in how a personal interpretation of perspective might be offered in print. We can cite Stevin's dictum that "the practise of perspective produces the true image of the thing."[129] The phrase appears aimed at assuring readers that Stevin had all the answers, a confidence Vredeman's book—written under duress, in exile, almost as a set of unresolved pictorial questions—did not share. Stevin even went on to define perspective as a *namaeksel*, an imitation of reality. Vredeman, the *rederijker* and describer of fantastic architecture, was differently attuned to what was "signified" by perspective—again, Vitruvius's term—and how it could drift depending upon its form.

Yet in seventeenth-century France, where perspective's modern history would be written, Stevin proved prescient. *Van de Deursichtighe* anticipated highly influential treatises by the Royal Academicians Vauzelard (1630), Niceron (1638), and Debreuil (1642), which instigated new mathematical approaches to perspective as projective geometry. Engravings from Abraham Bosse's book on the principles of his teacher, Gerard Desargues, were collected in the tract *Maniere Universelle De Monsieur Desargues* (1648). They restaffed the humble woodcut illustrations of earlier artists at work with visibly aristocratic practitioners (Figure 5.35). Bosse used engravings to demonstrate "a tangible way [*un moyen sensible*] to aid the imagination in representing visual rays."[130] In one print he showed the lines of sight as strings held taut by the fingers of standing cavaliers, all dressed in contemporary finery, complete with swords and spurs. In his images the slack of the optical "rays" springs and uncoils playfully next to the beholders' eyes, from between pinched fingers. Bosse's perspectivists seem to have just paused in the midst of trooping somewhere else, stopping momentarily to consider the points of a square. They fully and easily master perspective's purview. The contrast with, say, Roder's struggling draughtsman of 1531 (Figure 5.17) is acute.

As Bosse reifies Vredeman's dictum that "every look creates another point" through three figures on a bright and expansive plain, Rodler's young master toils in a darkened workshop, trying to transcribe the sprawling landscape confronting him. The former print is about vision, the latter about making a painting, yet over the two a key relationship between hand and eye has been reversed; where Rodler's perspectivist

5.35
Abraham Bosse, *Manière universelle de Mr. Desargues, pour pratiquer la Perspective* (Paris, 1648), plate 2.
Special Collections, Getty Research Institute, Los Angeles.

labored to capture things manually which overwhelmed his gaze, Bosse's geometers blithely pull the world to their eyes, in a manner so effortless that extra string, in effect a surplus of vision, unfurls dandily aside their heads. We have, after the interregnum of Vredeman's long perspective tract, arrived at the baroque of Gilles Deleuze's formulation, an epoch and condition of excess, one that "twists and turns its folds, pushing them to infinity."[131] Gone is the self-enclosed net-world of Dürer's cut-outs. The detachment of perspective from all suggestions of labor, struggle, or manual crafting, is complete; it has dissolved into a purely mathematical, or purely optical, pursuit.

All but the last of Vredeman's Dutch, German, and French translations contain letterpress poems about his training and patrons. These mention Vredeman's home of Leeuwarden and his dedicatee, the young Prince Maurits.[132] In the first Leiden edition Vredeman even included his portrait beside that of Maurits, ringing it with an identification as governor of the Dutch Republic. Maurits's motto is couched in horticulture, *Tandem fit surculus arbor* (at last the slip becomes a tree), alluding on one level to the prince's move from Antwerp to a new court at The Hague, and, more broadly, to the Dutch Republic, a Protestant polity newly severed from Spain.[133]

Like that of many dedicatees in the seventeenth century, Maurits's visage is placed first in the order of pages, before even the bust of Vredeman.[134] Beside both portraits stems an acrostic aligned along the first letters of Vredeman's name. Descending from the letters IOHANNES VREDEMAN VRIES (Figure 5.36) it reads:

> I have forced myself to spend over forty years
> of my time studying this art/
> How much difficulty [*moyete*]/how much I have searched
> The passing of time in toil teaches much about it.[135]

Vredeman's autobiographical grounding, set at the beginning of the book, frames a discernibly personal poetic. Acrostic devices were actually used in German perspective books in the sixteenth century.[136] Yet the "I" in Vredeman's lyric is, of course, Vredeman himself, in a direct address to Maurits and the reader. In the Latin edition Vredeman even deployed the double emphatic "*Ipse ego*" (I, myself) to reiterate his own presence, beginning his address with a repetition—making his own image, as with his prints, a stuttered version among a set of copies.[137]

Vredeman has used the acrostic structure before: in the *Stadhuis* woodcut of 1564–65 (Figure 2.1). There, he inserted a description of the new building within a long paean to Antwerp, allowing the printed image to honor the building as site of a rhetorical presentation. In the *Perspective* Vredeman's modest admission of his difficulty with the subject fulfills a similarly rhetorical, biographical function. On the one hand, he means to calm readers' fears about their own abilities in perspective, reminding them that "In order to grasp the art/one must have exerted oneself heartily/for no one is born a master."[138] On the other, the poem links Vredeman's art to his handicraft, to his patrons, and his

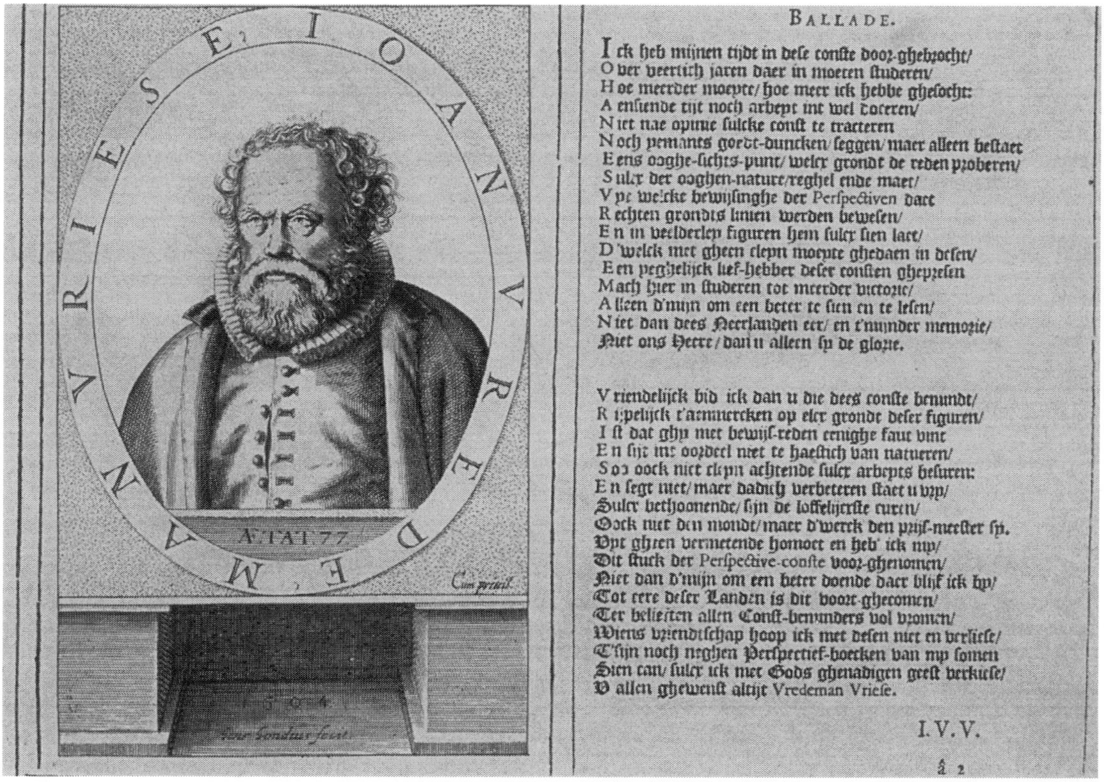

5.36
Hans Vredeman de Vries, *Perspective* I, fol. a2r, 1604. Letterpress and engraving. Universiteitsbibliotheek, Amsterdam.

wandering, via the letters of his name. Vredeman affirms himself as a figurative gatekeeper of Perspective.

In the end, any access to the *Perspective*'s plates is literally framed by Vredeman's own persona. Jacques Derrida once noted that a book's frontmatter—its introductions, preambles, and dedications—were generally the element of a publication written last, after the main sections had been completed and even rethought.[139] Vredeman's frontmatter to the *Perspective* was even produced separately from the main engravings: the title page and dedications were pressed in The Hague, while the images were struck in Leiden. The introductory section, rendered in four different languages and three different typefaces, even had different pagination from the plates. This standing-apart seems wholly consistent with Vredeman's own strategy of situating himself before his art. The book is literally a hybrid, echoing that of his ornament in its unnatural pairings of bodies and buildings.

At least in the initial versions of the *Perspective* the prefaces, portraits, and dedications manipulate the order in which his text was consumed. Dismantling the natural outlay of his text permits Vredeman's publisher a kind of authorial maneuvering, one familiar from Vredeman's own diction in the *Schilderboeck*. At the opening of Vredeman's treatise, the section written last, the artist fashions his own image specifically in relation to his patron, proposing it as an utopian contract which eluded him during his professional career—a "pact" with the reader, asserting authenticity, veracity, and the book's site of origin in his hand. Vredeman's round printed portrait stamps these views as his own, like an etched monogram, or giant trademark.[140]

*

Erwin Panofsky's reading of perspective, reconfigured by Bal, Bredekamp, Damisch, and many others, still dominates art history. In Panofsky's *Idea*, the Mannerist subversion of Renaissance perspective threatened to end, quickly after it had been born, a hermeneutics of modernity.[141] Those quintessentially humanist promises symbolized by Dürer's *Durchsehung*—the relativization of viewpoint, the triumph of reason over nature, the capacity to master and survey historical phenomena from afar—were betrayed when subverted by sixteenth-century space. As Panofsky complained in a letter to Aby Warburg the year of his "Symbolic Form" lecture (1924), Mannerism supplanted Renaissance theory with "metaphysics."[142]

The art historian Uwe Schneede once suggested that Vredeman's work, within the context of the early seventeenth century, represents a disquieting, almost Nietzschean moment in the history of representation, an early challenge to the idea that perspective was meaningful only as a humanist symbol. As Schneede put it, Vredeman's book spoke of seeing as a kind of knowledge, but one contingent, arbitrary, and—most dauntingly—ungraspable apart from real things.[143] This placement—a questionable one, certainly—of Vredeman in a history of technologized visuality[144] can lurch too easily into anachronism; at the same time, it suggests the intellectual conditions surrounding a very specific historical moment *after* Renaissance perspective had matured. Panofsky, the justly lauded founder of *Durchsehung*'s modern import, had implied that perspective was not just a technique, but a metaphor for the historian's task.[145] However the kind of perspective available at the end of the sixteenth century was not always a redemptive phenomenon, that is, a spatial allegory for the stabilization analysis could impart to a fragmented and distant artwork, seeing it into the present.

Shakespeare's *Hamlet*, first performed the year before *Perspective* was published (1603), raised a kindred uncertainty in its famous first line: "Who's there?"[146] Like Shakespeare's play, Vredeman's treatise thematized misrecognition, the potential of "nothingness" to speak volumes, and the plights and terrors confronting post-Reformation vision—and art—bereft of the capacity to impartially *see*. The form of Vredeman's book ultimately educes the exiled, migratory circumstances under which it was written. Its theory, meanwhile, grounded in the print medium, evinces the pressures besetting any "legitimate construction" at the moment of the Renaissance's demise.

Chapter 6

Epilogue

Vredeman and the modern

Is irony in architecture possible?

Frederic Jameson[1]

6.1
Schloss Johannisburg in Aschaffenburg, with gables after Hans Vredeman de Vries, April 1945.
Stadt. und Stiftarchiv, Aschaffenburg.

Vredeman died in Hamburg in 1609.[2] Into the nineteenth century (particularly in England) Vredeman's work was given consideration in academic guidebooks. J. M. W. Turner's notes for a series of illustrated lectures given in 1811 at the Royal Academy contained illustrations demonstrating the work of "*Vredeman Friese.*"[3] In fact, compendia of artist's biographies as early as the seventeenth century mentioned the *Perspective*, including books by Baldinucci (1687),[4] Orlandi (1704),[5] and Descamps (1753)[6]. John Evelyn even singled out prints after Vredeman of buildings and architecture for specific mention in his 1662 book on engraving techniques.[7]

Much of what architects and engineers do, and did, is the making of images—plans, sketches, sections, elevations, axionometrics, CAD diagrams, and perspectives. The litany of painters who practiced architecture is well known—Serlio, Altdorfer, Raphael, Michelangelo, Barbaro, du Cerceau, Cornelis Floris—these all used shared skills to make plans, paintings, drawings, and prints. As this book has tried to suggest, in many Vredeman works an architectural image represented an *encounter*, but a contentious and unstable one in terms of both production and of reception. As now, it was the images' indeterminacy between the realms of plan and structure that remained their allure, in their furnishing of alternatives to the programmatic, or aesthetic extremes of built environment or picture. Vredeman's images, to repeat, do not model architectural projects; they *are* the projects.

Historiographically, the desire among architectural and art historians to read Vredeman's works as manifesting the values of a particular style, nation, or epoch has often had the effect of attributing causality for Vredeman's images to his origins—as a Netherlander or, in one instance, as a Frisian[8]. At the same time, it has alerted audiences to the implicit relativism of their own historical viewpoint, their own *orison*. In 1885, Henri Hymans could observe how

> . . . il appartenait à notre temps, plus curieux sinon les autres en ce qui concerne les choses du passé, de voir en De Vries le maître distingué que le gout dominant au XVIIIe siècle, et davantage encore celui de la première moitié de XIXe, avaient en quelque sorte fait tomber dans l'oubli.[9]

Hymans, annotating his French translation of Van Mander, was aware of how changing tastes affected views of the sixteenth century. Indeed, when J. F. Waagen tapped Vredeman as "*Schöpfer der Architekturmalerei*" in 1866, he christened an appellation that Jantzen and others would see as his particular contribution to Dutch culture of the seventeenth century.[10] For Waagen, as for virtually an entire generation of art historians, it was Vredeman's relevance to the history of the specifically "Netherlandish" specialty of architectural painting, rather than ornament or architecture, which lifted him out of the unesteemed ranks of sixteenth-century contemporaries like Cornelis Floris.[11]

To collapse Vredeman's activities into an essentialist figure or activity is to ignore the role different factors played in foisting roles upon the artist, and the revisions which he was continually attempting to make to his own presentation of self. Vredeman was recently referred to as a "*uomo universale*" for his ambidexterity.[12] This appellation is apt but perhaps ultimately misleading—not so much for an overestimation of Vredeman's abilities as for the air of humanist mastery it imputes to his own career. The span of years surveyed in these last chapters marks not a process of artistic maturation; it reveals a sequence of roles that appear masterful only in retrospect, enacted for different patrons, under different circumstances, in different locales. An architect and rhetorician in Antwerp, a court painter in Prague, a garden designer in Wolfenbüttel, a painting teacher in Danzig—Vredeman's art was fashioned largely from the outside, predicated not so much on resolute *ingenium* as on intersubjective simulations and half-hearted court feints.[13]

The *Perspective*, dedicated to a youthful *stadhouder*, represents a last, furtive attempt to wield an artistic theme to stabilize a reputation. Completed near Vredeman's death, the *Perspective* seeks to picture this self-making from without, using a species of *contrefeyt* in the eyes of both a specific dedicatee and reading public, to look back to older traditions, and refashion those traditions to engender new things in the present. This Janus-like struggle between ingratiation and dissimulation is consistent, this book has tried to suggest, with the workings of late sixteenth-century perspective and its modern historiography. For while Vredeman's final project, and his autobiography in Van Mander's *Lives*, stakes a claim for prominence in a distinct kind of art, both sources, by nature of their illusive topic, must submerge the hand of their maker to truly engage. In this, the perspective tract resists dissolution into pure historical contextualization, forcing acknowledgment of our modern-day awareness of its peculiarity, its equivocal refuge-taking in older traditions. The struggles and exclusions that define Vredeman's prints answer the material forms he worked with all his life—wood, ink, plaster, paper—even as they surely bespeak—but hardly illuminate—a history of exile and performance. Rapturously scouring themselves of human bodies and acts, Vredeman's works revel in troubling alternatives to the notion of art as a history.

Unlike those by Stevin, Vredeman's perspective prints are no immaterial dupes for vision. Rather, they are tangible, stubborn acknowledgments that we, as patient readers, are crucial entanglements in a discourse of perspective. This makes us not doomed victims, however, but challenged participants, greeted at every angle with possibilities and limits—literal *orisons*—that we alone can take up. Such plurality signals both freedom and dread.[14] Once printed and in our hands, perspective is transformed, paradoxically rendered unfamiliar and strange; no longer a rational extension of our own space, it has become something alien, something separate and, indeed, chillingly modern: a succession of fictional worlds.

Notes

The source of this book's epigraph is "Transcript of the Discussion of Comrade Stepanova's paper, 'On Constructivism,' December 1921", James West (trans.), in *Art into Life: Russian Constructivism 1914–1932*, Seattle: Henry Art Gallery, University of Washington, 1990, p. 74.

Introduction Iconoclasm's faces

1 Universiteitsbibliotheek Leiden, Resoluties van Curatoren, A.C. Nr. 20, 8/9 February 1604, fol 128r: "Gepresenteeert zynde Requeste by eenem hans vredeman de vriese met brieven van Recommedndatie van zyn Excel.it ten einde hij mogte wordern geburck't in't doceeren van de perspective Ingenie ende architecture als darinne zeer ervaren zyndes ende zulx hebben de verschiede boekens daerop uit goen gaans, ende als nog verscheyden onderhanden hebben de die hy in coopere platen zoudan laten snyden ende ter eeren van de Universiteit alhier doen drucken. Is naar deliberatie de voorse professie niet nedig bevonden ende de staat van de Univ. niet suffisant is om te veel nyewe proffessoren aen te nemen", see P.C. Molhuysen, *Bronnen tot de Geschiedenis der Leidsiche Universiteit*, The Hague: Martinus Nijhoff, 1913, p. 156.

2 Giuliana Bruno, *Atlas of Emotion: Journeys in Art, Architecture, and Film*, London: Verso, 2004, p. 179.

3 Van Mander, fol. 267r: "eene Babelschen thoren/daer hy veel werck in ghedaen/en zijn ghesicht door hed ghebroken". On the Antwerp episode, see F. Blockmans, "Een krijgstekening, een muurschildering en een schilderij van Hans Vredeman de Vries te Antwerpen, *Antwerpen: Tijdschrift der Stad* 8, 1962, pp. 22–38, and Heiner Borggrefe, *Hans Vredeman de Vries und die Renaissance im Norden*, Munich: Hirmer, 2002 (hereafter Borggefe, *Norden*), p. 45; On Wolfenbüttel: Friederich Thöne, "Hans Vredeman de Vries in Wolfenbüttel", *Braunschweigisches Jahrbuch*, 41, 1960, pp. 47–68. In Danzig, the Netherlander was the Mechelen artist Anthonie von Opbergen (1543–1611), on whom see Georg Cuny, *Danzigs Kunst und Kultur im 16. Und 17. Jahrhunderts*, Frankfurt am Main: Heinrich Keller, 1910, p. 47, and Bernard Vermet, "Architectuurschilders in Danzig", *Gentse Bijdragen tot de kunstgeschiedenis* 31, 1996, pp. 27–57.

4 Alois Nedoluha, *Kulturgeschichte des technischen Zeichens*, Vienna: Springer, 1960, p. 12.

5 L. R. Shelby, "Medieval Masons' Tools II: Compass and Square", *Technology and Culture*, vol. 6:2, 1965, pp. 236–48.

6 Petra Sophie Zimmermann, *Die Architectura von Hans Vredeman de Vries*, Munich: Deutscher Kunstverlag, 2002, p. 15.

7 Samuel von Hoogstraten, *Inleyding tot de hoogh schoole der schilderkonst . . .*, Rotterdam: François van Hoogstraten, 1678, p. 274.

8 Van Mander, fol. 261v: ". . . om de wreetheyt van den Const-uytandigen Mars te wijcken . . ".

9 Theodor W. Adorno, *Aesthetic Theory*, Robert Hullot Kentor (trans.), Minneapolis: University of Minnesota Press, 1997, p. 183.

10 Joseph Leo Koerner, *The Reformation of the Image*, Chicago: Chicago University Press, 2004, pp. 27–37.

11 G. W. F. Hegel, *Vorlesungen über die Ästhetik* (1835–38) in *Hegel's Philosophy of Fine Art*, F. P. B. Osmaston (trans.), vol. 3, London: G. Bell and Sons, Ltd, 1920, pp. 333–7.

12 See, for example, "Blood" in Rebecca Zorach, *Blood, Ink, Milk, Gold: Abundance and Excess in the French Renaissance*, Chicago: University of Chicago Press, 2005, pp. 33–81.

13 Julius von Schlosser, " 'Stilgeschichte' und 'Sprachgeschichte' der bildenden Kunst: Ein Rückblick", *-hist. Abteilung der Bayerischen Akademie der Wissenschaftlen 1935*, Munich: Verlag der Akademie in Kommission bei C. H. Beck, 1935, vol. 1, p. 35.

14 Jaap Bolten, *Method and Practice: Dutch and Flemish Drawing Books 1600–1750*, Landau: Editions PVA, 1985, pp. 15–16.

15 On signature in print see Lisa Pon, *Raphael, Dürer, and Marcantonio Raimondi: Copying and the Renaissance Print*, New Haven: Yale University Press, 2004, pp. 1–13; 67–94. On signatures and architecture, *Architecture and Its Image: Four Centuries of Architectural Representation*, exh. cat., Montréal: Canadian Centre for Architecture, 1989, pp. 188–9.

16 As in Harry Francis Malgrave, "Dancing with Vitruvius: Corporeal Fantasies in Northern Classicism" in *Body and Building: Essays on the Changing Relation of Body and Architecture*, Cambridge, MA: MIT Press, 2002, p. 128.

17 See, for example, B. McCewan et al., *Emancipating Space*, London and Manchester: Manchester University Press, 1998; Brian Rotman, *Signifying Nothing*, Palo Alto: Stanford University Press, 1987.

18 On the Zeuxis/Parrhasius myth in the Renaissance: Erwin Panofsky, *Idea: Ein Beitrag zur Begriffsgeschichte der alten Kunsttheorie* (1924), J. J. S. Peake (trans.), New York: Harper and Row, 1968, p. 49; and in the Netherlands, specifically, Walter Melion, *Shaping the Netherlandish Canon*, Chicago: University of Chicago Press, 1992, pp. 28–32, and Philips Angel, *Lof der Schilderkunst*, Leiden: Willem Christaens, 1642, p. 12, translated in Michael Hoyle, "In Praise of Painting", *Simiolus* 24, 1996, pp. 227–58.

19 Cicero, *De Inventione* II. i, 3, H. M. Hubble (trans.), Cambridge, MA: Harvard University Press, 1949, p. 169.

20 Boudewijn Bakker, "Nederland naar t'leven, een inleiding" in B. Bakker and H. Leeflang, *Nederland naar t'leven*, Zwolle: Waanders, 1993, pp. 6–17. On the use of the term in Dutch art theory, Claudia Swan, "*Ad vivum, naar het leven*, from the life: defining a mode of representation", *Word and Image*, 11:4, 1995, pp. 353–72, esp. 354–8.

21 Heiner Borggrefe (see Borggefe, *Norden*, pp. 15–38) conclusively places Vredeman's date of death at 1609, on the basis of documents referring to his widow back in Amsterdam; the annotations to Van Mander by Hessel Miedema (see Van Mander, vol. V, pp. 48–64) is also extensive on Vredeman's biography, but do not conclusively confirm this date. Vredeman is the first living artist to receive a chapter in the biography part of Van Mander's *Schilderboeck*; see Henri Ekhard Greve, *De bronnen van Carel Van Mander* 's- Gravenhage: Nijhoff, 1903, p. 161.

22 *SAA*, Certificatieboek 146, fol. 102r. City records attesting to Vredeman's stays in many of these early towns have been lost, but see the introduction to A. Schoy, "Hans Vredeman de Vries (Les grands architectes de la Renaissance aux Pays-Bas)", *Journal des Beaux-Arts et de la Littérature*, 10, 1876, pp. 1–36; and Wopke Eekhoff, *Geschiedkundige Beschrijving van Leeuwarden* Leeuwarden: Eekhoff, 1846, vol. 1.

23 See Miedema's comments in Van Mander, vol. V, p. 50, commentary at 266r, line 6.

24 Emmanuel Neeffs, *Histoire de la peinture et de la sculpture a Malines I*, Ghent: Eugene Vanderhaegen, 1876, pp. 166–7, 303.

25 Ria Fabri, "Perpsectives in Wood" in Piet Lombaerde, *Hans Vredeman de Vries and the Artes Mechanicae Revisited*, Brepols: Turnhout, 2005, pp. 153–7.

26 The painting is Michael Coxcie's *Circumcision*, now in Mechelen, St Romboutskathedral; see Mary H. Stone, "Michael Coxcie in Rome", Ph.D. dissertation, New York University, 1957, 11, cat. 24. On Vredeman and the tapestry industry, S. Schneebalg-Perelman, "Les Neuf Preux et les Sept vertus", *Bulletin des Musees royaux d'Art et d'Histoire*, 45, 1973, pp. 201–27; Elizabeth Mahl, "Ein fürstlicher Baldachin des 16. Jahrhunderts", *Jahrbuch der kunsthistorischen Sammlungen in Wien*, 64, 1968, pp. 93–118, and Cecilia Pardes, "Vredeman de Vries and Tapestry Design" in Lombaerde, *Artes*, pp. 169–186.

27 Van Mander (fols. 266r–267v) relates an anecdote wherein Bruegel secretly added "eenen Boer", (a peasant) figure to an architectural composition Vredeman had left standing on an easel. See

A. Monballieu, "Een werk van P. Bruegel en H. Vredeman de Vries voor de tresorier Aert Molckman", *Jaarboek van het Koninklijk Museum voor Schone Kunsten Antwerpen*, 1969, pp. 113–135. The evidence marshaled by Monballieu supporting Van Mander's story is not particularly convincing, but the Buregel/Vredeman tale has itself become a trope; see, for example, Aldous Huxley's bizarre *The Elder Pieter Bruegel*, New York: Wiley, 1938, p. 50.

28 *SAA, Certificatieboek* 33, fol. 351r.

29 This sentence, and this chapter's understanding of post-biographical models of studying individual artitsts, is indebted on Matthew Jesse Jackson, "Answers of the Experimental Group", Ph.D. dissertation, University of California, Berkeley, 2003. My passage exerpts Jackson's superb introductory section, p. 23.

30 Cennino d'Andrea Cennini, *Il Libro dell Arte*, Daniel V. Thompson (trans.), New York: Dover, 1933, p. 97, in Chapter LXXXVII, "How Buildings are to be Painted, in Fresco and in Secco (*Como si de'colorire i casamenti, in fresco in secco*)".

31 Georgio Vasari, as in *Vasari on Technique*, Louisa S. Maclehose (trans and ed.), New York: Dover, 1960, p. 214.

32 Van Mander, fol. 250v.

33 Karel Van Mander, *Den Grondt der edel vry schilderkonst*, Hessel Miedema (ed.), Utrecht: Haentjens, Dekker, and Gumbert, 1972, vol. 1, part V, pp. 34–5.

34 Georgio Vasari, *The Lives of the Painters*, George Bull (trans.), London: Penguin, 1987, vol. 2, pp. 369–371 (in the life of Franciabigio).

35 Utrecht: Catharijneconvent, 99 × 230, inv. no ABM S104; see Caroline Henriette de Jonge, *Catalogus der schilderijen Centraal Museum Utrecht*, Utrecht: Centraal Museum, 1933, no 501, and J. Dijkstra et al., *De schilderijen van Museum Catharijneconvent*, Zwolle: Waanders, 2002, pp.136–7.

36 Truus van Bueren and W. C. M. Wüstefeld, *Leven na de dood: Gedenken in de late Middeleeuwen*, Turnhout: Brepols, 1999, p. 166. On the history of the crypt painting: Utrecht, Kunsthistorisch Instituut, exh. cat., *De Jeruzalemvaarders van Jan van Scorel: Een schilderij central 2*, Utrecht, Centraal Museum, 1979, pp. 12–14.

37 Karl M. Birkmeyer, "The Arch Motif in Netherlandish Painting of the Fifteenth Century: Part One", *Art Bulletin* 43:1, March 1961, pp. 1–20.

38 See Erich Auerbach, "Figura", (1944) in *Scenes from the Drama of European Literature*, Minneapolis: Minnesota University Press, 1984, pp. 11–16, and for a adaptation of the approach, which picks up where Auerbach left off, Hans Ulrich Gumbrecht, *The Production of Presence: What Meaning Cannot Convey*, Palo Alto: Stanford University Press, 2004, p. 128. Christopher Wood and Alexander Nagel, "Towards a Renaissance Anachronism", *Art Bulletin* 87:1, September 2005, pp. 403–15, have suggested the lingering efficacy of the "figura" in the Renaissance.

39 Vitruvius V.6.8, p. 70.

40 H (Hieronymus Cock), nos 482–509.

41 H (Hieronymus Cock), nos 22–46.

42 ". . . Sic Orbis Reginam, illam, lachrimabile, Romam/Vastarunt, fatis nimirum vrgentibus: ecquae/ Seruandis reliquis vaquam fidicia regnis?" Included on dedicatory page of H IV (Hieronymus Cock), no 22, exemplar in Vienna, Kunsthistorisches Museum, no 6638. See Timothy Riggs, *Hieronymus Cock (1510–1570): Printmaker and Publisher in Antwerp at the Sign of the Four Winds*, Ph.D. dissertation, Yale, 1971, p. 257, on which see also regarding the notion of Cock's ruins as *schilderachtig*, or picturesque.

43 On the Babel tradition in Antwerp: Ulrike B. Wegner, *Die Faszination des Maßlosen: Der Turmbau zu Babel von Pieter Bruegel bis Athanasius Kircher*, Hildesheim/Zürich: Olms, 1995, pp. 9–72; also S. Mansbach, "The Language of Contradiction in Bruegel's *Tower of Babel*", *Res: Anthropology and Aesthetics* 5, 1983, pp. 40–8.

44 H (Hieronymus Cock), no 8: "Veerderleye ordinantien van landtschappen, met fine historien daer in gheordineert, wt den ouden ende niewen testament . . ".

45 The preliminary drawing is in Prague: Nardoni Galerie, inv. no K4493. See K. Arndt, "Unbekannante Zeichnungen von Pieter Bruegel d. Ä.", *Pantheon* 24, 1966, pp. 207–16.

46 Jakob Rosenberg et al. (eds), *Dutch Art and Architecture 1600–1800*, Harmondsworth: Penguin, 1966, p. 255, and Hans Vlieghe, "Flemish Art, Does it Really Exist?", *Simiolus* 26, 1998, pp. 187–200.

47 Lewis Mumford, *The Culture of Cities*, London: Harcourt, Brace & Co., 1938, p. 131.

48 G. F. Waagen, *Die vornehmsten Denkmäler in Wien*, Vienna, Braumüller, 1866, p. 200; see also *idem*, "Epoche von 1530 bis 1600" in *Handbuch der Geschichte der Malerei IV*, Stuttgart: Ebner & Seubert, 1862, p. 319.

49 Hans Jantzen, *Das niederländische Architekturbild*, Leipzig: Klinkhardt & Berman, 1910, p. 20: "Mit seinen Zeichnungen gibt Vredeman der Architekturdarstellung ein festes Gerüst, das zum erstenmal auf nichts anderes als auf die konstruktive Sicherheit Rücksicht nimmt".

50 Jantzen, *Architekturbild*, p. 129: ". . . Die Gegensätzlichkeiten formaler Art zwischen vlämischer Bilderscheinung und holländischer Bilderscheinung wird sich letzten endes Endes stets als eine Gegensätzlichkeit taktischer und optischer Auffasung aller Sichtbarkeit characterisieren". The language of Alois Riegl's "haptic" and "optic" is quite clear.

51 Alois Riegl, unpublished lecture notes from academic year 1896/7, Institut für Kunstgeschichte, Universität Wien, VO WS, 1900/01, carton 6, p. 433.

52 Hubert Damisch, *The Origin of Perspective*, Cambridge, MA, MIT Press, 1994, pp. 236–77; Hanneke Grootenboer, *The Rhetoric of Perspective*, Chicago: University of Chicago Press, 2005, especially pp. 9–13, 97–133.

53 An effect which renders the early modern artist a kind of magus: cf. Ernst Kris and Otto Kurz, *Legend, Myth, and Magic in the Image of the Artist: An Historical Experiment*, A. Lang (trans.), New Haven: Yale University Press, 1979, pp. 77–9.

54 Leonard Barkan, "The Heritage of Zeuxis" in Alina Payne et al. (eds), *Antiquity and its Interpreters*, Cambridge: Cambridge University Press, 2000, pp. 102–4.

55 Alexander Nagel and Christopher S. Wood, "Interventions: The Authors Reply", *Art Bulletin*, 87:1, September 2005, pp. 430–1.

56 For example: Gregorio Comanini, *Il Figino, overo del fine della Pittura. Dialogo . . . ove quistionandosi se'l fine della pittura sia l'utile overo il diletto, si tratta dell' uso di quella nel Christianesimo*, Manuta, 1591.

57 Plato, *Sophist*, 235c–236e; here, as in Plato, *Sophist*, N. P. White (trans.), Indianapolis and Cambridge: Hackett, 1993, pp. 22–5.

58 *Epistolae* 7; see Karl Swoboda, *L'esthetique de Saint Augustin et ses sources*, Brno: Spisy Filosoficke fakulty Masarykovy university v Brno, 1933, p. 101.

59 See the discussion in David Summers, *Michelangelo and the Language of Art*, Princeton: Princeton University Press, 1981, pp.109–10.

60 "Ut doceat indecora & absurda fictione soedari Dei maiestatem, du incorporeus mastera corporea [. . .] Restat igitur vt ea fola pingantur ac sculpantur quorum sint capaces oculi, Dei maiestas, quae oculorum sensu longe superior est, ne indecoris ipecaris corrumpatur", John Calvin, *Institutio Christianae religionis*, Basel, 1559, 1.11.12, edition London: Thomas Vautrollerius, 1576, fols 31, 37.

61 Calvin, Second Helvetic Confession, 1566, as cited in S. Michalski, *The Reformation and the Visual Arts*, London and New York: Routledge, 1993, p. 182. However, on Calvin's complex relation to the concept of *figura*, see Ann Kibbey, *The Interpretation of Material Shapes in Puritanism*, Cambridge University Press, 1986, pp. 44–8.

62 Jan Gerrtz Versteghe, *Der Leken Wechwijser*, 1554, fol. Clxiii recto, as in *Bibliotheca Reformatica Neerlandica* 4, 1906, p. 289: "schone spreken mit grooten letteren an die meuren schrijven ende gar mit sonder figuren laten blyven".

63 Van Mander wrote that, "on account of the new preaching in 1566, art was at a standstill", Van Mander fol. 258r, itself an echo of German laments from the 1530s.

64 J. M. B. C. Kervyn de Lettenhove (ed.), *Relations politiques des Pays-Bays et de L'Angleterre sous le regne de Philippe II*, 4th edition, Brussels: F. Hayez, 1885, pp. 338–9.

65 M. van Varnewijk, *Troubles Religieux en Flandre en dans le Pays-Bas au XVIe siecle*, H. van Duyse (trans.), Ghent: Maison d'editions d'art, 1905, vol. II, p. 138.

66 Cf. Johannes Weyer, *Von den Teufeln, Zaubrern, Schwartzkünstlern, Teuffels beschwerern, Hexen oder*

Unholden u. Gifftbereitern, Frankfurt am Main: Basse, 1577, John Shea (trans.), Asheville, NC: Pegasus Press, 1998, p. 62, who discusses the devil *Deikelos* who brings "fear with faces and pictures".

67 Koerner, *Reformation*, p. 99. On early modern theories of non-image art, see Georges Didi-Huberman, *Devant le Temps*, Paris: Minuit, 2000, pp. 9–55.

68 Cited in Phyllis Mack Crew, *Calvinist Preaching and Iconoclasm in the Netherlands*, Cambridge: Cambridge University Press, 1978, p. 24.

69 G. N. de Vooys, "De Dordtse bundel met Christelijcke en Schriftuerlijcke Refereynen", *Nederlandsch archief voor kerkgeschiedenis*, n.s.: 21:4, 1928, p. 277.

70 Thomas Gresham (1519–79), as in Christine Goettler, "Ikonoklasmus als Kirchenreinigung: zwei satirische Bildfiktionen zum niederländischen Bildersturm 1566", *Georges-Bloch-Jahrbuch des Kunstgeschichtlichen Seminars der Universität Zürich*, 4, 1997, pp. 61–87.

71 Heinrich Vogtherr, *Ein frembdes und wunderbarliches kunstbuechlin* . . . Strasbourg: Christian Mueller, 1543, fol. A2r.

72 Hillel Schwartz, *The Culture of the Copy: Striking Likenesses, Unreasonable Facsimiles*, New York: Zone, 1996, pp. 211–57. But see also Jacques Derrida, *The Post Card*, 1977, Chicago: University of Chicago Press, 1987. I am indebted for this reference to Amy K. Powell, who articulates a related application in "The Origins of Early Netherlandish Painting", *Art Bulletin*, 88: 4, 2006, pp. 707–28, especially pp. 708–16.

73 Richard Schechner, *Performance Theory*, 3rd ed., New York: Routledge, 2003, p. 207. On performance and early modern architecture: Marvin Carlson, *Places of Performance: The Semiotics of Theatre Architecture*, Ithaca: Cornell University Press, 1989, pp. 1–37; Alice Jarrard, *Architecture as Performance in Seventeenth Century Europe*, Cambridge: Cambridge University Press, 2003, pp. 4–10.

74 A. van Dixhoorn, "Als retorica regeert. Rederijkersregels rond taalgebruik en gedrag in de zestiende en zeventiende eeuw", *De Zeventiende Eeuw*, 18, 2002, pp. 17–30; and in general on concepts of rehearsal in the Netherlands, see Dirck Coigneau, "Bedongen creativiteit. Over retoricale productieregeling" in R. Jansen-Sieben et al. (eds), *Medioneerlandistiek. Een inleiding tot de Middelnederlandse letterkunde*, Hilversum: Verloren, 2000, pp. 129–37.

75 Henry Hexam, *Copious English and Netherduytsch Dictionarie*, London, 1648; see Tiffany Stern, *Rehearsal from Shakespeare to Sheridan*, Oxford: Oxford University Press, 2000, pp. 22–2, 43–5.

76 Immanuel Kant, *Critique of Judgement*, Berlin and Libau, 1709, James Creed Meredith (trans. and ed.), Oxford: Clarendon, 1952, fol. 68, § 14–18.

77 Jacques Derrida, *Truth in Painting*, 1978, Geoff Bennington and Ian McLeod (trans.), Chicago: University of Chicago Press, 1987, p. 64.

78 See Anthony Vidler, "The Ledoux Effect: Emil Kaufmann and the Claims of Kantian Autonomy", *Perspecta*, 33, 2002, pp. 16–29.

79 Zorach, *Blood*, pp. 152–3.

80 Jacques Rancière, *The Philosopher and His Poor*, Durham, NC: Duke University Press, 2004, pp. 6–7.

81 Dieter Nuyten, *Hans Vredeman de Vries' "Architectura Oder Bauung der Antiquen aufs dem Vitruvius . . . Analyse en evaluatie van een architekturaal voorbeldenboek van de 16de eeuw"*, Ph.D. dissertation, Universiteit Leiden, 1994, 2 vols; Borgreffe, *Norden*, Dutch-language edition with different title: *Tussen Stadspaleizen en Luchtkastelen. Hans Vredeman de Vries en de Renaissance*, Ghent: Ludion, 2002; Peter Führing et al., *De Wereld is een Tuin. Hans Vredeman de Vries en de Tuinkunst van de* Renaissance, exh. cat., Antwerp: Rubenshuis, Ghent: Ludion, 2002; Zimmermann, *Architectura*; B. J. J. Krieger, *Hierarchie der ornamenten? De ontmoeten van het classicisme met de rolwerkcartouche in de Architectura (1577) van Hans Vredeman de Vries*, Ph.D. dissertation, Universiteit van Amsterdam, 2002; Heiner Borgreffe and Vera Lüpkes (eds), *Hans Vredeman de Vries und die Folgen: Studien zur Kultur der Renaissance*, Marburg: Jonas Verlag, 2005; P. Lombaerde, *Artes*, Adam Koperkiewicz (ed.), *Hans Vredeman de Vries: Niderlandzcy artyzci w Gdańsku*, Gdańsk: Muzeum Historyczne Miasta Gdańska, 2006.

82 Hal Foster, "Frank Gehry: Why all the Hoopla?", *London Review of Books*, 23, August 6, 2001; *idem*, "Image Building", *Artforum*, October 2004, pp. 270–6.

83 See Robert E. Somol (ed.), *Autonomy and Ideology: Positioning an Avant-Garde in America*, New

York: Monacelli, 1997, especially fol. 73, and Neil Leach, *Against Architecture*, Cambridge: MIT Press, 2000.

84 Theodor Adorno, "Heine the Wound", (1956) in *Notes to Literature: Volume One*, Shierry Weber Nicholsen (trans.), New York: Columbia University Press, 1991, pp. 80–5.

85 As importantly noted by Zorach, *Blood*, pp. 21–2. On how this presents specific problems to the monograph, see Gabriele Guercio, *Art as Existence: The Artists' Monograph and its Subject*, Cambridge MA: MIT Press, 2006, pp. 2–23.

86 Erik Forssman, *Säule und Ornament. Studien zum Problem des Manierismus in den nordischen Säulerbüchern und Vorlageblättern des 16. und 17. Jahnhunderts*, Stockholm: Almqvist and Wiskell, 1956, p. 13.

87 On which see Paul de Man, "Criticism and Crisis", *Blindness and Insight*, Minneapolis: University of Minnesota Press, 1971, p. 12.

Chapter 1 Unbuilt architecture in the world of things

1 C. H. Harford and Percy Simpson (eds), *Ben Jonson: Works*, Oxford: Oxford University Press, 1925, vol. III, pp. 78–9.

2 Paul Valéry, "Petit Discours aux peintre graveurs" in *Oeuvres*, II, Paris: Gallimard, 1960, p. 1299.

3 Mario Carpo, *Architecture in the Age of Printing: Orality, Writing, Typography, and Printed Images in the History of Architectural Theory*; Cambridge MA: MIT Press, 1998, p. 6.

4 John Ruskin, *The Stones of Venice*, London: Smith, Elder and Company, 1851–53, vol. III, p. 194.

5 Nadine Orenstein, *Hendrick Hondius and the Business of Prints in Seventeenth-Century Holland*, Rotterdam: Sound and Vision International, 1996; Manfred Sellinck, *Philips Galle 1537–1612: Engraver and Print Publisher in Haarlem and Antwerp*, Proefschrift: Vrije Universiteit Amsterdam, 1997, 3 vols; and *idem, The New Hollstein Dutch and Flemish Etchings, Engravings, and Woodcuts 1450–1700: Philips Galle*, Rotterdam: Sound and Vision Interactive, 2001, 4 vols.

6 Borggefe, *Norden*, p. 188; Uwe M Schneede, "Interieurs von Hans und Paul Vredeman de Vries", *Nederlands Kunsthistorisch Jaarboek* "hereafter NKJ"18, 1967, pp. 125–66, and Jean Ehrmann, "Hans Vredeman de Vries (Leeuwarden 1527–Anvers 1606)", *Gazette des Beaux-Arts*, nos 5, 93, January 1979, pp. 15–19.

7 On Beuckelaer and his master Pieter Aertsen's specific interest in the Mary and Martha narrative, see Hans Buijs, "Voorstellingen van Christus in het huis van Martha en Maria in het zestiende-eeuw keukenstuk", *Nederlands Kunsthistorisch Jaarboek*, 40, 1989, pp. 93–128; the classic work on the supposed "juxtapositions" of secular and religious subjects in the works is J. A. Emmens, " 'Eins aber is nötig'—Zu Inhalt und Bedeutung von Markt- und Küchenstücken des 16. Jahrhunderts" in J. Bruyn (ed.), *Album Amicorum J.G. van Gelder*, The Hague: Nijhoff, 1973, pp. 93–101. A critique of Emmens' thesis in the context of a larger investigation of Aertsen's space is found in Elizabeth Honig, *Painting and the Market in Early Modern Antwerp*, New Haven: Yale University Press, 1999, pp. 29–39.

8 The formative essay on Flemish "inverted" still-lifes is Max Dvořák, "Ein Stilleben der Beuckelaer oder Betrachtungen über die Enstehung der neuzeitigen Kabinettmaler", *Jahrbuch der Kunsthistorischen Sammlungen in Wien*, 36, 1923, pp. 1–14.

9 Anna Jameson, *Sacred and Legendary Art*, London: Longmans, Green and Co., 1870, vol. 1, p. 370: "At Hampton Court there is a curious picture of this subject by Hans Vries, which is an elaborate study of architecture: the rich decoration of the interior has been criticized, but, according to the legend, Mary and Martha lived in great splendour, and there is no impropriety in representing their dwelling as a palace, but a very great impropriety in rendering the decorations of the palace more important than the personages of the scene".

10 Van Mander, fol. 266r. My translation differs slightly from Miedema's.

11 See, for example, *C'est l'ordre qui a este tenv a la novvelle et ioyevse entrée que treshault, tresexcellent & trespuissãt Prince, le Roy treschrestien Henry deuzieme de ce nom, à faicte en sa bonne ville & cité de Paris, capitale de son royaume, le sezieme iour de iuin M.D.XLIX*, Paris: Jean Dallier, 1549, fol. 7v: "La paisage se monstroit doulx & entremesse. & les traicts menez par industries perspective, abusoyent tellement la veue, qu'elle estimoiit veoir bien loiung en pais. Ce neanmoins la superficie en estoit eoute vnie".

12 Most of these inventories are from the seventeenth century. For example, the 1615 inventory of the estate of Amsterdam wine merchant, Albert Martsz, lists "een stuck perspectieff gedaen bij den Ouden de Vries waarin Pieter Isaacx de beelden gedaen heft". (A perspective piece by the elder de Vries with figures done by Pieter Issacx); see Abraham Bredius, *Künstler-inventare; urkunden zur Geschichte der hollandischen kunst des XVIten, XVIIten und XVIIIten Jahrhunderts*, The Hague: Nijhoff, 1915, vol. VI, p. 639.

13 The document is from a 1619 manuscript inventory of Anne of Denmark's collection; see Lorne Campbell, *The early Flemish pictures in the collection of Her Majesty the Queen*, Cambridge: Cambridge University Press, 1985, p. 118.

14 Mark Evans, *Princes as Patrons*, London: Merrel Holberton, 1998, p. 30.

15 See B. Gutfleisch and J. Menzhauzen, "How a Kunstkammer should be formed: Gabriel Kaltemarkt's advice to Christian I of Saxony on the formation of an art collection", *Journal of the History of Collections*, 1:2, 1989, p. 26.

16 Immo Wagner-Douglas, *Das Maria und Martha Bild: Religiose Malerei im Zeitalter der Bildersturme*, Baden-Baden: V. Koerner, 1999, pp. 170–85.

17 Giles Constable, *Three Studies in medieval religious and social thought: the intepretation of Mary and Martha, the ideal of the imitation of Christ*, Cambridge: Cambridge University Press, 1995, pp. 34–57.

18 Jantzen, *Architekturbild*, p. 22.

19 Campbell, *Flemish Pictures*, p. 120.

20 Sergiusz Michalski, "Fleisch und Geist: zur Bildsymbolik bei Pieter Aertsen", *Artibus et historiae*, 22, 2001, pp. 167–86, 247.

21 Christine Christ-von Wedel, "Die Perikope von Martha und Maria bei Erasmus und der Reformatoren", *Zwingliana*, XXVII, 2000, pp. 103–15; on the responses to the translation: Erika Rummel, *Erasmus and His Catholic Critics*, Niewkoop: de Graaf, 1989, pp. 35–61.

22 Bremen, Kunstsammlungen Bötterstrasse, Roseliushaus, inv. no 343; also Uwe Schneede, *Das repräsentative Gesellschaftbild in der niederländischen Malerei des 17 Jahrhunderts und seine Grundlagen bei Hans Vredemann de Vries*, Ph.D. dissertation, Kiel University, 1965, cat. no 1/16a. The London picture was formerly in the Erskine collection: see Ellis Waterhouse, *Painting in Britain 1530–1790*, New Haven: Yale University Press, 1954, p. 241.

23 See G. Janssens (ed.), *Les Granvelle et les anciens Pays-Bas*, Leuven: Universitaire Pers, 2000, especially pp. 389–409, on Granvelle's art collecting.

24 Claudia Banz, *Höfisches Maezenatentum in Brussel*, Berlin: Mann, 2000, pp. 64–5.

25 See Nils Büttner, *Die Erfindung der Landschaft*, Göttingen: Vandenhoek & Ruprecht, 1999, p. 28.

26 On Ghisi see H. Zerner, "Ghisi et la gravure manieriste a Mantoue", *L'Oeil*, 80, 1962, pp. 26–32; and Riggs, *Cock*, p. 76.

27 H (Vredeman), nos 27–222. On Cock's career generally, see Riggs, *Cock*, and *Graven Images: The Rise of Professional Printmakers in Antwerp and Haarlem, 1540–1640*, exh. cat., Evanston, Mary and Leigh Block Gallery, Evanston: Northwestern University Press, 1993, pp. 1–45. Details of the business transactions are in Jan van der Stock, *Printing Images in Antwerp. The Introduction of Printmaking to a City: Fifteenth Century to 1585*, Rotterdam: Sound and Vision Interactive, 1998, pp. 143–72.

28 "laet de Cock coken om tvolckx Wille". In its subsequent repressing by Philips Galle (H. (Vredeman), no 31/II) the inscription was effaced. The phrase may also allude to a henpecked husband; Volcken is shown standing behind Cock in the engraving.

29 The lack of moving waterpower (owing partly to the Netherlands flat topography) meant that local paper manufacturing was virtually nonexistent in Antwerp. Most paper was imported from French mills or purchased at book *Messen*, like that held at Frankfurt, with Italian-made reams fetching a premium price. In the middle of the sixteenth century, paper prices spiked as part of a larger inflationary trend. See Charles Verlinden, *Dokumenten voor de geschiedenis van prijzen en lonen in Vlaandern en Brabant (XVe–XVIIIe eeuw) Working papers from the Rijksuniversiteit Gent*, nos 125, 1959, pp. 361–2. Also the booklet Andrew Robison, *Paper in Prints*, exh. cat., Washington DC: National Gallery, 1977.

30 See Max Rooses, *Christophe Plantin, imprimeur anversois*, Antwerp: Maes, 1882, p. 263, and A. J. J. Delen, "Christoffel Plantin als prentenhandelaar", *De Gulden Passer*, 10, 1932, pp. 1–24. Also L. Voet,

The Golden Compasses: A History and Evaluation of the Printing and Publication Activities of the Officiana Plantiniana at Antwerp, 2 vols, Amsterdam: Vangendt, 1969–72; and *idem, The Plantin Press (1555–1589): a bibliography of the works printed and published by Christopher Plantin at Antwerp and Leiden*, Amsterdam: Van Hoeve, 1980–82, 2 vols; and *Plantin of Antwerp: Books and prints from the Plantin-Moretus Museum*, exh. cat., Jerusalem: Israel Museum, 1981.

31 J. B. van der Straelen and P. T Moons-van der Straelen (eds), *Jaarboek der vermaerde en konstryke gilde van Sint Lucas binnen de stad Antwerpen*, Antwerp, Peeters-Genechten, 1855, p. 7.

32 Hans-Jörg Künast, "Die Augsburger Frühdrucker und ihre Textauswahl" in Johannes Jarota and W. Williams-Krapp (eds), *Literarisches Leben in Augsburg während de 15. Jahrhunderts*, Tubingen: Niemeyer, 1995, pp. 47–57.

33 Kurt Köster, "Gutenberg's Aachenspiegel-Unternehmen van 1438–1440", *Gutenberg-Jahrbuch* 1983, 24–44. On the distribution of pilgrimage badges in the Netherlands, see J. M. Baart, "Pilgrimeren: mobiliteit en economie" in H. J. E. van Beuningen and A. M. Koldeweij, eds., *Heilig en Profaan: 1000 Laatmiddeleeuwse Insignes uit de Collectie H. J. E. van Beuningen*, Amsterdam: Van Soems, 1993, pp. 186–87.

34 Werner Schultheiss, "Ein Vertrag Albrecht Dürers über den Vertreib siener graphischen Kunstwerke", *Scripta Mercaturae*, 1/2, 1969, pp. 77–81. Lucas van Leyden's role as a *peinture-graveur* is discussed in Jan Piet Filedt Kok, *Lucas van Leyden—grafiek*, exh. cat., Amsterdam: Rijksmuseum, 1978.

35 Alistair Hamilton, *The Family of Love*, Cambridge: James Clarke, 1981, pp. 43–8.

36 Fabienne Emile Hellendoorn, *Influencia del Maniersmo-Nordico en la Arquitectura Virreinal Religiosa de Mexico*, Proefschrift TU Delft, 1980, pp. 5–9, 302; Filip Vermeyen, "Exporting Art across the Globe: The Antwerp Art Market in the Sixteenth Century", *Nederlands Kunsthistorisch Jaarboek*, 50, 1999, pp. 23–39.

37 Bernhard Fabian (ed.) *Die Messekatalog Georg Willers* (facsimilie Hildesheim: Olms, 1978), vol. II, p. 414; vol. III, p. 124; vol. IV, p. 175.

38 On labor divisions and Antwerp printmaking generally, see still A. J. J. Delen, *Histoire de la gravure dans les anciens Pays-Bas et dans les provinces belges*, Paris: Librarie G. von Oest, 1935, vol. 1, pp. 61–100, and Konrad Oberhuber, *Die Kunst der Graphik IV: Zwischen Renaissance und Barock; das Zeitalter von Bruegel und Bellange, Werke aus dem Besitz der Albertina*, Vienna: Albertina, 1967.

39 This breakdown is traced in Riggs, *Cock*, pp. 6–7, based on Hans Widmann, *Geschichte des Buchhandels vom Altertum bis zur* Gegenwart, Wiesbaden: Harrasowitz, 1952.

40 Van der Stock, *Printing*, pp. 144–6.

41 Van Mander, fol. 232r.

42 See Dan Ewing, "Marketing Art in Antwerp 1460–1560: Our Lady's Pand", *Art Bulletin*, 72, 1990, pp. 558–94.

43 For example, Montréal, Centre Canadien d'Architecture, inv. DR 1992: 0003; see Lucia De Pauw-De Veen, "Archivalische gegevens over Volcxken Diercx, weduwe van Hieronymus Cock" in *Bijdragen tot de geschiedenis van de grafische kunst opgedragen aan Prof. Dr. Louis Lebeer ter gelelgenheid van zijn tachtigste verjkaardag*, Antwerp: Vereeniging van de Antwerpsche Bibliophilen, 1975, p. 240.

44 The groundplan of a house owned by Cock's widow on this street survives, and Van der Stock, *Printing*, pp. 144–5, suggests that the etchers may have worked in an adjoining address down the block.

45 ". . . umb das Jahr 1570 haben zwei gebrüder Joan and Lucas van Deutecum eine ganz newe und uberkünstige art von etzen erfunden/also das sie allerley Figuren Landtaffelen, mit allen Schrifften und Littem darin/so rein/geeff/lind und verblasen un Kupffer etzen kundten und noch kunnen/das es lange zeit von vielen verstandigen fur keine etzung sonder einer reinen Schnnitt ist angesehen worden" in Matthias Quod von Kinckelbach, *Teutscher Nation Herligkeitt*, Cologne: Lutzenkirchen, 1609, p. 431.

46 Raymond de Roover, "The Business Organization of the Plantin Press in the Setting of Sixteenth Century Antwerp", *De Gulden Passer*, 34, 1959, pp. 104–20.

47 *SAA*, IB 479, *Journael van Gerard Grammaye 1561–1565*, fol. 39r.

48 Walter Melion, "Hendrick Goltzius's Project of Reproductive Engraving", *Art History*, 13, 1990, pp. 458–87.

49 Guido Marnef, "Repressie en censuur in het Antwerps boekbedrijf, 1567–1576", *De zeventiende*

eeuw, 8:2, 1992, pp. 221–2. See also Maria E. Kronenberg, *Verboden boeken en opstandige drukken in de Hervormingstijd*, Amsterdam: van Kampen, 1948; on earlier developments. Van der Stock, *Printing*, pp. 143–4, rehearses the whole trial.

50 For example, the sheets Pieter Bruegel produced in the 1550s specifically for prints, such as the Virtues and Vices series: H (Bruegel), nos 20–39.

51 See H (Vredeman) nos 181–2.

52 Evelyn Lincoln supplies both a useful history of the idea and a methodological critique of it in *The Invention of the Italian Renaisssance Printmaker*, New Haven: Yale University Press, 2000, pp. 11–15. On study of signatures as tools for clarifying aspects of ownership and identity, see Andre Chastel et al., "L'art de la signature", *Revue de l'Art*, 26, 1974, pp. 8–26, and Creighton Gilbert, "A preface to signatures (with some cases in Venice)" in Mary Rogers (ed.), *Fashioning Identities in Renaissance Art*, Aldershot: Ashgate, 2000, pp. 79–90.

53 Van Mander, *Grondt*, Ch. 2, §16: "Datmen uyt zijn selve doe moet, im inventie te hebben".

54 *De Ratione Dicendi (Rhetorica ad Herennium)*, Harry Caplan (trans.), Cambridge, MA: Harvard University Press, 1965, p. 7.

55 Vitruvius I.2.1–2; see Ingrid D. Rowland and Thomas N. Howe (eds), *Vitruvius: Ten Books on Architecture*, Cambridge: Cambridge University Press, 1999, p. 24.

56 Van Mander, fol. 266r: ". . . quam [Vredeman] weder in Vreslandt/tot Collum/daer hy schilderende een Tafel van Oly-verwe/cont een kist-maker oft Schrijnwercker/die hadde de Boecke van Sebastiaen Serlius oft Vitruvij, uytgegeve door Pieter Koeck: dese schreef Vries nacht en dagh vlijtich uyt/zo den grooten als den cleene. Quam weder van daer te Mecchel by een Schilder/gehechte Glaude Dorici, welcken hem het maken verscheyden dingen daer Metselrijen in quame. Hem was oock doen volmaken een Tafereel van Perspective/daer enne Cornelius van Vianen was over gestorben/desen hadde redelrijk verstandt van dese dingen/doch op een zware manier".

57 Pieter Coecke van Aelst, *Die Inventie van Columnen*, Antwerp: Coecke van Aelst, 1539. On the extremely rare book (less than four exemplars survive), see Rudi Rolf, *Pieter Coecke van Aelst en Zijn Architectuuruitgaves van 1539*, Amsterdam: s.p., 1978, and more recently, Krista de Jonge, " '*Anticse Wecken*': Le Decouverte del L'Architecture Antique dans la Practique Architecturale des Anciens Pays-Bas. Livres de Modeles et Traites" in Michele-Caroline Heck, Frederique Lemerle, and Yves Pauwels (eds), *Theorie des arts et creation artistique dans l'Europe du Nord du XVIe au debut du XVIIIe siecle*, Lille: Université Charles-de-Gaulle-Lille, 3, 2002, pp. 59–61. Zimmermann, *Architectura*, pp. 158–65, notes that Coecke's books, like Serlio's, were not aimed specifically at builders.

58 T. J. Bruyn, "Tekeningen uit de werkplaats van Pieter Coecke van Aelst", *Nederlands Kunsthistorisch Jaarboek*, 38, 1987, pp. 73–86. Bruyn doubts the Pieter Bruegel connection.

59 For an overview of the book's history and survival, see Krista de Jonge, "Les Éditions du Traité de Serlio par Pieter Coecke van Aelst" in Sylvie Deswarte-Rosa (ed.), *Sebastiano Serlio a Lyon: Architecture et Imprimerie*, Lyon: Mémoire Active, 2004, pp. 263–7, and Sune Schéle, "Pieter Coecke and Cornelis Bos", *Oud Holland*, 77, 1962, pp. 235–40.

60 In 1542, the Antwerp engraver Cornelis Bos was contracted to sell 300 copies of Coecke van Aelst's Serlio at 14 sols apiece, and, later, 650 copies of the *Inventie* at one sol apiece. Bos seems to have sold 79 copies of the translation of Serlio's larger book before 1544. See J. Cuvelier, "Le graveur Cornelius van den Bossche", *Bulletin de l'Institut Historique de Rome*, 20, 1939, p. 10.; and de Jonge, "Les Editions", p. 264.

61 See Van Mander, fol. 218v, and Lampsonius, *Pictorum Aliquot Celebrum Germaniae Inferioris Effigies*, Antwerp: Hieronymus Cock, 1572, no. 16.

62 Joseph Rykwert, "The Roots of Architectural Bibliophilia", *Scroope: Cambridge Architectural Journal*, 8, 1996, pp. 111–17.

63 The two main sources for Coecke van Aelst's illustrations were Caesarino's Vitruvius (Como, 1521) and Diego de Sagredo's *Medidas del Romano* (Roman measurements), printed in Toledo in 1526. See Diego de Sagredo, *Medidas del Romano*, Toledo: Ramon de Petras, 1526, on which see Nigel Llewellyn, "Diego de Sagredo's Medidas del Romano and the Vitruvian Tradition", M.Phil. dissertation, Warburg Institute, University of London, 1977. In the North, however, Walther Ryff's *Vitruvius Teutsch*,

Nürenberg: Petreuis, 1548, retained a closer eye on the original antique treatise of Vitruvius, retaining terms like "architectus", in conjunction with Serlio's other copyists. Both publications would have been available on the Antwerp book market soon after their publication. See Forssman, *Säule*, pp. 239–51.

64 See Françoise Choay, "Le *de re aedificatoria* comme texte inagural" in Jean Guillaume (ed.), *L'Emploi des Ordres dans l'Architecture de la Renaissance*, Paris: Pichard, 1992, pp. 85–90.

65 Pieter Coecke van Aelst, *Het derde Boeck, handelende van de aldervermaertse Antique edificen*, Antwerp: Coecke van Aelst, 1540, fol. Aiv. ". . . in desen tegenwoordighen boeck niet allenlijk lesen en moghen wat ten lesen na alle andere natien de Romeynen ghebouwen hebben/maer hebben eenen alsulcken auteur voorhanden die figuren (sulckx alsmense noch in wesen vindt) van stuck tot stucke/niet alleene by roeden/ellen/vouten/ende palmen/maer oock by minuten scherpelijk ghemeten ende wel conterfeyt ons voorghestelt heeft". Van Aelst's text is a gloss of Serlio's original preface to the reader from his own 1539 *Third Book;* Coecke's was used for the first English version of Serlio; London: Robert Peake, 1611.

66 Cf. Coecke van Aelst, *Inventie*, fols. a2v, a3r.

67 This term is Coecke van Aelst's explanation for the notion of the "theoretical" aspect of architecture, which stands in opposition to the practical. See Hessel Miedema, "Over de waardering van architect en beeldende kunstenaar in de zestiende eeuw", *Oud Holland*, 94, 1980, p. 73.

68 Coecke van Aelst, *Inventie*, fol. a4v. "Architectura (dats overbouwmeesterie) . . . is verciert met veel andere consten en geleertheden, doer wiens von nis ende regel geprobeert worden alle werken die vande anderern consten volmaect worden. Dese spruit wt timmeringe en wt overlegginge. Timmeringe is een gecotinueerde ingebroken oefeninge van gebruike, welcke volbracht wort metten handen alsmen iet maect wt eeniger materien hoedanich datse is. Overlegginge is een cloecheit die can wtlegge getimmerde dingen, ende bewisen wat maniere van proportie daerinne is". Cf. Vitruvius, I.1.1–2, 21–2.

69 See Miedema, "Over de waardering", pp. 72–4, and Rudolf Meischke, "Het Architonisch Ontwerp in de Nederlanden gedurende de Late Middeleeuwen en die Zestiende Eeuw", *Bulletin KNOB*, 5, 6th series, 1952, cols. 199–227. German craftsmen seem to have encountered the term somewhat earlier; see P. A. Rose, "Wolf Huber Studies", Ph.D. dissertation, Columbia University, 1973, pp. 207–8.

70 On Dutch masons' guilds see H. Janse and D. J. de Vries, *Werk en Merk van de Steenhouwer: het Steenhouwerambacht in de Nederlanden voor 1800*, Zwolle: Waanders, 1991.

71 Vitruvius I.1.3–4, 22.

72 Coecke van Aelst, *Inventie*, fol. a5r: "Hy [the architect] moet ooc gelittereert sijn, ende conne betrecken oft ontworpe". On a different kind of distinction between craft and theory in contemporary Italian and French architectural practice, see Catherine Wilkinson, "The New Professionalism in the Renaissance" in Michael W. Cole (ed.), *Sixteenth Century Italian Art*, London: Blackwell, 2006, pp. 246–74.

73 Meischke, "Het Architonisch Ontwerp", cols. 232–233. See also Miedema, "Over de waardering", pp. 76–7.

74 S. Muller Fz, "Getuigenverhoor te Antwerpen. Over het maken van ontwerpen van Gebouwen in de 16e Eeuw door Schilders, Goudsmeden, Timerlieden en Metselaars", *Archief voor Nederlandsche Kunstgeschiedenis*, 4, 1881–1882, pp. 227–45. The testimony records the following statement: ". . . architectura, is een wetenschap ofte conste, die verciert is van veel onderwijsingen ende diversche geleertheden, duer wiens oerdel allen wercken, die dueren anderen consten volmaict worden".

75 Muller Fz, "Getuigenverhoor", p. 245: "Is dan wel claerlicken te vertstaen, dat achitectura onder geen particulaer contse begrepen en is, als te weten onder scilderie, steenhouden, cleensteecken, metseloen, tymmeren ofte diergelicken, mer dese syn alle mer deelen ende also limaten, onder die architectura begrepen". On this conclusion see also Piet Lombaerde, "Antwerp in its golden age: one of the largest cities in the Low Countries and one of the best fortified in Europe" in Patrick O'Brien (ed.), *Urban Achievement in Early Modern Europe: Golden Ages in Antwerp, Amsterdam, and London*, Cambridge: Cambridge University Press, 2001, pp. 113–15.

76 Hans Vredeman de Vries, *Architectura, Oder Bauung der Antiquen*, Antwerp: Gerard de Jode, 1577, fol. 5v. On van den Broeke: J. Duverger and M. J. Onghena, "Enkele nieuwe gegevens betreffende beeldhouwer W. van den Broeke alias Paludanus (1530 tot 1570 of 1580)", *Gentse bijdragen tot de kunstgeschiedenis*, 5, 1938, pp. 75–130.

77 "Dat ter contratrien notoor is, bij alle persoonen van verstande, date alle sunderlinghe ende excellente edifice ende werken . . . bij de beeltsnijders ende architecten geprojecteert, geordonnert ende tot perfectie gebracht moeten wordden, dewelcke de metsers moeten leeren ende de forme prescriberen, die sij moeten naevolghen. Soodat de beeltsnijders ended architecten dienaengaande in effecte de leeraers ende schoelmeesters van de metsers sijn, delwelcke in alsulke wercken nyet eenen steen en souden connen leggen, dan bij ordonnacien van den architecten". Van den Bloecke's testimony is transcribed in J. Rylant and M. Casteels, "De metsers van Antwerpen tegen Paludanus, Floris, de Nole's en anderen beeldhouwers", *Bijdragen tot de geschiedenis*, 31, 1940, pp. 185–203, with additional commentary by Krista de Jonge, "Interiors, Chimneypieces, and Portals" in Lombaerde, *Artes*, p. 144.

78 Coecke van Aelst, 1539, fol. a5r: "In allen dingen, ende bisonder in Architectura, zijn dese twee dingen, het gene dat beteekent; het voergeleide dink daerme af seit, is datter beteeket wort. De selve dinck beteekent dat onderwijs dat wtgesproken wort en betoont met redden vaconsten . . ". The relevant passage is in Vitruvius, 1.1.3, on which see F. Pellati, "Quod significatur et quod significat. Saggio d'interpretazione di un passo di Vitruvio", *Historia* 1, 1927, pp. 53–9. The German translation of the passage, which Vredeman likely saw, is nearly identical; see Ryff, *Vitriuvius Teutsch*, Nuremberg, 1548, fol. Aiiv.

79 Indra McEwan, *Vitruvius: Writing the Body of Architecture*, Cambridge, MA: MIT Press, 2003, pp. 76–7.

80 See John Onians, *Bearers of Meaning: The Classical Orders in Antiquity, the Middle Ages, and the Renaissance*, Princeton: Princeton University Press, 1989, p. 264.

81 Robin Evans, "Architectural Projection", in Montréal, *Image*, p. 21.

82 Vredeman, *Architectura*, fol. A1r. ". . . tis een excellent Conste, dwelck sijnen meester laudeert".

83 Mario Carpo, "How do you imitate a building you have never seen? Printed images, ancient models, and handmade drawings in Renaisssance architectural theory", *Zeitschrift für Kunstgeschichte*, 64: 2, 2001, p. 223.

84 Wolfang Lotz, "The Rendering of the Interior in Architectural Drawings of the Renaissance" in W. Lotz (ed.), *Studies in Italian Renaissance Architecture*, Cambridge, MA: MIT Press, 1977, pp. 1–65, and Myra Nan Rosenfeld, "Sebastiano Serlio's Contribution to the Creation of the Modern Illustrated Architectural Manual" in C. Thoenes (ed.), *Sebastiano Serlio*, Milan: Electa, 1996, pp. 102–10.

85 Francoise Choay, *The Rule and the Model: on the theory of architecture and urbanism*, Cambridge, MA: MIT Press, 1997, pp. 190–1.

86 Beatriz Colomina, "Media as Modern Architecture" in *Thomas Demand*, London: Serpentine Gallery, 2006, p. 44. Colomina argues that what defined twentieth-century modern architecture was less buildings than exhibition pavilions, photographs, advertisements, and models: "Modern architecture is produced within the space of photographs and publications, this space is for the most part two dimensional . . . Architects act as if their buildings were mainly images; they design the image", p. 37.

87 C. H. Peters, "Hans Vredeman de Vries. Mededelingen omtrent het leven en de werken van dezen Nederlandschen kunstenaar", *Bouwkundig Weekblad*, 26,1895, pp. 126–68.

88 Pietro Bembo, as quoted in Pon, *Raphael*, p. 22.

89 Jeroen Jansen, "Anders of beter: Emulatie in de renaissance literatuurtheorie", *De zeventiende eeuw*, 21:2, 2005, pp. 181–97; also Maria H. Loh, "New and Improved: Repetition as Originality in Italian Baroque practice and theory", *Art Bulletin*, 86:3, 2004, pp. 477–504; Alexander Nagel, "The Copy and its Evil Twin: Thirteen Notes on Forgery", *Cabinet*, 14, 2004, pp. 102–5.

90 Van Mander, fol. 267r.

91 William Ivins, *Prints and Visual Communication*, London: Routledge, 1953, p. 70. On this extremely problematic claim, see Lorraine Daston and Peter Galison, "The Image of Objectivity", *Representations*, 40, Fall 1992, pp. 81–128.

92 Vasari, *Lives*, vol. I, p. 47.

93 Andre Chastel, "Les vues urbaines peintes et le théâtre" in *Bollettino del Centro Internazionale di Studi di Architettura Andrea Palladio*, 1974, Paris, 1978, vol. 1, pp. 497–501. On the role of perspective in early architectural design processes, see particularly Alberto Pérez-Gómez and Louise Pelletier, "Architectural Representation Beyond Perspectivism", *Perspecta: The Yale Architectural Journal*, 27, 1992, pp. 21–39, and Caroline van Eck, "Verbal and visual abstraction: the role of pictorial techniques of representation in Renaissance architectural theory" in Christy Anderson (ed.), *The Built Surface, Vol 1: Architecture and the Pictorial Arts from Antiquity to the Enlightenment*, Aldershot: Ashgate, 2002, pp. 162–79.

94 Sebastiano Serlio, *I sette libri dell' architettura*, book II, fol. 25v, Vaughn Hart and Pieter Hicks (trans.), in *Sebastiano Serlio on Architecture*, New Haven: Yale University Press, 1996, p. 37.

95 Roger Tarr, "Brunelleschi and Donatello: Placement and Meaning in Sculpture", *Artibus et Historiae*, 16: 32, April 1995, pp. 101–40.

96 Alberti, *de re aedificatoria*, book II, ch. 1, as cited in Hart, "Serlio and Representation" in Hart, Vaughn Hart and Peter Hicks, *Paper Palaces: The Rise of the Renaissance Architectural Treatise*, New Haven: Yale University Press, 1998, p. 177.

97 Wolfgang Lotz, "Das Raumbild in der italienischen Architekturzeichnung der Renaissance", *Mitteilungen des kunsthistorischen Instituts in Florenz*, 7, 1956, pp. 193–227, attributes this trend to Italian architects' lack of familiarity (and interest) in architectural treatises.

98 ". . . con [perspective] quale saerebbe impossibile, or almeno difficilisimo, redurre tal cose nelle proprie forme . . "., John Shearman, *Raphael in Early Modern Sources*, New Haven: Yale University Press, 2004, vol. 1, p. 526. See Werner Oeschlin, "Architektur, Perspektive, und die hilfreiche Geste der Geometrie", *Daidalos*, 11, 1984, pp. 38–54; and the annotations to the passage in Vaughn Hart and Peter Hicks, *Palladio's Rome*, New Haven: Yale University Press, 2006, p. 191. On the letter to Leo X: Francesco Paolo Di Teodoro, *Raffaello, Baldassar Castiglione e la letter a Leone X*, Bologna: La Nuova Alfa, 1994.

99 Gotz Pöchat, *Theater und Bildende Kunst in Mittelalter und in der Renaissance in Italien*, Graz: Akademische Druk, 1990, p. 313.

100 See Th. H. Lunsingh Scheurleer, "Pieter Aertsen en Joachim Beuckelaer en hun ontleeningen aan Serlio's architectuurprenten", *Oud Holland*, 62, 1947, fol. 123; Keith Moxey, *Pieter Aertsen, Joachim Beuckelaer, and the rise of secular painting in the context of the Reformation*, Ph.D. dissertation, University of Chicago, 1974, pp. 41–112, and M. Meadow, "Aertsen's *Christ in the House of Martha and Mary*: Serlio's Architecture and the Meaning of Location" in Jelle Koopmans et al. (eds), *Rhetoric-Rhétoriqueurs-Rederijkers*, Koninklijke Nederlandse Akademie van Wetenschappen Verhandelingen, Afd. Letterkunde, new series, no 162, Amsterdam/Oxford/New York/Tokyo: North Holland, 1995, pp. 175–92.

101 See, for example, *Da Tiziano a El Greco: Per la storia del Manierismo a Venezia*, exh. cat., Venice, 1981, no 24.

102 Damisch, *Origin*, 271. Emphasis added.

103 Christopher Wood, review of Hubert Damisch, *The Origin of Perspective*, in *Art Bulletin*, 77, December 1995, p. 678.

104 That certain Italian perspective systems were devoted to the rendering of objects rather than spaces is argued in James Elkins, "Renaissance Perspectives", *Journal of the History of Ideas*, 53:2, 1992, pp. 209–30.

105 Jean-Paul Sartre, "Saint Georges et la Dragon", *Situations*, IX, Paris: Gallimard, 1972, pp. 202–26.

106 Janzten, *Architekturbild*, 22: "Sie [the prints] sind stets so angelegt, dass das Auge wie zwischen Eisenbahnscheinen auf den Augenpunkt hingezogen wird".

107 See, for example, Vredeman, *Architectura* (Dutch) title page, 1577 edition.

108 On the historical conditions under which prints were viewed, see Umberto Eco, "Interpreting Serials", in *The Limits of Interpretation*, Bloomington, IN: Indiana University Press, 1990, pp. 83–100. On the sixteenth century, specifically, see Peter Parshall, "The Print Collection of Ferdinand of Tyrol", *Jahrbuch der Kunsthistorischen Sammlungen in* Wien, 88, 1982, pp. 139–84, and Beatrice Hernad, *Die Graphiksammlung des Humanisten Hartmann Schedel*, Munich: Prestel, 1990, pp. 53–65.

109 Roland Barthes, *S/Z*, Richard Miller (trans.), New York: Farar, Strauss, & Giroux, 1974, p. 12. For a related application of this passage see Powell, "Origins", p. 724.

110 H. A. Gronewagen-Frankfurt, *Arrest and Movement: An Essay on Space and Time in the representational art of the ancient near east*, London: Faber and Faber, 1951, pp. 3–7.

111 Serlio, 37, Book II, fol. 25v.

112 Van Mander, *Grondt*, Chapter 8, § 17–26.

113 Alois Riegl, *Historical Grammar of the Visual Arts*, Jacqueline Jung (trans.), New York: Zone, 2004, pp. 172–78.

114 Anthonis Blocklandt (1533/4–1583) was named as the painter of the human figures when the painting was inventoried at Whitehall (London), sometime in the reign of Charles I (1600–1649). Few subsequent scholars have disputed the account; see Jadwiga Vuyk, "Anthonie Blocklandt van Montfoort II", *Oud Holland*, 46, 1929, pp. 108–9. Kristof Michiels, "Gillis Mostaert (1528–1598)" in Arnout Balis, et al. (eds), *Florissant: Bijdragen tot de kunstgeschiedenis der Nederlanden (15de—17de eeuw)*, Brussels: VUB Press, 2005, pp. 215–18, shows that the extant figures of Mary and Martha were painted over earlier figures. The architecture of the picture, however, is clearly signed in two places by Vredeman de Vries, and Campbell (*Flemish Pictures*, pp. 118–20) suggests that the staffagist painted *over* early human figures originally by Vredeman. The alterations could have been executed at the behest of a doctrinally concerned patron who sought a more legible subject; the copies now at Bremen (Roselius-Haus) and sold at London art market (Christies, King Street, March 12, 1926, lot 2), suggests that the original figures were much larger.

115 Van Mander, fol. 261r. Gillis Mostaert had a twin brother, Frans, who was also a painter. On Gillis, see Sander Pierron, *Les Mostaert: Jean Mostaert die le Maitre d'Oultremont. Gilles et Francois Mostaert. Michel Mostaert*, Brussels: van Oest, 1912, and Giorgio T. Faggin, "Gillis Mostaert als landschapschilder", *Jaarboek Koninklijke Museum voor schone Kunsten Antwerpen*, 1964, pp. 142–54, and Ekkhard Mai (ed.), *Gillis Mostaert (1528–1598): ein Antwerpener Maler zur Zeit der Bruegel-Dynastie*, Wolfratshausen: Edition Minerva, 2005.

116 Stanley Ferber, "Peter Bruegel and the Duke of Alva", *Renaissance News*, 19, 1966, pp. 205–19.

117 Vasari, *Lives*, Book I, p. 497.

118 Edward Norgate, *Miniatura, or, The Art of Limming* (1649–1650), J. Muller (ed.), New Haven: Yale University Press, 1996, pp. 86–7: "The only Inconvenience to Perspective, and whereof I have heard [architectural painter] Mr. Steinwicke complaine with indignation, was that soe many were the lines perpendicular perralell and the rest, that another Painter could compleat a piece, and get his money, before he could draw his lines".

119 Particularly in the later seventeenth century. On Antwerp see Zirka Zaremba Filipczak, *Picturing Art in Antwerp 1550–1700*, Princeton: Princeton University Press, 1987, pp. 31–44, and Katelijne van der Stighelen. "Productiviteit en samenwerking in het Antwerpse kunstenaarmilieu, 1620–1640", *Gemeentekrediet: Driemaandelijks Tijdschrift van het Gemeentekredit van Belgie*, 172, 1990–92, pp. 5–15. Collaborative practices were not limited to minor artists: see Marie-Louise Hairs, "Collaboration dans les tableaux de fleurs flamands", *Revue belge d'archaeologie et de l'histoire de l'art*, 26:3, pp. 149–162. 1957, and more recently, Anne Wollett and Arianne van Suchtelen (eds), *Rubens and Bruegel: A Working Friendship*, Los Angeles: Getty Museum, 2005, pp. 29–35.

120 See Thomas Da Costa Kaufmann, *The School of Prague*, Chicago: University of Chicago Press, 1988, p. 288. On Dirck Quade van Ravensteyn: J. Neumann, "Rudolfski umeni II profily maliru a soschru", *Umění*, 26:4, 1978, pp. 303–47; and Nicole Dacos, "Dirck Quade van Ravensteyn avant Prague: des Pays-Bas à Fontainbleau et à Sienne", in *Kunst des Cinquicento in der Toskana*, Munich: Brinkmann, 1992, pp. 292–307.

121 Bredius, *Künstler-Inventare*, V, p. 639.

122 J. Denucé, *Kunstuitvoer in de 17de Eeuw te Antwerpen: de Firma Forschoudt*, Antwerp: De Sikkel, 1931, p. 131, n. 9.

123 Denucé, *Kunstuitvoer*, p. 108, n. 7: "1 perspectief van de Vries, de figuren van langen Peer daer ons Heer Matthias van den Tol roept".

124 *SAA, Privilegiekamer*, 2203, fol. 39v: "Gelycke acte op de specificatie van Peeteren Leys, ter causen

van het spannen ende schilderen vande doecken den grondt daeraff . . . de perspective de voeyeren ende stofferen van kleyne figuere, volgende de specificatie daeradd zynde Actum XXVIII July 1583".

125 Sold by J. Viet, Amsterdam, October 12, 1774, no. 236. See Schneede, "Interieurs", cat. 11/9. On the definition of *stofferen* in terms of collaboration see Honig, *Painting*, pp. 179–80.

126 Marburg, Bildarchiv, inv. 79.240. In at least one other example Vredeman distinguishes himself by name from the "executor" of a painting; see Vienna, Kunsthistorisches Museum, inv. 2335, signed: "*Vredeman Vriese inv PA Vredeman fec*".—the PA is Vredeman's son, Pauwels.

127 See, for example, Otto Benesch (ed.), *Die Zeichnungen der niederländischen Schulen des XV. und XVI. Jahrhunderts: Beschreibender Katalog der Handzeichnungen in der Graphischen Sammlung Albertina:* Vienna: A. Schroll, 1928, vol. 2, nos 302, 299.

128 Katelijne van der Stighelen, "Productiviteit en samenwerking". Yet, as the preceding paragraphs have made clear, I am again drawing upon the discussion in Honig, *Painting*, pp. 177–89. Honig supplies the important reminder that economic influences alone cannot account for the different species of collaboration that took place in Antwerp, and later, Brussels, workshops.

129 See Mikhail Bakhtin, *The Dialogic Imagination*, Caryl Emerson and Michael Holquist (trans.), Austin: Texas University Press, 1978, and Tzvetan Todorov, *Bakhtin: The Dialogic Principle*, Wlad Godzich (trans.), Minneapolis: University of Minnesota Press, 1984.

130 Mieke Bal, "Seeing Signs: The Use of Semiotics for the Understanding of Visual Art" in Cheetham et al., *The Subjects of Art History: Historical Objects in Contemporary Perspective*, Cambridge: Cambridge University Press, 1998, pp. 78–9.

131 Cicero, *De Inventione*, 1.7, 19. See also *De Oratore*, p. 99, Book I, xxxi, 14.2: "[the orator] must first hit upon what to say, then manage and marshal his discoveries". Cf. Thomas Wilson, *The Arte of Rhetorique*, London: R. Graftonus, 1553, fol. 6: "the finding out of apt matter, called otherwise Invention, is a searching out of things true, or things likely, the which may reasonablie set forth a matter, and make it appear probable". On invention across Renaissance rhetoric and art theory, see, among others, Mark W. Roskill, *Dolce's Aretino and Venetian Art Theory of the Cinquecento*, New York: NYU Press, 1968, p. 118, and Michael Baxandall, *Giotto and the Orators*, New Haven: Yale University Press, 1971, p. 101.

132 Polydoro Vergilio, *Von der erfyndern der dyngen*, Augsburg: Heinrich Steiner, 1533; see Polydore Vergil, *On Discovery*, Brian P. Copenhaver (trans.), Cambridge, MA: Harvard University Press, 2002. See Plato, *Phaedrus* 236 A, and Aristotle, *Rhetorica* 1.2 on the initial stages of discourse.

133 Van Mander, *Grondt*, Chapter 2, fol. 9v. See Van Mander, fol. 284r: ". . . besonder had ick groot behaghen in eenighen Historikens van Lucretia, die hy selfs gheinventeert en gesneden hadde".

134 Walter Melion, in *Shaping the Netherlandish Canon*, Chicago: University of Chicago Press, 1991, argues for a distinction between Van Mander's use of the term *inventy* in the biographies of the Italian and the Netherlandish painters. In the northern *Lives*, Melion suggests, Van Mander collapses the twin concepts if *inventy* and *handelingh* (treatment, carrying-out) into a single definition of *teyckenkonst* (drawing), which denotes a practice more material and process-based than the Italian concept of *disegno*. Melion: "The *inventy* that promulgates oils [in the life of Jan and Hubert van Eyck] generates new models of rendering . . . *Inventy*, then, is the source of *handeligh* and initiates both the material basis and concomitant dexterity that precipitate the history of northern art. It intensifies the imitation of nature and differentiates the action of the brush from that of the stylus, serving finally to separate Netherlandish from Italian painting", p. 54. In a review (in *Oud Holland*, 107:1, 1993, pp. 152–9) Hessel Miedema attacked Melion's thesis by producing a long list of citations from the *Schilderboeck* showing parallel uses of *inventy* in the antique, Italian and northern *Lives*. Variously synonymous with "design", "concept", "drawing ability", "discovery", or even "ornament", *inventy* in Miedema's list indeed reveals interchangeable use of the term throughout: "the conclusion is that no single noticeable difference exists between [Van Mander's] use of the term in the lives of the antique, the Italian, and the Netherlandish 'Lives' ", p. 158, he writes. Van Mander surely sought to connect, rather than to separate, theories underpinning art making in the Netherlands and in Renaissance Italy, and

"invention" was clearly a key element in this project. But Miedema's overt refusal to entertain the possibility that *inventy* in the Schilderboeck is not always securely defined, and that, despite multiple uses, slippages exist between them—largely due to Van Mander's use of a variety of sources—weakens his argument significantly; surely when one looks at a passage from the life of Michiel Mierveldt, such as "[he] is seer genege tot inventie/en heeft een goet begin van Schilderen" (he is quite inclined towards inventions, and began well in painting), *Lives*, fol. 281v, the notion of invention is hardly explicit? On *inventy*, see the *Grondt*, Book II, fol. 9v, and Miedema's *Kunst, kunstenaar en kunstwerk bij Karel van Mander; een analyse van zijn levensbeschrijvingen*, Alphen aan den Rijn: Canaletto, 1980, pp. 139–45. On invention in the sixteenth century see R. Schleier, "Inventio als Maßstab der Kunstkritik" in *Bilder nach Bildern*, exh. cat., Münster: Landschaftsverband Westfalen-Lippe, 1976, pp. 78ff.; Svetlana Alpers, "Ekphrasis and Aesthetic Attitudes in Vasari's *Lives*", *Journal of the Warburg and Courtauld Institutes*, 23, 1960, pp.190–215; on *inventio* and printmaking, see Lincoln, *Invention*, pp. 7–9. Among the (enormous) literature on invention in rhetorical theory and architecture, see D. J. Gordon, "Poet and Architect" (1949) in *The Renaissance Imagination*, Berkeley: University of California Press, 1975, pp. 77–101, and Caroline van Eck, "Architecture, Language, and *Rhetoric* in Alberti's *De re aedificatoria*" in Georgia Clarke and David Crossley (eds), *Architecture and Language*, Cambridge: Cambridge University Press, 2000, pp. 72–81.

Chapter 2 Antwerp: the city rehearsed

1 Gottfried Semper, "Style in the Technical and Tectonic Arts or Practical Aesthetics", *The Four Elements of Architecture and Other Writings*, Harry F. Malgrave (trans.), Cambridge: Cambridge University Press, 1989, p. 256.

2 Adrian van Haemstede, *Historie ofte Geschiedenis vromer martelaren . . .*, Sedan: Goosen Gebbens, 1566, p. 518: "Want (seyde hy) Antwerpen is ghelijcke een werelt/men mach he daer wel in vereborgen houde/sonder daer wt to vlien".

3 "Ghenven in alder odimoet te kennen Uwe Magisteit onderdanige, die borgermeesteren, scepenen, tresoirs ende rentmeesteren der stadt van Antwerpen hoe dat, mits de cleynichheyt, bevanchheyt, ende ouderdom van den tegenwoirdighen stadthuys, zij bevonden, ende een yeglycken is kennelyck ende notoir, dat van noode is een nyeuwe stadhuys te makende, tenzij dat men die dubite ruyne, ten grooten pericle van denghenen die 't selve frequenteren, ende moeten frequenteren, wille verwachten". Letter from Antwerp City Magistrate to Philip II and Margaret of Parma, August 2, 1560, cited in Floris Prims, *Het Stadhuis te Antwerpen: Geschiedenis en Beschrijving*, Antwerp, Standaard, 1930, pp. 51–2.

4 Holm Bevers in *Das Rathaus von Antwerpen: Architektur und Figurenprogramm*, Hildesheim: Olms, 1985, pp. 159–60, transcribes the section of the 1561 document, referring to an "enclosed plan", which, sadly, has not survived. The transcription in Prims, *Stadhuis*, p. 52, is incomplete.

5 "Son Altesse . . . consent aux suppliants de edificier une nouvelle maison de ville de la longeur de 236 piedz et de 88 piedz de largeur, selon de patron par eulx exhibé". Letter from Margaret of Parma to Antwerp City Magistrates, August 29, 1560, Prims, *Stadhuis*, p. 52.

6 ". . . nullum Europa par habet aedificium, aequandum etiam stupendis illis mundi miraculis", quoted in Leon Voet, *De gouden eeuw van Antwerpen: Bloei en uitstraling van de Metropool in de zestiende eeuw*, Antwerp: Mercatorfonds, 1973, p. 146.

7 H (Vredeman) 181. Stockholm, Kungliga Biblioteket, sig. De la Gardie 160.

8 As cited in Guido Marnef, *Antwerp in the Age of Reformation*, Baltimore: Johns Hopkins University press, 1996, p. 14. The present chapter owes much to Marnef's "lucid analysis".

9 Simon Schama, "Mr. Europe: Peter Paul Rubens and the Universalist Ideal", *The New Yorker*, May 5, 1997, p. 214. Original italics.

10 Ad Meskens, *Wiskunde tussen Renaissance en Barok: aspecten van wiskundebeofening te Antwerpen 1550–1620*, Antwerp: AMVC, 1994, p. 180.

11 H (Vredeman) no 182:2. Two exemplars of the second state exist: Vienna, Kunsthistorisches Museum 6623, fol. 15, no 27, and *SAA*, inv. Icon. D-24/B.6.

12 Michel de Certeau, *The Practice of Everyday Life*, Stephen F. Randall (trans.), Berkeley and London: University of California Press, 1988, especially pp. 284–91; on sociological approaches to sixteenth-century urban history, see Rose Marie San Juan, *Rome: A City out of Print*, Minneapolis: University of Minnesota Press, 2001, pp. 9–21.
13 On early modern definitions of public, see Christine Klapisch-Zuber, "Kins, Friends, and Neighbors", in *Women, Family, and Ritual in Renaissance Italy*, Chicago: Chicago University Press, 1985, pp. 68–93.
14 W. Brulez, "Bruges and Antwerp in the 15th and 16th Centuries: An antithesis?", *Acta Historiae Neerlandica*, 6, 1973, pp. 1–26, and R. van Uyten, "Brabantse en Antwerpse centrale plaatsen (14de-19de eeuw)" in *Het Stedelijke netwerk in Belgie in historische perspectief (1350–1850)*, Brussels: Gemeentekrediet, 1992, pp. 29–79, and Filip Vermeylen, *Painting for the Market: Commercialization of Art in Antwerp's Golden Age*, Turnhout: Brepols, 2003, pp. 15–34.
15 Leon Voet, in Jan van der Stock (ed.), *Antwerp: Story of a Metropolis, 16th–17th Century*, Ghent: Snoeck-Ducaju & Zoon, 1993, p. 15.
16 Hermann van der Wee, *The Rise and Decline of Urban Industries in Italy and the Low Countries*, Leuven: Leueven University Press, 1963, p. 201.
17 H. Soly and A. K. L. Thijs, "Nijverheid in de Zuidelike Nederlanden" in Blok et al., *Algemene Geschiedenis der Nederlanden*, Haarlem: Fibula-Van Dishoeck, 1979, vol. VI, pp. 27–57.
18 The largest cities in Europe by population in 1550 were (in descending order): Naples, Venice, Paris, Lisbon, Antwerp. See Jan van Roey, "De bevolking" in *Antwerpen in de XVIde* eeuw, Antwerp: Mercurius, 1975, pp. 95–108.
19 Jan-Albert Goris, *Lof van Antwerpen: Hoe reizigers Antwerp zagen, van de XVe tot XXe Eeuw*, Brussels: N.V. Standaard, 1940, p. 42. On Guicciardini: P. Desan, "Lodovico Guicciardini et le discours sur la ville a la Renaissance", in P. Jodogne (ed.), *Lodovico Guicciardini (1521–1589). Actes du Colloque international des 28, 29, et 30 mars 1990*, Leuven: Universiteit Press, 1991, pp. 135–50.
20 G. E. Wells, "Antwerp and the Government of Philip II, 1555–1567", Ph.D. dissertation, Cornell University, 1982, pp. 5–18.
21 Wells, "Government", p. 275.
22 Marnef, *Antwerp*, pp. 5–20.
23 Marnef, *Antwerp*, p. 5.
24 See, for example, Willem Brulez, "Anvers de 1585 a 1650", *Vierteljahrsschrifte für Sozial- und Wirtschaftsgeschichte*, 53, 1967, pp. 75–99.
25 e.g. H (Vredeman), nos 183–200, 201–22.
26 Marnef, *Antwerp*, p. 21.
27 Van de Wee, *Rise and Decline*, pp. 245–51.
28 See *SAA*, Huiweliken, 1566, fol. 368r. Sara van Elsmaer's father, Wouter, was a sculptor who later worked with Vredeman in Wolfenbüttel. See Borggefe, *Norden*, p. 18.
29 See Ph. Rombouts and Th. van Lerius, *De liggeren en andere historische archieven der Antwerpsche Sint Lucasgilde, onder zinspreuk "Wt lonsten Versaemt"*, Antwerp: de Baggeman, 1864 (reprint Amsterdam, 1961), vol. I.
30 Van Mander, fol. 266r.
31 On the pardon, see E. M. Braekman, "Het Lutheranisme in Antwerpen", *Bijdragen tot de Geschiedenis*, 70, 1987, pp. 23–38.
32 *SAA* Collegieactienboek, April 29, 1581. See also Floris Prims, "De huisraad van Oranje te Antwerpen", *Antwerpiensa*, 7, 1933.
33 *SAA* Privilegiekamer 659, Requestboek 1581, fol. 8r, for February 4, 1581: ". . . Met Hans van Schille ingeniaur gemaeckt nyet half soe lastigen dienst enz . . ."., Vredeman also designed a small military encampment called Fort Veer on the western bank of the Schelde in 1584; see *AA*, vol. XIV, pp. 329–30, and Blockman's, "Een krijgstekening", p. 36.
34 *SAA* Requestboek, fol. 1972r.
35 *SAA*, Inv. G7A, 4830, fol. 198v. Notably, only citizens registered as Catholics could serve on the *wacht*.
36 J. van Roey, "De Antwerpse schilders in 1584–1585", *Jaarboek van het Koninklijk Museum voor Schone Kunsten te Antwerpen*, 1966, p. 119.

37 The painting was in the Stadsarchief, Antwerp after 1946. A 1615 inventory of the Stadhuis, however, makes no mention of it; see Klauss Bussman et al. (eds), *Kreig und Frieden in Europa*, Münster: Westfalisches Landesmuseum, 1999, pp. 29–30.

38 See Anne-Marie van Passen, "Antwerp under the Magnifying Glass. An Anthology", in Van der Stock, *Metropolis*, p. 63.

39 Peter Paul Rubens to Pierre Dupuy, May 28, 1627, in *The Letters of Peter Paulus Rubens*, Ruth Saunders Magurn (trans. and ed.), Cambridge, MA: Harvard University Press, 1955, p. 185. Conversely, on Antwerp's "Indian summer", c.1585–1650, see R. Baetens, *De nazomer van Antwerpens welvaart. De diaspora en het handelshuis Dr Groote tijdens de eerste half der 17de eeuw*, Brussels: Gemeentekrediet, 1976, 2 vols.

40 Rutger Tijs, "Antwerpen als invoerhaven en draaischrift van renaissance-ideeën" in Ed Taverne and I. Visser, *In't land van belofte: in de nieuwe stad. Ideale en werkelijkheid van de stadsuitleg in de Republiek 1580–1680*, Maarssen: Schwartz, 1978, pp. 93–102.

41 The wheel was the most used form of execution for perpetrators of property crimes between 1550–1600; see Mitchell B. Merback, *The Thief, the Cross, and the Wheel: Pain and the Spectacle of Punishment in Medieval and Renaissance Europe*, London: Reaktion, 1999, pp. 158–64.

42 H.G. Jelgesma, *Galgebergen en Galgevelden*, Zutphen: De Walburg Pers, 1978, pp. 8–13.

43 Hans Mielke, in Berlin, Kunstbibliothek, *Fünf Architekten aus fünf Jahrhunderten*, Berlin: Volker Mann, 1976, p. 8, attributes this in part to the print medium, ". . . die grellen Schwarzwieß-Kontraste (bei Ätzungen haufig) passen besser zu den geisterschaften, fast menschenleeren Straßenschluchten mit ihrem gewaltsamen Tiefenzog, den übersteilen, unwirklichen Häusern, deren Fenster z.T. schmal werden wie Schießscharten, einer beklemmenden Alptraumwelt . . ".

44 Lucia De Pauw-De Veen, "Archivalische gegevens", p. 231.

45 Van Mander, fols 266r–266v: ". . .en eergh stracx te Brussel te schilderen [Vredeman] voor den Tresorier Aert Molckeman, een Somer-huys in Perspectief/daer verseierende onder een open deur/waer in/in't afwesen va de Vries/Pieter Bruegel vindende hier de reetschap/hadde ghemaeckt een Boer met een beseghelt hemde/vaste doende met een Boerinne/waerom seer ghelachten/en den Heer [i.e. Molckman] seer aengenaem was/die on t'groot gelt niet hadde laten uytdoen".

46 Fedja Anzelewsky (ed.), *Pieter Bruegel d. Ä. als Zeichner*, Berlin: Staatliche Museen Preussischer Kulturbesitz, 1975, pp. 139–44; and for another view, Walter Gibson, *Pleasant Places: the Rustic landscape from Bruegel to Ruisdael*, Berkeley: University of California Press, 2000, p. 17.

47 Riggs, *Hieronymus Cock*, cat. nos 98–109.

48 Although this changed as the century progressed; using straw to thatch roofs was formally prohibited only in 1503, and in 1546 wooden gables were outlawed with little success. See R. Thijs, *Crowning the City*, Antwerp: Mercator, 1991; Voet, *Antwerpen*, pp. 439–42.

49 These plates, in turn, appear in an inventory of Galle's widow from 1636. See J. Denucé, "Prenthandel Theodoor Galle en Catharina Moerentorf", *Antwerpsche Archivenblad*, 2:1, January 1927, p. 146.

50 See Mielke, *Verzeichnis*, pp. 6–17; Riggs, *Hieronymus Cock*, p. 207.

51 e.g. Biblioteca Escorial, Album no 28–II–14. See J. A. DeLasarte and A. Casanovas, "Catalogo de la Coleccion de Grabados de la Biblioteca de la Escorial", *Anales y Boletin de los Museos de Arte de Barcelona*, XVI–XVII, 1963–66, and J. Gonazles de Zarate (ed.), *Real Coleccion de Estampas de San Lorenzo de El Escorial*, Vittoria/Gasteiz: Instituto Municipal de Estudios Iconográficos, 1992–96, 11 vols. More recently M. MacDonald, "The Print Collection of Philip II at the Escorial", *Print Quarterly*, XV, 1998, pp. 15–35.

52 Heuer, "Between the Histories of Art", pp. 29–32.

53 Van Mander, fol. 266r: "26. stucken/insiende en van boven siende Paleysen/uytwendigh en inwendigh . . ".

54 J. Denuce, *De Antwerpsche "Konstkamers" Inventarissen van kunstverzamelingen te Antwerpen in de zestiende en zeventiende eeuw*, Amsterdam: de Spiegel, 1932, p. 112.

55 Ian Buchanan, "Dürer and Abraham Ortelius", *Burlington Magazine*, CXXIV, 957, 1982, pp. 73–4; on "travel" in Bruegel's prints, Julius Müller-Hofstede, "Zur Interpretation von Bruegels Landschaft" in Otto von Simson and Matthias Winner (eds), *Pieter Bruegel und Seine Welt: Ein Colloquium*

veranstaltet vom Kunsthistorischen Institut der freien Universitat Berlin und dem Kupferstichkabinett der Staatlichen Museen Stiftung Preussischer Kulturbesitz, Berlin: Mann, 1979, pp. 73–142; Joseph Leo Koerner, "Unmasking the World: Bruegel's Ethnography", *Common Knowledge*, 10:2, 2004, pp. 221–3.

56 See Gunter Irmscher, "Hans Vredeman de Vries als Zeichner (I)", *Kunsthistorisches Jahrbuch Graz*, 21, 1985, pp. 123–42.

57 Mielke, *Verzeichnis*, p. 8. Erik Forssman, meanwhile, called the prints "a Northerner's dream of southern colonnades and ornate plazas", (den Traum des Nordlaenders von südlandischen saeulen- und laubengeschmückten Plaetzen); see Forssman, *Säule*, p. 86.

58 Paul Valéry, *Eupalinos; or, The Architect*, W. M. Stewart (trans.), Oxford: Oxford University Press, 1932, pp. 24–33.

59 Hugo Soly, *Urbanisme en kapitalisme te Antwerpen in de 16de eeuw*, Brussels: Gemeentekrediet, 1977, pp. 153–9.

60 City Magistrate to Parma, May 2, 1567, quoted in Marnef, *Antwerp*, p. 6. On the housing data, see Soly, "De Megalopolis Antwerpen" in L. Voet et al., *De stad Antwerpen van de Romeinse tijd tot de 17de eeuw: Topografische studie rond het plan van Virgilius Bononeisus 1565*, Brussels: Gemeentekrediet, 1978, pp. 95–119.

61 Soly, *Urbanisme*, p. 377.

62 Hugo Soly, "L'urbanisation d'Anvers au XVI siecle", *Revue du Nord*, LXIII, April/June 1981, pp. 391–413, especially p. 395–7.

63 Barbara Uppenkamp, "The Influence on the Cityscape Constructed Like a Picture", in Lombaerde, *Artes*, p. 121–2.

64 Soly, "L'urbanisation d'Anvers", p. 392.

65 Ria Fabri, "Het Vlaamse staadsbeeld in de 16de end 17de eeuw" in Ed Taverne and I. Visser (eds), *Stedebouw: de geschiedenis van de stad in de Nederlanden van 1500 tot heden*, Nijmegen: SUN, 1993, pp. 72–7, and Piet Lombaerde, "Continutieit, verniewingen en verschillen: Het concept van de stad in de Noordelijke en Zuidelike Nederlanden rond 1600", *Bulletin Koninklijke Nederlandse Oudheidkundige Bond* (hereafter *KNOB*), 5/6, 1999, p. 240. On the Calvinist building edicts, see F. Prims, *De kolonellen van de "Burgensche Wacht" te Antwerpen (December 1577–Augustus 1585)*, Antwerp: Kryn, 1942.

66 An edict of February 16, 1566, records 400,000 guilders in taxes levied specifically for the citadel. See *AA* I, p. 290 (fol. 77r.)

67 Federico Badero, as quoted in van Passen, in van der Stock, *Metropolis*, p. 61.

68 e.g.. August 18, 1508, "Varkens lang de straten niet te lateen gaen oft stouwen" in *AA* I, p. 142 (fol. 41v).

69 Voet, *Antwerp*, p. 448.

70 "De straeten daghelijcx vol van volcke, wagens, ende peerden, die dickmael maer dan een half ure in malcanderen soe verveerdt waeren, datmer miet duer en cost ende om't groot gewevel te mijden, so liep men dickmael ofte view straten omme", quoted in Soly, *Urbanisme*, p. 187.

71 Soly, *Urbanisme*, p. 187.

72 The so-called *nachtwerkers* were responsible for three separate tasks; the *moosmeieren* ("mud-minders") collected food and workshop-related waste; the *gruismeesters* ("dust- or debris masters") collected dry brick and rubble from crumbling buildings and streets, and the *pachters van de beerput* (literally, "tenants of the cesspit"), probably the least salubrious of the three posts, monitored cess pools and cesspits, emptying them when levels became too high. The stones and earthwork collected by the *gruismeesters* were often re-used as building material, and filled in much of the fortifications built after 1542. See Peter Poulussen, *Van Burenlast tot milieuhinder. Het stedelijk leefmilieu 1500–1800*, Kapellen: Pelckmans, 1987, pp. 2–30.

73 Illustrated in a pen sketch once associated with Jan Bruegel the Elder, The Hague, Rijksbureau voor Kunsthistorisch Documentatie, photo 30/3–1. See *The Paul Oppé Collection: English Watercolurs and Old Master Drawings*, London: Royal Academy, 1958, no 406, p. 62.

74 From 1578. See *AA* , p. 343 (fol. 163r.).

75 John Evelyn, *Diary*, October 5, 1641, Oxford: Clarendon Press, 1955, vol. II, p. 67. On the Mier: "this is a very faire and noble streete; cleare and sweete to admiration".

76 Peter Arnade, "Fertile Spaces: the Productivity of Urban Space in Northern Europe", *Journal of Interdisciplinary History*, 32:4, Spring 2002, p. 547.

77 On fire restrictions, see Voet, *Antwerp*, p. 440, and on urban design mandates, Piet Lombaerde, "Overzicht van de Opzoekingen over de Antwerpse Vestingbouw, De Architectuur en het Urbanisme", in *400 Jaar Scheiding der Nederlanden, 1585–1985*, Antwerp: Academie voor Culturele Werking, 1990, pp. 45–50.

78 "op pillerren, sulcx dat se dorluchtich zijn zellen ende also men de ghantse merckt sal moghen overseen", quoted in Soly, *Urbanisme*, p. 381.

79 Hans van Schille, *Form und weis zu bauwen . . .*, Antwerp: Gerard de Jode, 1573, fol. A2v. Very little is known of van Schille's work as a painter and architect; he was a "*vrijmeester*" in Antwerp in 1533 and a member of the St Lucasgild in 1585. See Rombouts and Th. van Lerius, *De liggeren*, vol. I., 98, and Theme-Becker, *Kunstler-Lexikon*, vol. XXX, p. 67.

80 Clifford Geertz, "Deep Play: Notes on the Balinese Cockfight", *Daedalus*, (101) Winter 1972, p. 25.

81 *Architectura* (French), appendix: "Non pas qu'en ceste Piece ou en ces Parties y sont observez aucunes particulieres & expresses mesures, que tant seulement formes ordinees, & delineations . . . ses distances & places bien situees embellissement accomoder, selon qu'on peult en ceste Piece (soubs correction) chascun a son commandement usurper, a la discretion de celuy qui entend ceste chose".

82 Spiro Kostof, *The City Assembled*, London: Phaidon, 1992, p. 138.

83 See, for example, edicts in *AA* I, 203, fol. 202r, from December 20, 1535; *AA* I, 289, fol. 72r, for July 21, 1567.

84 See edict from *AA* I, 192, fol. 152r, for November 19, 1530: "Mans en vrouwpersoonen van dissoluten en lichten leven, oneerbaere herbergen houdende, moeten vertrekken uyt de schoone straeten, te weten de Baghynestraet, den Rosier, de Vlierstege, de Bredestraet, St. Jans- en Steenbergstraet, waerdoor de geode leiden gaen van Sint Joriskerk naar St. Andrieskerke, nu onlankx in dese stad gemaekt; deselve oneerbaere persoonen mogen woonen aen den Blyenhoek en in andere plaetsen gedesigneerd, maer moeten hun regulieren naar d'orde van t'jaer 1519".

85 *AA* I, 292, fol. 8v, for September 3, 1568.

86 Both edicts are from 1580, *AA* I, 348, fol. 225, for January 13: "Sediteuse en scandaleuse liedekens op de straten niet te singen", and *AA* I, 348, fol. 226, for January 30: "Kindereren mogen op de vesten en straten niet vechten of spelen.'

87 Soly's revisionist account of labor unrest during Antwerp's large engineering projects argues that the *wet* actively targeted law-breakers, particularly on the new streets. See Soly, "L'Urbanisation", fol. 403.

88 Soly, "L'Urbanisation, pp. 391–413.

89 See *AA* I, 294, June 10, July 21, 1569.

90 See *AA* I, 309–10, for October 8, 9, 1572, fols 179, 179v.

91 H (Vredeman), no 91.

92 De Damhouder even specifies who is to be blamed for such crimes, in a move clearly meant to foster inter-apartment peer pressure: ". . . Alsmen den uytwerper niet en weet, dan worden zij al ghepuniert die inde camere present waeren". (!) See Joost de Damhouder, *Praktyck ende handebouck in criminele zaeken*, Leuven: Steven Wouters, 1555, p. 167. On the pamphlet, see E. J. Stubbe, "Joos de Damhouder als criminalist", *Studia Historica Gandensia*, 129, 1969, pp. 1–65.

93 The chamber was the prestigious *Violieren*. See *De liggeren*, vol. I. On the *Violeren*'s membership: A. Keersemakers, "De rederijkerskamers te Antwerpen: kanttekeningen in verband met onstaan, samenstelling, en ondergang" in *Verslag Vijfde Colloquium De Brabantse Stad, s'-Hertogenbosch 25–26 November 1977*, s'Hertogenbosch: PGKWNB, 1978, pp. 173–86.

94 But see E. van Autenboer, *Volksfeesten en Rederijkers te Mechelen (1400–1600)*, Ghent: Koninklijk Vlaamse Academie voor Taal- en Letterkunde, 1962, and Walter Gibson "Artists and Redeijkers in the Age of Bruegel", *Art Bulletin*, 63:3, September 1981, pp. 426–46. The reason why scholars have overlooked this part of Vredeman's career is simple: Van Mander's *Life* never mentions it.

95 Michel van Hamont, *Refereynen ende Liedekens van diversche Rethoriciens wt Brabant, Vlaenderen, Hollandt ende Zeelant*, Brussels, 1563, fols 80v–84r. Edition consulted: UBA, sig. 976 C 33. The publication seems to have been one of the Hamont firm's first; see F. Kossman, "De Refereyn- en Liedboekjes van de Antwerpsche Loterij (1574)", *Het Boek*, 1922, pp.136–9, and the annotations in G. Huyge, "Refereynen ende liedekens van diuersche rhetoricienen", Diss. lic. Germanse fil., Universiteits Gent, 1975, vol. 1.

96 See, for example, Van Mander, fol. 259r.

97 D. Coigneau, "Rederijkersliteratuur" in M. Spies, *Historische letterkunde*, Groningen: Wolters-Noordhoff, 1984, pp. 35–57.

98 See *Jaarboek van Retorica "De Fonteine" te Ghent*, XVIII, 1968, pp. 32–3, 48–9.

99 Van Mander, fol. 256v. The literature on the *Violieren* is vast. See, for example, J. van der Straelen, "Geschiedenis der Rederykerkamer de Violieren of Violettebloem", *Het Taalverbond*, 1853, pp. 213–32, C. P. Serrure, "de Violieren te Antwerpen", *Vaderlandsch Musem*, 1, 1855, pp. 103–8, and on the Antwerp chambers in general: A. Keersmaekers, "De rederijkerskamers te Antwerpen: kanttekeningen in verband met ontstaan, samenstelling, en ondergang", in *Verslag Vijfde Colloquium De Brabantse Stad*, Ghent: Rijksuniversiteit, 1978, pp.173–86, and Dirk Coigneau's introduction to the small exhibition catalog, *Uyt lonsten Versaemt. Het landjuweel van 1561 te Antwerpen*, Brussels: Bibliothek Albert Ier, 1994, pp. 17–26.

100 Van Mander, fols 236r (Scorel), 247v (Grimmer).

101 K. Bostoen, *Dichterschap en koopmanschap in de zestiende eeuw. Omtrent de dichters Guillaume de Poetou en Jan van der Noot*, Deventer: Sub Rosa, 1987, p. 35.

102 On van Schille as a *rederijker*, see *Uyt lonsten Versaemt*, pp. 86–7.

103 L. Maeterlinck, "L'art et les rhetoricians flamands", *Bulletin et du Bibliothecaire*, April 1906, pp. 293–8; W. S. Gibson, "Artists and Rederijkers in the Age of Bruegel"; Ilja Veldman, *Maarten van Heemskerck and Dutch Humanism in the sixteenth century*, Amsterdam: Muelenhoff, 1977, especially pp. 125–41; M. Meadow, *Pieter Bruegel the Elder's Netherlandish proverbs and the practice of rhetoric*, Zwolle: Waanders, 2002. The literature on connections between Netherlandish rhetoric and painting in the Netherlands is substantial, and largely centered on Pieter Bruegel; see, for example, J. J. Mak, "De wachter in het rederijkersdrama, naar aanleiding van de toneelvertoning op Bruegels Temperantia", *Oud Holland*, 66, 1949, pp. 162–74; B. A. M. Ramakers, "Bruegel en de rederijkers", *Nederlands Kunsthistorisch Jaarboek*, 47, 1996, pp. 80–105, and, for later development, A. Keersemaekers, "De schilder Sebastiaen Vrancx (1573–1647) als rederijker", *Koninklijk Museum voor Schone Kunsten Antwerpen*, 1982, pp. 165–86. The only historical overview of this material in English is Gary K. Waite, *Reformers on Stage: Popular Drama and Religious Propaganda in the Low Countries*, Toronto: University of Toronto Press, 2000, especially pp. 51–78.

104 H. Miedema, review of J. J. Emmens, *Kunsthistorische opstellen*, in *Oud Holland*, 84, 1969, pp. 249–56; a general overview of Renaissance architectural writings and rhetorical categories is C. Smith, *Architecture in the Culture of Early Humanism*, New York: Oxford University Press, 1992, pp. 82–96; specifically on Vredeman's relation to Italian traditions, see Zimmermann, *Architectura*, pp. 150–73.

105 On Renaissance categories of rhetorical "place" in architecture, see Y. Pauwels, "The Rhetorical Model in the Formation of French Architectural Language in the Sixteenth Century" in G. Clarke and P. Crossley (eds), *Architecture and Language: Constructing Identity in European Architecture c.1000–c.1650*, Cambridge: Cambridge University Press, 2000, pp. 134–47.

106 B. H. Erne and L. M. van Dis (eds), *De Gentse Spelen van 1539*, 2 vols, The Hague: Nijhoff, 1982.

107 Moxey, *Pieter Aertsen*, pp. 149–50.

108 Van Elslander, *Het Refrein*, pp. 187–230.

109 E. van Autenboer, "Rederijkers en schutters in de branding van de 16de eeuw", *Noordgouw*, 18, 1978, p. 93.

110 van Elslander, *Het Refrein*, pp. 212, 217.

111 On rhetorical formats at the *landjuweel*, Marieke Spies, " 'Op de questye . . .' Over de structuur van 16e-eeuwse zinnespelen", *De nieuwe taalgids*, 83:2, 1990, pp. 139–50; Dirk Coigneau, "Strofische

vormen in het rederijkerstoneel" in Bart A. M. Ramakers (ed.), *Spel in Verte: Tekst, structuur, en opvoeringspraktijk van het rederijkerstoneel*, Ghent: Fontaine, 1994, pp. 17–44, V. Moser, "De Strijd voor rhetorica: Poeticia en positie van rederijkers in Vlaanderen, Brabant, Zeeland en Holland Tussen 1450 en 1620", Ph.D. dissertation, Vrije Universiteit Amsterdam, 2001, pp. 178–80.

112 *Spele van Sinne*, fol. Biiiv; G. J. Steenbergen, *Het Landjuweel van der Rederijkers*, Leuven: Davisfonds, 1950–52.

113 Nina Serebrennikov, "Dwelck den Mensche, aldermeest tot Consten verwect" in Koopmans et al., *Rhetoric-Rhétoriqueurs-Rederijkers*, p. 236, n. 36.

114 On the *Peone*'s history and competition success, see van Autenboer, *Volkfeesten*, 159–60, and Dirk Coigneau, *Refreinen in Het Zotte Bij de Rederijkers*, Ghent: Koninklijke Academie voor Nederlandse Taal- en Letterkunde, 1980–83, vol. I, p. 149. The *Peone* of Mechelen's prizes are as follows: second prize for their entry decorations, first prize for their blazon, second prize for their "feest", and second prize for their spele's Prologue.

115 *Spelen van Sinne*, fol. Biiiiv.

116 *Spelen van Sinne*, fol. J2iir: "Dat is vedel Poentrature/Die stauere en faetsoen van elck creature/Wel rustich doet naer dleven/Tsghelijcx beelsnijden en dier aenclaeven. . ./Die oock te leere/voor en varde vrije/Consten/want sij is een stomme Poetrije. [. . .]/En sy besicht te sulcken tije/Geometriam/als sy de gronden/De perspectijve/ofte andere nieuwe vonden/Van wercken ondersoeckt seer constlich en cierlijk".

117 With specific regard to early modern Antwerp, see Carl van de Velde, *Frans Floris, leven en werk*, Brussels: Paleis der Academiën, 1975, vol. I, fol. 102, and Justus Müller Hofstede, "Ut Pictura Poesis': Rubens und die Humanistische Kunsttheorie", *Gentse Bijdragen*, 24, 1976–78, pp. 175–90.

118 See G. J. J. van Melckebeke, *Geschiedenis Aentekeninge Resstendede Peone*, Mechelen, 1862, pp. 43–4, 56.

119 *Violieren* member Crispijn van den Broek may have painted and built a stage near the Mier used by the Anwerp *Oliftak* in 1582. See F. J. van den Branden, *Geschiedenis der Antwerpsche Schilderschool*, Antwerp: J. E. Buschmann, 1883, p. 241.

120 On the Antwerp *toneel*, see, among others, W. M. H. Hummelen, "Illlustrations of Stage Performances in the Work of Crispin de Passe the Elder (c.1560–1637)", *Essays in Drama and Theatre. Liber Amicorum Benjamin Hunningher*, Amsterdam & Baarn: Standaard, 1973, fol. 67. The individuals involved with the Antwerp *landjuweel* preparations are listed in a document from 1561 in van de Velde *Floris*, pp. 442–3.

121 Published in Antwerp, Gerard de Jode, 1560. Suavius also submitted a losing entry for the Antwerp Town Hall competition of 1561. See Jean Puraye, "Lambert Suavius, Graveur Liegeois du XVIe Siecle", *Revue Belge D'Archéologie et D'Histoire de L'Art* XVI, 1946, pp. 27–45. In Wolfenbüttel, HAB inv. N37 Helmst 2°, this ruin series is bound with two contemporaneous print series by Vredeman, from 1560 and 1562.

122 *Spelen van Sinne*, fol. Aiiv: "Ende ghemerkt dat die ghemeynte zeer begherich is gheweest om dyer ghelijcke Poetijkse Acten ofte Spelen te siene/zoo heeftmen tot Athenen een Schoone Fabricke ghebout/dwelck alder in Griecsscher tale Theatrum werd genoemt/hebbende die forme van eenen halve circulen ofte rinck wesende [. . .] Zo heerlicke ende constlich getimmert/op date die burghers ende inwoenders der voorghemoemder stadt [Athens] bequaeme plaetse zouden hebben om die Spelen sittende beschedelijck te siene/perfectlijke te horen ende volcomelijcke te verstaen . . ".

123 Amsterdam, Rijksprentenkabinet, inv. no RP-Pp-1997-A-11746. The painting is in Brussels, Museum voor Schone Kunsten, inv. no 6950. See van de Velde, *Floris*, vol. I, pp. 239–44.

124 See *AA* I, 270, fol. 300, for August 2, 1561.

125 Frans de Potter, *Gent van de oudsten tijt tot heden* (1886–92), Brussels: Handzame, Familia et Patria, 1975, vol. IV, p. 9.

126 See C. de Baere, "Rhetoricale Feesten te Brussel" in Rob Roemans (ed.), *Miscellanea J. Gessler*, The Hague: Deurne, 1948, and Van Elslander, *Het Referein*, pp.189–99.

127 van Elslander, *Het Refrein*, pp. 212, 217.

128 On the 1562 *refreynfeest*, see Willem van Eeghem, "Het Brusselsche Rederijkerfeest (1565)", *Jaarboek van De Fonteyne*, 1944, pp. 57–82; C. de Baere, "De Brusselse Refereynen en Liedekens van 1562", *Koninklijke Vlaamse Academie voor Taal- en Letterkunde Verslagen en Mededelingen*, 1948, pp. 119–55, and Elslander, *Het Referein*, pp. 214–15. The prince of the Brussels *Corenbloem*, to whom officially all of the *refreynen* were directed, was Adrien Coninxloo, brother of the painter Gillis.

129 Hamont, *Refereynen*, fol. 81r: "Dese Wijsheyt vol alder Diligenten / Is en cracht Godts / en om exstimeren // t'hoot/Van alle constighe Excelentien/ Want sijt al deursoeckt / mids haerder Prudentien / En is bouen al / int triumpheren // groot:/ Sy maeckt elck van d'onverstandich vleren // bloot / Zijnde voorsichtich / vol Liefden / en verstandich".

130 Other species included the refreyen, *in 't amoureus* (dealing with the subject of love), and the refrain, *in 't zot* (comic matters). On these species see Dirk Coigneau, "en vreughdich liedt moet ick vermanen. Positie en gebruikswijzen van het rederijkerslied" in F. Wallaert, *Een zoet akkord: Middeleeuwse lyriek in de Lage Landen*, Amsterdam, 1992, pp. 264–6.

131 On refrein performance: E. van Elslander. "Refreinen 'Int Amoureuze' " in *Terugblik: opstellen en toespraken*, Ghent: Seminarie voor Nederlandse Literatuurstudie, 1986, pp. 27–53.

132 For overviews of Netherlandish poetic structures, see Marieke Spies, *Het Nederlandse renaissancetoneel als probleem en taak voor de literatuurhistorie*, Leuven: Universiteit Pers, 2002, and D. Coigneau, *Refreinen in Het Zotte Bij de Rederijkers*, Ghent, 1980–83, especially vol. I. A comparative study of the formal structures of *rederijker* addresses in relation to other European developments in vernacular rhetoric is needed. For Italy, see J. O'Malley, *Praise and Blame in Renaissance Rome*, Durham: Duke University Press, 1979, pp. 37–41; for France, Gerard Gros, *Le poète, la vierge et la prince du puy. Etudes sur les Puys marials de la France du Nord du XVIe siècle à la Renaissance*, Paris: Klincksieck, 1992.

133 Michael S. Halloran, "On the End of Rhetoric, Classic and Modern", *College English*, 36, February 1975, p. 625.

134 See, for example, Meadow, *Netherlandish Proverbs*, p. 90. On the idea of this space as a container, see George Lakoff and Mark Johnson, *Metaphors We Live By*, Chicago: University of Chicago Press, 1980, p. 31.

135 J. D. Lyons, *Exemplum: The Rhetoric of Example in Early Modern France and Italy*, Princeton: Princeton University Press, 1989, fol. 16.

136 Walter J. Ong, *Orality and Literacy: The Technologizing of the Word*, London: Methuen, 1982, pp. 281–3.

137 On the history and structure of *refreinen*, see Dirk Coigneau, "*De Const van Rhetoriken*, Drama and Delivery" in Koopmans et al., *Rhetoric-Rhétoriqueurs-Rederijkers*, pp. 124–8; the *locus classicus* for the definition of epidictic rhetoric remains Aristotle, *The Art of Rhetoric*, H. C. Lawson-Tancred (trans.), London: Penguin, 1991, I, 1358a, p. 80.

138 Matthijs de Castelijn, *De const van rhetoriken, alle ancommers ende beminners der zeluer, een zonderlijngh exemplaer, etc.*, Ghent: Gheeraert van Salenson, 1555.

139 Castelijn, *De const*, p. 28.

140 Hermogenes, *Progymnasmata*, 22–3, C. W. Wooten (trans.), Chapel Hill: UNC Press, 1987, p. 61.

141 Van Mander, fol. 266r: ". . . in t'Antwerp was hy doende ane de Triumph-bogen Ao 1549 doe Keyser Carel met zijn soon Philipe daer is gecome". See also E. Roobaert, "De Seer wonderlijcke schoone triumphelijcke incompst van den Hooghmogenden Prince Philips", *Bulletin Koninklijke Musea voor Schone Kunsten*, 8, 1959, doc. IV.

142 As illustrated in *De seer wonderlijcke, schoone, triumphelijcke incompst, van den hooghmogenden Prince Philips, Prince van Spaignen, Caroli des vijfden, Keysers sone: inde stadt van Antwerpen*, Antwerp; Cornelius Grapheus, 1550, fol. Liv-Liv. See W. Kuyper, *The Triumphant Entry of Renaissance Architecture into the Netherlands*, Alphen aan den Rijn: Canaletto, 1994, vol. 1, pp. 64–6.

143 Z. van Ruyven-Zeman, *Lambert van Noort Inventor*, Brussels: KAWLSK, 1995, pp. 74–7.

144 Grapheus, *De seer wonderlijcke*, fol. Liir: "Dese selve Sale was van buyten van geschilderte metselrijen/met vele boghen/na de Dorica/vander eerden op so constelijk gemaect/dates scheen niet van werven maer van levende steene gemect te wesene".

145 Grapheus, *De seer wonderlijcke*, fol. Liv: "Onder welche tribunael was gemaect eenen boghe/daer het volck onder duere paseren".

146 See Louis Marin, "Notes on a Semiotic Approach to Parade" in A. Falassi (ed.), *Time Out of Time: Essays on the Festival*, Albuquerque: University of New Mexico Press, 1987, pp. 220–7.

147 *AA* I, 235, fol. 2, for August 1549: ". . . premie van dry haemelen en twelf stadstoopen wyn voor de wyck die met meeste getal sal uytkomen".

148 Mark Meadow, " 'Met geschickter ordenene': The Rhetoric of Place in Philip II's 1549 Antwerp *Blijde Incompst*", *Journal of the Walters Art Gallery*, 57, 1999, pp. 1–11.

149 Kuypers, *Entry*, pp. 19–62, but see also the critical comments by Charles van den Heuvel in *Archis*, 11, November 1995, pp. 90–1.

150 Montréal, *Architecture and its Image*, p. 90. On transfigurative aspects of festival in an urban setting, see Karl M. Möseneder, *Zeremoniel und monumentale Poesis*, Berlin: Mann, 1983, pp. 11–17, Henri Zerner, "Looking for the Unknowable: The Visual Experience of Renaissance Festivals" in J. R. Mulryne et al. (eds), *Europa Triumphans: Court and Civic Festivals in Early Modern Europe*, Aldershot: Ashgate, 2004, vol. I, pp. 75–98; On Charles V's specific role in these processions: Sydney Anglo, *Spectacle, Pageantry, and Early Tudor Policy*, Oxford: Clarendon, 1969, pp. 170–206, and Roy Strong, *Splendour at Court: Renaissance Spectacle and Illusion*, London: Weidenfeld, 1973, pp. 79–120.

151 See, for example *AA* I, 235, for August 2, 1549, which appears a month before the September entry of Philip II and Charles V into Antwerp.

152 Andre Chastel, "Le Lieu de la fete" in Jean Jacquot and Elie Konigson (eds), *Les Fetes de la Renaissance*, III, Paris: Editions CNRS, 1975, vol. I, p. 420; on the fragments edict, see *AA* I, 236, fol. 102v.

153 H (Vredeman), no 468. Edition consulted: Berlin, Preußischer Kulturbesitz, Kunstbibliothek, inv. 2942. For Anjou's period in the Netherlands: Mack P. Holt, *The Duke of Anjou and the Politique Struggle during the Wars of Religion*, Cambridge: Cambridge University Press, 1986, and Susan Doran, *Monarchy and Matrimony: The courtships of* Elizabeth, London: Routledge, 1996, pp. 154–94.

154 Frances Yates, *The Valois Tapestries*, London: Warburg Institute, 1959, pp. 94–6.

155 Carl van de Velde, "Hans Vredeman de Vries und die Triumphalen Einzüge in Antwerpen" in Borggefe, *Norden*, p. 87, n. 10.

156 Raphael Holinshed, *The / Third volume of Chronicles, be- / ginning at duke William the Norman, / commonlie called the Con-queror: and / descending by degrees of yeeres to all the / kings and queenes of England in their / orderlie successions* . . ., London: Richard Hooke, 1586, p. 1339, following Plantin's 1582 book on the entry, fol. D4v.

157 *SAA* Pk. 660, fol. 47v. F. J. van den Branden made reference to Vredeman's role in Anjou's entry, but did not cite any sources. See van den Branden, 1883, pp. 240–1.

158 *AA* XXIV, fol. 375.

159 On the strangeness of money in Antwerp, see Honig, *Painting and the Market*, pp. 11–12.

160 W. M. Johnson, "Essai de critique interne des livres d'entrées Français au XVIe siecle" in Jean Jacquot and Elie Konigson (eds), *Les Fêtes de la Renaissance*, III, Paris: Editions CNRS, 1975, pp. 187–200.

161 Montréal, *Architecture and its Image*, p. 88.

162 Bertold Brecht, interview with Luth Otto, in John Willett (trans.), *Brecht on Theatre: the Development of an Aesthetic*, New York: Hill and Wang, 1964, pp. 70–1.

163 See Louis Marin, "Theses on Ideology and Utopia", *Minnesota Review*, 6, Spring 1976, pp. 71–5.

164 The market, as economically derived metaphor for social and visual representation, was the liveliest site for such change; see Elizabeth A. Honig, "Looking into Jacob Vrel", *Yale Journal of Criticism*, 1990, pp. 37–56.

165 Hubert Damisch, "The Scene of the Life of the Future", in *Skyline: the Narcissistic City*, 1996, John Goodman (trans.), Palo Alto: Stanford University Press, 2001, p. 94.

166 Berlin, Kupferstichabinett inv. nos 1191–1200, Paris, École Nationale Supériere des Beaux-Arts, inv. 647.

167 The attribution of the Amsterdam sheet to Valkenborch is in Karel G. Boon, *Catalogue of the Dutch and Flemish Drawings in the Rijksmuseum II: Netherlandish Drawings of the XVth and XVIth Century*, The Hague: Staatsuijgeverij, 1978, cat. 450, who also draws attention to the landscape's similarity to that around the Schelde; see also Alexander Wied, *Lucas und Marten van Valkenborch*, Freren: Luca, 1990. On the Master of the Small Landscapes, see Simson and Winner (eds), *Pieter Bruegel und seine Welt*, pp. 130–45, in which Mielke first drew attention to the connection between the figures in Vredeman's drawings and the Landscapes, pp. 139–40. On the latter, see also Nadine Orenstein, et al., *Pieter Bruegel the Elder. Drawings and Prints*, exh. cat., Rotterdam and New York, New Haven: Yale University Press, 2001, pp. 296–9, and H. Johannes and Lucas van Doetecum, vol. 1, pp. 94–109.

168 See, for example, Egbert Haverkamp Begemann, "Joos van Liere" in von Simson and Winner (eds), *Pieter Bruegel und seine Welt*, pp. 17–28.

169 "Vele ende seer fraeye gheleghentheden van diversche Dorphuysingeh, houven, Beldem, Straten, ende dyer ghelijcken, met alderhande Beestjens verciert. Al te samen ghcoterfeyt naer dleven, ende meest rontom Antwerpen ghelegen sinde", title page to *Small Landscapes*, Antwerp: Hieronymus Cock, 1559.

170 Peter Parshall, "*Imago Contrafacta:* Images and Facts in the Northern Renaissance", *Art History*, 16:4, December 1993, pp. 571–3.

171 Hans Mielke (ed.), *Pieter Bruegel d. Ä. Als Zeichner*, exh. cat., Berlin, Staatliche Museen Preussischer Kulturbesitz, 1975.

172 Detlef Zinke, *Patinirs "Weltlandschaft": Studien und Materialien zur Landschaftsmalerei im 16. Jahrhundert*, Frankfurt: Lang, 1977, and Jay Appleton, *The Experience of Landscape*, London: John Wiley, 1975, pp. 194–219.

173 Erlangen, Universitätsbibliothek, inv. 955. See *Die Zeichnungen in der Universitätsbibliothek Erlangen*, Frankfurt am Main: Prestel, 1929, vol. I, p. 239.

174 Koerner, "The Printed World", pp. 24–6; also Müller-Hofstede, "Zur Interpretation", in von Simson and Winner (eds), *Pieter Bruegel und seine Welt*, pp. 120–5.

175 Rodler, *Eyn schön nützlich büchlin*, p. 28.

176 Seneca, *Four Dialogues*, ed. C.D.N. Costa, Warminster: Aris & Phillips, 1994, p. 97.

177 Van Mander, *Grondt*, book V, fol. 16, § 12, 131; "Want ons ordinancy moete ghenieten/Eenen schoonen aerdt, naer one sins ghenoegen, als wy doer een insien oft doorsien lieten . . .daer t'ghesicht in heeft te ploeghen".

178 See R. Hoecker, *Das Lehrgedicht des Karel Van Mander*, The Hague: Nijhoff, 1916, p. 214.

179 De Certeau, *Everyday Life*, 1984, pp. 99–100.

180 Ann Roberts, "The Landscape as Legal Document: Jan de Henry's View of the Zwin", *Burlington Magazine*, 133, 1991, pp. 82–6. On Flemish mapmaking in general see H. van der Haegen et al. (eds), *Oude kaarten en plattegronden: Bronnen voor de historische geografie van de Zuidelijke Nederlanden (16de–18de eeuw)*, Brussels: Archief en Bibliotheekwezen in Belgie, 1986, as well as on the use of representations of property in early modern Europe.

181 Jan van Doetecum, *Karte des Esperwaard*, in Stadsbibliotheek, Deventer, 11 G 4. See Nils Büttner, *Die Erfindung der Landschaft*, p. 244; M. J. Onghera, "Landkaarten in tapijtwerk", *Artes textiles*, 10, 1981, p. 292.

182 *SAA* Inv. nr. PK 566, Collegiale Actenboeken 1582–83, fol. 97. Also in *AA*, I26, fol. 250r.

183 *AAI*, fol. 250r: "Geordonneert Tresoriers ende Rentmeestere vuyt te reyckene ende te betalen aen Hans de Vriese de somme van xxx gulden, ter causen van het maken van sekere caerte van Brabant, daerinne affgeteekent syn de vaert loopende door de Kampen naar Maestricht. Actum vii May 1583". That the map hung in the Stadhuis is clear from a further passage, see fols 294v–295r.

184 Borggrefe, *Norden*, pp. 224-5.

185 Landau and Parshall, *The Renaissance Print*, pp. 220–3.

186 ". . . gedenct dan (ghy eersame const-beminders) dat dit [book] niet zonder groote moeyte en conste te weggebracht is . . . daaromme (met uwe goet-jonstighe affectie) dat ghy t'selfde wilt voorderen, ende niet verachteren"., *Perspective*, vol. I (Dutch), fol. Ar.

Chapter 3 Guidebooks to chaos

1 Dürer, *Unterweyssung*, fol. G4r. My translation modifies that in Walter L. Strauss, *Albrecht Dürer: The Painter's* Manual, New York: Abrams, 1977, p. 195.

2 Goda Juchheim, "Das 'Neuw Grottessken Buch' Nuremberg 1610 von Christoph Jamnitzer", Ph.D. dissertation, Munich, 1976; Carsten-Peter Warnke, "Christoph Jamnitzers 'Neuw Grotteßken Buch'—ein Unikat in Wolfenbüttel", *Wolfenbütteler Beiträge*, 3, 1978, pp. 65–87, details the drawings for the book; more generally, see Peter A. Wick, "A New Book of Grotesques by Christoph Jamnitzer", *Museum of Fine Arts Boston Bulletin*, LX: 321, 1962, pp. 83–104, and Günther Irmscher, "Modern oder altfränkisch? Zur 'Nachgotik' bei Hans Vredeman de Vries und Christoph Jamnitzer", *Barockberichte*, 13, 1996, pp. 475–94.

3 Hans Rupprich, *Dürers Schriftlicher Nachlass*, Berlin: Deutscher Verein für Kunstwissenschaft, 1956–9, vol. III, p. 291.

4 Günther Irmscher, "Zur Koöperation zweier Nürnberger Goldschmiede", *Weltkunst*, 61, no. 18, September 15, 1991, pp. 242–3.

5 Heuer, "Between the Histories of Art", pp. 29–31.

6 Vasari, *Lives*, vol. 1, p. 265.

7 Heinrich Wölfflin, *Prolegomena zur ein Psychologie der Architektur*, Inaugural Dissertation, Universität Munich, 1886, in Joseph Ganter (ed.), Heinrich Wölfflin, *Kleine Schriften*, Basel: Benn Schwabe, 1946, translated as "Prolegomena" in Harry Francis Mallgrave and Eleftherios Ikonomou (eds), *Empathy, Form, and Space: Problems in German Aesthetics 1873–1893*, Los Angeles: Getty Research Institute, 1994, p. 185.

8 Frederic Schwartz, "Cathedrals and Shoes, Concepts of Style in Wölfflin and Adorno", *New German Critique*, 76, 1999, pp. 3–48, especially 12–13.

9 Gerard Raulet, Burghart Schmidt, "Einleitung" in Gerard Raulet, Burghart Schmidt (eds), *Kritische Theorie des Ornaments*, Vienna: Böhlau, 1993; on Wölfflin's view of ornament, see Frank-Lothar Kroll, *Das Ornament in der Kunsttheorie des 19. Jahrhunderts*, Hildesheim/Zürich: Olms, 1987, pp. 59–65, 112–26.

10 As noted by Andrea Hauser, "Grundbegriffiliches zu Wölfflin's 'Kunstgeschichtlichen Grundbegriffen' ", *Jahrbuch des Schweizerischen Instituts für Kunstwissenschaft*, 1984–86, pp. 39–53.

11 Michel de Montaigne, "De l'amité" in *Michel de Montaigne: The Complete Essays*, M. A. Screech (trans.), London: Penguin, 1987, p. 205.

12 Alina Payne, *The Architectural Treatise in the Italian Renaissance*, Cambridge: Cambridge University Press, 1999, p. 6.

13 But see Rebecca Zorach's excellent "Ink" in Zorach, *Blood*, pp. 135–88. Early compendia of photolithographic reproductions of Vredeman's work concentrated precisely upon such ornament: for example, F. Ewenbeck, *Documents classes de l'art dans les Pays-Bas du Xe au XIXe siècle*, Brussels: n.p., 1880–89). Vredeman describes his audience for such works on the title page of *Den Eersten Boek*, H (Vredeman) no 183a: "Schilders, Beeltsnyders, Steenhouwers, Schrynwerkers, Glaesmakers, en allen Constbeminders . . ".

14 H (Vredeman), nos 180–200.

15 H (Vredeman), nos 201–22; H (Vredeman) nos. 442–53.

16 John Onians, *Bearers of Meaning: The Classical Orders in Antiquity, the Middle Ages and the Renaissance*, Princeton: Princeton University Press, 1989, pp. 263–71.

17 A Dutch version of Blüm's earlier edition of Vitruvius was also on the Antwerp book market by 1550. See Forssman, *Säule*, p. 239.

18 *Den Eersten Boeck* (Dutch), fol. 1v: "Soo ick my eertijts langhe heb gheexcerceert/In de leeringhge Vitruuijen immer ander boecken/Van de oude Antique edificen gecopieert/Inhoudende vijf Colomnen, telcx ondersoecken [. . .] Om dat somminghe Vitruuius leere sijn soo subiect/Niet datse om verbeteren

is (t'waer ignorantie)/Maer zijn bewysen tot groote zware wercken strect/ En Schilders, Beeltsnyders, Schrynwerkers instantie/Tenderen haer wercken tot de meeste plaisante".

19 *Den Eersten Boeck* (Dutch), fol. 1v: "Hier toe noch diende zijn ghesocht en ghevonden/Diversche ghecompertimenteerde cieraten [. . .]/Men macht oock schilderen, soot elck dient sonder ghequell/Oft maken van houte, elck mach hier in doen en laten/Nae dat hem goet dunct in hun bestel".

20 Georg Simmel describes asymmetrical social relations in this way. See Georg Simmel, "Sociological Aesthetics" in K. Peter Etzkorn (ed.), *The conflict in modern culture and other essays*, New York: Teacher's College Press, 1968, pp. 68–80.

21 *Den Eersten boeck*, fol. 1v: ". . . elck mach hier in doen en laten/nae dat hem goet dunct in hun bestel".

22 Alberti, *On the Art of Building*, Book I: 9, J. Rykwert et al. (trans.), Cambridge, MA: MIT Press, 1988, p. 24.

23 J. A. Simpson and E. S. C. Weiner, *The Oxford English Dictionary*, vol. X, Oxford: Clarendon Press, 1989, p. 939.

24 Quintilian, *Institutio Oratoria*, H. E. Butler (trans.), Cambridge, MA: Harvard University Press, 1965, 8.3, pp. 62, 82.

25 Cicero, *De Oratore*, pp. 134–5.

26 André Robinet, *Aux sources de l'esprit cartesien: L'axe la Ramea-Descartes*, Paris: Vrin, 1986, p. 56.

27 See, for example, Peter Furhing, *Ornament Prints in the Rijksmuseum*, Rotterdam: Sound and Vision, 2004, vol. 1, pp. 2–5.

28 Max Lehrs, *Geschichte und kritischer Katalog des deutschen, niederlandischen, und französischen Kupferstichs im XV. Jahrhundert*, Vienna: Gesellschaft für Vervielfältigende Kunst, 1908–34, vols 1–6, especially no 540.

29 On the Hopfer family of etchers, see Augsburg, Rathaus and Zeughaus, *Welt im Umbruch: Augsburg zwischen Renaissance und Barok*, exh. cat., 1980–81, no 12, and Ed Eyssen, "Daniel Hopfer van Kaufbeuren", Ph.D. dissertation, Heidelberg, 1904. On the *kleinen meistern*, see J. E. Wessely, *Das Ornament und die Kunstinustrie in ihrer Geschichtlichen Entwickelung auf dem Gebiete des Kunstdruckes*, Berlin: Nicolaische Verlags, 1877, especially vol. I, and Herbert Zschelletzschky, *Die drie gottlossen Maler von Nuremberg*, Leipzig: Seemann, VEB, 1975, and Stephen Goddard, *The World in Miniature: Engravings of the German Little Masters 1500–1550*, Lawrence, Kansas: Spencer Museum, 1986.

30 Till-Holger Berchaert, *Rondom Dürer: Duitse prenten en tekeningen ca 1420–1525 uit de collectie van Museum Boijmans-van Beuningen*, Ghent: Ducaj & Zoon, 2000, pp. 14–15; Peter Fuhring, "Hans Vredeman de Vries und das Ornament als Vorlage und Modell" in Borggefe, *Norden*, pp. 61–70.

31 C. Van Veen, *Centsprenten: Nederlandse volks-en kinderprenten*, Amsterdam: Rijksprentenkabinet, 1976, p. 91. In the first quarter of the sixteenth century, decorative woodcuts were even pasted onto the walls of the Antwerp cathedral in rhythmic patterns: see Bernard Delmotte, "De Onze-Lievevrouwkatedrale te Antwerpen", *Bulletin 1994 bis van de beroepsveringingen voor conservatie/restaurateur van kunstvoorwerpen*, 1994, pp. 21–9; and A. K. L. Thijs, "Behangpapier Anno 1582", *Ons Heem*, XXV: 3, 1971, pp. 112–14.

32 Van der Stock, *Printing*, pp. 13–15.

33 Sixteenth-century printed wallpaper patterns found in Antwerp were also found in Wienhausen and Malmö; see Geert Wisse, "Manifold Beginnings: Single-Sheet Papers" in *The Papered Wall: History, Pattern, Tradition*, New York: Abrams, 1994, pp. 10–11.

34 In one extraordinary case, Italian cartouches (likely after Marcantonio Raimondi) were shipped to India and pasted into an illuminated manuscript of Mughal love poems. See Milo Cleveland Beach, "The Gulshan Album and its European Sources: European Engravings and the Mughal Adaptations", *Bulletin of the Boston Museum of Fine Arts*, 63, 1965, pp. 63–91. On the cutting and recombination of early prints for use as pictures, see Landau and Parshall, 1993, pp. 81–8.

35 Jutta Funke, *Beiträge zum Graphischen Werk Heinrich Vogtherrs d. Ä*, Ph.D. dissertation, Freie Universität Berlin, 1967, pp. 90–105, and Frank Müller, *Heinrich Vogtherr l'ancien: un artiste entre Renaissance et Reforme*, Wiesbaden: Harrassowitz, 1997, no 231, 296–9.

36 Vogtherr 1543, fol. A2r.

37 B. 368, *The Illustrated Bartsch*, vol. 20 (Amman), nos 4–29. On Amman and ornament, see Ilse O'Dell-Franke, "Etienne Deleaune and Jost Amman", *Print Quarterly*, 7, December 1990, pp. 414–19.

38 Many of the disputes were over the inappropriate use of metalsmithing motifs. See Ilse O'Dell-Franke, *Kupferstiche und Radierungen aus der Werkstatt des Virgil Solis*, Wiesbaden: Steiner, 1977, pp. 13–14.

39 "Den gleich wie die Bienen/in dem Honig machen/vie und macherley blumen uberfliegen/und nur das jenige/so ihnen bequamlich außfaugen und darvon nemen/die andern blumen aber lassen sie nichts desto minder ganz und unversehret", Jost Amman, *Kunst und lehrbüchlein . . .*, Frankfurt am Main: Sigmund Fayerbend, 1580, fol. 3r. On apiarian metaphors in the Renaissance, see Claire Preston's remarkable *Bee*, London: Reaktion, 2006, pp. 76–83.

40 In an elephant folio dated 1616 in the Kungliga Biblioteket, Stockholm: Isak Collijn, *Katalog der Ornamentstichsammlung des Magnus Gabriel de la Gardie*, Stockholm/Uppsala: Almqvist & Wiksells, 1933, pp. 91–8.

41 Michael Snodin and Maurice Howard, *Ornament: A Social History since 1450*, New Haven: Yale University Press, 1996, p. 24. On the "delay" effect of style in sixteenth-century collection trends, also Jean Adhémar, "L'Estampe et la transmission des formes maniéristes", *Le Triumphe du Maniérisme européen*, exh. cat., Amsterdam: Rijksmuseum, 1955, and Jonathan Brown, *Kings and Connoisseurs: Collecting Art in Seventeenth-Century Europe*, Princeton: Princeton University Press, 1995.

42 See "The School of Paris and the Dissemination of the Fontainebleau Style", in Los Angeles, Gruenwald Center for the Graphic Arts, *The French Renaissance in Prints from the Bibliothèque Nationale de France*, exh. cat., 1994, p. 296; and Zorach, *Blood*, pp. 135–88. Chimneypieces and frames based on these Fontainbleau prints, for example, were being built in southern England from the 1580s through the early seventeenth century; see Anthony Wells-Cole, *Art and Decoration in Elizabethan and Jacobean England*, New Haven: Yale University Press, 1997, pp. 33–42.

43 See Teréz Gerszi, "Zeichnung und Druckgraphik" in Essen, *Prag*, vol. 1, pp. 301–27, and Dorothy Limouze, "Taking the High Road: Netherlandish Engravers at the Courts of Munich and Prague", *Blockpoints: Annual Journal of the Block Gallery, Northwestern University*, 1993, pp. 28–45.

44 See, for example, Hans and Pauwels Vredeman de Vries, *Architectura*, Amsterdam: Hondius, 1606, fol. A2r, which Zimmermann, *Architectura*, pp. 76–9, convincingly attributes to Paul Vredeman de Vries.

45 Coecke van Aelst, *Regelen*, fol. R3v.-S2v.

46 Coecke van Aelst, *Regelen*, fol. S3r: "Ick en wil niet sustieniere dat dese lettere de beste sijn, elck neme die he best behaeghe. Ten is ook geen noot om elcke cleine lettere desen arbeyt te doene . . ".

47 Herman de la Fontaine Verwey, "Pieter Coecke van Aelst and the publication of Serlio's book of architecture", in *Quaerendo*, VI, 1976, p. 182.

48 Van Mander, IV, p. 124.

49 On the early history of the *grotte*, Nicole Dacos, *La découverte de la Domus Aurea et la formation des grotesques à la Renaissance*, London: Warburg Institute, 1969, pp. 57–117, Friederich Piel, *Die Ornament-Groteske in der italienischen Renaissance: zu ihrer kategorialen Struktur und Entstehung*, Berlin: de Gruyter, 1962.

50 Floris's son, also named Cornelis, scratched his name in the Domus Aurea in 1574. See Nicole Dacos, "Graffitti de la Domus Aurea", *Bulletin de l'Institut historique belge de Rome*, 38, 1967, p. 149. August Schmarsow described how contemporary Romans thought that artists who descended into the dank grottos to study the works were as bizarre as the paintings themselves; see his classic article "Der Eintritt der Grottesken in die Dekoration der Italienischen Renaissance", *Jahrbuch der Königlich Preussischen Kunstsammlungen*, 2, 1881, pp. 131–44.

51 Rudolf Berliner, *Ornamentale Vorlagblätter des 15. bis 18. Jahrhunderts*, Leipzig: Klinkhardt & Biermann, 1926, pp. 132–7.

52 H. D. L. Verliet, *Sixteenth Century Printing Types of the Low Countries*, Amsterdam: Menno Hertzberger, 1968; on confessional uses of different kinds of typography, see also Virgil Moser, "Begriffsunterscheidung durch Faktur und Antiquamajuskeln", *Luther-Jahrbuch*, XVIII, 1936, pp. 83–96.

53 Livy, Book VII, ch. 5, in B. O. Foster (trans.), *Livy in Fourteen volumes*, vol. 3, Cambridge, MA: Harvard University Press, 1968.

54 Alexi Larinov, "Entwurfszeichnung", in Borggrefe, *Norden*, pp. 248–9.

55 Horace, *Ars Poetica*, Book I, pp. 1–5, in H. Rushton Fairclough (trans.), *Horace: Satires, Epistles, and Ars Poetica*, Cambridge, MA: Harvard University Press, 1970, p. 451.

56 Vitruvius, VI.5, pp. 3–4.

57 Philippe Morel, *Les Grotesques: Les Figures de l'Imaginaires dans la Peinture Italienne de la Fin de la Renaissance*, Paris: Flammarion, 1997, pp. 75–86, 115–17.

58 As in Hellmut Wohl, *The Aesthetics of Italian Renaissance Art*, Cambridge: Cambridge University Press, 1999, p. 217.

59 A. Roggen and J. Withof, "Cornelis Floris", *Gentsche Bijdragen tot de Kunstgeschiedenis*, VIII, 1942, pp. 79–171, especially docs. 12, 148.

60 Summers, *Michelangelo*, pp. 496–7, n. 106, whose helpful discussion has informed some of what follows.

61 Henri Focillon, *The Life of Forms in Art*, George Kubler (trans.), New York: Zone Books, 1989, p. 68.

62 Ernst Kris, *Psychoanalytic Explorations in Art*, 1952, New York: Schocken, 1964, pp. 64–84.

63 "una spezie di pittura licenziosa e ridicola molto", cited in Andre Chastel, *Chronique de la peinture italienne a la Renaissance, 1280–1580*, Paris: Editions Vilo, 1983, p. 12.

64 Dacos, *La découverte*, pp. 161–82; see also D. R. Coffin, "Pirro Ligorio and the Decoration at Ferrara", *Art Bulletin*, 37, 1955, p. 183.

65 Fischart's text appears in a broadsheet published by Tobias Stimmer; see Dieter Koepplin, *Spätrenaissance am Oberrhein. Tobias Stimmer 1539–1582*, Basel: Kunstmuseum, 1984, pp. 263–5, and the discussion in Koerner, *Reformation*, pp. 52–6.

66 John Calvin, "Epistre", I, 42.5, in *Institutio*, 1559.

67 Coecke van Aelst, *Regelen*, fol. PIIIv: "Hoewel dat Vitruvius leert iiiimaniere van colomen te sine, dats Dorica, Ionica, Corinthia, en Tuschana: gevede hier bycans vader Architecture deerste en simpele ornamente, so heb ick niettemin aende voersz. iiii eene (bicans) vijfte maniere wille voege, gemegt vade simpel voersz . . . En ieder waerheit de voer sichtichheyt des Architects behoort sulx te sine dathy na dathet behoeve sal, me nichwert van de voersz. simpelheyt een menghinge behoort te maken, aensiende de nature en tsubiect".

68 Anton Francesco Doni, *Disegno*, Venice, 1549, cited in Roland Kanz, "Capriccio und Grotteske", in Ekkhard Mai and Joachim Rees (eds), *Kunstform Capriccio: Von der Groteske zur Spieltheorie der Moderne*, Cologne: Walter König, 2001, pp. 21–2.

69 Montaigne, *Essays*, I, ch. 28, p. 92. On this passage and its context, see Rebecca Zorach, "Desiring Things", *Art History*, 24, 2001, pp. 195–212.

70 Alina Payne, "Introduction" to Payne, *Antiquity and its Interpreters*, p. 4.

71 Peter Stallybrass and Allon White have argued that the grotesque models an image of social relations as well: bourgeois class consolidation results in popular culture constructed as a "grotesque otherness"— in its proximity to the popular, this middle-class transforms society itself into a colossal, monstrous hybrid. See Peter Stallybrass and Allon White, *The Politics and Poetics of Transgression*, Ithaca: Cornell University Press, 1986, pp. 191–6: "When the bourgeoisie consolidated itself as a respectable and conventional body by withdrawing itself from the popular, it constructed the popular as grotesque otherness; but by this act of withdrawal and consolidation it produced *another grotesque* . . ".", p. 196. The concept of grotesque as "another place of being" comes from Geoffrey Galt Harpham, *On the Grotesque: Strategies of Contradiction in Art and Literature*, Princeton: Princeton University Press, 1982, especially pp. 23–47.

72 Alina Payne, "Creativity and *bricolage* in architectural literature in the Renaissance", *Res*, 34, 1998, pp. 32–4.

73 Hans Vredeman de Vries, *Das ander Buech*, Antwerp: Hieronymus Cock, 1565, fol. 1r: "Denn es schickt sich nicht ubel, wenn man das alte mit dem newen maessiglich schmucket".

74 See Vladimir Juren, "Fecit-Faciebat", *Revue de l'Art*, 26, 1974, pp. 27–30; William Hood and Charles Hope, "Titian's Vatican Altarpiece", *Art Bulletin*, 59, 1977, p. 535; and Aileen June Wang, "Michelangelo's Signature", *Sixteenth Century Journal*, 35/2, 2004, pp. 447–73, especially pp. 459–61.

75 H (Vredeman), no 183:1a, 1b, 1c.

76 On Vredemania in Gdańsk: J. Z. Łozinski and A. Miłobedszki, *Guide to Architecture in Poland*, Warsaw: Polonia, 1967, pp. 115–16; Arnold Bartetzky, "Niederlande versus Polen: Zur Rezeption nordischen-manieristischer Architektur in Danzig", in Andrea Langer and Georg Michels (eds), *Metropolen und Kulturtransfer im 15./16. Jahrhundert*, Stuttgart: Franz Steiner, 2001, pp. 171–84. Brian Knox, *The Architecture of Poland*, New York: Praeger, 1971, p. 111, indicates that in the years following World War II, restorers used Vredeman's pattern books to rebuild those sections of Gdańsk's neighborhoods destroyed by artillery.

77 Wells-Cole, *Art and Decoration*, pp. 61–2, 69.

78 Ojars Sparitis, "Untersuchungen zur Formensprache der Renaissance in der Architektur und bildenden Kunst Lettlands" in *Beitrage zur Renaissance zwischen 1520 und 1570*, Marburg: Jonas Verlag, 1991, pp. 273–93. Barbara Uppenkamp, "Die Influss von Hans Vredeman de Vries auf Architektur und Kunstgewerbe" in Borggrefe, *Norden*, p. 93. For an exhaustive list of German buildings based on Vredeman's prints, see Uppenkamp's "Roll- und Beschlagwerk in der 'Weserrenaissance' " in Petra Krutisch and G. U. Grossmann (eds), *Baudekoration als Bildungsanspruch (Materialien zur Kunst- und Kulturgeschichte in Nord- und Westdeutschland 5*, Marburg: Jonas Verlag, 1993, pp. 9–120. Specifically on the Riga building, Janis Krastins, *Rigas Ratslaukums*, Riga: Madris, 1999, pp. 21–5.

79 George Kubler, *Portuguese Plain Architecture: Between Spices and Diamonds 1521–1706*, Middletown: Wesleyan University Press, 1972, pl. 87.

80 Santiago Sebastian, "La Decoration Llamade Plateresca en el Mundo Hispanico", *Boletin de Centro de Investigaciones Historicas y Estheticas*, 6, 1966, pp. 61–80.

81 See Augusto Fabella Vilalon, "Baroque Churches of the Philippines", *UNESCO Courier*, 49: 11, November, 1996, pp. 44–8.

82 See the section "Renaissance—Planung und Technik" in Jose Kastler, Regina Fristsh (ed.), *Renaissance im Weserraum*, Berlin/Munich: Deutscher Kunstverlag, 1989, vol. I, pp. 121–42.

83 Fabienne Emilie Hellendoorn, *Invloed van het Noordelijk-Manierisme op de Mexicaanse Religieuze Archtiectuur in de Periode van 1600–1750*, Proefschrift TH Delft, 1980, pp. 5–7, pl. 136; George Kubler and Martin Soria, *Art and Architecture in Spain and Portugal and their American Dominions, 1500–1800*, Harmondsworth: Penguin, 1959, pp. 17–18. More research on the subject of Vredeman's impact on South American design is needed. For now, see two case studies: Patricia Díaz Cayeros, "La recreación de modelos europeos en la sillería del coro de la Catedral de Puebla" in Helga von Kügelgen (ed.), *Herencias indígenas, tradiciones europeas y la mirada europea—Indigenes Erbe, europäische Traditionen und der europäische Blick*, Madrid and Frankfurt: Vercuert, 2002, pp. 166–98, and Rodney Palmer, "Adaptions of European Print Imagery in two Andean *Sillerias* of circa 1600" in Lauren Golden (ed.), *Raising the Eyebrow: John Onians and World Art Studies*, Oxford: Archaeopress, 2001, pp. 183–8.

84 As pointed out by, for example, Linda Nochlin, in *The Body in Pieces: The Fragment as a Metaphor of Modernity*, London: Thames and Hudson, 1994. On how the fragment relies upon a physical manifestation of temporality, see Karen Lang, "The Dialectics of Decay: Rereading the Kantian subject", *Art Bulletin*, LXXIX: 3, September 1997, pp. 413–39. On architectural fragments as physical components of early collections, see Krzysztof Pomian, *Collectionneurs, amateurs, et curieux*, Paris: Gallimard, 1987, pp. 30–58.

85 As is argued of Serlio's work by Mario Carpo, *La mashera e il modello*, Milan: Jaca, 1993, pp. 85–105.

86 Vredeman, *Architectura*, fol. 17r.

87 Walter Benjamin, "The Work of Art in the Age of its Technological Reproducibility" (Second Version), in *Selected Writings*, vol. 3, Edmund Jephcott et al. (trans.), Cambridge, MA: Harvard University Press, 2003, pp. 119–20.

88 Georg Simmel, "Excurs über den Schmuck" in *Soziologie. Untersuchungen über die Formen der Vergesellschaftung*, 1908, in Orthein Rammstedt (ed.), *Georg Simmel: Gesamtausgabe*, vol. 11, Frankfurt am Main: Suhrkamp 1992, pp. 418–19. Deleuze and Guattari's notion of "faciality" is clearly akin to this definition of adornment. Cf. G. Deleuze and F. Guattari, *A Thousand Plateaus: Capitalism and Schizophrenia*, Brian Massumi (trans.), Minneapolis: Minnesota University Press, 1987, p. 168: "Faces are not basically individual . . . [the face] constructs the wall that the signifier needs in order to bounce off . . ".

89 Craig Owens, "The Allegorical Impulse: Towards a Theory of Post-Modernism", *October*, 12, Spring 1980, pp. 67–86.

90 Benjamin, "Work of Art", p. 243, n. 2.

91 Roger Chartier, *The Order of Books: Readers, Authors, and Libraries in Europe between the Fourteenth and Eighteenth Centuries*, Lydia G. Cochrane (trans.), Palo Alto: Stanford University Press, 1994, p. viii; on Benjamin's figure of the "expert", a "politically active manipulator of documents", see Frederic J. Schwartz, *Blind Spots*, New Haven: Yale University Press, 2005, pp. 38–9, 86–101.

92 Otto Karl Werckmeister, "Walter Benjamin's Angels of History, or the Transfiguration of the Revolutionary into the Historian", *Critical Inquiry*, 22: 2, Winter 1996, pp. 239–67.

93 Much of the quarrel centered specifically on grotesques; cf. Dacos, *La découverte*, p. 122, for example: "Le debat souleve en effect le problem complexe de la rupture avec la tradition classique et de l'expression libre de l'imagination". On the controversy, see Summers, *Michelangelo*, p. 152, and on its historiographical ramifications, Stanley Rosen, *The Ancients and Moderns: Rethinking Modernity*, New Haven: Yale University Press, 1991, pp. 37–64.

94 Cited in Payne, *Architectural Treatise*, p. 16; on Michelangelo's *invenzione* and its criticism: Joseph Connors, "Ars tornandi: Baroque Architecture and the Lathe", *JWCI*, 53, 1990, pp. 217–36. The classic study of the grotesque in relation to the decorum/license debate in architecture is David Summers, "Michelangelo on Architecture", *Art Bulletin*, 54:2, June 1972, pp. 146–57.

95 Christof Thoenes, "Vignola's 'Regola delle cinque ordini' ", *Römisches Jahrbuch für Kunstgeschichte*, 20, 1983, pp. 354–76.

96 Vredeman, *Architectura*, 1st ed. (French), fol. 9r: "Combien que les tres-renomee *Vitruvius, Sebastian Serlio, & l'expert Iacobeus Androuetus Cerceau* ont mis enauent beaucoup d'aulture diverse sortes de Fronteaue, enz . . . selon qu'on le treuue en leurs livres & patron des aultres Maistres, a la mode, coustume & facon de ce pais la. . . . Mais en ce Pais Bas, on a une aultre condition, singulierment aux villes des grandes negotiations, ou les places sont petites & bien cheres, la ou il fault practiser & chercher les places en hault, a la plus grande commodotie, pour en avoir la clarte, chacus sa place & sa commodite . . "., exemplars consulted: Amsterdam, Universiteitsbibliotheek inv. 1151, A34; Montréal, Canadian Centre for Architecture, inv. no W9502). No Dutch editions of the 1577 impression survive.

97 For a full discussion of Vredeman's definitions of "antique" and "modern", see Dieter Nuytten, "Hans Vredeman de Vries ARCHITECTURA Oder Bauung der Antique aus dem Vitruvius . . "., Ph.D. dissertation, Katholieke Universiteit Leuven, 1994, pp. 70–92; Krista de Jonge, " '*Anticse Wercken*': La découverte de l'architecture antique dans la practique architecturale des anciens Pays-Bas. Livres de Modèles et Traités (1517–99)" in Michèle-Caroline Heck et al. (eds), *Théorie des arts et création artistique dans l'Europe du Nord du XVIe au début du XVIII siècle*, Lille: Collection UL3 Traveaux Recherches, 2002, pp. 55–74.

98 *Architectura*, 1st ed. (French), ff. 3r; 8v, 16r, 21r.

99 On bodily metaphors in Vitruvius, see Drew Leder, *The Absent Body*, Chicago: University of Chicago Press, 1990.

100 Hubert Damisch, "The Column and the Wall", *Architectual Design*, 49: 8–9, 1979, pp. 18–25; Paul Davies, "The Double Life of Alberti's Column", *Art History*, 13:1, March 1990, pp. 126–8.

101 Christian Norberg-Schulz, "Das Licht und der Genius des Ortes" in Ingebord Flagge (ed.), *Architecktur Licht Architektur*, Stuttgart: K. Krämer, 1991, p. 143. On architecture as a confrontation between light and shadow, see *Das Geheimnis des Schattens: Licht und Schatten in der Architektur*, exh. cat., Frankfurt am Main: Deutsches Architektur Museum, 2001.

102 See Francoise Choay, "La Ville et le domaine bati comme corps", *Nouvelle Revue de Psychoanalyse*, 9, Spring 1974, pp. 239–52.

103 Forssman, *Säule*, p. 97, which refers to Vredeman's *Eersten Boeck* as "das Elementarbuch des reifen nordischen Manierisme".

104 Dagobert Frey, *Gotik und Renaissance als Grundlagen der modernen Weltanschauung*, Augsburg: B. Filser, 1929, p. 24.

105 H (Vredeman), nos 435–41. The first edition (1577) was published by Peter Baltens, and etched by Hieronymus Wierix. These plates were later sold to Theodor Galle as "*vii platen van dleven van menssche*" and republished in 1600. See Peter Karstkarel, "Het allegorisch theater. Enkele opmerkingen bij de herdruk van het Theatrum Vitae Humanae van Hans Vredeman de Vries", *Akt* 2, 1978, pp. 18–36. On Baltens as an engraver, see Richard Jung, "Peeter Baltens, a forgotten draughtsman of the Bruegel circle", *Nationalmuseum Bulletin*, 9:1, 1985, pp. 46–59. The *Theatrum* will be the subject of a forthcoming study by Heiner Borggrefe.

106 In 1606, Vredeman collaborated with his son Pauwels on prints that linked the orders to the five senses; see H (Vredeman), nos 615–19; preliminary drawings in ink and wash for four prints from the series are in Paris, Ecole Nationale Supérieure des Beaux-Arts, inv. 648 (d), 2238, 2239, 2240. See *Renaissance et Manierisme dans les Ecoles du Nord*, exh. cat., Paris, ENSBA, 1985. On Vredeman's typology as a metaphor for architectural completeness, see Juan A. Ramirez, *Edificios u sueños; estudios sobre arquitectura y utopaia*, Madrid: Nerea, 1991, p. 166. On bodily projection in architecture, see Joseph Rykwert, *The Dancing Column*, Cambridge, MA: MIT Press, 1996; Anthony Vidler, "Architecture Dismembered" in *The Architectural Uncanny: Essays in the Unhomely*, Cambridge: MIT Press, 1992, pp. 69–73.

107 H (Vredeman) no 436, "En genus humanum Deus et natura creatrix/Mobillus e cunis gravidaque parentis ab alvo/Ducit ad aerumnas; his mobillus aeducat umbris/Illos fortunam jubet incusare potentem".

108 Yves Pauwels, "Les origines de l'ordre composite", *Annali di Architettura*, 1, 1989, pp. 29–49.

109 Marc Wilson-Jones, *Principles of Roman Architecture*, New Haven: Yale University Press, 2000; Dieter Nuytten, "Theory and Example" in Lombaerde, *Artes*, p. 47.

110 Ernst Gombrich, *The Sense of Order*, Ithaca: Cornell University Press, 1979, p. 178.

111 Gombrich, *Sense*, p. 281.

112 Henri Zerner, "The Sense of Sense", *New York Review of Books*, XXVI: 11, June 28, 1979, pp. 18–21. A similar point was made regarding architectural prints in a book review by George Hersey: see *JSAH* XXXIX, 1, March 1980, pp. 91–2.

113 Aryeh Finkelberg, "On the History of the Greek κοσμοξ", *Harvard Studies in Classical Philology*, 98, 1998, pp. 116–17; Clemente Marconi, "Kosmos: the Imagery of the Archaic Greek temple", *Res* 45, Spring 2004, p. 211.

114 Franciscus Junius, *De pictura veterum*, 1637, Book III, ch. 7, § 12, Keith Aldritch, Phillip Fehl, Raina Fehl (trans.), *The Painting of the Ancients*, Berkeley: California University Press, 1991, vol. 1, p. 11.

115 Geoffrey Galt Harpham, *On the Grotesque: Strategies of Contradiction in Art and Literature*, Princeton, Princeton University Press, 1982, p. 37. On *kosmos*/ornament, see Angus Fletcher, *Allegory: Theory of a Symbolic Mode*, Ithaca: Cornell University Press, 1964, pp. 108–9; Joseph Leo Koerner, "The Fate of the Thing: Ornament and Vessel in Chou Bronze Interlacery", *Res* 10, Autumn 1985, p. 29; on how late sixteenth-century ornament was singularly "narrative", see Ethan Matt Kavalaer, "Renaissance Gothic: Pictures of Geometry and Narratives of Ornament", *Art History*, 29:1, February 2006, pp. 1–46.

116 Zorach, *Blood*, pp. 160–4.

117 See M. P. R. van den Broecke, P. van der Krogt, and P.H. Meurer (eds), *Abraham Ortelius and the First Atlas*, 't Goy-Houten: HES Publishers, 1998, pp. 55–78; Dirck Imhof, *De wereld in kaart: Abraham Ortelius (1527–1598) en de eerste atlas*, Antwerp: Museum Plantin-Moretus, 1998. On Vredeman's cartouches in the atlas, see Beatrijs Vuylsteke, "Het Theatrum Orbis Terrarum van Abraham Ortelius (1595): een studie van de decoratief elementen en de ghehistoriceerde voorstellingen", Ph.D. dissertation, Katholiek Universiteit Leuven, 1985, 2 vols; and James A. Welu, "The Sources and Development of Cartographic Ornamentation in the Netherlands" in David Woodward (ed.), *Art and Cartography: Six Historical Essays*, Chicago: University of Chicago Press, 1987, pp. 147–73.

118 Jean Puraye, "Abraham Ortelius' Album Amicorum", *De Gulden Passer*, 45, 46, 1967, 1968, pp. 1–23, 1–99.

119 H (Vredeman) no 191; see also Peter H. Meurer, *Fontes cartographici Orteliani: das "Theatrum orbis terrarum" von Abraham Ortelius und seine Kartenquellen*, Weinheim: VCH, 1991, pp. 10–11. On the

1570 *Theatrum* as an epistimological model derived from the sixteenth-century stage: John Gillies, *Shakespeare and the Geography of Difference*, Cambridge: Cambridge University Press, 1994, pp. 70–98.

120 "Descriptione Orbis terrarum absoluta, en candide lector tres hae seuqentes Tabulae, quas in gratia veretis tam sacrae quam profanae historiae studiosorum a me delinatasm seorsum publicarae decreueram, nihil enim ad nostrum in hoc Theatrum, quo tantum hodiernum regionum situm exhibere proposueram . . ".

121 For the 1592 edition, published in Antwerp, see Cecile Kruyfthooft, "A recent discovery: Utopia by Abraham Ortelius", *The Map Collector*, 16, 1981, pp. 10–14; and on the *Parergon*'s relation to landscape painting, Walter Melion, "*Ad ductus itinerus et dispositionem mansionum ostendendam*: Meditation, Vocation, and Sacred History in Abraham Ortelius' *Parergon*", *Journal of the Walters Art Gallery*, 57, 1999, pp. 49–72, especially 50–2. On early modern maps of imaginary places, see E. S. Schaffer's fascinating "Samuel Butler's fantastic maps: Erewhon, the 'New Jerusalem,' and the periplus of Odysseus", *Word and Image*, 4: 2, 1988, pp. 510–22.

122 Nils Büttner, "De verzamelaar Abraham Ortelius" in P. Cockshaw and Fritz de Nave (eds), *Abraham Ortelius (1527–1598), cartograaf en humanist*, exh. cat., Museum Plantin Moretus/Koninklijke bibliotheek van België, Turnhout: Brepols Publishers, 1998, pp. 168–80.

123 Van Mander, fol. 82r.

124 Junius, *Painting*, pp. 310–11. When the Dutch and English translations of Junius appeared in 1641, the discussion of *parerga* was placed at the end, thus literally serving as a "supplement". This passage is discussed insightfully in Christopher S. Wood, "Curious Pictures and the Art of Description", *Word and Image*, 11: 4, 1995, p. 344.

125 Junius, *Painting*, glossing Plutarch, *Pericles*, 13, pp. 2–3, in Bernadotte Perrin (trans.) *Plutarch Lives III: Pericles and Fabius Maximus Nicias and Crassus*, Cambridge, MA: Harvard University Press, 1996, p. 41.

126 Wölfflin, *Prologomena*, p. 178. On the methodological background of this passage see Peter Meyer, *Das Ornament in der Kunstgeschichte*, Zürich: Schweizer Spiegel, 1944, pp. 5–10, 58–66.

127 Wölfflin's notion of the "physical" apprehension of architectural forms was taken from Wilhelm Wundt and Wilhelm Dilthey, his teachers in experimental psychology and sociology at Basel and Munich. See Meinhold Lurz, *Heinrich Wölfflin: Biographie einer Kunsttheorie*, Worms: Werner'sche Verlagesellschaft, 1981; on the underpinnings of "empathy" and ornament, see Joan G. Hart, "Heinrich Wölfflin: An Intellectual Biography", Ph.D. dissertation, University of California, Berkeley, 1981, pp. 9–21, and Juliet Koss, "On the Limits of Empathy", *Art Bulletin*, 88: 1, March 2006, pp. 139–57.

128 See Alois Riegl, *Volkskunst, Hausfleiss, und Hausindustrie* (1894), Darmstadt: Maander, 1978, pp. 9–10.

129 A more redemptive view of this estrangement is found in Gianni Vattimo, "Ornament/Monument" in *The End of Modernity: Nihilism and Hermeneutics in post-modern culture*, Jon Snyder (trans.), Cambridge, UK: Polity Press 1988, pp. 79–89.

Chapter 4 The vanishing self

1 Theodor W. Adorno, *Negative Dialectics*, E. B. Ashton (trans.), New York: Continuum, 1973, p. 140.

2 *AA* IV, 1868, p. 253, doc. VI: "Alle de voors. Borgheren ende Inghesetenen sullen aldaer moghen blijven houden hun residentie, den termijn van vier gehele Jahren, sonder aldaer ondersocht oft geinquieteert te worden in stuc van hunne conscientien, oft ghedwonghen te worden tot nieuwen Eedt om tfeyt vande Religie. Midst aldaer levende in stillicheyt ende sonder desordre ende shadel, om hen daerentusschen inde exercitie van de oude Catholijke, Apostolijcke, Roomsche Religie, om inghevalle niet, hen alsdan binnen den selven tijt te morgen vrielijck vuyten lande vertrecken, als hun goet duncken sal/"

3 *SAA*, Inv. G & A 4830, 198v; see Blockmans, "Een krijgstekening", p. 26.

4 The painting is now in the St Gummaruskerk, Lier. See Hans Vlieghe, "Het altaar van de Jonge

Handboog in de Onze-Lievevrouwkerk te Antwerpen" in J. Bruyn et al. (eds), *Album Amicorum J. G. van Gelder*", The Hague: Nijhoff, 1973, pp. 342–6; and F. Prims, "Het Altaar van den Jongen Handboog", *Antwerpiensia*, XII, 1938, p. 324.

5 Michael Miller, "Zur Frage der Zweiten Reformation in Danzig" in Heinz Schilling, *Die Reformierte Konfessionaliserung in Deutschland—Das Problem der "Zweiten Reformation"*, Gütersloh: Gerd Mohn, 1986, pp. 251–65.

6 See Eugeniusz Iwanoyko, *Sala Czerwona Ratusza Gdańskiego*, Wrocław: Zakład Narodowy im. Ossolińskich, 1986, p. 31.

7 Horst Ponczek, *Spurensuche: die Wahrheit uber den Untergang Danzigs 1945*, Helmstedt: Ponczek, 2001.

8 Susan Tipton, *Res publica bene ordinata: Regentenspiegel und Bilder vom guten Regiment*, Hildesheim: Olms, 1996, pp. 239–92.

9 Friedrich Ohly, *Gesetz und Evangelium: zur Typologie bei Luther und Lucas Cranach: zum Blutstrahl der Gnade in der Kunst*, Münster: Aschendorff, 1985, pp.16–47.

10 E. Erahart (ed.), *Dictionnaire Etymologique de la Langue Latine*, 4th ed., Paris: Editions Klinckenseck, 1994, pp. 639–41.

11 The indispensable case-study of *trompe l'oeil* and authorial semantics in early modern Europe is Celeste Brusati, *Artifice and Illusion: The Art And Writing of Samuel van Hoogstraten*, Chicago: University of Chicago Press, 1995, see especially pp. 9–15, 138–68. On *trompe l'oeil* and "absence", particularly, see Pierre Charpentrat, "Le trompe l'oeil", *Nouvelle revue de psychoanalyse*, 4, 1971, pp. 160–8, and the response by Louis Marin, "Representation and Simulacrum" in *On Representation*, Palo Alto: Stanford University Press, 1994, pp. 309–19. Both readings counter a conventional interpretation of *trompe l'oeil* as imbricated with presence and sheer visuality alone (cf: Jean Baudrillard, "The *Trompe L'Oeil*" in Norman Bryson (ed.), *Calligram: Essays in New Art History from France*, Cambridge: Cambridge University Press, 1988, p. 58).

12 Amsterdam, Gemeentearchief, Rapiamus Thesauriren nr 286, fol. 66r, "27 Juli 1600: Hans Vredeman de Vries van Leeuwarden, architekt, heeft zyn poorter eedt gedaen ende den Tresorieren het poortergheldt betaelt". On April 27, 1601, Vredeman was further listed as living with his son and daughter-in-law; see Jan Briels, *Vlaamse schilders en de dageraad van Hollands Gouden Eeuw 1585–1630*, Antwerp: Mercatorfonds, 1997, p. 404.

13 Van Mander, fol. 266r.

14 According to an entry in the ducal accounts, May 25, 1587: see Peter Scheliga, "A Renaissance Garden in Wolfenbüttel", *Garden History*, XXV: 1, 1997, pp. 11, 25. On the relatively common practice of aristocratic women as supervisors of gardens in the Holy Roman Empire, see Ursula Härting (ed.), *Garten und Höfe der Rubenszeit*, Munich: Hirmer, 2000, pp. 49–57.

15 Christof Römer, "Wolfenbüttel und Halberstadt unter Herzog Henirich Julius im Rahmen der mitteleuropäischen Konstellationen 1566–1613", *Beiträge zur niedersächsischen Landesgeschichte*, 1982, pp. 165, which draws heavily on still-important researches of Friedrich Thöne, "Wolfenbüttel unter Herzog Julius", *Braunschweigisches Jahrbuch*, 33, 1952, pp. 1–74.

16 Christa Graefe (ed.), *Staatslugkeit und Frommigkei: Herzog Julius von Braunschwieg-Lüneberg*, Weinheim: VDC, 1989, pp. 13–16.

17 See, for example, Peters, "Mededelingen", p. 3.

18 Borggefe, *Norden*, no 151.

19 See Van Mander, V, pp. 48–9.

20 The literature on the Family of Love is vast. A helpful overview is: Christopher Marsh, *The Family of Love in English Society, 1550–1630*, Cambridge: Cambridge University Press, 1993, which, despite its title, deals with all of North Europe. See also Janet E. Haley, "Heresy, Orthodoxy, and the Politics of English Discourse", *Representations*, 15, Summer 1986, pp. 98–120.

21 Hendrick Niclaes, *Dicta H.N.*, Cologne, n.p., 1574, fol.16v.

22 Hermann de la Fontaine Verwey, "De geschriften van Hendrick Niclaes", *Het Boek*, 26, 1940–42, pp. 161–271, and *idem*, "Was Plantin a Member of the Family of Love?", *Quaerendo*, 23:1, Winter 1993, pp. 3–23.

23 See Dirck Volkertszoon Coornhert, *Wercken*, 3 vols, Amsterdam: Colum Press, 1930, vol. 2, for example, and Herman de la Fontaine Verwey, "The Family of Love", *Quaerendo*, 6: 3, 1976, pp. 219–71.

24 Hendrick Niclaes, *Terra pacis. Ware Getügenisse van idt geistelicke Landtschop des Fredes*, 2nd ed., Cologne: N. Bohmberg, 1580, here cited in *Terra Pacis: A True Testification of the Spirituall Lande of Peace*, Cologne: N. Bohmberg, 1575, fol. 4r.

25 Hendrick Niclaes, *Der Spiegel der Richtigkeit*, 1575?, lost but known today only through a seventeenth-century English translation: see *An introduction to the holy understanding of the glasse of righteousnesse*, London: George Whittington, 1649, as cited in Jean Dietz Moss, "Godded with God: Henrick Niclaes and His Family of Love", *Transactions of the American Philosophical Society*, 71: 8, 1981, p. 18.

26 See Hamont, *Refreynen ende Liedekens*, fol. 81r.

27 Jan Briels, *Zuid-Nederlandse Immigratie, 1572–1630*, Haarlem: Fibula-van Dishoek, 1978, p. 57.

28 On the Saverys and Bol: H. G. Frans, *Niederländische Landschaftsmalerei im Zeitalter des Manierismus*, Graz: Akademische Druck- u. Verlagsanstalt, 1969, pp. 182–97, fol. 295.

29 Briels, *Zuid-Nederlandse Immigratie*, p. 52.

30 Thomas Da Costa Kaufmann, *Court, Cloister, and City*, Chicago: University of Chicago Press, 1995, p. 211.

31 Thomas Da Costa Kaufmann, "Die Kunstmetropole Antwerpen und ihr Einfluss auf Europa und die Welt", in Borggrefe, *Norden*, fol. 44.

32 In general, on religious emigration to the Holy Roman Empire, see Heinz Schilling, *Niederländische Exulanten im 16. Jahrhundert*, Gütersloh: Mohn, 1972, pp. 83–139.

33 Martin Warnke, "Künstler in der Emigration", and Ilja M. Veldman, "Protestant Emigrants: Artists from the Netherlands in Cologne" in Thomas W. Gaehtgens (ed.), *Künstlerischer Austauch/Artistic Exchange: Akten ds XXVIII. Internationalen Kongresses für Kunstgeschichte, Berlin, 15–20 July 1992*, Berlin: Akademie-Verlag, 1993, vol. 1, pp. 161–2, 163–74. For an excellent overview of the situation of *Glaubensfluchten* in the Holy Roman Empire, see Heinz Schilling, "Religion, Politik, und Kommerz. Die europäische Konfessionsmigration des. 16. Jahrhunderts und ihr Folgen" in Edgar J. Hürkey (ed.), *Kunst, Kommerz, Glaubenskampf: Frankenthal um 1600*, exh. cat., Frankenthal: Erkenbert-Museum, 1995, Worms: Wernersche Verlagsgesellschaft, 1995, pp. 29–36.

34 Eddy Stols and Eduardo Dargent-Chamot, "Avontiers des Pays-Bas en Amérique hispano-portigaise" in Eddy Stols and Rudi Bleys (eds), *Flandre et Amérique latine: 500 ans de confrontation et métissiage*, Antwerp: Mercatorfonds, 1993, pp. 40–67.

35 Martin Papenbrock, *Landschaften des Exils: Gillis van Coninxloo und die Frankenthaler Maler*, Cologne/Wiemar/Vienna: Böhlau, 2001, fol. 45, with extensive bibliography. On Frankfurt, see specifically Thea Vignau-Wilberg, "Niederländischen Emigranten in Frankfurt und ihre Bedeutung für die realistische Pflanzendarstellung am Ende des 16. Jahrhunderts" in K. Wettengl (ed.), *Georg Flegel 1566–1638, Stilleben*, Frankfurt am Main: Historisches Museum Frankfurt, 1993, pp. 157–63.

36 Roy Strong, *The English Icon: Elizabethan and Jacobean Portraiture*, London and New York: Pantheon, 1969, pp. 151–7.

37 Rotterdam, Museum Boymans-van Beuningen, *Perspectiven: Saenredam en de architectuurschilders van de 17de eeuw*, exh. cat., 1991, p. 65; on the Steenwycks, see also Timothy T. Blade, "Hendrick van Steenwyck the Younger's 'Aeneas Rescuing Anchises from Burning Troy' ", *Museum Studies*, Chicago, 1970, pp. 38–52.

38 On Flemish artists' emigration in general, see Hub Devogherlaere, *De Zuidnederlandsche schilders in het buitenland, van 1450 tot 1600*, Antwerp: Nederlandsche Boekhandel, 1944, and Briels, *Immigratie*, 1978. On the various sites, see the following: on England, Lionel Cust, "Foreign Artists of the Reformed Religion Working in London from about 1560 to 1600", *Proceedings of the Hugenot Society*, 7, 1905, pp. 45–82; to the Baltic rim, Teresa Hrankowska (ed.), *Niderlandyzm w sztuce polskie* (Netherlandism in Polish Art), Warsaw: Wydawn Nauk, 1995 and Maria Bogucka, "Towns in Poland and the Reformation. Analogies and Differences with other Countries", *Acta Poloniae Historica*, XL, 1979, pp. 55–74. On Antwerp painters' flights to the Dutch Republic: *Dawn of the Golden Age: Northern Netherlandish Art 1580–1629*, exh. cat., Amsterdam: Rijksmuseum, 1993, pp. 55–64; Briels, *Immigratie*, pp. 9–20.

39 The pre-war appearance of the work is discussed in Hans Jantzen, "Hans Vredeman in Hamburg", *Hamburger Nachrichten*, October 10, 1910.

40 Wolfenbüttel, Niedersächsisches Staatsarchiv, Inv. 2, Alt 3468; see Thöne, "Hans Vredeman", 1960, pp. 50–2.

41 It was Specklin who advised William of Orange to demolish the Antwerp citadel in 1577. The Wolfenbüttel plan appears on fol. 70 recto of the untitled 1583 manuscript, Strasbourg, Musées du Strasbourg, Cabinet des Estampes, Ms. 1583.

42 *Architectura von Vestungen, wie die zu unsem zeiten mögen erbawen warden*. . . Strausburg: Bernhart Jobin, 1589.

43 Krzytof Biskup, "Planungen zum Ausbau Wolfenbüttels als einer Idealstadt er Renaissance" in *Herzog Julius zu Braunschweig-Luneburg, ein norddeutscher Landesherr des 16. Jahrhunderts*, exh. cat., Wolfenbüttel: Herzog August Bibliothek, 1989, pp. 34–9.

44 Barbara Uppenkamp, "Die Scenographiaen und Gartenentwürfe des Hans Vredeman de Vries und seine Tätigkeit in Wolfenbüttel im Lichte neuer Quellen" in Lubomír Komečný (ed.), *Rudolf II, Prague, and the World*, Prague: Artefactum, 1998, pp. 111–16, and *idem*, "The Influence of Hans Vredeman de Vries on the Cityscape constructed like a picture", in Lombaerde, *Artes*, pp. 123–4.

45 Wolfenbüttel, HAB sig. N37 Helmst 2°. Instances of this print series in other collections are detailed in Heuer, "Between the Histories of Art", pp. 29–31.

46 Nuremberg, Germanisches Nationalmuseum, inv. no 3473.

47 The attribution appeared first in Thöne, "Hans Vredeman", pp. 58–60. On town expansion in Wolfenbüttel, see Barbara Uppenkamp, 'Ordnung und Geometrie. Die Wolfenbütteler Heinrichstadt—eine deutsche Idealstadt um 1600" in *Pasqualini-Studien I (Jülicher Forschungen 4)*, Jülich: Jülicher Geschichtsvereins, 1995, pp. 7–30.

48 Document in the Hauptstaatarchiv Hannover, Cal. Br. 22, Nr 1039, fol. 33v. On Vredeman as horticulturist, see Thomas Scheliga, "Renaissance Gärten der Herzoge von Braunschweig-Lüneberg in Wolfenbüttel" in Vera Lüpkes (ed.), *"zur zierde und schmuck angeegt . . ".: Beitrage zur frühneuzeitlichen Garten- und Schloßbaukunst*, Marburg: Jonas Verlag, 1996, pp. 9–52, and most recently, Chris de Maegd, "Tuinbezit, Tuinen, en Tuinlui: Een Licht op de Praktijk in de Tijd van Vredeman de Vries" in *De Wereld is een Tuin: Hans Vredeman de Vries en de Tuinkunst van de Renaissance*, exh. cat., Antwerp: Rubenshuis, 2002, pp. 69–87.

49 Thierry Lamirault, *La Nature mise en Perspective dans l'art de la peinture et l'art des jardins*, Paris: Economica, 1997, pp. 87–100.

50 The contents of a 1589 inventory of the Wolfenbüttel gardens are listed in Scheliga, "Renaissance Gärten", pp. 20–6.

51 Thöne, "Hans Vredeman", p. 50.

52 Wolfenbüttel, Niedersächsisches Staatsarchiv, Inv. 50, Slg 1053, nr 1. On the drawing, see Charles van den Heuvel, "Hydraulic Projects" in Lombaerde, *Artes*, pp. 113–15.

53 See Gerd Spies, *Technik der Steingewinnung und der Flußschiffahrt im Harzvorland in früher Neuzeit*, Braunschweig: Waisenhaus, 1992, pp. 119–35.

54 See Irmscher, "Zeichner (II)", p. 101, cat. 15.

55 On the definition of *Abriß* (sketch, or concept): *Wasmuth Lexikon der Baukunst*, Berlin: Wasmuth, 1929, vol. 1, p. 11.

56 *SAA* Icon. 26/6. The various stages of reconfiguration of the Antwerp citadel are discussed in Charles van den Heuvel, "Il problema della cittadella: Anversa" in Cesare de Seta and Jacques Le Goff (eds), *La città e le mura*, Rome: Laterza, 1989, pp. 166–86, and, more recently, in Piet Lombaerde, "New Techniques for Representing the Object: Hans Vredeman de Vries and Hans Van Schille" in Borggrefe and Lüpkes et al., *Die Folgen*, p. 104.

57 Piet Lombaerde, "Cutting and Pasting Fortifications" in Lombaerde, *Artes*, pp. 92–5.

58 Thöne, "Hans Vredeman", p. 56.

59 The altarpiece is now in Wolfenbüttel, disassembled and housed at three separate locations within the city: the main panel depicting a *Crucifixion with Allegory of Sin and Redemption* is in the Church of the Beatified Virgin, two outer wings are in the Schloßmuseum Wolfenbüttel, and the retable by Walter van

Elsmaer is in the Johaniskirche. For a visual reconstruction, see Thomas Scheliga, "Ein neuer Aktenfund zum Altar der Schloßkapelle Hessen", *Heimatjahrbuch für Landkreis Wolfenbüttel*, 1996, pp. 58–60, and on the work's rather heavy-handed Lutheran iconography: Oliver Glißmann, "Hans Vredeman de Vries: Allegorie auf Sünde und Erlösing", *Niedersächsische Denkmalpflege*, 16, 2001, pp. 242–59.

60 Van Mander, fol. 266r.

61 Most documents related to Vredeman's activity in Danzig were destroyed in 1945; those transcribed by Cuny, *Danzigs Kunst*, pp. 47–8, 125, remain the chief sources on the stay. See, however, Bernard M. Vermet, "Architectuurschilders in Dantzig: Hendrick Aerts and Hans en Paul Vredeman de Vries", *Gentse bijdragen tot de kunstgeschiedenis*, 31, 1996, pp. 27–57.

62 See G. Schramm, "Danzig, Elbing, und Thorn als Beispele städtisches Reformation (1517–1558)" in *Historia Integra. Festschrift für E. Hasinger zum 70. Geburtstag*, Berlin: Duncker und Humbolt, 1977, pp. 125–54.

63 B. Woelderink, "Het bezoek van Simon Stevin aan Danzig", *Tijdschrift voor de gescheidenis van de geneeskunde, natuurwetenschappen, wiskunde, en techniek*, 3, 1980, pp. 178–86. On cultural circumstances in Danzig c.1500–1600, see Teresa Grzybkowska (ed.), *Aurea Porta Rzeczypospoliteij*, exh. cat., Gdańsk, Muzeum Narodowe w Gdańsku, 1997, 2 vols.

64 Cuny, *Danzigs Kunst*, p. 47.

65 Gustav Köhler, *Geschichte der Festungen Danzig und Weichselmünde bis zum Jahre 1814*, Brelsau: W Köbner, 1893, vol. 1, pp. 283–4. The document survives in the Stadtsarchiv Danzig (Gdańsk). On Anton van Opbergen, who went on to work in Denmark using Vredeman's ornament books, see Eugeniusz Gasiriowski, "Anthonis van Opbergen", *Hafnia*, 3, 1976, pp. 71–90.

66 ". . . dennach ich [that is, Vredeman] aber von Hamburg abgefordert und von dannen mit Weib und Kind mit nicht geringem Verlust und Schaden, indem ich allda in guter Nahrung gesessen und und mein Brodt wohl habe werben können . . ". in Cuny, *Danzigs Kunst*, p. 47.

67 Cuny, *Danzigs Kunst*, p. 47.

68 Formerly with Frye & Sohn, Münster. See Antwerp, Koninklijke Museum voor Schone Kunsten, *Van Bruegel tot Rubens*, exh. cat., 1992, nr. 144.

69 Bernard M. Vermet, "Hendrick Aerts", *Gentse Bijdragen tot de kunstgeschiedenis en oudheidkunde*, 30, 1995, pp. 107–17.

70 See, for example, Timothy T. Blade, "The Paintings of Dirck van Delen", Ph.D. dissertation, University of Minnesota, 1976, pp. 153–64; Walter Liedtke, "Faith in Perspective", *Connoisseur*, 193, 1976, pp. 264–73.

71 Calvin, *Institutes* IV.1.7–9; see John Calvin, *Institutio Christianae religionis*, Basel, 1536, Ford Lewis Battles (trans. and annotated), Grand Rapids, MI: Eerdmans, 1986, pp. 62–3.

72 Calvin, *Institutes* IV. 10. 29–31. Calvin, *Institutio*, p. 206.

73 I am indebted for this observation and phrasing to Cammy Brothers, unpublished seminar paper, Harvard University, Fall 1999.

74 John Michael Montias, "Perspectiven in zeventiende-eeuwse bodelbeschrijvingen", in Rotterdam, *Perspectiven*, pp. 19–29.

75 Cuny, *Danzigs Kunst*, p. 48, n. 73. Seven of the paintings are intact and remain in their original settings in Gdańsk, now as part of the Muzeum Historii Miasta Gdańska (Historical Museum of Gdańsk). For the Council chamber painting cycle and its visual sources, see Teresa Grzybkowska, *Zwischen Kunst und Politik der Rote Saal des Rechtstädischen Rathausen in Danzig*, Warsaw: Agencja Reklamowo, 2003, pp. 30–56.

76 Cuny, *Danzigs Kunst*, p. 48.

77 Lommel was a Flemish confectioner from Antwerp, in Hamburg since 1591; further *trompe l'oeil* decoration was added by Vredeman to his ceiling; see Wilhelm Sillem, "Zur Geschichte der Niederländer in Hamburg von ihrer Ankunft bis zum Abschlußes niederländischen Contracts 1605", *Zeitschrift des Vereins für hamburgische Geschichte*, 7, 1883, p. 518.

78 On Prague as religious haven: Nicolette Mont, "Political and Religious Ideas of the Netherlands at the Court in Prague", *Acta historiae neerlandicae*, 9, 1976, pp. 1–29.

79 Van Mander in the "Voor-reden", fol. iiiiv.

80 On the history of Hapsburg collecting in Bavaria and the Tyrol, see Alphons Lhotsky, *Die Geschichte der Sammlungen*, vol. 2, part 1 of *Festschrift des Kunsthistorischen Museums*, Vienna, F. Berger, 1941–45, and on Ambras, generally, Elisabeth Scheicher, *Ambras: Die Kunstkammer*, Innsbruck/Vienna: Kunsthistorisch Museum, 1977.

81 Transcribed in H. Zimmerman (ed.), "Urkunden, Akten, und Regesten aus dem Archiv des K.K. Ministerium des Innern", *Jarhrbuch der Konigliche Sammlungen der Allerhöchsten Kaiserhauses*, 7, 1888, p. 2, n. 4607.

82 Lubomír Komečný, "Picturing the Arts in Rudolfine Prague" in Lubomír Komečný, Beket Bukovinska, and Ivan Muchka (eds), *Rudolf II, Prague, and the World*, Prague: Artefactum, 1998, pp. 107–12.

83 See Hessel Miedema, "Kunstschilders, gilde, en academie: Over het probleem van de emancipatie van de kunstschilders in de Noordelijke Nederlanden van de 16de en 17de eeuw", *Oud Holland*, 101, 1987, p. 27; and for an alternative view of the effects of the 1593 letter, Thomas da Costa Kaufmann, "The eloquent artist: towards an understanding of the stylistics of painting at the court of Rudolf II" in *The Eloquent Artist*, London: Pindar, 2004, p. 144.

84 Of the enormous literature on art and artists in Rudolfine Prague, the following sources are particularly relevant to the Vredemans' stay: H. G. Franz, "Niederländische Landschaftsmalerei im Künstlerkreis Rudolfs II", *Umeni*, 18, 1970, pp. 222–45; *Artis pictoriae amatores: Evropa v zrcadle prazskehs barokniho sberatelvi*, exh. cat., Prague: Nardoni Galerie, 1993; Karl Vocelka, *Rudolf II und seine Zeit*, Vienna: Böhlau, 1985, and Komečný et al., *Rudolf II*, pp. 2–72.

85 On Spranger at court: Michael Henning, *Die Tafelbilder Bartholomäus Sprangers (1546–1611): Höfische Malerei zwischen "Manierismus" und "Barock"*, Essen: Blaue Eule, 1987, pp. 16–57.

86 Vienna, Kunsthistorisches Museum, inv. no 2335.

87 Van Mander, fol. 267r, and commentary in Van Mander, vol. V, 61, p. 257, n. 108.

88 Lhotsky, *Sammlungen*, pt 2, pp. 237–98.

89 Lothar Dittrich and Sigrid Dittrich, "Tiere in Höfen und Gärten von Palästen auf Bildern von Hans und Paul Vredeman de Vries", *Niederdeutsche Beiträge zur Kunstgeschichte*, 32, 1993, pp. 90–107, especially 92–3. On the "merry companies" tradition, see Elmer Kolfin, "Een geselschap jonge luyden: productie, functie, en betekenis van Noord-Nederlandse voorstellingen van vrolijke gezelschappen 1610–1645", Proefschrift: Universiteit Leiden, 2002, pp. 4–23.

90 Juub Bosmans, "Hans Vredeman de Vries", *Fries Museumbulletin*, September 1991, pp. 6–8.

91 Martin Warnke, *The Court Artists: On the Ancestry of the Modern Artist*, Cambridge: Cambridge University Press, 1993, p. 252. For the specific situation at Prague: Jaroslava Hausenblasová, "Die 'Höfflinge' des Kaisers Rudolf II—Beitrage zur Begriffsbestimming", in Komečný et al., *Rudolf II*, pp. 239–43.

92 Eliška Fučíková, "Die Kunstkammer und Galerie Kaiser Rudolfs II als eine Studiensammlung" in *Der Zugang zum Kunstwerk: Schatzkammer, Salon, Ausstellung, "Museum": Akten des XXV International Kongresses für Kunstgeschichte, Wien*, Vienna: Bohlau, 1986, vol. 4, pp. 53–8; Georg Kugler, "Rudolf II als Sammler" in Essen, *Prag*, vol. 2, p. 11. A later inventory of the kunstkammer section appears in R. Bauer and H. Haupt, "Das Kunstkammerinventar Kaiser Rudolfs II, 1607–1611", *Jahrbuch der Kunsthistorischen Sammlungen in Wien*, LXXII, 1976. On the kunstkammer's physical layout, in which the Vredemans' paintings could have eventually hung alongside naturalia, weapons, globes, books, gems, sculptures and other precious objects, see also Komečný et al., *Rudolf II*, pp. 199–208, 469–72.

93 The painting is lost, but a small *Babel* canvas sold at Christie's, London (King Street) on July 10, 2002, lot 17, as "Circle of Abel Grimmer", monogrammed "HV", which is stylistically approximate to both Hans Valkenborch and Hans Vredeman.

94 Jarmilia Krválová, "Die rudolfinische Architecktur", *Leids Kunsthistorisch Jaarboek*, I, 1982, pp. 271–308; Eliška Fuíková, "The collection of Rudolf II at Prague: cabinet of curiosities or scientific museum?" in Oliver Impey and A. MacGregor (eds), *The Origins of Museums: the cabinet of curiosities in sixteenth- and seventeenth-century Europe*, Oxford: Oxford University Press, 1985, pp. 47–53.

95 Karl Köpl, "Urkunden, Acten, und Regesten aus dem K. K. Staathaltererei-Archiv in Prag", *Jahrbuch der Kunsthistorischen Sammlungen des Allerhöchsten Kaiserhauses*, 12, 1891, fol. LXXXV, docs 8309, 8320.

96 Köpl, "Urkunden", doc. 8320: "Dort, wo man aus den grossen Saal zum Vorbau oder Sommerhaus der Kaisers geht, sei ihnen eine Perspective genannte Maleriei in Oelfarben gezeigt worden".

97 See Jaroslaus Schaller, *Beschriebung der Köninglichen Haupt- und Residenzstadt Prag sammet allen darin befindlichen sehenswürdingen Merkwürdigkeiten*, Prague: F. Gerzabeck, 1794–97, vol. 1, p. 345, which mentions "von hartem Metal gogossene Fountain".

98 Van Mander, fol. 267r: "maken dat [the Emperor] mocht gaen sonder te connent zijn gesien".

99 On the castle architecture at Prague: Maria Brykowska, "The Architecture of the Prague Castle in light of the Plan of the Uffizi" in Komečný et al., *Rudolf II*, pp. 220–5, and for reconstructions, Ivan Muchka, "Die Architecktur unter Rudolf II, gezeigt am Beispel der Prager Burg" in Essen, *Prag*, vol. 2, pp. 85–95.

100 Leopold Chatenay, *Vie de Jacuqes Esprinchard Rochelais et Journal de ses Voyages au XVIe siècle*, Paris: S.E.V.P.E.N., 1957, pp. 169–70: "L'Empereur a de grandes galeries couvertes en son chasteau desquelles il peult aller par tout ou il veult, voire mesme jusques en ses jardins et au jeau de paume, sans ester apperceu d'aucun".

101 George Kubler, *Building the Escorial*, Princeton: Princeton University Press, 1982, p. 88, describes "tortuous, and strangely proportioned corridors" leading from Philip's royal apartments, described in a 1597 letter from the English courtier Jehann Lhermite.

102 In a series of publications: see Thomas da Costa Kaufmann, "Remarks on the Collections of Rudolf II: the *Kunstkammer* as a form of *Representatio*", *Art Journal*, 38, 1978, pp. 22–8; and Da Costa Kaufmann, *School*, pp. 11–17.

103 An entry in the Amsterdam *Kerckenboeck* is cited in A. D. de Vries, "Biographische aanteekeningen betreffende voornamelijk Amsterdamsche schilders, plaatsnijders, enz. en hunne verwanten", *Oud Holland*, 4, 1886, p. 298: "Ondertr. 24. April 1601. Paulus Vredeman de Vriese, van Antwerpen, oudt 34 jaren, won. in de Hoogstrate, geass. met Johan de Vriese, sijn vader, en Mayken Godelet, oudt 37j., won inde Geertruydenstraet".

104 See, for example, Borggrefe, *Norden*, pp. 353–6.

105 Mönchengladbach, Städisches Museum Schloss Rheydt, inv. M. 101. See *Wallraf-Richartz Jahrbuch*, 41, 1980, p. 312.

106 See *Architekt und Ingenieur*, exh. cat., Wolfenbüttel: Herzog-August Bibliothek, 1984, pp. 263–7.

107 As has been suggested of two drawings in Gdańsk: see *Nie Tylko o Mapach—Holandia W Zbiorach Biblioteki Gdańskiej Polskiej Akademii Nauk*, exh. cat., Gdańsk: Polish Academy of Science, 2000, p. 32, n. 61. Reverse copies of *Perspective* plates from a Milan collection have also been regarded as copies after preliminary drawings; see Guilio Bora, "Quattro Disegni: Hans Vredeman de Vries e un Doppio Scambio Italia-Fiandria", *Incontri*, 9: 1, 1994, pp. 57–62.

108 Melion, *Shaping*, pp. 31–3, Brusati, *Artifice and Illusion*, pp. 10–11, Van Mander, V, pp. 58–9.

109 Miedema likens Vredeman's canvases to those executed by Federico Zuccaro for the reception of Joanna of Austria. See Van Mander, V, p. 58, n. 122.

110 Brusati, *Artifice and Illusion*, p. 10.

111 Jürgen Müller, *Concordia Pragensis: Karel Van Manders Kunsttheorie im Schilder-Boeck (Veröffentlichen des Collegium Carolinium 77)*, Munich: Oldenbourg, 1993, pp. 111–14.

112 Melion, *Shaping*, pp. 31–2.

113 Van Mander, fol. 265v.

114 Stephen Bann, *The True Vine: On Visual Representation and the Western Tradition*, Cambridge: Cambridge University Press, 1989, pp. 27–40. On the Zeuxis myth in art historiography: Norman Bryson, *Vision and Painting*, New Haven: Yale University Press, 1983, pp. 1–12, but also Carl Goldstein, "The image of the artist reviewed", *Word and Image*, 9: 1, 1993, especially pp. 9–10. Rupert Shepard has pointed out that the whole *topos* of image conflated with its prototype relies upon what is essentially an aesthetic of naturalism; see his "Art and life in Renaissance Italy: a blurring of Identities?" in Mary Rogers (ed.), *Fashioning Identities in Renaissnace Art*, Aldershot: Ashgate, 2000, pp. 63–72.

115 Van Mander, fol. 266r: ". . . maekt by een groot Perspect/als een doorsien in eenen Hof. Nier mede werden namaels begrogen eenige duytsche Edelluyden/en den Prins van Orangien/meenende dat het een natuerlijck gebouw een doorsie was".

116 Van Mander, fol. 266v: "Ao. 1591. quam hy t'Hamborgh, daer hy onder ander heeft gheschildert in S. *Pieters* Kerck, in een Capelle, voor een Iuwelier *Iacob Moor*, zijn begraefnis, een groot Perspectijf, daer *Christus* Duyvel, Doot, en Helle heeft onder voeten. Onder comen twee half open staende deuren, daer veel om wort verwedt: want men sieter of men saegh door een Portael op eenen trap. Onder ander eenen Poolschen Wewode, oft Hertogh, opperste Hofmeester des Conings, souder wel duysent Poolsche gulden om verwedt ebben, dat het een natuerlijcke open deur was. Ander verwedden een gelach biers, een ton boter, en dergheliјcke: wenschende de verliesers dat des Schilders handen mochten bedreckt wesen".

117 Van Mander, fol. 266v: "maeckte voor d'Heer *Hans Lomel* een aleryken in eenen hof, met een doorsien van groenicheyt:recht teghen over de Galerije, in't self Hof, een houten schutsel, een Prospect van een opstaende deur, toonende eenen Vijver met Swanen, en onder gheschildert de Boomstammen, welcker toppen natuerlijck men boven t'schutsel siet, wort van velen met verwonderen gesien . . ".

118 Vienna, Kunsthistorisches Museum, inv. no 6436. Da Costa Kaufmann, *School*, p. 291, indicates that the altarpiece was probably used for the altar of the *Allerheiligenkapelle* of the church in the Hradcany castle. The *Annunciation* figures on the shutters, attributed by Ehrmann to Paul Vredeman, are convincingly attributed by Da Costa Kaufmann to Hans van Aachen.

119 See Da Costa Kaufmann, *School*, p. 291.

120 I owe this insight to Daniel Arasse, *L'annonciation italienne: une histoire de perspective*, Paris: Hazan, 1999, especially pp. 20–50.

121 Van Mander, fol. 267r. "heeft *Vries* uytwendigh gheschildert een Perspect, latende eerst de deuren glat effen maken, bracht neffens de sluytende vergaderinghe eenen viercanten Pijler datmen geen vergaderinge can sien, t'welck den Keyser met verwonderen wel beviel".

122 Van Mander, fol. 267r: "*Pauwels* ter begheerte van den Keyser maeckte noch in de Salette een Perspect met een doorsiende Galerije, in eenen Hof met een Fonteyne, alwaer den Keyser als hem vergissende dickwils meende door heen te gaen".

123 On the linguistic contexts of these terms in Dutch art theory, see Walter S. Melion, "Karel Van Mander et les origins du discours historique sur l'art dans les Pays-Bas au XVIIe siecle" in Edouard Pommier (ed.), *Histoire de l'histoire de l'art: Tome I: de l'Antiquite au XVIIIe siecle*, Paris: Klincksieck, 1995, pp. 179–219.

124 On "disguise" tropes in the *Schilderboeck:* James J. Bloom, "Mastering the Medium: Reference and Audience in Goltzius' print of the *Circumcision*", *NKJ*, 52, 2002, pp. 79–99, especially 81–6.

125 See the outline in Hessel Miedema, *Karel Van Mander: Het bio-bibliografisch materiaal*, Amsterdam: n.p., 1972, and the introductory section of Werner Waterschoot, *Ter liedfde der const: uit het Schilderboeck Van Karel van Mander*, Leiden: Nijhoff, 1983.

126 Greve, *de Bronnen*, pp. 30–5. On the use of letters for research, see Irene Baldriga, "The role of correspondence in the transmission of collecting patterns in seventeenth-century Europe" in F. Bethencourt (ed.), *Correspondence and Cultural Exchange in Early Modern Europe*, Cambridge: Cambridge University Press, 2007, pp. 187–216.

127 Van Mander, fol. 258r.

128 Van Mander, fol. 227r.

129 Or in Van Mander, fol. 220v, on the life of Hans Holbein: "I wrote to Basel and sent for information but unfortunately the person from whom I would have been able to get much of the information had died eight or ten years earlier", fol. 242v; on the life of Crispin van den Broeke: "I do not know any more particulars about him because my request to those who knew him was not granted".

130 For some remarks on the unusual length of Ketel's biography in the *Schilderboeck*, see Wolfgang Stechow, "Cornelis Ketels Einzelbildnisse", *Zeitschrift fur bildende Kunst*, 63, 1929–30, pp. 200–6.

131 Paul Taylor's untitled review article of Van Mander/Miedema, in *Oud Holland*, 115: 2, 2001/2002, pp. 131–55.

132 Charles Hope has made a claim about Vasari's summative use of letters, suggesting that the author—if he was involved at all—wrote only a small part of the seven-volume *Vite*, and should be recognized chiefly as a compiler of other biographies. See Charles Hope, "Can you trust Vasari?", *New York*

Review of Books, October 5, 1995, pp. 10–13, and its expansion in *idem*, "Le Vite Vasariane: un esempio autore multiplo" in Anna Santioni (ed.), *L'Autore Multiplo*, Pisa: Scuole Normale Superiore, 2005, pp. 59–74. Thomas Frangenberg has shown that the prefaces to Vasari's *Lives*, too, were, probably written by others: see T. Frangeberg, "Bartoli, Giambullari, and the Prefaces to Vasari's *Lives* (1550)", *JWCI*, 65, 2002, pp. 244–58.

133 Helen Noë, *Carel Van Mander en Italië, beschouwingen en notities naar aanleiding van zijn "Leven der dees-tijtsche doorluchtighe Italiensche schilders"*, The Hague: Nijhoff, 1954, and Greve, *de Bronnen*, p. 124; Van Mander, II, pp. 172–6.

134 On conventions of artistic biography in general, see the classic Ernst Kris and Otto Kurz, *Legend, Myth, and magic in the image of the artist* (1934), New Haven: Yale University Press, 1979; in specific reference to the Netherlands, Eric Jan Sluijter, "*Herscheppingen* in prenten van Hendrick Goltzius en zijn kring (I)", *Delineavit et sculpsit*, 4, 1990, pp. 1–23.

135 Van Mander, fol. 261v. On the seventeenth-century adoption of "perspective" as a label for a variety of crafted objects, see John Michael Montias, "How Notaries and Scribes Recorded Works of Art", *Simiolus*, 30, no 3/4, 2003, pp. 227–9.

136 However, in the life of Gillis Mostaert (Van Mander/Miedema, fol. 261v) we read about "een Perspekt in de Nacht" (a nocturnal perspective); Gillis (d. 1598), worked closely in Antwerp with Vredeman as a staffagist; information about his life could also have come from Hans himself.

137 It does appear in Van Mander's Italian lives (fol. 193v), in the life of Giovanni da Udine, apparently lifted straight from Vasari's 1568 edition.

138 Miedema, *Italienische Schilders*, p. 73.

139 Paul Taylor, "The Concept of *Houding* in Dutch Art Theory", *JWCI*, 55, 1992, pp. 210–32. Another important discussion of *doorsien*, one that distinguishes the term from the Latin *perspect*, is Martha Hollander, *An Entrance for the Eyes: Space and Meaning in Seventeenth-Century Dutch Art*, Berkeley and London: UC Press, 2002, pp. 7–18.

140 The word "*doorsien*", however, appears in legal proceedings from the fourteenth century to refer to "examination". See E. Wewijs (ed.), *Middelnederlandsch Woordenboeck*, 2nd ed., The Hague: Nijhoff, 1899, vol. 2, pp. 338–9; in the seventeenth century, Dutch poets like Vondel and Hooft periodically used "*doorzien*" to describe a kind of optical illusion; see J. A. N. Knuttel (ed.), *Woordenboek der Nederlandsche Taal*, The Hague: Nijhoff, 1916, vol. 3, pp. 3121–3.

141 Van Mander, fol. 272r: "Den Spranger maeckt hier nae een stucken . . . daer Mercurius in den Raedt der Goden Pysche bringt/het welck met een aerdich doorsien der wolcken uytnemende wel geordineert en wel ghedaen was". The painting is discussed in Da Costa Kaufmann, *School*, p. 250, cat. 20.3; also Henning, *Die Tafelbilder Bartholomäus Sprangers*, p. 178.

142 On the dating and bibliographic circumstances of the *Schilderboeck*'s first editions, see Werner Waterschoot, "Karel Van Mander's *Schilder-Boeck*: a description of the book and its setting", *Quaerendo*, XIII: 4, Autumn 1983, pp. 260–86.

143 "*Doorsien*" does, however, appear twice in the Italian lives (in the life of Giulio Romano, fol. 137v), and then again in the life of Geerard Horebout (fol. 204v). I am indebted to Paul Taylor for this observation (personal correspondence, January 2007).

144 See Van Mander, fol. 209r. On the exact hanging of the works in the Prague castle versus Rudolf's *kunstkammer*, see Beket Bukovinská, "The Kunstkammer of Rudolf II: Where It Was and What It Looked Like" in Komečný et al., *Rudolf II*, pp. 199–208.

145 Van Mander, vol. V, p. 52.

146 Cited in Taylor, "Review", p.153, n. 275.

147 Van Mander, fol. 266v: "Op de nieuw Raedt-camer zijn oock van hem acht stucken Perspecten, met Histori*e*n va*n* de Regeringe. Eerst, *Iustitia* en *Injustitia*. Tweedst, *Consilium*. Derdst, *Pietas* in eenen Moderne*n* Tempel. Vierdst, *Concordia*. Vijfst, *Libertas*. Sest, *Constantia*. Sevenst, het Oordeel. Achtst, een stuck, datmen des Somers stelt in de schoorsteen, met een Perspect van eenen boogh: hier in sit op trappen de Reden, en eene*n* Hondt nae t'leven voor de Trouwe. Dese houden hier binnen gevange*n* *Discordiam, Seditionem, Traditionem, Calumniam falsam, Invidiam*,en alle quaet gespoock".

148 On the locations of the *Schilderboeck*'s composition, see Van Mander, vol. II, p. 171.

149 Van Mander, fol. 267r.

150 "*Punct*" (point), as "vanishing point", appears twice in the life of Vredeman, and nowhere else in the entire *Schilderboeck*, save for once in the life of Hans Holbein (fol. 222v).

151 e.g. Van Mander, fol. 232r.

152 Taylor, "Review", p. 142.

153 On the growing interest in self-explanation in artistic and architectural treatises of the sixteenth century, see Long, *Openness, Secrecy*, pp. 222–43.

154 Michael Leja, "*Trompe L'Oeil* painting and the deceived viewer" in Robert Maniura and Rupert Shepherd, *Presence: The Inherence of the Prototype within Images and Other Objects*, Aldershot: Ashgate, 2006, pp. 173–90; also, Louis Marin, "Mimesis and Representation" in *On Representation*, Palo Also, Stanford University Press, 2001, pp. 252–68.

155 Paul de Man, "Autobiography as De-Facement" in *The Rhetoric of Romanticism*, New York: Columbia University Press, 1984, pp. 67–81.

Chapter 5 Hidden terrors: the *Perspective* (1604–05)

1 Carl Einstein, "The Etchings of Hercules Seghers", Charles W. Haxthausen (trans.), *October*, 107, Winter 2004, p. 154.

2 See Alberti, *On Painting*, pp. 23–45. The best overview of the colossal literature on Alberti's specific method is Luigi Vagnetti, "De naturali et artificali perspectiva", *Studi e documenti di architettura*, IX/X, 1979, pp. 195–226, with some newer references in Francesco Furlan, *Leon Battista Alberti: Actes du Congrés International de Paris*, Paris: J. Vrin, 2000, vol. 1, pp. 575–88, vol. 2, pp. 589–632. On the *De Pictura* as a treatise, specifically, see Samuel Edgerton, "Alberti's Perspective, A New Discovery and a new evaluation", *Art Bulletin*, XLVIII, 1966, pp. 367–78, and Branko Mitrovic, "Alberti and Spatium" in *Serene Greed of the Eye*, Berlin: Deutsche Kunstverlag, 2005, pp. 73–100.

3 Joel Snyder, "Picturing Vision", *Critical Inquiry*, 6, 1980, pp. 499–526, and James Elkins, *The Poetics of Perspective*, Ithaca: Cornell University Press, 1994, particularly pp. 117–80; the latter source has shaped some of the thinking of the present chapter.

4 Fritz Novotny, *Die Monatsbilder Pieter Bruegels d. Ä*, Vienna: Franz Deuticke, 1948, pp. 3–9.

5 Yet see Michael Kubovy, *The Psychology of Perspective and Renaissance Art*, Cambridge: Cambridge University Press, 1986, pp. 104–26.

6 On early twentieth-century architectural critiques of perspective projection, and Taut's interest in detaching vision from perspectival models, see Iain Boyd White, *Bruno Taut and the Architecture of Activism*, Cambridge: Cambridge University Press, 1982, and Hanno-Walter Kruft, *A History of Architectural Theory from Vitruvius to the Present*, Ronald Taylor et. al. (trans.), Princeton: Princeton University Press, 1994, pp. 372–7; for Helmholtz's take on perspective, see Jonathan Crary, *Techniques of the Observer*, Cambridge: MA: MIT Press, 1990, p. 70.

7 But one whose mechanisms, paradoxically, have driven art-historical obsessions with painting at the cost of other media: see Rosalind Krauss, *The Optical Unconscious*, Cambridge: MIT Press, 1993, pp. 213–14.

8 Michel Foucault, "Nietzsche, Genealogy, History", Donald F. Bouchard and Sherry Simon (trans.) in *Michel Foucault: Language, Counter-Memory, Practice: Selected Essays and Interviews*, Donald F. Bouchard (ed.), Ithaca, NY: Cornell University Press, 1977, pp. 139–64.

9 Robin Evans, *The Projective Cast*, Cambridge, MA: MIT Press, 1994, pp. 126–7.

10 See *Leonardo on Painting* (ed.), Martin Kemp, New Haven: Yale University Press, 1989, pp. 53–61.

11 See the appendix of Kim Veltman, "Military surveying and topography: the practical dimension of Renaissance Linear Perspective" in *Revista da Universidade de Coimbra*, XXVII, 1979, pp. 263–79.

12 On "inversion" as a function of printmaking, Claudia Swan, "The Praxis of Inversion: Jacques de Gheyn II's *Preparation for the Sabbath* ca. 1610", *Print Quarterly*, 16, 1999, pp. 327–9.

13 *Perspective, dat is De hoochgheroemde conste eens schijnende in oft door-siende ooghenghesichtespunt op effen staende muer, penneel oft doeck, eenige edifitien t'sy van kercken, tempelen, palleysen, salen, cameren . . . alhier bethoont, gestelt op sijne gronts-linien, ende 't fondement der selver met beschrijvinge claerlijck uyt-geleyt, nut, dienstelijck ende grootelicx van noode voor allen*

schilders, plaet-snijders . . ., The Hague and Leiden: Hendrick Hondius, 1604–05. Unless otherwise noted, all citations come from this edition.

14 H (Vredeman), nos 517–91; the relevant *Schilderboeck* passage is in Van Mander, fol. 267r. There is, to date, no comprehensive study of Vredeman's *Perspective* as treatise. There are, however, partially annotated facsimiles of the plates to the 1604–05 Latin edition, New York: Abrams, 1968, and Paris: Gallimard, 1977, and a full impression of the Dutch with translation and commentary annotated by Peter Karstkarel, Mijdrecht: Tableau, 1979. On the engravings, see Mielke, *Verzeichnis*, pp. 1–13, Nadine Orenstein, *Hendrick Hondius and the Business of Prints in 17th Century Holland*, Rotterdam: Sound and Vision, 1996, cat. no 629, pp. 116–19; H (Hondius), no 197, and H (Vredeman), no 591. A considerably larger literature has examined Vredeman's method, usually in relation to painting in the Dutch republic; see Gezienius ten Doesschate, *Perspective: fundamentals, controversials, history*, Nieuwkoop: De Graaf, 1964, pp. 152–5; see also Heinz Roosen-Runge, "Perspektive und Bildwircklichkeit in Hollandischen gemälden des 17. Jahrhunderts", *Kunstschronik*, XX, 1966, p. 304; Schneede, *Gesellschaftbild*; Arthur Wheelock, *Perspective, Optics, and Delft Painters Around 1650*, New York: Garland, 1977, pp. 9–14; Martin Kemp, *The Science of Art*, New Haven: Yale University Press, 1986, pp. 108–11; Pascal D. Glatigny, "Hans Vredeman de Vries und die Perspektive" in Borggrefe, *Norden*, pp. 127–32; Michael Gnehm, "Die 'alte und newe manier' in Vredeman de Vries' *Perspektive*" in Lüpkes, et al., *Die Folgen*, pp. 190–8.

15 Thomas Fusenig and Bernard Vermet, "Der Einfluss von Hans Vredeman de Vries auf die Malerei" in Borggrefe, *Norden*, pp. 161–78; Prosper Arents, *De Bibliotheek van Pieter Pauwel Rubens: een reconstructie*, Antwerp: Vereniging der Antwerpse Bibliofielen, 2001, pp. 296–7.

16 Ramon Solar I Fabregat, "Libres de perspectiva a biblioteques d'artistes espanyols (Sieglos XVI–XVIII)" in *D'art: Revista del Department d'Histoire d'art Universidad de Barcelona*, 20, 1994, pp.167–79; Ivan P. Muchka, "Hans Vredeman de Vries in den Böhmischen Bibliotheken", *Studia Rudolphina*, 3, 2003, pp. 29–40.

17 Norgate, *Miniatura*, p. 110: "For designe of Perspective there are in Marolois, Vredeman, Vries, and others soe goed rules, and easy a method, as try drawing, which in all other painting is the hardest, is in this the easiest . . ".

18 Michel Poudra, *Histoire de la Perspective Ancienne et Moderne*, Paris: Librarie Militaire, Maritime, et Polytechnique, 1864, pp. 240–5.

19 Lawrence Wright, *Perspective in Perspective*, London: Routledge, 1983, p. 130.

20 Karsten Harries, "Les Arquitectures Fantastiques I La Transcendencia Espiritual de La Perpsectiva", in *La ciutat que mai no existí : arquitectures fantàstiques en l'art occidental*, Barcelona: Centre de Cultura Contemporània de Barcelona, 2003, pp. 27–37.

21 Wheelock, *Perspective*, p. 10.

22 See, for example, Jennifer L. Roberts, *Mirror Travels: Robert Smithson and History*, New Haven: Yale University Press, 2004, pp. 76–9.

23 Vredeman, *Perspective* (Dutch), title page.

24 Tatiana V. Senkevitch, "Ce n'est pas chose facile de demonstrer cet art pour escrit", Textual and Visual in the Preliminaries of Perspective Treatises in Seventeenth-Century France', unpublished dissertation chapter, University of Michigan, Ann Arbor, 2006, pp. 2–14.

25 On frontispieces in the Netherlands: W. G. Hellinga, *Kopij en druk in de Nederlanden. Atlas bij de geschiedenis van de Nederlanse typographie*, Amsterdam: Noord-Hollandsche Uitgevers, 1962. On the frontmatter of scientific books: L. Tongiorgi Tomasti, "Image, Symbol and word on the title pages and frontispieces of scientific books from the sixteenth and seventeenth centuries", *Word and Image*, 4: 1, 1988, 372–82; on portrait conventions, see, broadly, Koerner, *The Moment of Self-Portraiture*, and Joanna Woods-Marsden, *Renaissance Self-Portraiture: the Visual Construction of Identity and the Social Status of the Artist*, New Haven: Yale University Press, 1998, pp. 241–53.

26 Wolfgang Schäffner, "Die Punkt" in Helmar Schramm (ed.), *Kunstkammer—Laboratorium—Bühne*, Berlin and New York: Walter de Gruyter, 2003, pp. 57–73.

27 Such as H (Vredeman), no 581. Peter Karstkarel, *Perspective*, 25, attributes the plates marked ("BD") to Theodor de Bry, but Orenstein, *Hendrick Hondius*, pp. 106–8, on the basis of payments in Hondius's

shop, shows Dolendo was most probably the etcher. On Dolendo: Thieme and Becker, vol. IX, pp. 390–1; Eddy de Jongh, "Réalisme et réalisme apparent dans la peinture hollandaise du 17e siècle" in *Rembrandt et son temps*, Brussels, Palais des Beaux-Arts, 1971, pp. 174–5.

28 Karsten Harries, "Les Arquitectures Fantastiques", p. 29.

29 *Perspective*, I (Dutch), fol. Ar: ". . . vele cude, ervane, constrijcke masters bevint, hen ghemoeyt te hebben met de voorseyde conste der Perspectiven, ende in veel verscheydene goet-dunckende opinien, met figuerlijcke linimenten ende sirkelen, haren gront, sin ende meyninghe uytgheggeven, den dat by diverseche Natien, soo by Italianen, Francoysen, ende Hooch-dutyschen, alsomen sien mach aen hare wercken in druck uytghegaen: order welcker den voornamsten is Albertus Dürer, die mijnes bedunckens de bestegevveest sy, die de redden der naturen aldernaest gheobsserveert, ende met zijne wercken oock bethoont heeft. Dien volgende sullen wy met reghe, mate, en gront, de selve nature-reden in figuren bethoonen, hoe wel hier voor desen wel negen-boeken oft stucken der Perspective-conste, by my ghinventeert, ende by Hieronymus Cock, Geerart de Iode, Philips Galle, ende Pieter Baltens zijn uytgegaen, soo en is nochtans onder deselve gheen onderricht der Perspective-konst, noch oock by eenighe Neerlanders in Nederlant oyt gemaectoft uytgegaen".

30 On nationalistically based definitions of perspective (e.g. "Italian" concepts of "mere technique" versus "Anglo-Saxon" equivalences of the art with optics), see Yve-Alain Bois, "Perspective: Vision, Geometry, and Imagination" (review of Damisch, *Origin*), *Journal of Art*, 3, December 1990, p. 48.

31 Alberti, 1972, fol. I.19. The metaphor of the *aperta finestra* remains, Joseph Mascheck has pointed out, precisely that, a metaphor. See J. Masheck, "Alberti's Window: Art Historiographic Note on an Antimodernist Misprision", *Source: Notes in the History of Art*, VIII/IX, no 4/1, Summer/Fall, 1989, pp. 13–17.

32 On "pre-Renaissance" perspective and "modern" subjectivity, Thomas Cramer, "Über Perspektive in Texten des. 13. Jahrhunderts oder: wann beginnt in der Literatur die Neuzeit?" in Thomas Cramer (ed.), *Wege in die Neuzeit (Forschungen zur Geschichte der älteren deutschen Literatur, Bd. 8)*, Munich: W. Fink, 1988, pp. 100–21.

33 Snyder, "Picturing Vision", pp. 499–526.

34 On the early histories of perspective as optics versus perspective as draughsmanship, see specifically Guilo Argan, "The Architecture of Perspective and the origins of Perspective Theory", *JWCI*, 9, 1946, pp. 96–121, and Robert Klein, "Pomponius Gauricus on Perspective", *Art Bulletin*, 44, 1961, pp. 211–30.

35 On print's debatable effect upon the nature of scientific investigation, see generally: Elizabeth L. Eisenstein, *The printing press as an agent of Change*, Cambridge: Cambridge University Press, 1979, vol. I, pp. 45–62; Cynthia Hay (ed.), *Mathematics from manuscript to print, 1300–1600*, Oxford: Clarendon Press, 1988, and Adrian Johns, *The Nature of the Book: Print and Knowledge in the* Making, Chicago: University of Chicago Press, 1998, fol. 378. On the mediating function of print in science see: Bruno Latour, "Drawing Things Together" in Mike Lynch and Steve Woolgar (eds), *Representation in Scientific Practice*, Cambridge: MIT Press, 1990, pp. 19–68.

36 *Perspective* I (Dutch), title page.

37 Cennini, *Handbook*, §87.

38 On the *tiers points*, see Thomas Frangenberg, "The Image and Moving Eye: Jean Pélerin (Viator) to Guidobaldo del Monte", *JWCI*, 49, 1986, pp. 150–71; for Jean's Pélerin's biography see Liliane Brion-Guerry, *Jean Pélerin Viator: sa place dans l'histoire de la perspective*, Paris: Belles Lettres, 1962, and Jean Bombardier, "Jean Pélerin et son temps", *Etudes Toulouses*, 1979, pp. 3–24.

39 Published as *Von der Konstperspektive*, Nuremberg: Jörg Glockendon, 1509.

40 Jean Pélerin, *De artificiali perspectiva*, 2nd ed., Toul: Petra Jacobi, 1509, fol. A4r.

41 Jean Cousin, *Livre de perspective de Iehan Cousin, senonois, maistre painctre a Paris . . .*, Paris: Iehan de Royer, 1560, fol. Liiv: "En cette example est traite les poincts Accidenteaux, lesquels peuuence beaucoup feurir pour la coduitte ds plans & corpres solides qui ont plusiers faces . . ". The methological relationship between Pèlerin and Vredeman is the subject of Andres de Mesa, "Entre le practica artesenal y la teoria de la vision. El concepto de piramide visual en el tradado de perspectiva de Jean Pèlerin Viator", *D'art*, 20, 1994, pp. 74–83.

42 Pélerin 1509, fol. B4r.

43 Pélerin 1509, fols A4r, B2v.

44 Svetlana Alpers, *The Art of Describing*, Chicago: University of Chicago Press, 1983, pp. 53–5. A small book on perspective by one Sterck van Ringelbergh, however, known as Fortius, can claim to be the first original "Netherlandish" book on perspective. Ringelbergh, about whom little in known, was born in Antwerp and studied at Leuven in the early 1520s, where he appears to have met Erasmus, and become something of a humanist dilettante, publishing nearly 30 tracts on subjects as diverse as language, astrology, mathematics, and physiology. In his writings he discussed perspective as a subset of rhetoric; in an octavo printed at Lyon around his death in 1531, he included a short discussion on perspective that reveals familiarity with the *tiers points* method. In the book, skeletal illustrations appeared alongside several linguistic *stemma* explaining the parts of oratory; like much of Ringelbergh's *oeuvre*, this section was less a feat of original pedagogy than of compilation. However, Ringelbergh intended to present perspective as an explicit extension of one of the liberal arts—rhetoric. The explanatory mode, in Ringelbergh's account, assumed that perspective represented a rhetorical form of address and positioning, reliant upon compositional models of space. See Luc Indestige, "Joachim Sterck von Ringelberg, humanist en encyclopedische geest", *Verslagen medelingen van de Koninklijke Academie voor Nederlandse Taal- en Letterkunde*, 1, 1972, pp. 74–9.

45 *Perspective* I (Dutch), fol. A1:, ". . . ende onse meyninghe en is niet, de Lief-hebbers deser consten met veel te lessen zwaermoedich te maken, allenlijck alles op t'conste (doch so veel als wy des nodich ende genouch achten) ende inde figuren levendich voorte stellen, achten wy in dese materie het aldernoodichste te wesen tot de leere van dien".

46 *Perspective* I (Dutch), fol. A1v.

47 James Elkins, "Response to Tomás Garcia-Salgado", *Leonardo*, 29: 1, 1999, pp. 82–3.

48 *Perspective* I (Dutch), fol. B1r., ". . . ende so veel dit belangt, bevinden wy inder naturen met reden de rechte aerdte ende gront der vercortende viercanten naer de Perspective wesen te sijn . . . so iemant beter weet t'staet hem vry te bewisen, ende dit opt conste voor d'eerste instantie, als grondt van Perspective".

49 *Perspective* I (Dutch), fol. A1r.

50 *Perspective* I (Dutch) fols Hr–Hv.

51 This became an exercise as early as the fifteenth century; see Karl Rathe, *Die Ausdrucksfuncktion extrem verkürzter Figuren*, London: Warburg Institute, 1938, especially pp. 10–16, 34–6.

52 Bruno, *Atlas*, pp. 178–80.

53 Dürer, *Unterweyssung*, p. 426. On Dürer's pedagogical method in the tract, see specifically Eberhard Schröder, *Dürer: Kunst und Geometrie*, Berlin: Akademie Verlag, 1980.

54 On which, see A. Margaret Hagen, *Perception of Pictures 2: Dürer's Devices*, New York: Academic Press, 1980.

55 Erwin Panofsky, *Dürers Kunsttheorie*, Berlin: G. Reimer, 1915, p. 259. Gilles Deleuze cites the section of Panofsky's 1943 Dürer monograph on the "nets" (p. 269) in a footnote to his own meditation on folding as a post-Platonic ontology, *Le Pli*; see Gilles Deleuze, *The Fold*, 1988, Tom Conley (trans.), Minneapolis: University of Minnesota Press, 1991, p. 147, n. 8.

56 Dürer, *Unterweyssung*, p. 426.

57 Rupprich, *Schriftlicher Nachlass* as in Walter Strauss, *The Painters Manual*, New York: Abaris, 1977, p. 31.

58 Wenzel Jamnitzer, *Perspectiva Corporum Regularum*, Nuremberg: s.p, 1568; see Albert Flocon, "Etude sur la Perspectiva Corporum Regularium" in a modern facsimile of Jamnitzer, *Perspectiva Corporum Regularum*, Paris: n.p, 1964.

59 Hans Lencker, *Hierinnen auffs kürtzte beschrieben mit Exempeln eröffnet und an Tag gegeban wird, ein newer . . . unnd sehr leichter Weg, wie allerley Ding*, Nuremberg: D. Gerlatz, 1571, fol. Vr; Heinrich Lautensack, *Des Cirkels und Richtscheyts auch der Perspectiva und Proportion der Menschen . . .*, Frankfurt am Main, 1564, fol. 4r, as cited in Rupprich, *Schrifter Nachlass*, vol. III, p. 468, n. 38a.

60 Rodler, *Eyn schön nützlich büchlin*, fol. Aiir. On the authorship of this remarkable tract, see Elsbeth Bonnemann, *Die Presse des Hieronymus Rodler in Simmern*, Leipzig: Harrassowitz, 1938, pp. 11–12,

and Werner Wunderlich, "Poet, Scholar, Sovereign: The Discovery of the Unknown Author Johann II of Simmern", *Renaissance Studies*, 10: 4, December 1996, pp. 451–61.

61 Rodler, *Eyn schön nützlich büchlin*, fol. Hiiir: "So las dir eye rame machen (wie vor gemelt) die grosse den fenster begriff".

62 Frankfurt am Main: Städelisches Museum, inv. no 1856. The work has been also been attributed to one Bartolomeus Pons. See Joshua Bruyn, "Over de betekenis van het werk van Jan van Scorel omstreeks 1530 voor oudere en jongere tijdgenoten, IV", *Oud Holland*, 98, 1984, pp. 98–110, and Jochen Sander and Bodo Brickmann (eds), *Italian, French, and Spanish Painting before 1800 at the Städel*, Frankfurt: Blick in de Welt, 1997, no 94.

63 Fritz Hellwag, *Die Geschichte des Deutschen Tischler-Handwerks* (1924), Reprint, Hannover: Schäfer, 1995, p. 222.

64 See, for example, Robert Keil, "Die Rezeption Dürers in der Deutschen Kunstbuchliteratur des 16. Jahrhunderts", *Wiener Jahrbuch für Kunstgeschichte*, 38, 1985, pp. 133–50. On German perspective after Dürer: the catalog, *Nützliche Anweisung zur Zeichenkunst: Illustrierte Lehr- und Vorglagbücher*, Nuremberg: Germanisches Nationalmuseum, 1980, esp. pp. 2–6, and Jeanne Peiffer, "La fabrique de la perspective à Nuremberg au XVIe siècle", *Les cahiers de la recherché architecturale et urbaine*, 17, September 2005, pp. 49–60.

65 M. M. Kleerkooper, *De Boekhandel te Amsterdam*, The Hague: Nijhoff, 1914–16, pt 2, p. 838.

66 On Loy, see Strauss, *The German Single-Leaf Woodcut 1550–1600: Vol 2: K–R*, New York: Abaris, 1975, pp. 617–32; Linda S. Stiber et al., "The Triumphal Arch", *The Book and Paper Group Annual*, 14, 1995, p. 3, n. 11; Wood, "Ruins", pp. 251–2.

67 *Kunstnijverheid Middeleeuwen en* Renaissance, exh. cat., Rotterdam, Museum Boymans-van Beuningen, 1994, nos 310, 319.

68 See, for example, Lieselotte-Möller, *Der Wrangelschrank und die Verwandten Süddeutschen Intarsiamöbel des 16. Jahrhunderts*, Berlin: Deutcher Verein für Kunstwissenschaft, 1956, pp.15–20; Gerdi Maierbach-Legl, *Truhe und Schrank*, Munich and Berlin: Deutscher Kunstverlag, 1997, pp. 124–5.

69 Leuven: Stedelijk Museum Vanderkelen-Mertens, inv. 82. See Jan van der Stock (ed.), *Stad in Vlaandern: Cultuur et Maatschappij 1477–1787*, Brussels: Gemeentekrediet, 1991, p. 467, cat. 233.

70 Hermann Ryff, *Der Architectur angehören Mathematischen und mechanischen Kunst eigenliche Bericht* . . ., Nuremberg: Petreius, 1547, fol. Ir.

71 Ryff, *Der Architectur*, fol. IXr: "Darumb merckt mit fleis/Und für das erst wird dir von note sein/das du auff die fleche oder superficien/darauff dien gemehl/oder was du in die Perspectiva bringe wilt verzeichnet werden soll/was materi die sey/ein vierung ordnen und setzen wir als ein fenster dat durch die Histori/oder was man in die Perspectiva der gestalt bringen wil/zuschawen ist". See Peiffer, "La fabrique de la perspective", p. 58.

72 Hans Lencker, *Perspectiva literaria*, Nuremberg, Lencker, 1567.

73 Now Wolfenbüttel, Herzog-August Bibliothek, 36.2.1 Geom (2), in its original binding.

74 Wood, "Ruins"; see also, for example, Lieselotte Möller, *Der Wrangelschrank*, fol. 119, cats 135–40, and Helmut Flade, "Die Intarsia in Deutschland" in Helmut Flade (ed.), *Intarsia: Europäische Einlegkunst aus sechs Jahrhunderten*, Munich: Beck, 1986, pp. 122–8. Perspective and plagiarism have a long history in this vein: in 1538, Agnes Dürer successfully blocked the publication of a perspective book by Hans Beham which copied Albrecht Dürer's—her late husband's—work.

75 Gerd Unverfehrt, *Da sah ich viel köstliche Dinge: Albrecht Dürers Reise in die Niederlande*, Göttingen: Vandenhoek & Ruprecht, 2007, pp. 185–95.

76 See *Vorbild Dürer: Kupferstiche und Holzschnitte Albrecht Dürers im Spiegel der europaischen Druckgraphik des 16. Jahrhunderts*, exh. cat., Nuremberg, Germanischen Nationalmuseum, 1978, Munich: Prestel, 1978, and on later editions and adaptations of the Jerome engraving, Christiane Andersson and Charles Talbot, *From a Mighty-Fortress: Prints, Drawings, and Book in the Age of Luther*, Detroit: Institute of Arts, 1983, no. 281. On the copying of Dürer prints in Prague, see Eliska Fucikova, "Umelci na Dvove Rudolf II, A Jejich vztah tvoba Albrechta Dürera", *Umeni*, 20, 1972, pp. 149–66, and Thomas Da Costa Kaufmann, "Hermeneutics in the History of Art" in Jeffrey Chipps

Smith (ed.), *New Perspectives on Renaissance Nuremberg: Five Essays*, Austin: Texas University Press, 1985, pp. 22–6.

77 Kurt Pilz, "Nurenberg und die Niederlande", *Mitteilungen des Vereins fur Geschichte der Stadt Nurnberg*, 43, 1952, pp. 1–224, especially 69–77.

78 Hans Kaufmann, "Dürer in der Kunst und im Kunsturteil im 1600" in *Vom Nachleben Dürers; Beiträge zur Kunst der Epoche von 1530 bis 1650*, Berlin: Mann, 1954, pp. 18–47, and Bernhard Decker, "Im Name Dürers. Dürer Renaissance um 1600", *Pirckheimer Jahrbuch*, 6, 1991, pp. 9–50.

79 Erwin Panofsky, *Perspective as Symbolic Form*, Christopher S. Wood (trans.), New York: Zone Books, 1991, p. 69.

80 Walter Benjamin drew this distinction: ". . . centuries ago [printing] began gradually to lie down, passing from the upright inscription to the manuscript resting on sloping desks before finally taking to bed in the printed book", Walter Benjamin, *Einbahnstrasse* (1928) in "Attested Auditor of Books" in Edmund Jepcott (trans.), *One-Way Street and Other Writings*, London: New Left Books, 1979, p. 62.

81 See, for example, Alan G. Debus (ed.), *Robert Fludd and his Philosophicall key: being a transcription of the manuscript at Trinity College, Cambridge*, New York: Science History Publications, 1979, as discussed in Francis A. Yates, *Theatre of the World*, Chicago: University of Chicago Press, 1969, p. 45.

82 Jamnitzer, *Perspectiva*, fol. Aiiiv: ". . . die *Perspectiva* zu nenne pflegen/Nemlich ein kunst die da lehret/ von eigenschafft/art vnd natur/der Linien und Strom so von unserem gesicht auff.andere ding hin und wider geworssen werden/dan alles das/so inn der ganzen welt dutch undere Menschliche augen angeschawet wirdt/es senen die himlichen Corper/und Firmament/oder aber die irdische/ als Geprage/ Gründe/Gebewe/Schlosser/Stett/dörffer und Landschafft oder andere Copora/und in Summa alles das/ so durch das gesicht gefast und begriffen werden mag".

83 For example, L. Meijers, *Woordenschat*, Amsterdam: Jan Hendrick Boon, 1669, p. 627, where perspective is a "science of seeing through [or] in" ("*doorzichtkunde, inzichtkunde*").

84 On the idea of *der Falsch*, and its status as a legal category in the Middle Ages, see Karl Elben, *Zur Lehre der Warenfäschung—hauptsächlich in geschichtlicher Hinsicht*, Freiburg/Tübingen: Mohr, 1881, pp. 2–30.

85 Ben Jonson, *The Alchemist* III, iv, 87, as in Douglas Brown (ed.), New York: Hill and Wang, 1966, p. 80.

86 Van Mander, *Grondt*, Chapter 8, § 17–26.

87 C. S. Singleton (ed.), *Nuori conti caravaleschi del Rinascimento*, Modena, 1940, p. 18, as cited in Cladio Gullién, *Literature as System*, Princeton: Princeton University Press, 1971, p. 299.

88 Baldassare Castiglione, *The Book of the Courtier* (1588), London: Penguin, 1976, p. 80.

89 Lucien Febvre, *The Problem of Unbelief in the Sixteenth Century: The Religion of Rabelais*, Beatrice Gottlieb (trans.), Cambridge, MA: Harvard University Press, 1982, p. 432.

90 Montaigne, *Essais*, I: 38, 107. See also Craig Bush, *From the Perspective of the Self: Montaigne's self-portrait*, New York: Fordham University Press, 1994.

91 Vasari, *Lives*, vol. I, p. 104.

92 Ulm, Ulmer Museum, inv. no 2124. See Wood, "Ruins", p. 256, n. 37.

93 Escorial, Monastery, Cloister apartments. See Joscijka Gabriele Abels, *Erkenntnis der Bilder*, Frankurt/ Main: Campus, 1985, p. 219, and Jan Bialostocki, "Renaissance artists as philosophers in meditation", *Acta historiae atrium*, XXIV: 4, 1978, pp. 207–10.

94 Adam von Bartsch, *Le peinture-graveur* IX, Vienna: Degen, 1808, vol. I, p. 462.

95 B. 87, London, British Museum, no 1850, 0810.268; 7.5 × 5 cms. Franz Isaac Brun (c.1559–1596?) also published prints of peasant scenes and ornament.

96 H (Vredeman), no 51/I, 1562, and H (Vredeman), no 51/II; Mielke, *Verzeichnis*, p. 206.

97 Robert Scribner, "Popular Piety and Modes of Visual Perception in Late-Medieval and Reformation Germany", *The Journal of Religious History*, 15: 4, December 1989, pp. 448–69.

98 Heinz Lüdecke, *Lucas Cranach der Altere im Spiegel seiner Zeit*, Berlin: Mann, 1953, p. 55.

99 Alberti, *On Painting*, p. 78. On the *Rückenfigur* tradition: Marguerite Koch, *Die Rückenfigur im Bild von Antique bis Giotto*, Recklinghausen: Bongen, 1965, and Joseph Leo Koerner, *Caspar David Friedrich and the subject of landscape*, New Haven: Yale University Press, 1990, pp. 162–6.

100 See David Freedberg, "The Hidden God: Image and Interdiction in the Netherlands in the Sixteenth Century", *Art History*, 5: 2, 1982, pp. 133–53.

101 Thomas Puttfarken, *The discovery of pictorial composition: Theories of Visual Order in Painting 1400–1800*, Yale University Press, 2000, pp. 67–71.

102 Louis Althusser, "Ideology and Ideological State Apparatuses", *Lenin and Philosophy and other Essays*, New York: Monthly Review Press, 1971, pp. 165–83.

103 Vredeman, *Perspective* I (Dutch), fol. E1v: "Volgende de seventwintichste figure, op gront ende linamenten als voren, inde welcke ghestelt is een edefitie der Architecturen, in een fatie drie boghen, nare de Antique maniere der columnen, waer van de middelste boghe begrijpt vijf deelen, ende de twee sy-boghen elck drie drie deelen uyten grondt . . . wat het vercorten der boghen-welssel belangt, is vooren beswesen, ende de figure sal den lief-hebber dat lichtelijck aenwijsen".

104 Isaac de Ville, *T'Samen-spreeckinghe Betreffende de Architecture ende Schilderkonst . . .*, Gouda: Pieter Rammaseyn, 1628.

105 de Ville, *T'Samen-spreeckinghe*, 16: ". . . het blyck wel aen het gene dat Pauwel de Vries daer van in printen heeft laten drucken/waer uyt het alzoo ghemackelijck om leeren is als een Voghel inde lacht met de handt te grypen: Uyt die oorsake en hebbe ick noyt ymant gesproken die het selfde grondich uyt zijn printen gheleert heeft".

106 See, for example, Theodor Hetzer, *Das deutsche Element in der italienischen Malerei des sechezehnten Jahrhunderts*, Berlin: Deutsche Kunstverlag, 1929; *idem*, "Paolo Veronese" in *Römisches Jahrbuch fuer Kunstgeschichte*, 1940; Hans Sedlymayr, "Mannerism and the Nearness of Death", *Art in Crisis*, London: Hollis and Carter, 1957, pp. 189–95; Further, Max Dvořák, "Über Greco und den Manierismus", *Jahrbuch für Kunstgeschichte des kunsthistorischen Instituts des Bundesdenkmalamtes*, 1, 1921–22, pp. 22–42. On the interest in mannerism as a concept rather than a style in the 1930s, see especially Edwin Lachnitt, "Zur Geschichtlichkeit des Manierismusbegriffs" in Werner Hoffmann (ed.), *Zauber der Medusa: Europäischen Manierismen*, Vienna: Löcker, 1987, pp. 32–42, and Peter Klein, "El Greco's 'Burial of Count Orgaz' and the concept of mannerism of the Vienna School" in Nikos Chatzenikolau (ed.), *El Greco of Crete*, Iraklion: Municipality of Iraklion, 1995, pp. 507–32.

107 Cristoforo Landino, as cited by Margaret Iversen, "The Discourse of Perspective in the Twentieth Century", *Oxford Art Journal*, 28: 2, 2005, p. 194.

108 Yet the idea of a single "classic" perspective is nonetheless crucial to art-historical narratives that privilege some rupturing heterogeneity in modernism. See Christopher Wood, "Introduction" to Panofsky, *Perspective as Symbolic Form*, pp. 14–16.

109 Elkins, *Poetics*, p. 263.

110 Friedrich Nietzsche, in the *Wille zur Macht*, explicitly melds "point of view" and subjectivity using the imagery of a "picture". See Oscar Levy (ed.), *The Complete Works of Friedrich Nietzsche*, New York: Gordon Press, 1974, vol. 15, p. 120, §636. On this kind of "perspectivism", paradoxically as a somehow Manneristic contrast to "perspective" as an objective structure, see Wolfgang Kemp, "Narrative" in Nelson (ed.), *Critical Terms for Art History*, Chicago: University of Chicago Press, 1996, pp. 58–69.

111 On Florensky, see the essays in Norbert Franz, Michael Hagemeister, and Frank Haney (eds), *Pavel Florenskij—Tradition und Moderne: Beiträge zum Internationalen Symposium an der Universität Potsdam 5. bis 9. April 2000*, Frankfurt am Main: Peter Lang, 2001. On the "pre-perspective" of icons, also Bruno Latour, "How to be Iconophilic in Art, Science, and Religion?" in Caroline Jones and Peter Galison, *Picturing Science, Producing Art*, London: Routledge, 1998, pp. 430–3.

112 Pavel Florensky, "Reverse Perspective" (1920), Wendy Salmond (trans.) in Nicoletta Misler (ed.), *Beyond Vision: Essays on the Perception of Art*, London: Reaktion, 2002, p. 242.

113 Or in the Church of Sts Peter and Paul in Prague, for example, which housed Bohemian icons. See Jannic Durand, "Precious-Metal Icon Revetments" in Helen C. Evans (ed.), *Byzantium: Faith and Power (1261–1557)*, New Haven: Yale UP, 2004, p. 250, and Anton Legner, *Die Parler und der schone Stil 1350–1400*, Cologne: Museen der Stadt, 1978–80, vol. 3, pp. 217–35. On Florensky's art history, see Vyacheslav Ivanov, "Florensky: A Symbolic View", *Elementa*, II, 1995, pp. 1–22.

114 Florensky, "Reverse Perspective", p. 208. Italics as original.

115 Florensky, "Reverse Perspective", p. 208.

116 e.g. Panofsky, *Early Netherlandish Painting*, New York: Harper and Row, 1953, vol. I, pp. 140–1.

117 Cornelisz. Pietrz. Biens, *De Teecken-Conste*, Amsterdam: Johannes Janssonius, 1636: "Om [perspective] wel te verstaen, zijn verscheyden boecke in 't lichte gekomen, onder anderen de wercken van Hans Vredeman Vriese, de Cock ende andere". The small drawing guide is known only through a nineteenth-century transcription in Basel, Kunstmuseum, inv. Brosch. A 1222, made by C. Müller-Hofstede. See E. A.. de Klerck, "*De Teecken-Const*, een 17de eeuws Nederlands Traktaatje", *Oud Holland*, 96, 1982, pp. 16–60.

118 Samuel Marolois, *Opticae sive perspectivae*, The Hague: Hondius, 1614. Hendrick Hondius's own book on perspective, *Institutio Artis Perspectivae*, was issued in Latin (1622) and French (1625) and copied directly from its plates.

119 At the same sale Dutch translations of Vitruvius appear to have gone for 3 to 4 guilders. See H. Meeus, "Jan Moretus en de Noordnederlandse Boekhandel 1590–1610" in *Ex Plantiana officiana: Studien over het Drukkersgeschlicht Moretus*, Antwerp: Antwerpsche Bibliophilen, 1996, p. 361.

120 P. A. Tiele (ed.), *Catalogus der Bibliotheek van Joannes Thysius*, Leiden: Brill, pp. 187, 316.

121 See, for example, Ramon Solar I Fabregat, "Libres de perspectiva", *D'art: Revista del Department d'Histoire d'art Universidad de Barcelona*, 20, 1994, pp. 167–9, and Badeloch Noldus, *Trade in Good Taste: Relations in Architecture and Culture between the Dutch Republic and the Baltic World in the Seventeenth Century*, Turnhout: Brepols, 2004, pp. 161, 169.

122 Bredius, *Künstler-Inventare*, vol. I, no 175: "Een d. van de Vries"; vol. II, 1494: "1 perspectief boek van de Vries"; and vol II, no 1747: "1 boek met prenten van Hans de Vries".

123 Thomas Fusenig and Bernard Vermet, "Der Einfluss von Hans Vredeman de Vries auf die Malerei", in Borggrefe, *Norden*, pp. 161–78.

124 On Stevin's biography: E. J. Dijksterhuis, *Simon Stevin*, The Hague: Nijhoff, 1943, pp. 1–32; and the materials collected in the small exh. cat., Martine de Reu (ed.), *Simon Stevin*, Ghent: Universiteitsbibliotheek, 1998.

125 Simon Stevin, *Wisconstige gedachtenissen, inhoudende t'ghene daer hem in gheoeffent heeft . . .*, Leiden: Jan Bouwensz, 1605, II, fol. A2r, "Aen den Leser". Stevin claims that Prince Maurits had taken a keen interest in fortification design and drawing, seeking, "een voorghestelde verschaeulicke saeck volcomelick afteycknen, met kennis der oirsaken en sijn wiscontlich bewijs". There is a large literature on Stevin's method: see D. J. Struik (ed.), *The principle works of Simon Stevin*, 6 vols, Amsterdam: C.V. Swets, 1958–84, vol. IIB, pp. 787–93; K. Andersen, "Stevin's theory of perspective: the origin of a Dutch academic approach to perspective", *Tractrix*, 2, 1990, pp. 25–62.

126 Stevin, *Wisconstige gedachtenissen*, II, fol. H2r: "Ettlicke meesters in dadelick verschaeuwen, houdent daer voor, datmen int verschaewen niet heel volcomelick en moet navolghen de reghelen deser const, maer somwillen wat beghaelicker voor t'oogh stellen dat teghen de reghel gaet . . . Maer al dit is ghemist . . ".

127 There are, however, two woodcut diagrams (e.g. fol. H2r) of the kind found in Italian treatises from the same time, for example Guidobaldo del Monte's *Perspectivae libri sex* published at Pesaro in 1600. Stevin does include in his seventh chapter a woodcut illustration of the "glass" [*glas*], a kind of perspective machine modeled after the devices Dürer described in the last two folios of the *Unterweyssung*.

128 Robert Ruurs, "Pieter Saenredam: Zijn boekenbezit", *Oud Holland*, 93: 2, 1983, pp. 59–68.

129 Stevin, *Wisconstige gedachtenissen*, II, fol. A3v: ". . . de selve dadelijke verschaeuwing, voortbrengt de ware schaeu van het verschaeuwing".

130 Abraham Bosse, *Maniere Universelle de Mr. Desargues pour practiquer la Perspective part Petit-Pied . . .*, Paris: Pierre Des-Hayes, 1648, fol. Hiir.

131 Deleuze, *The Fold*, p. 3.

132 This juxtaposition represents a common enough publishing strategy in books around this time; other perspective authors had included poems; the mystic Charles de Bouelles, for example, began his *Geometrie* Practique, Paris, 1551, with a sonnet warning readers about the hard work of perspective.

And a 1583 edition of Giacomo Vignola's treatise tacked on a rare bust portrait of the author on the title page.

133 On Mauritian iconography in the Dutch Republic: Arthur Eyffinger, " *'Een Stil Proces van Vervreemding . . .'* Prins Maurits en Hugo de Groot" in Kees Zandvliet (ed.), *Maurits, Prince van Oranje*, exh. cat., Amsterdam, Rijksmuseum, Zwolle: Waanders, 2000, pp. 92–105.

134 Along the lines suggested in Roger Chartier, "Princely Patronage and the Economy of Dedication", in *Forms and Meaning: Texts, Performances and Audiences from Codex to Computer*, Philadelphia: Pennsylvania University Press, 1995, pp. 25–42. On authorial frontispieces in the Dutch Republic, specifically, see M. A. Schenkenveld-van der Dussen, "Word and Image in Huygens' *Otia*, the author as hidden persuader" in *Word and Image*, 4: 1, 1988, pp. 238–45.

135 Vredeman, *Perspective* (Dutch), fol. a2 r: "Ik heb mijnen tijdt in dese conste door-ghebracht/Over veertich jaren daer in moeten studeren/ Hoe meerder moeyte/hoe meer ick hebbe ghesocht; Aensiende tijt noch arbeyt int wel doceren".

136 On acrostics in the Netherlands: "Naamdicht" in Cornelius Buddingh (ed.), *Lexicon der poëzie*, Amsterdam: De Arbeiderspers, 1977, fol. 112; also S. M. Noach, "Een naamdicht van Bredero", *Nieuwe Taalgids*, 32, 1938, pp. 176–7; F. Willaert, "Vier acrostichons in het Haagse Liederhandschrift", *'t Ondersoeck leert*, 1986, pp. 93–104. Hieronymus Rodler's perspective tract of 1531 began with an acrostic in its first 54 initials. See Wunderlich, "Poet, Scholar", pp. 456–7.

137 Vredeman, *Perspective* (Latin) fol. a2r: "Ipse ego, qui primis Artem veneratus ab annis . . ".

138 Vredeman, *Perspective* I (Dutch), fol. a1v: "Om s'Consts wete/elck hem te bevlijtighen heeft/Want noyt en was neymadt meester geboren".

139 Jacques Derrida, "Outwork" in *Disseminations*, Barbara Johnson (trans.), Chicago: University of Chicago Press, 1981, pp. 2–59.

140 Philippe Lejeune, *Le pacte autopbiographique* (1975), Katharine Leary (trans.), *On Autobiography*, Minneapolis: University of Minnesota Press, 1989; Gottfried Boehm, *Bildnis und Individuum: Über den Ursprung der Porträtmalerei in der italienischen Renaissance*, Munich: Prestel-Verlag, 1985, argues for a connection between Renaissance portrait frontispieces and early modern autobiography; another view is that of Peter Burke, "Reflections on the frontispiece portrait in the Renaissance" in Andreas Köstler and Ernst Seidl (eds), *Bildnis und Image: das Portrait zwischen Intention und Rezeption*, Vienna: Bohlau, 1998, pp. 151–62.

141 "[Mannerism] abandoned the classic style's comfortingly clear rendering of space based on rational perspective construction in favor of that peculiar, almost medieval manner of composition that pressed shapes into a single, often 'unbearably crowded' plane", Panofsky, *Idea*, pp. 73–4. On the centrality of "Renaissance" perspective, specifically, in the early Panofsky's idea of history, see Georges Bazin, "Panofsky et la notion d'espace", *Gazette des Beaux Arts*, LXXI, May/June 1968, pp. 252–68; Steven Melville, "The Temptation of New Perspectives", *October*, 52, 1990, p. 11; and Keith Moxey, "Perspective, Panofsky, and the Philosophy of History", *New Literary History*, 26:4, 1995, pp. 775–86. Karl Clausberg, "Zwei Antipoden der Kunstwissenschaft und einer versunkener Kontinent: Zum methodischen von Pächt, Panofsky, und Wygotski", *Kritische Berichte*, 6: 3, 1978, pp. 5–12, as well as Joseph Leo Koerner, "The Shock of the View", *New Republic*, April 26, 1993, pp. 32–4, point to the way Cassirer's "symbolic forms" in history suggested a means, close in time and place to Panofsky, to defend Enlightenment rationalism intellectually against National Socialism.

142 Letter from Erwin Panofsky to Aby Warburg, February 14, 1923, in Dieter Wuttke (ed.), *Erwin Panofsky: Korrespondenz 1910–1936*, Wiesbaden; Harrasowitz, 2001, p. 119.

143 Schneede, *Gesellschaftbild*, pp. 102–8, who cites Guido Hauck's version of "subjective" perspective: Guido Hauck, *Die subjektive Perspektive und die horizontalen Curvaturen des dorischen Styls: Eine perspektivische-ästhetische Studie*, Stuttgart: Konrad Wittwer, 1879. Cf. Anton Ehrenzweig, *A Psycho-Analysis of Art, Vision, and Hearing*, New York: Braziller, 1958, p. 101: "perspective served in its first place to an express an irrational symbolism", also cited by Schneede.

144 See Jonathan Crary, *Suspensions of Perception: Attention, Spectacle, and Modern Culture*, Cambridge, MA: MIT Press, 1999, pp. 64–96. On Panofsky's own concept of subjectivity, indebted to

Cassirer, see especially Marisa Dalai's introduction to the French translation of the perspective essay, *La Perspective comme forme symbolique*, Paris: Minuit, 1975.

145 Erwin Panofsky, "Dürer and Classical Antiquity" (1921) in *Meaning in the Visual Arts*, Garden City, NY: Doubleday, 1955, pp. 236–85; Dana Polan, "History in Perspective, Perspective in History: A Commentary on *L'Origine de la Perspective* by Hubert Damisch", *Camera Obscura*, 24, 1992, pp. 89–97, and Wood, "Une Perspective Oblique", 1996, especially pp. 107–15.

146 Harold R. Whaley, "The Dates of *Hamlet* and Marston's *The Malcontent*", *Review of English Studies*, 9, no 36, October 1933, pp. 397–409. The play was first printed in 1603.

Epilogue: Vredeman and the modern

1 Frederic Jameson, "Is Space Political?" in Cynthia Davidson (ed.), *Anyplace*, Cambridge, MA: MIT Press, 1995, p. 194.

2 According to Jan C. G. Briels, *Peintres flamands, 1585–1630*, Antwerp: Fonds Mercator, 1997, p. 405, in August of 1607, Vredeman was in Hamburg. In a document of August 18, 1609, *SAA* Scherpenregister, fol. 482, pp. 287–8, Hans Vredeman's wife, Sara van Elsmaer, was back in Antwerp as: "*weduwe wylen Jan Vredemans*". See also Borggefe, *Norden*, p. 38, n. 188.

3 These drawings and notes are now in the British Museum. See J. Ziff, "Backgrounds, Introduction to Architecture and Landscape", *Journal of the Warburg and Courtauld Institutes*, XXVI, 1963, pp. 124–47. Among many other perspective books mentioning Vredeman: Joshua Kirby, *Dr. Brook's Taylor's Method of Perspective made easy both in Theory and in Practice*", Ipswich: W. Craighton, 1754; Thomas Malton, *A Complete Treatise on Perspective in Theory and Practice*, London, W. Taylor, 1779.

4 F. Baldinucci, *Notize de Professori*, Florence: Gio Battista Stecchi, 1687, pt II, pp. 72–4.

5 Fra Pellegrino Antonio Orlandi, *Abcedario pitturico*, Venice: Giambattista Pasquali, 1704, p. 309.

6 Jean-Baptiste Descamps, *La Vie des Peintres Flamands, Allemands, et Hollandois*, Paris: Bailleu, 1753, vol. I, pp. 135–7

7 John Evelyn, *Sculptura, or, the History and Art of Chalography, AND engraving in copper, etc.*, London: G. Beedle, 1662, p. 65: ". . . JEROME COCK, a Fleming, cut for VRISSE, a painter, the Perspectives, which pass under his name, with twenty leaves of several Buildings . . ".

8 See Willem Eekhoff, *De Stedelijke Kunstverzameling van Leeuwarden*, Leeuwarden: H. Bokma, 1875, pp. 282–3.

9 Henri Hymans (trans.), *Le Livre des Peintres de Carel Van Mander, Vie des Peintres flamands, hollandaise et allemands*, Paris: Rouam, 1885, vol. II, p. 107.

10 Jantzen, *Architekturbild*, p. 138. An important examination of this book's methodological context is in J. Boomgaard, "Bronnenstudie en stilistiek: Van de Kunst der werkelijkheid tot de werkelijkheid der kunst" in F. Grijzenhout and H. van Veen (eds), *De Gouden Eeuw in Perspectief*, Nijmegen: Sun, 1992, pp. 269–71.

11 Waagen, *Die vornehmsten Denkmäler in Wien*, p. 200. Waagen's views on the Antwerp school in the sixteenth century were elaborated in "Über den Maler Petrus Paulus Rubens", *Historisches Taschenbuch*, Leipzig: Brockhaus, 1833, pp. 137–282.

12 Petra Zimmermann, "Hans Vredeman de Vries—ein 'uomo universale'?", *Bulletin KNOB*, 100:1, 2001, pp. 2–13.

13 Sustained critique of the autonomous Renaissance self, first described by Jakob Burckhardt and later given a philosophical nuance in Ernst Cassirer, *Individual and the Cosmos in Renaissance Philosophy* (1927), W. Domandi (trans.), Oxford: Oxford University Press, 1963, is now more than three generations old. The key critical authors remain Geertz, Orgel, Greenblatt, and the Foucault of *Power/Knowledge: Selected Interviews and Other Writings, 1972–1977*, Colin Gordon (trans.), New York: Viking, 1980. On the general question of interiority in early modern Europe, see Natalie Zemon Davis, "Boundaries of the Sense of Self in Sixteenth-Century France" in Thomas C. Heller et al. (eds), *Reconstructing Individualism: Autonomy, Individuality, and the Self in Western Thought*, Palo Alto: Stanford University Press, 1986, pp. 53–63, 332–6.

14 On horizon and historicism: Hans Georg Gadamer, *Truth and Method*, George Cumming and J. Barden (trans.), New York, Seabury Press, 1975, pp. 269–75.

Bibliography

I: Primary Materials (includes modern editions)

Alberti, Leon Battista, *On Painting*, John R. Spencer (trans.), 1435–36, New Haven: Yale University Press, 1972.

—— *On the Art of Building in Ten Books*, Joseph Rykwert, Neil Leach, and Robert Tavenor (trans.), Cambridge, MA: MIT Press, 1988.

Arcus Triumphal Aliqvot Triumphal et Monumenta Victor Classicae in Honor Iani Austriae Victoris non Qvientri . . ., Antwerp: Philips Galle, 1572.

Angel, Philips, *Lof der Schilderkonst*, Leiden: Willem Christaens, 1642.

Arphe Y Villafañe, Joan, *De Vara Commensuracion para le Escultura, y Architectura* . . ., Seville: Andrea Persciono, 1585.

Bellesforest, François, *La Cosmographie Universelle de Toute Monde*, Paris: Michael Sonnu, 1575.

Beschreibung des gluchieligen Einzugs des aller Durchleuchti . . ., Prague: Johann Schumann, 1594.

Beste, Charles van de, *Architectura. Dat is Constelicke Bouwinghen huilt die Anticken ende Modernen* . . ., unpublished manuscript, Brussels: Koninklijk Bibliotheek Albert I, MS II 7617, 1599.

Biblioteki Gdańskiej Polskeij Akademii Nauk (Gdańsk Library of the Polish Academy of Sciences), *Nie Tylko o Mapach—Holandia w Zbiorach*, Gdańsk: PAN, 2000.

Bochius, Johannes, *Historica narratio profectionis et inavgvrationis serenissimorvm Belgii principvm Alberti et Isabellæ, Avstriæ archidvcvm : et eorum optatissimi in Belgium aduentus, rerumque gestarum et memorabilium, gratulationum, apparatuum, et spectaculorum in ipsorum susceptione et inavgvratione hactenus editorum accurata description*, Antwerp: Jan Moretus, 1602.

Bouquet, S, *Bref et Sommaire recueil de ce qui a este faict & de l'ordre tenue a la ioyeuse & triumphante Entrée de tres-puissant, tres magnanime & tres-chrestien Prince CHARLES IX, dece nom Roy de France &c.*, presentation copy to Catharine de Medici, London, British Library C33, m. 1, Paris: Denis du Pre, 1572.

Calvin, John,*Institutio Christianae religionis*, Basel, 1536, Ford Lewis Battles (trans. and ann.), Grand Rapids, MN: Eerdmans, 1986.

—— *Institutio Christianae religionis*, Geneva, 1559, *Institutes of the Christian Religion*, Ford Lewis Battles (trans. and ann.), Philadelphia: The Westminster Press, 1960.

Castelijn, Matthijs de, *De const van rhetoriken*, Ghent: Ian Cauweel, 1555.

Cennini, Cennino D'Andrea. *The Craftsman's Handbook* (Il Libro Dell'Arte), Daniel V. Thompson (trans.), New York: Dover, 1933.

Cicero, Marcus Tullius, *De Oratore*, E. W. Sutton and H. Rackham (trans.), Cambridge: Harvard University Press, 1959.

—— *De Inventione, De Optimo Genere Oratorum, Topica*, H. M. Hubbell (trans.), Cambridge: Harvard University Press, 1960.

Coecke van Aelst, Pieter, *Die Generale Regelen der Architectvren*, Antwerp: Pieter Coecke van Aelst, 1539.

—— *Die Inventie der Colommen* . . ., Antwerp: Coecke van Aelst, 1539.

Damhouder, Joost de, *Praktyck ende handbouck in criminele zaeken, verchiert met zommeghe schoone figuren* . . ., Leuven: Steven Wouters, 1555.

De Bray, Salomon, *Architectura Moderna ofte Bouwinge van Onsen Tyt*, 1631, reprint, Soest: Davaco, 1971.

Dietterlin, Wendel, *Architectura*, Nuremberg: Caymox, 1594–98.

Diversche Refereynen ende Liedekens seer playsant om lessen . . ., Brussels: van der Aa, 1574.

Du Cerceau, Jacques Androuet, *Leçons der Perspective Positive*, Paris: Mamert Patisson, 1576.

Dürer, Albrecht, *Vnderweysung der Messung : mit dem Zirkel vn[d] Richtscheyt in Linien, Ebnen vnnd gantzen Corporen; durch Albrecht Dürer züsamen gezogen zu Nutz allen Kunstliebhabenden mit zü gehörigen Figuren in Truck gebracht im Jar MDXXv*, Nuremberg : s.n., 1525.

—— *Etliche underricht, zu befestung der Stett, Schloß, und flechen*, Nuremberg: s.p., 1527.

Erasmus, Desiderius, *Encomium moriae*, 1515, *The praise of folly*, Hoyt Hopewell Hudson (trans.), Princeton University Press, 1971.

—— *De Copia. The Collected Works of Erasmus*, Craig R. Thomson (ed.), London and Toronto: University of Toronto Press, 1978, vol. 24.

Grapheus, Cornelius, *De seer wonderlijke, schoone, triumphelijcke incompst, van den hooghmogenden Prince Philips, Prince van Spaignen, Caroli des vijfden, keysers sone: inde stadt van Antwerpen*, Antwerp: Pieter Coecke van Aelst, 1550.

Guicciardini, Ludivico, *Description de Tout les Pays-Bas*, Antwerp: William Silvius, 1568.

Heere, Lucas de, *Beschrijving van het ghene dat vertoocht werde ter Incomste van d'Excellentie des Princen van Orangien binnen der Stede van Ghendt/den xxix Decembris Anno M.D.Lxxvii*, Ghent: n.p., 1578.

Hondius, Hendrick, *Les cinq rangs de l'architecture, a savoir: tuscane, dorique, ionique, corinthiaque, et composee, avec l'instruction fondamentale . . .*, Amsterdam: J. Jeansson, 1620.

—— *Grondige Onderrichtinge in de Optica ofte Perspective Konste*, Amsterdam: 1640.

Hoogstraten, Samuel van, *Inleyding tot de hooge schoole der schilderkonst: anders de zichtbaere werelt; verdeelt in negen leerwinkels, yder bestiert door eene der zanggodinnen; ten hoogsten noodzakelijk, tot onderwijs, voor alle die deeze edele, vrye, en hooge konst oeffenen, of met yver zoeken te leeren, of anders eenigzins beminnen . . .*, Rotterdam: François van Hoogstraten, 1678.

Houwaert, Johan Baptista, *Sommaire beschrijvinghe vande triumphelijcke Incomste vanden doorluchtighen ende hooghgheboren Aerts-hertoge Matthias/binnen die Princelijcke stadt van Brussele . . .*, Antwerp: Christoffel Plantijn, 1578.

Huygens, Constantijn, *Stede-Stemmen en Dorpen*, C. de Kruyter (ed.), Zutphen: WJ Thieme, 1981.

La Joyeuse & Magnifique Entree de Monsigheur Francoys, fils de France . . . d'Anvers, Antwerp: Plantin, 1582.

Mander, Karel Van, *Den Grondt der edel vry schilderconst*, 2 vols, Hessel Miedema (ed. and trans.), Utrecht: Haentjens, Dekker en Gumbert, 1973.

—— *Het schilder-boek : het leven van der doorluchtige Nederlandshe en Hoogduitsche schilders*, Haarlem: Paschier van Wesbuch, 1604, 6 vols, Hessel Miedema (ed.), Michael Hoyle, J. Pennial-Boer, and C. Ford (trans.), Doornspijk: Davaco, 1994–99.

Marolois, Samuel, *Opera mathematica*, Amsterdam: J. Jeansson, 1644–47.

Norgate, Edward, *Miniatura, or, the Art of Limming*, c.1649–50, Jeffery Muller and Jim Murrell (eds), New Haven: Yale University Press, 1996.

Pèlerin, Jean, *De artificiali perspectiva: pinceaux, burins, acuilles, lices, pierres, bois metaulx, artifices Viator: secundo*, Toul: n.p., 1505.

Quintilian, *Institutio Oratoria*, H. E. Butler (trans.), Cambridge: Harvard University Press, 1965.

Refereynen ende Liedkens van diversche Rhetoricien uyt Brabant/Vlandern/Hollant en Zeelant Ghelesen en ghesongen op de Corenbloem Camer binnen Brussel/op haer jaerlicxse Prinsfeste/zeer lustich om te lessen en te singhere, Brussels: Michel van Hamont, 1563.

Rodler, Hieronymus (publisher), *Eyn schön nützlich büchlin und underweisung der kunst des Messens/mit dem Zirkel/Richtscheidt oder Lineal*, Simmern: 1531, reprint, Trude Aldrian Graz (comm.), 1970.

Roffet, Jacques, *C'est l'ordre qui a este tenu a la nouvelle et joyeuse entree, que treshault, tresexcellet, & trespuissant Prince*, Paris: Roffet, n.d.

Sachs, Hans, *Eygentliche Beschrieibung Aller Stände auff Erden/Hoher und Nidgriger/Geistlicher und Weltlicher . . .*, Frankfurt au Main: Feyerbend, 1568.

Schille, Hans van, *Form und weis zu bauwen*, Antwerp: Gerard de Jode, 1573.

Serlio, Sebastiano, *I sette libri dell' architettura*, Books I–V, Venice, 1537–57, in *Sebastiano Serlio on Architecture*, Vaughn Hart and Pieter Hicks (trans. with comm.), New Haven: Yale University Press, 1996.

Serres, Oliver de, *Le theatre d'Agriculture et Mesnage des Champs*, Paris: Chouet, 1600.

Shute, John, *The First and Chief Groundes of Architecture*, London: Ion Shute, 1563.

Specklin, Daniel, *Architectura von Vestingen . . .*, Strasbourg: Zetzner, 1608.

Spelen van Sinne vol scoone moralisacien vvtlegginge ende bediedenissen . . ., Antwerp: Willem Silvius, 1562.

Stevin, Simon, *Vita Politica, Het Burgherlijck Leven . . .*, Leiden: Franchoys van Ravelenghien, 1590.

—— *Van de Deursichtighe*, Leiden: Jan Bouwensz, 1605, in *The Principal Works of Simon Stevin: Volume IIB: Mathematics*, Ernst Crone et al. (eds), Amsterdam: C.V. Swets & Zeilinger, 1958.

Vasari, Giorgio, *The Lives of the Painters, Sculptors, and Architects*, 1568, George Bull (trans.), London: Penguin, 1987.

—— *Vasari on technique; being the introduction to the three arts of design, architecture, sculpture and painting, prefixed to the lives of the most excellent painters, sculptors and architects*, Louisa S. Maclehose (trans. and ed.), New York: Dover, 1960.

Ville, Issac de, *T'Samen-spreeckinghe Betreffende de Architecture ende Schilderkonst . . .*, Gouda: Pieter Rammaseyn, 1628.

Vitruvius, *de Architectura*, 1st c. AD, first printed text, Rome, 1486, English ed., Ingrid D. Rowland and Thomas N. Howe (eds.), *Vitruvius: Ten Books on Architecture*, Cambridge: Cambridge University Press, 1999.

Vogtherr, Heinrich, *Ein Frembdes und wunderbarliches kunstbuechlin . . .*, Strasbourg: Christian Mueller, 1538.

Vredeman de Vries, Hans (des.), *Multarum variarum' que protractionum (Compartimenta vulgus pictorum vocat)*, Antwerp: Gerard de Jode, 1555, facs., Brussels, 1870.

—— *Variarum protractionum (vulgus Compartimenta vocat)*, Antwerp: Gerard de Jode, 1555.

—— *Pictores, statuarii, architecti . . . uarias caenotphiorum . . .*, Antwerp: Hieronymus Cock, 1563.

—— *Scenographiae, sive perspectivae (ut aedificia, hoc modo as opticam excitata)*, Antwerp: Hieronymus Cock, 1560, 2nd ed., 1563, enlarged as *Variae architectura formae* Antwerp, 1601, facs., Brussels, 1870, Amsterdam, 1979.

—— *Den eersten Boeck, ghemaect opde twee columnen Dorica en Ionica*, Antwerp: Hieronymus Cock, 1565, 2nd ed., 1565.

—— *Den ander Buech, gemacht auff die zway Colonnen, Corinthia und Composita*, Antwerp: Hieronymus Cock, 1564–65.

—— *Architectura, ou Bastiment, prins de Vitruue & des Ancient Escrivains . . .*, Antwerp: Gerard de Jode, Dutch and French eds, 1577, German ed., 1581.

—— *Hortarum viridariorumque elegantes & multiplices formae*, Antwerp: Philips Galle, 1583.

—— *Theatrum vitae humanae*, Antwerp: Petrus Balt, 1583.

—— *Perspective. Dat is de hooch-ghereomde conste een schinende in oft door-siende ooghen ghesichtes punt/op effen staende muer oft doeck/eenige Edifitein/t van ercken/Templen . . .*, 1st Dutch, French, German, Latin eds., The Hague and Leiden, 1604–05,

Vredeman de Vries, Hans and Paul (des.), *Architectura: Die hoogh en vermerde conste bestaende in vijf manieren van edifitien*, 1st ed., The Hague: Hondius, 1606, 11th ed., 1662.

Wilson, Thomas, *The Arte of Rhetorique, for the use of all soche as are studious of Eloquence . . .*, London: John Kingston, 1560.

II: Secondary Literature

Abels, Joscijka Gabriele, *Erkenntnis der Bilder. Die Perspektive in der Kunst der Renaissance*, Frankfurt: Campus, 1985.

Ackerman, James, *The Villa*, Princeton: Princeton University Press, 1990.

Adorno, Theodor W., *Negative Dialectics*, A. B. Ashton (trans.), New York: Continuum, 1966.

—— *The Jargon of Authenticity*, Knut Tarnowski and Frederic Will (trans.), Evanston: Northwestern University Press, 1974.

Albertina, Vienna, *Die Kunst der Graphik IV: Zwischen Renaissance und Barock: das Zeitalter von Bruegel und Bellange, Werke aus dem Besitz der Albertina*, exh. cat., with entries by Konrad Oberhuber, Vienna: Graphische Sammlung Albertina, 1967.

Alpers, Sveltana, *The Art of Describing*, Chicago: University of Chicago Press, 1983.

Ames-Lewis, Francis, *The Intellectual Life of the Early Renaissance Artist*, New Haven: Yale University Press, 2000.

Amsden, Jon, "Historians and the Spatial Imagination", *Radical History Review*, 1979, 11–30.

Andersen, Kirsti, "Stevin's Theory of Perspective: The Origin of A Dutch Academic Approach to Perspective", *Tractrix*, 2, 1990, pp. 25–62.

Arnscheidt, Grit, "Vom Prospectus zum Prospekt" in B. Kirchgässner (ed.), *Stadt und Repräsentation*, Sigmaringen: Jan Thorbecke, 1995, pp. 9–23.

Auerbach, Erich, *Mimesis: The Representation of Reality in Western Literature*, 1946, Willard R. (trans.), Trask: Princeton University Press, 1968.

Autenboer, E. van, *Volksfeesten en Rederijkers te Mechelen (1400–1600)*, Ghent: Koninklijk Vlaamse Academie voor Taal- en Letterkunde, 1962.

—— *Het Brabants landjuweel der rederijkers (1515–1561)*, Middelburg: Merlijn, 1981.

Badiou, Alain, *Handbook of Inaesthetics*, Alberto Toscano (trans.), Palo Alto: Stanford University Press, 2005.

Bakker, Boudewijn, "De eerste gezichten van de Dam", *Kunstschrift*, 36: 2, March/April 1992, pp. 14–16.

Bal, Mieke, *Narrativity: Introduction to the theory of Narrative*, Christine van Boheemen (trans.), Toronto: Toronto University Press, 1985.

—— "First Person, Second Person, Same Person: Narrative as Epistimology", *New Literary History*, 24, 1993, pp. 293–320.

Ballegeer, J. P. C. M., "Enkle voorbeelden van de invloed van Hans en Paulus Vredeman de Vries op de architectuurschilders in de Nederlanden gedurende de XVIe en XVIIe eeuw", *Gentse Bijdragen tot de Kunstgeschiedenis en Oudheidkunde*, 20, 1967, pp. 55–70.

Barrocchi, Paola (ed.), *Trattati d'arte del Cinqucento, Fra Manierismo e Controriforma*, 3 vols, Bari: Laterza, 1960–62.

Baudrillard, Jean, *Simulations*, Paul Foss (trans.), New York: Semiotext(e), 1983.

Baxandall, Michael, *Giotto and the orators: humanist observers of painting in Italy and the discovery of pictorial composition, 1350–1450*, Oxford: Clarendon Press, 1971.

Beaujean, Dieter, "Druckgraphik als Vorlage für Bilder in Bildern", *Bulletin des Musées royaux des beaux-arts de Belgique*, 41–42: 1–4, 1992–93, pp. 63–96.

—— *Bilder in Bildern: Studien zur niederländischen Malerei des 17. Jahrhunderts*, Weimar: VDG, 2001.

Behringer, Wolfgang et al. (eds), *Stadt im Bild in fruhen Neuzeit 1400–1800*, Munich: Beck, 1999.

Benesch, Otto (ed.), *Die Zeichnungen der niederländischen Schulen des XV. und XVI. Jahrhunderts: Beschreibender Katalog der Handzeichnungen in der Graphischen Sammlung Albertina: Bd. 2*, Vienna: A. Schroll, 1928.

Benjamin, Walter, "Die Reflexion in der Kunst und in der Farbe", 1914/15, in H. Böhme and Y. Ehrenspeck (eds), *Walter Benjamin: Aura und Reflexion*, Frankfurt am Main: Suhrkamp, 2007, pp. 11–12.

—— "The Work of Art in the Age of its Technological Reproducibility: Second Version" in *Selected Writings*, vol. 3, Howard Eiland and Michael W. Jennings (eds), Cambridge, MA: Belknap, 2006, pp. 101–33.

—— *The Origin of German Tragic Drama*, George Steiner (trans.), London: Verso, 1998.

Berger, Harry Jr, "The System of Early Modern Painting", *Representations*, 62, Spring 1998, pp. 1–57.

Bevers, Holm, "Die Meerwesen vom Antwerpener Rathaus und der Handel der Scheldestadt", *Jaarboek Koninklijk Museum voor Schone Kunsten*, 1982, pp. 97–117.

—— *Das Rathaus von Antwerpen: Architektur und Figurenprogramm*, Hildesheim: Georg Olms, 1985.

Blockmans, F., "Een krijgstekening, een muurschildering en een schilderij van Hans Vredeman de Vries te Antwerpen (1577–86)", *Antwerpen: Tijdschrift der Stad Antwerpen*, 8, April 1962, pp. 20–42.

Bodar, Antoine, "Vitruvius in de Nederlanden" in *Bouwen in Nederland*, Delft: DUM, 1985, pp. 55–71.

Boersma, H. L., "Hans Vredeman de Vries en diens Naamgenooten", *Bouwkundige Bijdragen*, 26, 1881, pp. 23–52.

Bois, Yve-Alain, *Painting as Model*, Cambridge, MA: MIT Press, 1993.

Boon, Karel G., *Catalogue of the Dutch and Flemish Drawings in the Rijksmuseum II: Netherlandish Drawings of the XVth and XVIth Century*, The Hague: Staatsuijgeverij, 1978.

Bora, Giulio, "Quattro Disegni: Hans Vredeman de Vries e un Doppio Scambio Italia-Fiandria", *Incontri*, 9: 1, 1994, pp. 57–68.

Borggrefe, Heiner et al. (eds), *Hans Vredeman de Vries und die Renaissance im Norden*, exh. cat., Lemgo: Schloss Brake, Antwerp: KMSK, 2002.

Borggrefe, Heiner and Lüpkes, Vera (eds), *Hans Vredeman de Vries und die Folgen*, Marburg: Jonas Verlag, 2005.

Boyer, M. Christiane, *The City of Collective Memory*, Cambridge: Cambridge University Press, 1996, pp. 73–127.

Branden, F. J. van den, *Geschiedenis der Antwerpsche Schilderschool*, Antwerp: J. E. Buschmann, 1883.

Braudel, Fernand, *The Structures of Everyday Life I: Civilization and Capitalism 15th–18th Century*, New York: Abrams, 1981.

Braunfels, Wolfgang, *Urban Design in Western Europe: Regime and Architecture, 900–1900*, Chicago: University of Chicago Press, 1988.

Braungart, W., *Die Kunst der Utopie: Von Späthumanismus zur frühen Augkläring*, Stuttgart: J. B. Metzler, 1989.

Bredius, A., *Künstler-Inventare. Urkunde zur Geschichte der holländischen Kunst des XVIter XVIIter, und XVIIIter Jahrhunderts*, The Hague: Nijhoff, 1915.

Briels, J., *Zuid-Nederlandse Immigratie 1572–1630*, Haarlem: Fibula-van Dishoek, 1978.

Brion-Guerry, L., *Jean Pélerin Viator. Sa place dans l'histoire de la perspective*, Paris: Les Belles Lettres, 1962.

Broadfoot, Keith, "Perspective Yet Again: Damisch with Lacan", *Oxford Art Journal*, 25.1, 2002, pp. 71–94.

Brües, Eva, "Hans Vredeman de Vries: ideal architektur" in Herzog August Bibliothek, *Architekt und Ingenieur: Baumeister in Kreig und Frieden*, exh. cat., Wolfenbüttel, 1984, pp. 263–7.

Brusati, Celeste, *Artifice and Illusion: The Art and Writing of Samuel von Hoogstraten*, Chicago: University of Chicago Press, 1996.

Bruyne, Jan de, *Refereinen en Andere Gedichten uit de XVIe Eeuw*, 3 vols, Antwerp: P. Kockx, 1880.

Buck-Morss, Susan, "The City as Dreamworld and Catastrophe", *October*, 73, Summer 1995, pp. 3–25.

Burke, Peter, *Popular Culture in Early Modern Europe*, London: Temple Smith, 1979.

Burns, Elizabeth, *Theatricality: A Study of convention in the theatre and in social life*, New York: Harper and Row, 1972.

Burroughs, Charles, "Absolutism and the Rhetoric of Topography" in Çelik, Zynep et al. (eds), *Streets: Critical Perspectives on Public Space*, Berkeley: University of California Press, 1994, pp. 189–202.

Büttner, Nils, *Die Erfindung der Landschaft. Kosmographie und Landschaftkunst im Zeitalter Bruegels*, Göttingen: Vandenhoeck & Ruprecht, 2000.

—— " 'Quid Scivitas Sequeris Per Mille Pericula Terras?' Ein Beitrag zur Biographie 'Pieter Bruegels d Ä und zur Kulturgeschichte der niederländischen Italienreise' ", *Marburger Jahrbuch für Kunstwissenschaft*, 27, 2000, pp. 209–42.

Campbell, Lorne, *The early Flemish pictures in the collection of Her Majesty the Queen*, Cambridge, New York: Cambridge University Press, 1985.

Carpo, Mario, "How do you imitate a building you have never seen? Printed images, ancient models, and handmade drawings in Renaisssance architectural theory", *Zeitschrift für Kunstgeschichte*, 64: 2, 2001, pp. 223–33.

—— *Architecture in the Age of Printing: Orality, Writing, Typography, and Printed Images in the History of Architectural Theory*, 1998, Sarah Benson (trans.), Cambridge, MA: MIT Press, 2001.

Cassirer, Thomas, "Awareness of the City in the *Encyclopédie*", *Journal of the History of Ideas*, 24, 1963, pp. 387–96.

Cavallo, Guglielmo and Chartier, Rogier, "Introduction" to *A History of Reading in the West*, Lydia G. Cochrane (trans.), London: Polity Press, 1997.

Cave, Terence, *The Cornucopian Text: Problems of Writing in the French Renaissance*, Oxford: Clarendon, 1979.

Caws, Mary Ann (ed.), *City Images: Perspectives from Literature, Philosophy, and Film*, New York: Gordon and Breach, 1991.

Centraal Museum, Utrecht, *Nederlandse architectuurschilders 1600–1900*, exh. cat., Utrecht: 1953.

Chartier, Roger, "From Court Festivity to City Spectators" in *Forms and Meanings Texts, Performance, and Audiences from Codex to Computer*, Philadelphia: Pennsylvania University Press, 1995.

—— *The Cultural Uses of Print in Early Modern France*, L. G. Cochrane (trans.), Princeton: Princeton University Press, 1987.

Chastel, André, "Marquetrie et Perspective au XVe Siècle", *La Revue des Arts*, 5: 3, 1953, pp. 141–54.

Chatenay, Leopold, *Vie de Jacques Esprinchard Rochelais et Journal de ses voyages au XVIe siècle*, Paris: S.E.V.P.E.N, 1957.

Choay, Françoise, *The Rule and the Model: On the Theory of Architecture and Urbanism*, 1980, London and Cambridge: MIT Press, 1997.

Coigneau, Dirk, *Refreinen in Het Zotte Bij de Rederijkers*, 3 vols, Ghent: Koninklijke Academie voor Nederlandse Taal- en Letterkunde, 1980–83.

—— "Rederijkersliteratuur" in *Historische Letterkunde. Facetten van vakbeofening*. Groningen: Wolters-Nordhoff, 1984, pp. 35–57.

—— "Matthijs de Castelein: Excellent Poete Moderne", *Verslagen en Mededelingen van de Koninklijke Academie voor Nederlandse Taal- en Letterkunde*, new series, 1985, pp. 451–75.

—— "Strofische vormen in het rederijkerstoneel" in B. A. M. Ramakers (ed.), *Spel in Verte: Tekst, structuur, en opvoeringspraktijk van het rederijkerstoneel*, Gent: Koninklijk Vlaamse Academie voor Taal- en Letterkunde, 1994, pp. 17–44.

Coo, J. de, "Verscholen Antwerps stadsbeeld bij Jan Brueghel I en bij Hans Vredeman de Vries", *Jaarboek van het Koninklijk Museum Antwerpen*, 1970, pp. 121–31.

Corbet, August, *Cornelis Floris en de Bouw van het Stadhuis van Antwerpen*, Antwerp: De Sikkel, 1937.

Coubier, Heinz, *Europäische Stadt-Plätze: Genius und Geschichte*, Cologne: DuMont, 1985.

Crary, Jonathan, *Techniques of the Observer: On Vision and Modernity in the Nineteenth Century*, Cambridge, MA: MIT Press, 1990.

—— *Suspensions of Perception: Attention, Spectacle, and Modern Culture*, Cambridge, MA: MIT Press, 1999.

Crew, Phyllis Mack, *Calvinist preaching and iconoclasm in the Netherlands, 1544–1569*, New York: Cambridge University Press, 1978.

Cuny, Georg, *Danzigs Kunst und Kultur im 16. und 17. Jahrhundert*, Frankfurt am Main: Heinrich Keller, 1, p. 910.

—— "Johannes Fredemann de Fries und Aegidius Dickmann", *Mitteilungen des West-Preussischen Geschichtsvereins*, 26, 1927, pp. 65–77.

Dacos, Nicole, *Les peintres belges a Rome au XVIe siècle*, Brussels, Rome: Institut historique belge de Rome, 1964.

—— *La découverte de la Domus Aurea et la formation des grotesques à la Renaissance*, London, Warburg Institute, 1969.

Damisch, Hubert, "The Column and the Wall", *Architectural Design*, 48: 8–9, 1979, pp. 18–25.

—— *The Origin of* Perspective, 1987, John Goodman (trans.), Cambridge, MA: MIT Press, 1994.

—— *A theory of /cloud/: toward a History of Painting*, Janet Lloyd (trans.), Palo Alto: Stanford University Press, 2002.

Daniëls, G. L. M., "De verheerlijking van de Triumferende Kerk door Hans Vredeman de Vries (1526–1606)", *Antiek* 19: 8, March 1985, pp. 418–24.

David Winton Bell Gallery, Providence, *Philip II and the Escorial: Technology and the Representation of Architecture*, exh. cat., Providence, 1990.

Delen, A. J. J., *Iconographie van Antwerpen*, Brussels: L. J. Kryn, 1930.

—— *Histoire de la gravure dans les anciens Pays-Bas et dans les provinces belges, des origines jusqu'à la fin du XVIIIe siecle*, II, 1–2, Paris-Brussels, 1935.

Deleuze, Gilles, *Difference and Repetition*, Paul Patton (trans.), New York: Columbia University Press, 1994.

Denucé, J., "Prenthandel Theodoor Galle en Catharina Moerentorf: Inventaris van 1636", *Antwerpsche Archivenblad*, 2nd series, 2: 1, January 1927, pp. 136–51.

—— *Kunstuitvoer in de 17de Eeuw te Antwerpen: de Firma Fourschoudt*, Antwerp: De Sikkel, 1931.

—— *De Antwerpsche "Konstkamers" Inventarissen van kunstverzamelingen te Antwerpen in de zestiende en zeventiende eeuw*, Amsterdam: de Spiegel, 1932.

Devisscher, Hans (ed.), *Cornelius Floris 1514–1575: beeldhouwer/architect/ontwerper*, Brussels: Snoeck-Ducaju & Zoon, 1996.

Dittrich, Lothar and Dittrich, Sigrid, "Tiere in Höfen und Gärten von Palästen auf Bildern von Hans und Paul Vredeman de Vries", *Niederdeutsche Beiträge zur Kunstgeschichte*, 32, 1993, pp. 90–107.

Duverger, J., "Cornelius Floris II en het Stadhuis te Antwerpen", *Gentsche Bijdragen tot de Kunstgeschiedenis*, VII, 1941, pp. 37–72.

Eck, Caroline A. van, "Architecture, Language, and Rhetoric in Alberti's *De re aedificatoria*" in Georgia Clarke and Paul Crossley (eds), *Architecture and Language: Constructing Identity in European Architecture c.1000–c.1650*, Cambridge: Cambridge University Press, 2000, pp. 72–81.

Edgerton, Samuel Y., *The Renaissance Rediscovery of Linear Perspective*, New York: Abrams, 1975.

—— "Image and Word in Sixteenth-Century Printed Technical Books" in *The Heritage of Giotto's Geometry: Art and Science on the Eve of the Scientific Revolution*, Ithaca: Cornell University Press, 1991, pp. 148–92.

Eeghem, William van, "Het Brusselsche Rederijkersfeest (1565)", *Jaarboek Koninklijke Souvereine Hoofdkamer van Retorica van Vlaanderen*, 1944, pp. 457–82.

Ehrmann, Jean, "Hans Vredeman de Vries (Leeuwarden 1527–Anvers 1606)", *Gazette des Beaux-Arts*, n.s., 5, 93, January 1979, pp. 13–27.

Eisenstein, Elizabeth L, *The Printing Revolution in Early Modern Europe*, Cambridge: Cambridge University Press, 1983.

Eisler, William, "Celestial Meanings and Hapsburg Rule: Levels of Meaning in a Triumphal Arch for Philip II in Antwerp, 1549" in B. Wisch and S. Munschower (eds), *"All the world's a stage . . ".: Art and Pageantry in the Renaissance and Baroque*, University Park: Penn State University Press, 1990, pp. 332–56.

Elias, Norbert, *The Civilizing Process*, London: Blackwell, 1978.

—— *The Court Society*, New York: Pantheon, 1983.

Elkins, James, "Mannerism: Deformation of the Stage", *Storia dell' arte*, 67, 1989, pp. 257–62.

—— *The Poetics of Perspective*, Ithaca: Cornell University Press, 1994.

Elslander, Antonin van, *Het Refrein in Nederlanden tot 1600 (Koninklijke Vlaamse Academie Voor Taal- en Letterkunde Reeks, VI, nr 71)*, Ghent: Erasmus, 1953.

—— "Les Chambres de Rhetorique et les Fêtes du Regne de Charles Quint" in Jean Jacquot (ed.), *Fêtes et Cérémonies au Temps de Charles Quint*, Paris: ECNRS, 1960, pp. 281–5.

—— "Lijst van de Nederlandse rederijkerskamers uit de XVe end XVIe eeuw" in *Jaarboek Koninklijke Souvereine Hoofdkamer van Retorica "De Fontaine" te Gent*, XVIII, 1968, pp. 1–67.

Evans, Robin, *The Projective Cast*, Cambridge, MA: MIT Press, 1994.

Eversmann, Peter, *De Ruimte van het Theatre: Een studie naar de invloed van de theatreruimte op de beleving van voorstellingen door de toeschower*, Amsterdam: Academische Proefschrift, 1996.

Fauser, Alois, *Repertorium älterer Topographie: Druckgraphik von 1486–1750*, 2 vols, Wiesbaden: Reichert, 1978.

Febvre, L, *The Coming of the Book: The Impact of Printing*, D. Gerard (trans.), London: Albin Michael, 1958.

Filipczak, Zirka Zaremba, *Picturing Art in Antwerp 1550–1700*, Princeton: Princeton University Press, 1987.

Findlen, Paula, *Possessing Nature: Museums, Collecting, and Scientific Culture in Early Modern Italy*, Berkeley and London: University of California Press, 1994.

Fink, August, "Ein Altar des Hans Vredeman de Vries für die ältest Trinitatiskirche in Wolfenbüttel", *Braunschweigisches Jahrbuch*, 43, 1962, pp. 173–6.

Flade, Helmut, *Intarsia: europaische Einlegekunst aus sechs Jahrhunderten*, Munich: Beck, 1986.

Fleurkens, Anna C. G., *Stichtelighe Lust: De toneelspelen van D.V. van Coornhert 1522–1590*, Hilversum: Verloren, 1994.

Focillon, Henri, *The Life of Forms in* Art, George Kubler (trans), New York: Zone Books, 1989.

Fogg Museum of Art, *The Made Landscape: City and Country in Seventeenth Century Dutch Prints*, exh. cat., Cambridge, MA: Harvard University Art Museums, 1993.

Fontaine Verwey, H. de la, "Pieter Coecke van Aelst en de uitgaven van Serlio's architecturboek", *Het Boek*, vol. 31, 1952–54, pp. 251–70.

Forssman, Erik, *Säule und Ornament. Studies zum Problem des Manierismus in den nordischen Säulerbüchern und Vorlageblättern des 16. und 17. Jahnhunderts*, Stockholm: Almqvist and Wiskell, 1956.

—— *Dorisch, Ionisch, Korinthisch*, Stockholm: Almqvist and Wiskell, 1961.

Forster, Kurt W., "Monument/Memory and the Mortality of Architecture", *Oppositions*, 25, Fall 1982, pp. 2–19.

Foucault, Michel, *The Order of Things*, New York: Viking, 1970.

Frampton, Kenneth, "Towards a Critical Regionalism: Six Points for an Architecture of Resistance" in Hal Foster (ed.), *The Anti-Aesthetic: Essays on Postmodern Culture*, Port Townsend, Wash.: Bay Press, 1983, pp. 16–30.

Francastel, P, *Peinture et Societe: Naissance et Destruction d'Un Espace Plastique de la Renaissance au Cubisme*, Lyon: Audin, 1951.

Frangenberg, Thomas, "The Image and Moving Eye: Jean Pélerin (Viator) to Guidobaldo del Monte", *Journal of the Warburg and Courtauld Institutes*, 49, 1986, pp. 150–71.

Freedberg, David, "Johannes Molanus on Provocative Paintings", *Journal of the Warburg and Courtauld, Institutes*, XXXIV, 1971, pp. 229–45.

—— *Iconoclasm and painting in the Netherlands, 1566–1609*, Ph.D. dissertation, Oxford University, 1972.

—— "The Hidden God: Image and Interdictions in the Netherlands in the Sixteenth Century", *Art History*, 5: 2, June 1982, pp. 133–53.

—— "Prints and the Status of Images in Flanders" in H. Zerner (ed.), *Le Stampe e la diffusione delle Immagini e degli Stili (Atti del XXIV Congresso Internazionale di Storia dell'Arte)*, l979, vol. VIII, Bologna, 1983, pp. 39–54.

Friedlander, Max. J., *Early Netherlandish Painting*, E. Goldschmidt et al. (eds), 14 vols, Leiden: A. W. Sijthoff, 1967–76.

Frijhoff, Willem, "De stad en haar geheugen", OASE, 24, 1989, pp. 14–21.

Fuciková, Eliška (ed.), *Rudolf II and Prague: The Court and the City*, London: Thames & Hudson, 1997.

Fusenig, Thomas, "Hendrick van Steenwijks d. Ä 'Markplatz' im Herzog Anton Ulrich-Museum zu Braunschweig", *Niederdeutsche Beiträge zur Kunstgeschichte*, 36, 1997, pp. 55–72.

Gent, Lucy, *Picture and Poetry 1560–1620*, Leamington: James Hall, 1981.

Germanisches Museum, Nuremberg, *Jamnitzer, Lencker, Stoer: drei Nuremberger Konstructivisten des 16. Jahrhunderts*, exh. cat., 1969.

—— *Der Traum von Raum: Gemalte Architektur aus 7 Jahrhunderten*, Marburg: Wolfram Hitzeroth, 1986.

Gibson, Walter, "Artists and Rederijkers in the Age of Bruegel", *Art Bulletin*, 63: 3, September 1981, 426–46.

Giesecke, Michael, *Der Buchdruck in der frühen Neuzeit: Eine historische Fallstudie über die Durchsetzung neuer Informations- und Kommunikationstechnologien*, Frankfurt: Suhrkamp, 1991.

Gilbert, Creighton, "On Subject and Not-Subject in Italian Renaissance Pictures", *Art Bulletin*, XXXIV, 1952, pp. 202–16.

Gilman, Ernst, *The Curious Perspective: Literary and Pictorial Wit in the Seventeenth Century*. New Haven: Yale University Press, 1978.

Gombrich, Ernst, *Art and Illusion: a Study in the Psychology of Pictorial Representation*, New York: Phaidon, 1960.

—— *The Sense of Order*, Oxford: Phaidon, 1979.

Goodman, Nelson, "How Buildings Mean" in P. Alperson (ed.), *The Philosophy of the Visual Arts*, Oxford: Oxford University Press, 1992, pp. 368–76.

Goris, Jan-Albert, *Lof van Antwerpen: Hoe reizigers Antwerpen zagen, van de XVe tot de XXe Eeuw*, Brussels: N.V. Standaard, 1940.

Graaf, Floor de (ed.), *Een dansfestijn doorgrond: technisch en kunsthistorisch onderzoek naar een Vlaams schilderij*, exh. cat., The Hague: Mauritshuis, 1992.

Greve, Henri Ekhard, *De bronnen Van Carel van Mander voor "Het leven der doorluchtighe Nederlandtsche en Hoogduytsche schilders"*, 's-Gravenhage: M. Nijhoff, 1903.

Grondijs, Henderick Frederik (ed.), *Een Spul van Sinnen van den Siecke Stadt*, Borculo: P.G. Repko, 1917.

Grootenboer, Hanneke, *The Rhetoric of Perspective*, Chicago: University of Chicago Press, 2005.

Guillaume, Jean (ed.), *L'Emploi des Ordres dans l'Architecture de la Renaissance*, Paris: Pichard, 1992.

Guillen, Claudio, *Literature as System: Essays toward a theory of literary history*, Princeton: Princeton University Press, 1971.

Guillerme, André, *The Age of Water*, College Station, TX: A&M Press, 1988.

Gustav-Lubeck Museum, Hann, *Gärten und Höfe der Rubenszeit im Spiegel der Malerfamilie Brueghel*, exh. cat., Munich: Hirmer, 2000.

Gutschow, N. and Sieverts, T., *Stadt und Ritual/Urban Space and Ritual (Beiträge und Studienmaterialen der Fachgruppe Stadt, no 11)*, Darmstadt, 1977.

Habermas, Jürgen, *The Structural Transformation of the Public Sphere: An Inquiry into a Category of Bourgeois Society*, Thomas Burger (trans.), Cambridge, MA: MIT Press, 1991.

Hajos, E.M, "The Concept of an Engravings Collection in the Year 1565", *Art Bulletin*, 40, 1958, pp. 151–6.

Hale, J. R., "Sixteenth Century Explanations of War and Violence", *Past and Present*, 51, 1971, pp. 3–26.

Hart, Vaughn, "Decorum and the Five Orders of Architecture", *Res*, 34, Autumn 1998, pp. 75–84.

Hart, Vaughn and Hicks, P., *Paper Palaces: The Rise of the Renaissance Architectural Treatise*, New Haven: Yale University Press, 1998.

Haverkamp-Begemann, Egbert, "The Spanish View of Anton van den Wyngaerde", *Master Drawings*, VII: 4, 1969, pp. 375–99.

Hedicke, Robert, *Cornelis Floris und die Florisdekoration: Studies zur niederländischen und deutschen Kunst im XVI. Jahrhundert*, 2 vols, Berlin: Julius Bard, 1931.

Hegel, Georg Wilhelm Friedrich, *Aesthetics or the Philosophy of Fine Art—Selections*, Henry Paolucci (trans. and ed.), New York: Ungar, 1979.

Heidegger, Martin, "Building Dwelling Thinking" in *Poetry, Language, Thought*, A. Hofstadter (trans.), New York: Harper & Row, 1971, pp. 145–61.

Heiden, Th. C. J. van der and Boheemen, F. C. van, *Met minnen versaemt. De Hollandse rederijkers vanaf de middeleeuwen tot het begin van de achtiende eeuw. Bronnen en bronnenstudies*, Delft: Eburon, 1999.

Hellendoorn, Fabienne Emilie, *Invloed van het Noordelijk-Manierisme op de Mexicaanse Religieuze Archtiectuur in de Periode van 1600–1750*, Proefschrift TU Delft, 1980.

Hellinga, W., *Copy and Print in the Netherlands*, Amsterdam: Federatie der Werkgeversorganisatiën in het Boekdrukkersbedrijf, Noord-Holland, 1962.

Henning, Michael, *Die Tafelbilder Bartholomäus Sprangers (1546–1611): Höfische Malerei zwischen "Manierismus" und "Barock"*, Essen: Blaue Eule, 1987.

Herzog Anton Ulrich Museum, *Hofkunst der Spätrenaissance*, exh. cat., Braunschweig, 1998.

Herzog August Bibliothek, Wolfenbüttel, *Architekt und Ingenieur: Baumeister in Kreig und Frieden*, exh. cat., Wolfenbüttel, 1984.

—— *Weltblicke in Malerbüchern der Herzog-August Bibliothek: Ut pictura poesis*, exh. cat., Wolfenbüttel, 1991.

Het Stedelijk netwerk in Belgie in historische perspectief (1350–1850). Een statistische en dynamische benadering, Handelingen 15de Internationaal Colloquium, Spa, September 4–6, 1990, Brussels: Gemeentekrediet, 1992.

Heuer, Christopher P., "Perspective as Process", *Res*, 38, 2000, pp. 82–100.

—— "Between the Histories of Art and Architecture: Critical Reception of Hans Vredeman de Vries", *Bulletin Koninklijke Nederlandse Oudheidkundige Bond*, 100: 1, 2001, pp. 27–40.

—— "Perspectivebookjes, leering en vermaak", *Kunstschrift*, June 2002, pp. 34–6.

—— "Placing *Rederijkerskunst* in Antwerp" in Piet Lombaerde et al. (eds), *Hans Vredeman de Vries and the Artes Mechanicae Revisted* (*Architectura Moderna 2*), Turnhout: Brepols, 2004, pp. 192–220.

—— "A Copperplate for Hieronymus Cock", *Burlington Magazine*, CXLIX, no 1247, February 2007, pp. 96–9.

—— "Three Drawings in Gdańsk: Notes on the Limits of Influence", *Biuletyn Historii Sztuki*, 69, 3/4, Fall 2007, pp. 315–22.

Heuvel, Charles van der, *"Papiere bolwercken": de introductie van de Italiaanse stede- en vestingbouw in de Nederlanden*, Alphen aan den Rijn: Canaletto, 1991.

—— " 'T' Samenspreeckinghe betreffende de Architecture ende Schilderkonst: Schilders, architecten en wiskundigen over de uitbeelding van architectuur", *Incontri*, 9: 1, 1994, pp. 69–85.

—— "De Architectura (1599) van Charles de Beste", *Bulletin Koninklijke Nederlandse Oudheidkundige Bond*, 94: 1, 1995, pp. 11–23.

—— "Of marble columns and wooden piles; Hans Vredeman de Vries and Simon Stevin", unpublished typescript, 1999.

Historisch Museum, Amsterdam, *Opkomst en bloei van het Noordnederlandse stadsgezicht in de 17eeuw/ The Dutch Cityscape in the 17th Century and its Sources*, 1977, review, Lyckle de Vries, *Simiolus*, 9, Amsterdam, 1977, pp. 187–9.

Honig, Elizabeth Alice, *Painting and the Market in Early Modern Antwerp*, New Haven: Yale University Press, 1999.

Hummelen, W. M. H., *Repertorium van het Rederijkersdrama 1500 ca. 1620*, Assen: van Gorcum, 1968.

—— "Illustrations of Stage Performances in the Work by Crispin de Passe the Elder (c.1560–1637)", *Essays in Drama and Theatre. Liber Amicorum Benjamin Hunningher*, Amsterdam and Baarn: Standaard, 1973.

Huysmans, Antoinette, *Cornelis Floris, 1514–1575: beeldhouwer, architect, ontwerper*, Brussels: Gemeentekrediet, 1996.

Ingraham, Catherine, *Architecture and the Burdens of Linearity*, New Haven: Yale University Press, 1998.

Irmscher, Günter, *Kleine Kunstgeschichte des Europäischen Ornaments seit der frühen Neuzeit (1400–1900)*, Darmstadt: Wissenschaftliche Buchgesellschaft, 1984.

—— "Hans Vredeman de Vries als Zeichner (I)", *Kunsthistorisches Jahrbuch Graz*, 21, 1985, pp. 123–42

—— "Hans Vredeman de Vries als Zeichner (II)", *Kunsthistorisches Jahrbuch Graz*, 22, (1986), pp. 79–117.

Ivins, William M., " 'Ornament' and the Sources of Design in the Decorative Arts", *Bulletin of the Metropolitan Museum of Art*, XIII: 2, 1918, pp. 35–41.

—— *On the Rationalization of Sight*, New York: Metropolitan Museum of Art, 1938.

Iwanoyko, Eugeniusz, *Gdański okres Hansa Vredemana de Vries*, Poznan: Uniwersyet im Adama Mickiewicza, 1963.

—— "Zagadenienie Przestrzeni W Malarstwie Hansa Vredemana de Vries", *Biuletyn Historii* Sztuki, 26: 2, 1964, pp. 136–41.

—— *Sala Czerwona ratusza gdańskiego*, Wrocław: n.p., 1986.

Jackson, J. B., "By Way of Conclusion: How to Study the Landscape" in *The Necessity of Ruins and other Essays*, 1980, pp. 113–26.

Jacqout, Jean (ed.), *Les Fêtes de la Renaissance*, 3 vols, Paris: Editions CNRS, 1956–75.

Jameson, Frederic, "The Brick and the Balloon: Architecture, Idealism, and Land Speculation", *New Left Review*, 228, March/April 1998, pp. 25–46.

Jansen, G. H., *Een land van steden: het spoor van de tijd. Cultuurgeschiedenis van de Hollandse stad tot 1900*, The Hague: Staatsuitgeverij, 1984.

Jantzen, Hans, *Das niederländische Architekturbild 1600–1800*, Ph.D. dissertation, Freie Universität Berlin, 1908.

—— *Das niederländische Architekturbild*, Leipzig: Klinkhardt & Berman, 1910, 2nd ed. Braunschweig, 1979, review, Ernst Heidrich in *Zeitschrift für Aesthetik und allgemeine Kunstwissenschaft*, VII, 1912, pp. 117–43, published posthumously in Ernst Heidrich, *Beiträge zur Kunstgeschichte und Methode der Kunstgeschichte*, Basel: Benno Schwabe, 1917, pp. 82–109.

Jay, Martin, *Downcast Eyes: On the Denigration of Vision*, Berkeley and London: UC Press, 1993.

Jong, Johannes A. B. M. de, *Architektuur bij der Nederlandsche Schilders vóór de Hervorming*, Amsterdam: de Spieghel, 1934.

Jong, Marijnke de and de Groot, Irene, *Ornamentprenten in het Rijksprentenkabinet I: 15de & 16de Eeuw*, The Hague: Staatsuitgeverij, 1988.

Jonge, Krista de et al., "Building Policy and Urbanization during the Reign of the Archdukes" in Werner Thomas and Luc Duerloo (eds), *Albert and Isabella 1598–1621: Essays*, Turnhout: Brepols, 1998, pp. 191–220.

Joost-Gaugier, Christiane L., "Jacopo Bellini's Interest in Perspective and its Iconographical Significance", *Zeitschrift für Kunstgeschichte*, 38, 1975, pp. 1–29.

Judovitz, Dalia, "Vision, Representation and Technology in Descartes" in David Michael Levin (ed.), *Modernity and the Hegemony of Vision*, Berkeley and London: UC Press, 1993, pp. 63–86.

Kahn, Victoria, *Rhetoric, Prudence, and Skepticism in the Renaissance*, Ithaca: Cornell University Press, 1985.

Karstkarel, Peter, "Het allegorisch theater. Enkele opmerkingen bij de herdruk van he Theatrum Vitae Humanae van Hans Vredeman de Vries", *Akt: Aktueel kunsttijdschrift Instituut voor Kuntgescheidenis Groningen*, 2: 3, 1978, pp. 18–36.

—— "Hans Vredeman de Vries (1526–1606?) Vondsten", *Tableau*, 3, 1981, pp. 763.

—— "Johnnes Vredemannus Frisius Leovardiensis" in *30 jaar tijd genoten Vredeman de Vries: Geschiedkundig overzicht en catalogus in het kader van 30 jaar kunst-onderwijs*, Leeuwarden: Academie voor Beeldende Kunst, 1991.

Kassell, Lauren, "Reading for the Philosopher's Stone" in Marina Frasca-Spada and Nick Jardine (eds), *Books and the Sciences in History*, Cambridge: Cambridge University Press, 2000, pp. 132–50.

Kaufmann, Thomas da Costa, *The School of Prague: Painting at the Court of Rudolf II*, Chicago: University of Chicago Press, 1988.

—— "Addenda Rudolphinae", *Annales de la Galerie Nationale Hungaroise*, 1991, pp. 141–8.

—— *Court, Cloister, and City: The Art and Culture of Central Europe 1450–1800*, Chicago: University of Chicago Press, 1995.

—— "Planeten im kaiserlichen Universum" in Herzog Anton Ulrich Museum, Braunschweig, *Hofkunst der Spätrenaissance*, exh. cat., Braunschweig, 1998, pp. 9–30.

—— "Empiricism and Community in Early Modern Science and Art: Some Comments on Baths, Plants, and Courts" in A. Grafton and Nancy Siraisi (eds), *Natural Particulars. Nature and the Disciplines in Renaissance Europe*, Cambridge, MA: MIT Press, 1999, fol. 401.

—— *Toward A Geography of Art*, Chicago: University of Chicago Press, 2004.

Kavalaer, Ethan Matt, *Pieter Bruegel: Parables or Order and Enterprise*, Cambridge: Cambridge University Press, 1999.

—— "Renaissance Gothic in the Netherlands: the uses of Ornament", *Art Bulletin*, 82, 2000, pp. 226–51.

Keersmaekers, A., "De rederijkerskamers te Antwerpen: kanttekeningen in verband met onstaan, samenstelling, en ondergang" in *Verslag Vijfde Colloquium De Brabantse Stad, s'-Hertogenbosch 25–26 November 1977*, s'Hertogenbosch: PGKWNB, 1978, pp. 173–86.

Kelsch, Wolfgang, "Wolfenbüttel—eine geplante Idealstadt der Renaissance?", *Braunschweigisches Jahrbuch*, 71, 1990, pp. 139–46.

Kemp, Martin, "Geometrical Perspective from Brunelleschi to Desargues: A Pictorial Means or an Intellectual End?", *Proceedings of the British Academy*, LXX, 1984, pp. 90–132.

—— *The Science of Art*, New Haven: Yale University Press, 1990.

Kernodle, George, *From Art to Theatre: Form and Convention in the Renaissance*, Chicago: University of Chicago Press, 1944.

Kipling, Gordon, "The Idea of the Civic Triumph: Drama, Liturgy, and the Royal Entry in the Low Countries", *Dutch Crossing*, 22, April 1984, pp. 60–83.

Kloster, Elwin, "Stadsvorm en Traktaten" in J. L. de Jong and E. A. Kloster (eds), *Onverwacht Bijeengebracht. Opstellen voor Ed Taverne en Lyckle de Vries ter gelegenheid van hun 25-jarig jubileum in dienst van de Rijksuniversiteit Groningen*, Groningen: Instituut voor Kunst- en Architectuurgeschiedenis, 1996, pp. 83–8.

Kluge, Walter, "Die Stadt in der Utopie: Architektur als Modell der Gesellschaft" in Andreas Mahler (ed.), *Stadt-Bilder: Allegorie—Mimesis—Imagination*, Heidelberg: C. Winter, 1999, pp. 67–85.

Koerner, Joseph Leo, *The Moment of Self-portraiture in German Renaissance art*, Chicago: University of Chicago Press, 1993.

—— "The Printed World" in *The Printed World of Pieter Bruegel the Elder*, exh. cat., St. Louis Art Museum, 1995.

—— *The Reformation of the Image*, Chicago: University of Chicago Press, 2004.

Kofuku, Akira (ed.), *Bruegel and Netherlandish Landscape Painting from the National Gallery Prague*, exh. cat., Tokyo: National Museum of Western Art, 1990.

Koninklijke Bibliotheek Albert I, *Les Sadeler, graveurs et éditeurs*, exh. cat., Brussels, 1992.

—— *Uyt lonsten Versaemt. Het landjuweel van 1561 te Antwerpen*, exh. cat., Brussels, 1994.

Koninklijke Museum voor Schone Kunsten, *De schilderkunst in Belgie in de 16de Eeuw*, exh. cat., Brussels, 1963.

—— *Rondom plechtige intredes en feestelijke stadsversieringen Antwerp, 1594–1599–1635*, exh. cat., Antwerp, 1981.

—— *De Bruegel à Rubens: L'ecole de peinture aversoise 1550–1650*, exh. cat., Antwerp, 1992.

Koopmans, Jelle et al. (eds), *Rhetoric-Rhétoriqueurs-Rederijkers*, Koninklijke Nederlandse Akademie van Wetenschappen Verhandelingen, Afd. Letterkunde, new series, no 162, Amsterdam/Oxford/New York/Tokyo: North Holland, 1995.

Koska, I., "Hans Vredeman de Vries" in U. Thieme and F. Becker, *Allegemeines Künstlerlexikon*, 34, Leipzig, Engelmann, 1940, pp. 575–9.

Kostof, Spiro (ed.), *The Architect: Chapters in the History of the Profession*, New York: Oxford University Press, 1977.

Krauss, Rosalind, "Grids" in *The Originality of the Avant-Garde and Other Modernist Myths*, Cambridge, MA: MIT Press, 1985, pp. 9–40.

Krieger, Bart J. J., "Hierarchie der Ornamenten? De ontmoeting van het classicisme en het rolwerkcartouche in de *Architectura* [1577] van Hans Vredeman de Vries", unpublished typescript, Vrije Universiteit Amsterdam, 2000.

Krings, Wilfred, "Text und Bild als Informationsträger bei gedruckten Stadtdarstellungen der Frühen Neuzeit" in Stephan Füssel and Joachim Knape (eds), *Poesis et Pictura: Festschrift für Dieter Wuttke*, Baden-Baden: Koerner, 1989, pp. 295–335.

Kruft, Hanno-Walter, *A History of Architectural Theory from Vitruvius to the Present*, R. Taylor, E.Callander, A. Wood (trans.), Princeton: Princeton Architectural Press, 1985.

—— *Städte in Utopia: Die Idealstadt vom 15. bus 18. Jahrhundert zwischen Staatsutopie und Wirklichkeit*, Munich: C. H. Beck, 1989.

Kruyskamp, C., *Het Antwerpse Landjuweel van 1561*, Antwerp: Nederlandsche Boekhandel, 1962.

Kubovy, Michael. *The Psychology of Perspective and Renaissance Art*, Cambridge: Cambridge University Press, 1986.

Kulturstiftung Ruhr, Essen, *Prag um 1600: Kunst und Kultur am Hofe Rudolfs II*, 2 vols, Freren: Luca Verlag, 1988.

—— *Beiträge: Prag um 1600*, Freren: Luca Verlag, 1988.

Kunstbibliothek, Berlin *Architektenzeichnungen 1479–1979 von 400 europäischen und amerikanischen Architekten aus dem Bestand der Kunstbibliothek Berlin*, exh. cat., Berlin: Volker Spiess, 1979.

Kunsthistorisches Museum, Vienna, *Eros und Mythos: Kunst am Hof Rudolf II*, exh. cat., Vienna: 1995.

Kuyper, W., *The Triumphant Entry of Renaissance Architecture into the Netherlands*, 2 vols, Alphen aan den Rijn: Canaletto, 1994.

Lampert, Jay, "Why is there no Category of the City in Hegel's *Aesthetics?*", *British Journal of Aesthetics*, 41: 3, July 2001, pp. 312–24.

Landau, David and Parshall, Peter, *The Renaissance Print, 1470–1550*, New Haven: Yale University Press, 1994.

Landwehr, John, *Splendid Ceremonies: State Entries and Royal Funerals in the Low Countries 1515–1791*, Leiden: Brill, 1943.

Latour, Bruno, "Ces réseaux que la raison ignore: laboratories, Bibliothèques, collections" in Marc Baratin and Christian Jacob, *Le Pouvoir des Bibliothèques: La mémoire des livres en Occident*, Paris: Albin Michel, 1996, pp. 23–46.

Lefebvre, Henri, *Writings on Cities*, E. Kofman and E. Lebas (trans.), London: Blackwell, 1996.

Leigh Block Gallery, Evanston, *Graven Images: The Rise of Professional Printmakers in Antwerp and Haarlem, 1540–1640*, Evanston: Northwestern University Press, 1993.

Lhotsky, Alphons, *Festschrift des Kunsthistorischen Museums zur Feier des fünfzigjährigen Bestandes*, 2 vols, Vienna: F. Berger, 1941–45.

Liedtke, Walter A., "From Vredeman de Vries to Dirck van Delen: Sources of Imaginary Architectural Painting", *Bulletin of the Rhode Island School of Design*, 57: 2, December 1970, pp. 15–25.

Lombaerde, Piet, "Verschuivingen binnen het Planningsdenken over de Ruimte: van een perspectivische naar een semiologische benaderingswijze", Ph.D. dissertation, KU Leuven, 1982.

—— "Overzicht van den Opzoekingen over de Antwerpse Vestingbouw, de Architectuur en het Urbanisme" in *400 Jaar Scheiding der Nederlanden, 1585–1985*, Antwerp: Academie voor Culturele Werking en het Antwerps Museum en Archief, 1990, pp. 45–66.

—— "Continutieit, verniewingen en verschillen: Het concept van de stad in de Noordelijke en Zuidelike Nederlanden rond 1600", *Bulletin Koninklijke Nederlandse Oudheidkundige Bond*, 98: 5/6, 1999, pp. 237–48.

Long, Pamela O., *Openness, Secrecy, Authorship*, Baltimore: Johns Hopkins University Press, 2001.

Lootsma, Bart, "The Image and the Visual—a Plea for Unrestricted Architectural Photography", *Daidalos*, 66, December 1997, pp. 16–23.

MacGregor, W. B., "The authority of prints", *Art History*, 22: 3, September 1999, pp. 389–420.

Mak, J. J., *De Rederijkers*, Amsterdam: P.N. van Kampen & zoon, 1944.

—— "De Wachter in het Rederijkersdrama", *Uyt Ionsten Versaemt: Retoricale Studiën 1946–1956*, Zwolle: W. E. J. Tjeenk Willink, 1957, pp. 91–102.

Mallgrave, Harry Francis and Ikonomou, Eleftherios (eds.), *Empathy, Form, and Space: Problems in German Aesthetics 1873–1893*, Los Angeles: Getty Research Institute, 1994.

Marin, Louis, *Utopics: Spatial Play*, Robert A. Vollrath (trans.), Atlantic Highlands, NJ: Humanities Press, 1984.

Marlier, Georges, *La Renaissance Flamande: Pierre Coecke d'Alost*, Brussels: Finck, 1966.

Marnef, Guido, *Antwerp in the Age of Reformation*, J. C. Grayson (trans.), Baltimore and London: Johns Hopkins University Press, 1996.

Marx, Karl, *Capital*, vol. 1, Ben Fowkes (trans.), New York: Vintage, 1977.

Masheck, Joseph, "Alberti's 'Window': Art Historical Note on an Antimodernist Misprision", *Source: Notes in the History of Art*, 9/10: 4/1, 1989, pp. 13–17.

McClung, William, "A Place for a Time: The Architecture of Festivals and Theatres" in *Architecture and Its Image: Four Centuries of Architectural Representation*, Montréal: Canadian Centre for Architecture, 1989.

McPhee, Sarah, "The Architect as Reader", *JSAH* 58: 3, September 1999, pp. 454–61.

Meadow, Mark, "Ritual and Civic Identity in Philip II's Antwerp *Blijde Incompst*", *NKJ*, 49 1998, pp. 37–66.

—— " 'Met geschickter ordenen': The Rhetoric of Place in Philip II's 1549 Antwerp *Blijde Inkompst*", *Journal of the Walters Art Gallery*, 57, 1999, pp. 1–11.

Mehrtens, Ulbe Martin, "L' 'Hortorum Formae' di Johan Vredeman de Vries" in M. Mosser and G. Teyssot (eds), *L'architettura dei giardini d'Occidente dal Rinascimento al Novecento*, Milan: Electa, 1990, pp. 99–101.

Meijer, Hans, "Het beeld van de stad", *OASE*, 24, 1989, pp. 2–13.

Meischke, R., "Het Architonische Ontwerp in de Nederlanden gedurnede de Late Middeleeuwen en de Zestiende Eeuw", *Bulletin Koninklijke Nederlandse Oudheidkundige Bond*, 5, 6th series, 1952, cols 161–230.

Melion, Walter, *Shaping the Netherlandish Canon*, Chicago: University of Chicago Press, 1992.

Merleau-Ponty, M. *Phenomenology of Perception*, Colin Smith (trans.), London: Routledge, 1962.

Meskens, Ad, *Wiskunde Tussen Renaissance en Barok: Aspecten van Wiskunde-beoefening te Antwerpen 1550–1620*, Publikaties van de Stadsbibliotheek en het Archief en Museum voor het Vlaamse Cultuurleven, 41–3, Antwerp: Academic Press, 1994.

Miedema, Hessel, "Over de waardering van architect en beeldende kunstenaar in de zestiende eeuw", *Oud Holland*, 94, 1980, pp. 71–87.

—— *Karel Van Manders Leven der Moderne, Oft Dees-Tijtsche Doorluchtighe Italianensche Schilders en hun bron*, Alphen aan den Rijn: Canaletto, 1984.

—— "Kunstschilders, gilde, en academie: Over het probleem van de emancipatie van de kunstschilders in de Noordelijke Nederlanden van de 16de en 17de eeuw", *Oud* Holland, 101, 1987, pp. 1–34.

Mielke, Hans, *Hans Vredeman de Vries. Verzeichnis der Stichwerk und Beschreibung seines Stils sowie Beiträge zum Werk Gerard Groenings*, Ph.D. dissertation, Berlin, Freie Universität, 1967.

—— "Antwerpener Graphik in der 2.Halfte des 16. Jahnhunderts", *Zeitschrift für Kunstgeschichte*, 38, 1975, pp. 29–83.

—— "Hans Vredeman de Vries—Ornament", *Raggi*, 8, 1968, pp. 75–96.

—— *Pieter Bruegel: Die Zeichnungen*, Turnhout: Brepols, 1996.

Miłobędzki, Adam, "Niderlandzka I niderlandyzujaca architektura jako zjawisko kulturowe I artystyczne: 1550–1650" in *Niderlandyzm w Sztuce Polskiej* (Netherlandish Influences on Polish Art), Warsaw, 1995, pp. 51–8.

Möller, Lisette, *Der Wrangelschrank und die verwandten süddeutschen Intarsiaenmöbel des 16. Jahrhunderts*, Berlin: Deutscher Verein für Kunstwissenschaft, 1956.

Monballieu, A., "Een werk van P. Bruegel en H. Vredeman de Vries voor de tresorier Aert Molckman", *Jaarboek van het Koninklijk Museum voor Schone Kunsten Antwerpen*, 1969, pp. 113–35.

Morel, Phillipe, *Les Grotesques*, Paris: Flammarion, 1997.

Moser, Verselke, *De Strijd voor rhetorica: Poeticia en positie van rederijkers in Vlaanderen, Brabant, Zeeland en Holland Tussen 1450 en 1620*, Ph.D. dissertation, Vrije Universiteit Amsterdam, 2001.

Moss, Jean Dietz, *Novelties in the Heavens: Rhetoric and Science in the Copernican Controversy*, Chicago: University of Chicago Press, 1993.

Moxey, Keith P. F., *Pieter Aertsen, Joachim Beuckelaer, and the rise of secular painting in the context of the Reformation*, Ph.D. dissertation, Chicago: University of Chicago Press, 1974.

Mullaney, Steven, *The Place of the Stage: License, Play, and Power in Renaissance England*, Chicago: University of Chicago Press, 1988.

Muller Fz., S., "Getuigenverhoor te Antwerpen. Over het maken van ontwerpen van Gebouwen in de 16e Eeuw door Schilders, Goudsmeden, Timerlieden en Metselaars", *Archief voor Nederlandsche Kunstgeschiedenis*, 4, 1881–82, 227–45.

Müller, Jürgen, *Das Paradox als Bildform: Studien zur Ikonologie Pieter Bruegels d. Ä.*, Munich: Fink, 1999.

Museum Boymans-Van Beuningen, Rotterdam, *In de Vier Winden: de prentuitgeverij van Hieronymus Cock 1507/10–1570 te Antwerpen: uit de collectie tekeningen en prenten*, Jacqueline Burgers (ed.), Rotterdam, 1988.

—— *Perspectiven: Saenredam en de architectuurschilders van de 17de eeuw*, exh. cat., Rotterdam, 1991.

Museum Boymans-Van Beuningen, Rotterdam, and Metropolitan Museum of Art, New York, *Pieter Bruegel the Elder, Drawings and Prints*, exh. cat., New Haven: Yale University Press, 2001.

Museum voor Folklore, Amsterdam *Ommegangen end Blijde Inkomsten te Antwerpen*, exh.cat., Amsterdam, 1957.

Narondi Galerie, Prague, exh. cat., *Artis pictoriae amatores: Evropa v zrcadle prazskehs barokniho sberatelvi*, Prague, 1993.

National Galleries of Scotland, *The Stylish Image: Printmakers to the Court of Rudolf II*, exh.cat., Edinburgh, 1991.

Neeffs, Emmanuel, *Histoire de la peinture et de la sculpture a Malines*, 2 vols, Ghent: van der Haeghen, 1876.

Nelson, Robert S., "Descartes' Cow and Other Domestications of the Visual" in R. S. Nelson (ed.), *Visuality Before and Beyond the Renaissance*, Cambridge: Cambridge University Press, 2000, pp. 1–21.

Nuti, Lucia, "The Perspective Plan in the Sixteenth Century: The Invention of a Representational Language", *Art Bulletin*, 76: 1, March 1994, pp. 105–28.

Nuytten, Dieter, "Hans Vredeman de Vries' 'Architectura Oder Bauung des Antique aufs dem Vitruvius': Analyse en evaluatie van een architecturaal voorbeeldenboek van de 16e eeuw", unpublished Ph.D. dissertation, Katholijke Universiteit Leuven, 1994.

Oberhuber, Conrad, *Zwischen Renaissance und Barock*, exh. cat., Vienna: Graphische Sammlung Albertina, 1967.

Obreen, D. O., "Getuigenverhoor te Antwerpen", *Archief voor Nederlandsche kunstgeschiedenis*, 4, 1881–82, pp. 227–45.

O'Brien, Patrick et al. (eds), *Urban Achievement in Early Modern Europe: Golden Ages in Antwerp, Amsterdam, and London*, Cambridge: Cambridge University Press, 2001.

O'Malley, John, *Praise and Blame in Renaissance Rome*, Durham: Duke University Press, 1979.

Offerhaus, Johannes, "Pieter Coecke van Aelst et l'Introduction des traits d'architecture aux Pays-Bas" in Jean Guillaume (ed.), *Les Traités d'Architecture de la Renaissance*, Paris: Picard, 1988, pp. 443–52.

Ong, Walter J., *Orality and Literacy: The Technologizing of the Word*, London, Methuen, 1982.

Onians, John, "The System of the Orders in Renaissance Architectural Thought" in Jean Guillaume (ed.), *Les Traités d'Architecture de la Renaissance*, Paris: Picard, 1988, pp. 169–78.

—— *Bearers of Meaning: The Classical Orders in Antiquity, the Middle Ages, and the Renaissance*. Princeton: Princeton University Press, 1989.

Orenstein, Nadine M., *Hendrick Hondius and the Business of Prints in Seventeenth-Century Holland*, Studies in Prints and Printmaking, 1, Rotterdam: Sound and Vision Interactive, 1996.

Orgel, Stephen, *The Illusion of Power*, Berkeley and London: University of California Press, 1982.

Ottenheym, Konrad, "Possessed by such a Passion. Frederik Hendrik and Architecture" in Keblusek, M. and Zijlmans, J. (eds), *Princely Display. The Court of Frederik Hendrik of Orange and Amalia van Solms in The Hague*, The Hague/Zwolle: Waanders, 1997, pp. 105–25.

—— "Classicism in the Northern Netherlands in the Seventeenth Century" in Guido Beltramini et al., *Palladio and Northern Europe: Books, Travellers, Architects*, Milan: Skira, 1999, pp. 150–67.

Paleis voor Schone Kunsten, *Fiamminghi a Roma 1508–1608: Kunstenaars uit de Nederlanden en het Prinsbisdom Luik te Rome Tijdens de Renaissance*, exh. cat., Brussels: Snoeck-Ducaju & Zoon, 1995.

Panofsky, Erwin, *Dürers Kunsttheorie*, Berlin: George Reiner, 1915.

—— *Perspective as Symbolic Form*, 1924, Christopher S. Wood (trans.), New York: Zone Books, 1991.

—— *The Life and Art of Albrecht Dürer* (1943) Princeton: Princeton University Press, 2005.

—— *Deutschsprachige Aufsätze*, 2 vols, Berlin: Akademie, 1998.

Parshall, Peter, "Images and Facts in the Northern Renaissance", *Art History*, 16: 4, December 1993, pp. 554–79.

—— "Art and the Theatre of Knowledge: The Origins of Print Collecting in Northern Europe", *Harvard Art Museums Bulletin*, 2: 3, Spring 1994, pp. 7–36.

Payne, Alina A., "Between *giudizzio* and *auctoritas*: Vitruvius' *decor* and Its Progeny in Sixteenth-Century Italian Architectural Theory", Ph.D. dissertation, University of Toronto, 1992.

—— "Creativity and *bricolage* in architectural literature in the Renaissance", *Res*, 34, 1998, pp. 20–38.

—— *The Architectural Treatise in the Italian Renaissance: Architectural Invention, Ornament, and Literary Culture*, Cambridge: Cambridge University Press, 1999.

Peiffer, Jeanne, "La fabrique de la perspective à Nuremberg au XVIe siècle", *Les cahiers de la recherche architecturale et urbaine*, 17, September 2005, pp. 49–60.

Pérez-Gómez, Alberto, *Architectural Representation and the Perspective Hinge*, Cambridge, MA: MIT Press, 1997.

Pérez-Gómez, Alberto and Pelletier, Louise, "Architectural Representation Beyond Perspectivism", *Perspecta*, 27, 1992, pp. 21–39.

Peters, C. H., "Hans Vredeman de Vries. Mededelingen omtrent het leven en de werken van dezen Nederlandschen kunstenaar", *Bouwkundig Weekblad*, 1895, pp. 3–31.

Peters, John Durham, "Exile, Nomadism, and Diaspora: The Stakes of Mobility in the Western Canon" in H. Naficy (ed.), *Home, Exile, Homeland*, New York: Routledge, 1999, pp. 17–39.

Pleij, Herman, "De Stedelijke Literatuur 15de-16de eeuw" in Jan van der Stock (ed.), *Stad in Vlaanderen: Cultuur en Maatschappij 1477–1787*, Brussels: Gemeentekrediet, 1991, pp. 17–182.

Pochat, Götz, *Geschichte der Ästhetik und Kunsttheorie: von der Antike us zum 19. Jahrhundert*, Cologne: DuMont, 1986.

—— "Rhetorik und die bildende Kunst in der Renaissance" in *Renaissance-Rhetorik Renaissance Rhetoric*, Berlin: Walter de Gruyter, 1993, pp. 266–84.

Polan, Dana, "History in Perspective, Perspective in History: A Commentary on *L'Origine de la Perspective* by Hubert Damisch", *Camera Obscura*, 24, 1990, pp. 89–98.

Pollack, Martha, *Military Architecture, Cartography, and the Representation of the Early Modern European City*, Chicago: The Newberry Library, 1991.

Pon, Lisa, *Raphael, Dürer, and Marcantonio Raimondi: Copying and the Renaissance Print*, New Haven: Yale University Press, 2004.

Ponten, Josef, *Die Architektur die Nicht Gebaut Wurde*, 2 vols, Berlin and Leipzig: Deutsche Verlag, 1925.

Powell, Amy, "A Point 'Ceaselessly Pushed Back': The Origin of Netherlandish Painting", *Art Bulletin*, 88: 4, December 2006, pp. 707–28.

Pressouyre, Sylvia, "L'Image de la Maison dans la littérature du XVIe siècle" in A. Chastel and J. Guillaume (eds), *La Maison de Ville a la Renaissance*, colloquium proceedings, Paris: Picard, 1977.

Prims, Floris, "De ontwerpers van het Antwerpsch stadhuis", *Antwerpiensia*, 111, 1929, pp. 82–9.

—— *Het Stadhuis van Antwerpen. Geschiedenis en Beschrijving*, Antwerp: Standaard, 1930.

—— "Letterkundigen, geleerden en kunstenaars in de rekening der stad Antwerpen 1576–1650", *Verlsagen en Mededeelingen der Koninklinke Vlaamische Academie voor Taal- en Letterkunde*, 1931, pp. 171–211.

Puraye, Jean (ed.), *Abraham Ortelius. Album amicorum—Reproduit en facsimile*, Amsterdam: A. L. van Gendt & Co., 1969.

Rahmsdorf, Sabine, *Stadt und Architektur in der literarischen Utopie der frühen Neuzeit*, Heidelberg: C. Winter, 1999.

Randall, Catharine, *Building Codes: The Aesthetics of Calvinism in Early Modern Europe*, Philadelphia: University of Pennslyvania Press, 1999.

Rathe, K., "Die Ausdruckfuncktion Extrem Verkürzter Figuren", *Studies of the Warburg Institute*, 8, London: The Warburg Institute, 1938.

Ricoeur, Paul, "Narrative Time" in W. J. T. Mitchell (ed.), *On Narrative*, Chicago: University of Chicago Press, 1980, pp. 165–86.

Riegl, Alois, *Historical Grammar of the Visual Arts*, 1st German version, 1966, J. Jung (trans.), New York: Zone, 2004.

Riggs, Timothy, *Hieronymus Cock (1510–1570), Printmaker and Publisher in Antwerp at the Sign of the Four Winds*, Ph.D. dissertation, Yale University, 1971.

Rijksmuseum, Rijksprentenkabinet, *Het Profiel van de Stad*, exh. cat., Amsterdam, 1969.

—— *Kunst voor de beeldenstorm*, The Hague: Staatsuitgeverij, 1986.

—— *Kunst voor de beeldenstorm: Catalogus*, exh.cat., The Hague: Staatsuitgeverij, 1986.

—— *Dawn of the Golden Age: Northern Netherlandish Art 1580–1629*, exh. cat., Amsterdam, 1993.

Roeder-Baumbach, Irmengard von, *Versieringen Bij Blijde inkomsten gebruikt in de zuidelijke Nederlanden gedurende de 16de en 17de eeuw*, Antwerp: de Sikkel, 1943.

Roever, Margriet de and Bakker, Boudewijn, *Woelige tijden: Amsterdam in de eeuw van de beeldenstorm*, Amsterdam: Gemeentearchief, 1986.

Rolf, Rudi, *Pieter Coecke van Aelst en Zijn Architectuuruitgaves van 1539*, Amsterdam: s.p., 1978.

Roose, L., " 'Dwelck den Mensche Aldermeest tot Consten Verwect': de Poetica der Brabantse Rederikers in 1561" in *Hulde-Album Prof. Dr. J.F. Vanderheyden*, Langemark: Vonksteen, 1970, pp. 91–108.

Rosenfeld, Myra Nan, "Sebastiano Serlio's Contribution to the Creation of the Modern Illustrated Architectural Manual" in C. Thoenes (ed.), *Sebastiano Serlio*, Milan: Electa, 1996, pp. 102–10.

Ross, Kristin, "Streetwise: The French Invention of Everyday Life", *Parallax*, 2, 1996, pp. 67–75.

Rotman, Brian, *Signifying Nothing: The Semiotics of Zero*, Palo Alto: Stanford University Press, 1987.

Rupprich, Hans (ed.), *Dürer: Schriftlicher Nachlass*, 3 vols, Berlin: Deutscher Verein für Kunstwissenschaft, 1, 1956–69.

Ruurs, Robert, *Saenredam: The Art of Perspective*, Amsterdam: Benjamin Forsten, 1987.

Rykwert, Joseph, "The City as Spectacle" in Gutschow, N. and Sieverts, T., *Stadt und Ritual/Urban Space and Ritual (Beiträge und Studienmaterialen der Fachgruppe Stadt, no. 11)*, Darmstadt: Technische Hochschule, 1977, pp. 91–5.

—— "Translation and/or Representation", *Res*, 34, Autumn 1998, pp. 64–70.

Saenger, Paul, "Benito Arias Montano and the evolving notion of locus in sixteenth-century printed books", *Word and Image*, 17: 1 & 2, 2001, pp. 119–37.

San Juan, Rose Marie, *Rome: A City out of Print*, Minneapolis: Minnesota University Press, 2001.

Schechner, Richard. *Performance Theory*, New York: Routledge, 1988.

Schéle, Sune, *Cornelius Bos: A Study of the Origins of the Netherland Grotesque*, Stockholm: Almqvist & Wiskell, 1965.

Scheliga, Thomas, "Ein neuer Aktenfund zum Alter der ehemaligen Schlosskapelle Hessen", *Heitmatbuch fur das Landkriese Wolfenbüttel*, 42, 1996, pp. 58–60.

—— "Renaissance Gärten der Herzöge von Braunschweig-Lüneburg in Wolfenbüttel", in Vera Lüpkes (ed.), *"zur zierde und schmuck angeegt. . ".: Beitrage zur frühneuzeitlichen Garten- und Schloßbaukunst*, Marburg: Jonas Verlag, 1996, pp. 9–52.

—— "A Renaissance Garden in Wolfenbüttel, North Germany", *Garden History*, XXV: 1, Summer 1997, pp. 1–22.

Schleiner, Winfried, *Melancholy, Genius, and Utopia in the Renaissance*, Wiesbaden: Otto Harassowitz, 1991.

Schneede, Uwe M., *Das repräsentative Gesellschaftbild in der niederländischen Malerei des 17 Jahrhunderts und seine Grundlagen bei Hans Vredeman de Vries*, Ph.D. dissertation, Kiel 1965.

—— "Interieurs von Hans und Paul Vredeman de Vries", *NKJ*, 18, 1967, pp. 125–66.

Schöne, Günter, *Die Entwicklung der Perpektivbühne von Serlio dis Galli-Bibiena Theatergeschichtliche Forschungen*, 43, Leipzig: Leopold Voss, 1933.

Schoy, A., *Hans Vredeman de Vries (Les grands architectes de la Renaissance aux Pays-Bas)*, Brussels: s.p., 1876.

Sedlmayr, Hans, "Towards a Rigorous Study of Art", 1931, Tawney Becker (trans.), in Christopher S. Wood (ed.), *The Vienna School* Reader, New York: Zone Books, 2000.

Sellinck, Manfred, " 'As a guide to the highest learning': an Antwerp drawing book dated 1589", *Simiolus*, 21, 1992, pp. 40–56.

Sennett, Richard, *Flesh and Stone: The Body and the City in Western Civilization*, New York: Norton, 1994.

Silver, Larry, "Graven Images. Reproductive Engravings as Visual Models" in *Graven Images: The Rise of Professional Printmakers in Antwerp and Haarlem, 1540–1640*, exh. cat., Mary and Leigh Block Gallery, Evanston: Northwestern University Press, 1993, pp. 1–45.

Simson, Otto von and Winner, Matthias (ed.), *Pieter Bruegel und Seine Welt: Ein Colloquium veranstaltet vom Kunsthistorischen Institut der freien Universität Berlin und dem Kupferstichkabinett der Staatlichen Museen Stiftung Preussischer Kulturbesitz*, 1975, Berlin: Mann, 1979.

Simmens, J., *Ruinen-Faszination in der Graphik vom 16 Jahrhundert bis in de Gegenwart*, Dortmund: Harenberg, 1980.

Skelton, R. A., "Introduction" to Braun and Hogenberg, *Civitates Orbis Terrarum, 1572–1618*, vol. I, reprint, New York: World Publishing Company, 1966, pp. vii–xxii.

Smith, Pamela H. and Paula Findlen (eds), *Merchants and Marvels: Commerce, Science, and Art in Early Modern Europe*, New York and London: Routledge, 2002.

Snyder, Joel, "Picturing Vision", *Critical Inquiry*, 6, 1980, pp. 499–526.

Soly, Hugo, "Fortificaties, belastingen, en corruptie te Antwerpen in het midden der 16de eeuw", *Bijdragen tot de Geschiendenis*, 53: 3–4, 1970, pp. 190–210.

—— "The Betrayal of the Sixteenth-Century Bourgeousie: A Myth?", *Actae Historiae Neerlandicae*, VIII, 1975, pp. 31–49.

—— *Urbanisme en kapitalisme te Antwerpen in de 16de eeuw*, Brussels: Gemeentekrediet, 1977.

—— "L'Urbanisation d'Anvers au XVIe Siecle", *Revue du Nord*, LXIII: 249, April/June 1981, pp. 391–413.

—— "Openbare feesten in Brabantse en Vlaamse steden 16de-18de eeuw" in *Het Openbaar Initiatief van de Gemeenten in Belgie: Historische Grondslagen*, Brussels: Gemeentekrediet, 1984, pp. 606–36.

—— "Plechtige intochten in de steden van de Zuidlijke Nederlanden", *Tijdschrift voor Geschiedenis*, 97, 1984, pp. 341–61.

Spies, Marijke, " 'Op de questye . . .' Over de structuur van 16e-eeuwse zinnespelen", *De nieuwe taalgids*, 83: 2, 1990, pp. 139–50.

—— "Developments in Sixteenth-Century Dutch Poetics From 'Rhetoric' to 'Renaissance' " in *Renaissance-Rhetorik Renaissance Rhetoric*, Berlin: Walter de Gruyter, 1993, pp. 72–91.

Staatliche Museen Preussischer Kulturbesitz, *Pieter Bruegel d. Ä. Als Zeichner*, exh. cat, Berlin, 1975.

Starn, Randolf and Partridge, Loren, *Arts of Power: Three Halls of State in Italy, 1300–1600*, Berkeley: California University Press, 1992.

Steenbergen, G. J., *Het Landjuweel van der Rederijkers*, Leuven: Davisfonds, 1950–52.

Sterck, J. F. M., *Van Rederijkerskamer tot Muiderkring*, Amsterdam: De Spieghel, 1928.

Stock, Jan van der (ed.), *Stad in Vlaanderen: Cultuur en Maatschappij 1477–1787*, Brussels: Gemeentekrediet, 1991.

—— *Antwerp: Story of a Metropolis: 16th–17th century*, Antwerp: Hessenhuis, 1993.

Stock, Jan van der, *Printing Images in Antwerp. The Introduction of Printmaking to a City: Fifteenth Century to 1585*, Rotterdam: Sound and Vision Interactive, 1998.

Strauss, Walter (ed.), *The Illustrated Bartsch*, New York: Abaris Books, 1978–.

Stridbeck, Carl Gustaf, *Bruegelstudien*, Stockholm: Almquist & Wiskell, 1956.

Stumpel, Jeroen, "On grounds and backgrounds: some remarks about composition in Renaissance painting", *Simiolus*, 18: 4, 1988, pp. 219–43.

Summers, David, *Michelangelo and the language of art*, Princeton: Princeton University Press, 1981.

Szonyi, György E., "Architectural Symbolism and Fantasy Landscapes in Alchemical and Occult Discourse: Revelatory Images", *Glasgow Emblem Studies*, 3,1988, pp. 49–69.

Tafuri, Manfredo. *The Sphere and the Labyrinth: Avant-Gardes and Architecture from Piranesi to The 1970s*, 1978, Pelligrino d 'Acierno and Robert Connolly (trans.), Cambridge, MA: MIT Press, 1987.

Talbot, Charles, "Prints and the Definitive Image" in Gerald P. Tyson and Sylvia S. Wagonheim (eds), *Print and Culture in the Renaissance: Essays on the Advent of Printing in Europe*, Newark: University of Delaware Press, 1986, pp. 189–207.

Taverne, Ed, *In't land van belofte: in de nieue stad. Ideale en werkelijkheid van de stadsuitleg in de Republiek 1580–1680*, Maarssen: SDU/Schwartz, 1978.

Taverne, Ed. and Visser, I., (eds), *Stedebouw: De geschiedenis van de stad in de Nederlanden van 1500 tot heden*, Nijmegen: SUN, 1993.

Thijs, R., *Crowning the City: Vernacular Architecture in Antwerp from the Middle Ages to the Present Day*, Antwerp: Fonds Mercator, 1991.

Thøfner, Margit, "Marrying the City, Mothering the Country: Gender and Visual Conventions in Johannes Bochius' account of the Joyous Entry of the Archduke Albert and the Infanta Isabella into Antwerp", *Oxford Art Journal*, 22: 1, 1999, pp. 1–27.

Thomson, David, *Renaissance Architecture: Critics, Patrons, Luxury*, Manchester University Press, 1993.

Thöne, Friedrich, "Wolfenbüttel in der Spätrenaisssance", *Braunschweigisches Jahrbuch*, 35, 1954, pp. 1–116.

—— "Hans Vredeman de Vries in Wolfenbüttel", *Braunschweigisches Jahrbuch*, 41, 1960, pp. 47–68.

—— "Werke des Hans Vredeman de Vries in Wolfenbüttel", *Pantheon*, 20, 1962, pp. 248–55, 335–6.

Thrift, Nigel and Williams, Peter, "The geography of class formation" in Thrift and Williams (eds), *Class and Space: The making of Urban Society*, London: Routledge, 1987.

Thrupp, Sylvia. L., "The City as the Idea of Social Order" in Oscar Handlin and John Burchard (eds.), *The Historian and the City*, Cambridge, MA: MIT Press, 1968, p. 121–32.

Tittler, Robert, *Architecture and Power: The Town Hall and the English Urban Community, c.1500–1640*, Oxford: Clarendon, 1991.

Trachtenberg, Marvin, *Dominion of the Eye: Urbanism, Art and Power in Early Modern Florence*, Cambridge; Cambridge University Press, 1997.

Uppenkamp, Barbara, "Ordnung und Geometrie. Die Wolfenbüttler Heinrichstadt—eine deutsche Idealstadt um 1600" in *Jülicher Forschungen*, 4, 1995, pp. 7–30.

—— "Idealstadt Wolfenbüttel" in H. Hipp and E. Seidl (eds), *Architektur als Politische Kultur*. Berlin: Dietrich Reimer, 1996, pp. 115–29.

Uyten, Raymond van, "Scenes de la vie sociale dans les Villes des Pays-Bas", *Mémoires de la Société d'Agriculture, Science, et Arts de Douai*, 5th series, VIII, Douai: Lefebvre-L'eveque, 1983, pp. 11–31.

Van de Velde, Carl, *Frans Floris (1519/20–1570), leven en werk*, Brussels: Paleis der Academiën, 1975.

Vandevelde, L., *De Kamers van Rhetorica in de Lage Landen*, s.p., 1994.

Veldman, Ilja M., "Maarten van Heemskerck and the Rhetoricians of Haarlem", *Hafnia—Copenhagen Papers in the History of Art*, 4, 1976, pp. 96–112.

—— *Maarten van Heemskerck and Dutch humanism in the sixteenth century*, Amsterdam: Meulenhoff, 1977.

—— "Philips Galle, een inventiere prentenontwerper", *Oud Holland*, 105, 1991, pp. 262–90.

Vermet, Bernard M., "Tableaux de Dirck van Delen (v. 1604/1605–1671) dans les Musées français", *Revue du Louvre*, XLIII: 3, June 1995, pp. 30–44.

—— "Architectuurschilders in Danzig: Hendrick Aerts en Hans en Paul Vredeman de Vries", *Gentse Bijdragen tot de kunstgeschiedenis*, 31, 1996, pp. 27–57.

Vermeulen, F. A. J., *Handboek tot de geschiedenis der Nederlandsche bouwkunst*, 6 vols, The Hague: M. Nijhoff, 1928–41.

Vesely, Dalibor, "Architecture and the Conflict of Representation", *AA Files*, 8, 1985, pp. 21–38.

Vlieghe, Hans, *Flemish Art and Architecture 1600–1800*, 2nd ed., New Haven: Yale University Press, 1998.

Voet, Léon, *The golden compasses: a history and evaluation of the printing and publishing activities of the Officina Plantiana at Antwerp*, 2 vols, Amsterdam: Van Gendt & Co., 1969–72.

—— *Antwerp: The Golden Age*, Antwerp: Mercatorfonds, 1973.

Vries, A. D. de, "Biographische aanteekeningen betreffende voornamelijk Amsterdamsche schilders, plaatsnijders, enz. en hunne verwanten", *Oud Holland*, 4, 1886, pp. 295–304.

Vries, Jan de, *European Urbanization 1500–1800*, London: Cambridge University Press, 1984.

Warnke, Martin (ed.), *Politische Architektur in Europa von Mittelalter bis heute—Repräsentation und Gemeinschaft*, Cologne: DuMont, 1984.

—— *The Court Artist: On the Ancestry of the Modern Artist*, Cambridge: Cambridge University Press, 1993.

Wee, Hermann van de, *The Rise and Decline of Urban Industries in Italy and in the Low Countries*, 3 vols, Leuven: Leuven University Press, 1963.

Wells-Cole, Anthony, *Art and decoration in Elizabethan and Jacobean England: the influence of continental prints, 1558–1625*, New Haven: Yale University Press, 1997.

Welu, James A., "The Sources and Development of Cartographic Ornamentation in the Netherlands" in D. Woodward (ed.), *Art and Cartography: Six Historical Essays*, Chicago: University of Chicago Press, 1987, pp. 147–73.

Wesfälisches Landesmuseum für Kunst und Kulturgeschichte, *Bilder nach Bildern*, exh. cat., Münster: Landshcaftsverband Westfalen-Lippe, 1976.

Westra, Frans, *Nederlandse ingenieurs en de fortificatiewerken*, Alphen aan den Rijn: Canaletto, 1992.

Wheelock, Arthur K., *Perspective, Optics, and Delft artists around 1650*, Ph.D. dissertation, Harvard University, 1973, republished New York: Garland, 1977.

White, John, *The Birth and Rebirth of Pictorial Space*, Cambridge, MA: Harvard University Press, 1987.

Wick, Peter A., "A New Book of Grotesques by Christoph Jamnitzer", *Bulletin of the Museum of Fine Arts, Boston*, LX, 1962, pp. 83–104.

Winkel, Madeline van de, "Hans Vredeman de Vries" in J. Guillaume (ed.), *Les Traités d'Architecture de la Renaissance, Actes de la colloque Tours 1981*, Paris: Picard, 1988, pp. 453–8.

—— "Les ordres dans les facades des Pays-Bas du Sud" in J. Guillaume (ed.), *L'Emploi des Ordres dans l'Architecture de la Renaissance*, Paris: Picard, 1992, pp. 293–8.

—— "Hans Vredeman de Vries" in Jane Turner (ed.), *The Dictionary of Art*, vol. 32, London: Grove, 1996, pp. 724–7.

Wittkower, Rudolf, *Architectural Principles in the Age of Humanism*, New York, 1949, 2nd ed., New York: Norton, 1971.

Wood, Christopher S., *Albrecht Altdorfer and the Origins of Landscape*, Chicago: University of Chicago Press, 1993.

—— "Une Perspective Oblique. Hubert Damisch, La Grammaire du Tableau, et la *Strukturanalyse* Viennoise", *Les Cahiers du Musée national d'art moderne*, 58, Winter 1996, pp 107–29.

—— "Why Autonomy?", *Perspecta* 33, 2002, pp. 48–53.

—— "The Perspective Treatise in Ruins: Lorenz Stoer, *Geometria et perspectiva*, 1567" in Lyle Massey (ed.), *The Treatise on Perspective*, Washington DC: National Gallery of Art, 2003, pp. 234–57.

Wulff, Oskar, "Die umgekehrte Perspective und die Niedersicht" in Heinrich Weiszäcker, (ed.), *Kunstwissenschaftliche Beiträge. August Schmarsow gewidmet zum fünfzigsten semester seiner akademischen Lehertätigkeit.* Leipzig: Hiersmann, 1907, pp. 1–40.

Zerner, Henri, *The school of Fontainebleau: etchings and engravings*, London, Thames & Hudson, 1969.

—— "Du mot à l'image: le role de la gravure sur cuivre" in *L'Emploi des Ordres dans l'Architecture de la Renaissance*, Paris: Pichard, 1992, pp. 282–93.

Zimmermann, Petra Sophia, "Hans Vredeman de Vries—ein 'uomo universale'?", *Bulletin Koninklijke Nederlandse Oudheidkundige Bond*, 100: 1, 2001, pp. 2–13.

—— *Die Architectura von Hans Vredeman de Vries. Entwicklung der Renaissance-architektur in Mitteleuropa*, Munich & Berlin: Deutsche Kunstverlag, 2002.

Zorach, Rebecca, *Blood, Milk, Ink, Gold: Abundance and Excess in the French Renaissance*, Chicago: University of Chicago Press, 2005.

Zülch, Walter Karl, *Enstehung des Ohrmuschelstiles* [*Heidelberger Kunstgeschichtliche Abhandlungen* 12], Heidelberg: Carl Winters Universitätsbuchhandlung, 1932.

Index

Note: Page numbers in *italics* refer to illustrations.

Photographic credits

Amsterdams Historisch Museum, Bureau Monumenten & Archaeologie: 1.5; Albertina, Vienna: 1.2, 1.4, 1.6, 1.7, 1.13, 2.21; Avery Architectural and Fine Arts Library, Columbia University: 2.3a, 2.4, 2.5, 2.7, 2.10, 2.12, 3.3, 3.4, 3.5, 3.11, 3.12, 3.13, 3.19, 3.20, 5.30; Bildarchiv Preussischer Kulturbesitz/Art Resource NY: 2.11, 2.22, 3.6, plate III; BnF (Bibliothèque nationale de France): 5.8, 5.9; After Borggrefe 2002, p. 93: 3.15; British Museum, London: 5.26; Butler Library, Columbia University: 5.34; Marcel van den Broeke: 3.22; CCA, Montréal: 0.1, 0.3, 5.1, 5.3, 5.4, 5.5, 5.6, 5.7, 5.10, 5.11, 5.12, 5.13, 5.14, 5.33; Deventer Historisches Museum: 2.25; © Ursala Edelmann, Frankfurt au Main: 5.19; Frye and Sohn, Münster: 4.7; Getty Research Institute: 1.11, 5.35; After Hellendoorn 1980: 3.17; Herder-Institut, Marburg: 4.1; Herzog-August Bibliothek: 0.2, 3.1, 3.18, 4.3, 5.16; KHM, Vienna: 4.8, 4.11, 5.2, 5.20; Koninklijke Bibliotheek, The Hague: 4.2; Kungliga Biblioteket, Stockholm: 2.1; Metropolitan Museum of Art Image Library: 3.2, 3.7, 5.32; Museum Catharijneconvent, Utrecht: plate I, 0.4 © The National Gallery, London: 1.3; Niedersäschsches Landesarchiv: plate IV, 4.4 4.5; M. Novais: 3.16; Princeton University, Visual Resources: 4.10, 5.15, 5.25; Rijksmuseum, Amsterdam: 0.8, 2.6, 2.16, 2.18, 2.19, 2.20, 3.23; Rijksuniversiteit Leiden: 0.5, 0.7; The Royal Collection © Her Majestry Queen Elizabeth II: plate II, 1.1; Schloss Rheydt, Mönchengladbach: 4.9; Stadsarchief Antwerpen: 2.3, 2.8, 2.9, 4.6; Stadt- und Stiftarchiv, Aschaffenburg: 6.0; Stedelijke Prentenkabinet, Antewerp: 2.2, 5.24; Universitätsbibliothek, Erlangen: 2.23, 5.28; Universitietsbibliotheek, Amsterdam: 1.8, 2.14, 2.15, 2.17, 3.8, 3.21, 5.36; Universiteitsbibliotheek, Ghent: 1.9, 1.10; © Richard Wachert, Innsbruck: 5.2; © Wesleyan University Press: 3.16.